A TEXT BOOK OF

DESIGN OF MACHINE ELEMENTS - II

For
SEMESTER - II
THIRD YEAR DEGREE COURSE IN
MECHANICAL ENGINEERING

ACCORDING TO NEW REVISED SYLLABUS OF
SAVITRIBAI PHULE PUNE UNIVERSITY

Prof. L. S. Utpat
M.E. (Mech. Engg.)
Formerly Professor and Head of Mech. Engg. Deptt.
D.Y. Patil College of Engg.
Akurdi, Pune

L. V. Awadhani
M.E. (Mech. Engg.),
Assistant Professor, Mech. Engg. Deptt.
Pimpri-Chinchwad College of Engineering
Pune

Vikas R. Deulgaonkar
M.E. (Mech. Engg.),
Assistant Professor, Mech. Engg. Deptt.
MM Mandal's College of Engineering
Pune

N3307

DESIGN OF MACHINE ELEMENTS - II (T.E. Mechanical, Sem. II, PU)   ISBN 978-93-5164-357-9
First Edition : February 2015
© : **Authors**

The text of this publication, or any part thereof, should not be reproduced or transmitted in any form or stored in any computer storage system or device for distribution including photocopy, recording, taping or information retrieval system or reproduced on any disc, tape, perforated media or other information storage device etc., without the written permission of Authors with whom the rights are reserved. Breach of this condition is liable for legal action.

Every effort has been made to avoid errors or omissions in this publication. In spite of this, errors may have crept in. Any mistake, error or discrepancy so noted and shall be brought to our notice shall be taken care of in the next edition. It is notified that neither the publisher nor the authors or seller shall be responsible for any damage or loss of action to any one, of any kind, in any manner, therefrom.

Published By :	Printed By :
NIRALI PRAKASHAN	**REPRO INDIA LTD.**
Abhyudaya Pragati, 1312, Shivaji Nagar,	50/2 T.T.C. MIDC,
Off J.M. Road, PUNE – 411005	Industrial Area, Mahape, Navi Mumbai
Tel - (020) 25512336/37/39, Fax - (020) 25511379	Tel - (022) 2778 2011
Email : niralipune@pragationline.com	

DISTRIBUTION CENTRES
PUNE

Nirali Prakashan
119, Budhwar Peth, Jogeshwari Mandir Lane
Pune 411002, Maharashtra
Tel : (020) 2445 2044, 66022708, Fax : (020) 2445 1538
Email : bookorder@pragationline.com

Nirali Prakashan
S. No. 28/27, Dhyari,
Near Pari Company, Pune 411041
Tel : (020) 24690204 Fax : (020) 24690316
Email : dhyari@pragationline.com
bookorder@pragationline.com

MUMBAI
Nirali Prakashan
385, S.V.P. Road, Rasdhara Co-op. Hsg. Society Ltd.,
Girgaum, Mumbai 400004, Maharashtra
Tel : (022) 2385 6339 / 2386 9976, Fax : (022) 2386 9976
Email : niralimumbai@pragationline.com

DISTRIBUTION BRANCHES

NAGPUR
Pratibha Book Distributors
Above Maratha Mandir, Shop No. 3, First Floor,
Rani Jhanshi Square, Sitabuldi, Nagpur 440012,
Maharashtra, Tel : (0712) 254 7129

BENGALURU
Pragati Book House
House No. 1, Sanjeevappa Lane, Avenue Road Cross,
Opp. Rice Church, Bengaluru – 560002.
Tel : (080) 64513344, 64513355,
Mob : 9880582331, 9845021552
Email:bharatsavla@yahoo.com

JALGAON
Nirali Prakashan
34, V. V. Golani Market, Navi Peth, Jalgaon 425001,
Maharashtra, Tel : (0257) 222 0395
Mob : 94234 91860

KOLHAPUR
Nirali Prakashan
New Mahadvar Road,
Kedar Plaza, 1st Floor Opp. IDBI Bank
Kolhapur 416 012, Maharashtra. Mob : 9855046155

CHENNAI
Pragati Books
9/1, Montieth Road, Behind Taas Mahal, Egmore,
Chennai 600008 Tamil Nadu, Tel : (044) 6518 3535,
Mob : 94440 01782 / 98450 21552 / 98805 82331, Email : bharatsavla@yahoo.com

RETAIL OUTLETS
PUNE

Pragati Book Centre
157, Budhwar Peth, Opp. Ratan Talkies,
Pune 411002, Maharashtra
Tel : (020) 2445 8887 / 6602 2707, Fax : (020) 2445 8887

Pragati Book Centre
Amber Chamber, 28/A, Budhwar Peth,
Appa Balwant Chowk, Pune : 411002, Maharashtra,
Tel : (020) 20240335 / 66281669
Email : pbcpune@pragationline.com

Pragati Book Centre
676/B, Budhwar Peth, Opp. Jogeshwari Mandir,
Pune 411002, Maharashtra
Tel : (020) 6601 7784 / 6602 0855

PBC Book Sellers & Stationers
152, Budhwar Peth, Pune 411002, Maharashtra
Tel : (020) 2445 2254 / 6609 2463

MUMBAI
Pragati Book Corner
Indira Niwas, 111 - A, Bhavani Shankar Road, Dadar (W), Mumbai 400028, Maharashtra
Tel : (022) 2422 3526 / 6662 5254, Email : pbcmumbai@pragationline.com

www.pragationline.com   info@pragationline.com

PREFACE

It gives us immense pleasure to present this book **"Design of Machine Elements-II"** to the Students of Third Year (TE) Degree Course in Mechanical Engineering of Savitribai Phule Pune University.

The book is comprehensive and is written strictly as per New Revised Syllabus (2012 Pattern) which has been implemented from Academic Year (2013-2014). Design fundamentals are explained in a simple way and are supplemented with adequate numerical examples to explain the design procedure in detail.

Unit I: It covers different types of gears, their selection and materials, spur gear design parameters, procedure of design against bending and pitting and force analysis. Gear tooth failures - causes and remedies and gear lubrication are discussed in detail.

Unit II: It covers helical and bevel gear terminology, geometric relationships, virtual number of teeth for equivalence with spur gears and design of helical and bevel gears against bending and pitting.

Unit III: It covers types of rolling contact bearings, selection of bearing type, selection of bearings from manufacturer's catalogue, bearing mounting, bearing failures, preloading and lubrication.

Unit IV: It covers types of worm and worm gears, geometric relationships, selection of worm and gear pair, efficiency of pair, design of worm gear against wear, bending and thermal aspects.

Unit V: It covers introduction to belt and rope drives, power calculations, selection of belt from manufacturer's catalogue, design of pulley. Selection of rope and chain.

Unit VI: It covers introduction to various types of sliding contact bearings. Reynolds equation for 2D flow, Raimondi and Boyd method. Bearing design parameters and lubricants with their properties.

We take this opportunity to express thanks to all members of Nirali Prakashan for their excellent co-operation. A special thanks to Publisher Mr. Dineshbhai Furia, Mr. Jignesh Furia and Mr. M. P. Munde and team namely Mr. Akbar Shaikh (DTP), Mrs. Deepali Lachake (Co-ordinator), and Mrs. Roshan Shaikh, for showing full faith in us to write this book.

We are also thankful to Marketing Executives namely, Mr. Sachin Shinde, Mr. Ashok Bodke, Mr. Balasaheb Thorat, Mr. Nilesh Deshmukh, Mr. Mohsin Shaikh, Mr. Parag Ghamandi (Nashik) and Mr. Raju Shaikh (Ahmednagar) for their valuable help and efforts for promotion of our book.

Suggestions and comments are always welcome for the improvement of this book.

Authors

SYLLABUS

Unit I: Spur Gears (08 Hours)

Gear Drives: Classification of gears, Selection of types of gears, Selection of materials for gears, Standard systems of gear tooth, Basic modes of gear tooth failures, Gear Lubrication Methods.

Spur Gears: Number of teeth and face width, Types of gear tooth failure, Desirable properties and selection of gear material, Constructional details of gear wheel, Force analysis (Theoretical Treatment only), Beam strength (Lewis) equation, Velocity factor, Service factor, Load concentration factor, Effective load on gear, Wear strength (Buckingham's) equation, Estimation of module based on beam and wear strength, Estimation of dynamic tooth load by velocity factor and Buckingham's equation.

Unit II: Helical and Bevel Gears (08 Hours)

Helical Gears: Transverse and normal module, Virtual number of teeth, Force analysis (Theoretical Treatment only), Beam and wear strengths, Effective load on gear tooth, Estimation of dynamic load by velocity actor and Buckingham's equation, Design of helical gears.

Bevel Gears: Straight tooth bevel gear terminology and geometric relationship, Formative number of teeth, Force analysis (Theoretical Treatment only), Design criteria of bevel gears, Beam and wear strengths, Dynamic tooth load by Velocity factor and Buckingham's equation, Effective load, Design of straight tooth bevel gears.

Unit III: Rolling Contact Bearings (08 Hours)

Types of rolling contact Bearings, Static and dynamic load carrying capacities, Stribeck's Equation, Equivalent bearing load, Load-life relationship, Selection of bearing life, Selection of rolling contact bearings from manufacturer's catalogue, Design for cyclic loads and speed, bearing with probability of survival other than 90%.

Lubrication and mounting of bearings, Preloading of rolling contact bearings, Types of failure in rolling contact bearings – causes and remedies.

Taper roller bearing (Theoretical Treatment only).

Unit IV: Worm Gears (08 Hours)

Worm and worm gear terminology and geometrical relationship, Types of worm and worm gears, Standard dimensions, Force analysis of worm gear drives, Friction in Worm gears and its efficiency, Worm and worm-wheel material, Strength and wear ratings of worm gears, Thermal consideration in worm gear drive, Types of failures in worm gearing, Methods of lubrication.

Unit V: Belts, Rope and Chain Drives (08 Hours)

Belt Drive: Materials and construction of flat and V belts, geometric relationships for length of belt, power rating of belts, concept of slip and creep, initial tension, effect of centrifugal force, maximum power condition, selection of flat and V belts from manufacturer's catalogue, belt tensioning methods, relative advantages and limitations of flat and V belts, construction and applications of timing belts.

Wire Ropes (Theoretical Treatment Only): Construction of wire ropes, lay of wire ropes, stresses in wire rope, selection of wire ropes, rope drum construction and design.

Chain Drives (Theoretical Treatment Only): Types of power transmission chains, Geometry of Chain, Polygon effect of chain, Modes of failure for chain, Lubrication of chains.

Unit VI: Sliding Contact Bearings (08 Hours)

Lubricating Oils: Properties, additives, selection of lubricating oils, Properties and selection of bearing materials.

Hydrodynamic Lubrication: Theory of Hydrodynamic Lubrication, Pressure Development in oil film, 2D Basic Reynolds Equation, Somerfield number, Raimondi and Boyd method, Temperature Rise, Parameters of bearing design, Length to Diameter ratio, Unit bearing Pressure, Radial Clearance, minimum oil film thickness.

CONTENTS

1. SPUR GEARS   1.1 – 1.50

GEAR DRIVES

1.1	Introduction	1.1
1.2	Classification of Gears	1.1
1.3	Gear Tooth Terminology	1.3
1.4	Law of Gearing	1.5
1.5	Forms of Gear Tooth Profile	1.6
1.6	Selection of Types of Gears	1.8
	1.6.1 Selection of Materials for Gears	1.9
1.7	Standard Systems of Gear Tooth	1.10
1.8	Addendum Modification of Gears	1.11
1.9	Crowning of Gear Tooth	1.11
1.10	Basic Modes of Gear Tooth Failures	1.12
1.11	Gear Lubrication Methods	1.14

SPUR GEARS

1.12	Spur Gears - Number of Teeth and Face Width	1.14
	1.12.1 Number of Teeth	1.14
	1.12.2 Face Width	1.15
1.13	Desirable Properties and Selection of Gear Material	1.15
1.14	Constructional Details of Gear Wheel	1.15
1.15	Force Analysis	1.17
1.16	Design Considerations	1.18
1.17	Beam Strength (Lewis Equation)	1.19
1.18	Velocity Factor	1.21
1.19	Service Factor	1.21
1.20	Load Concentration Factor (C_L)	1.22
1.21	Effective Load on Gear (P_{eff})	1.23
1.22	Wear Strength (Buckingham's Equation)	1.25
1.23	Gear Design	1.28
	• Solved Examples	1.30
	• Exercise	1.50

2. HELICAL AND BEVEL GEARS   2.1 – 2.56

HELICAL GEARS

2.1	Introduction	2.1
2.2	Important Terms for Helical Gears	2.2
2.3	Force Analysis	2.6
2.4	Beam Strength of Helical Gear (Lewis Equation)	2.8
2.5	Wear Strength of Helical Gear	2.9
2.6	Effective Load	2.10
2.7	Helical Gear Design Procedure	2.11
	• Solved Examples	2.12

BEVEL GEARS

2.8	Introduction	2.26
2.9	Terminology of Bevel Gears	2.27
2.10	Virtual Number of Teeth (Z')	2.28
2.11	Force Analysis	2.29
2.12	Beam Strength of Bevel Gear	2.31
2.13	Wear Strength	2.33
2.14	Effective Load	2.34
2.15	Design of Straight Teeth Bevel Gears	2.35
	• Solved Examples	2.36
	• Exercise	2.55

3. ROLLING CONTACT BEARINGS   3.1 – 3.46

3.1	Introduction	3.1
3.2	Types of Rolling Contact Bearings	3.2
	3.2.1 Deep Groove Ball Bearing	3.2
	3.2.2 Cylindrical Roller Bearing	3.3
	3.2.3 Angular Contact Bearings	3.4
	3.2.4 Self-Aligning Bearings	3.4
	3.2.5 Taper Roller Bearings	3.5
	3.2.6 Thrust Ball Bearings	3.6
3.3	Static and Dynamic Load Carrying Capacities	3.7
	3.3.1 Static Load Carrying Capacity: Static Load [C_o]	3.7
	3.3.2 Dynamic Load Carrying Capacity [C]	3.8
3.4	Stribeck's Equation	3.8
3.5	Equivalent Bearing Load (F_e)	3.10
	3.5.1 Load-Life Relationship	3.13
3.6	Selection of Bearing Life	3.13
3.7	Load Factor in Rolling Contact Bearings	3.14
3.8	Design for Cyclic Loads and Speeds	3.15
3.9	Bearing with a Probability of Survival other than 90%	3.16
3.10	Lubrication and Mounting of Bearings	3.16
	3.10.1 Lubrication of Rolling Contact Bearings	3.16
	3.10.2 Mounting of Rolling Contact Bearings	3.17
	• Solved Examples	3.26
	• Exercise	3.45

4. WORM GEARS   4.1 – 4.36
    4.1   Worm/ Worm Gears   4.1
    4.2   Worm/Worm Gears – Dimensions and Proportions   4.3
    4.3   Gear Enveloping and Rim Constructions   4.7
    4.4   Strength of Worm and Worm Gear   4.9
    4.5   Force Analysis of Worm Gear Drive   4.9
    4.6   Coefficient of Friction and Sliding Velocity   4.13
    4.7   Efficiency of Worm/Worm Gear Pair   4.14
    4.8   Thermal Consideration in Worm Gear Drive   4.16
    4.9   Worm Drive - Type of Failures   4.17
- Solved Examples   4.17
- Exercise   4.35

5. BELTS, ROPE AND CHAIN DRIVES   5.1 – 5.48

BELTS

    5.1   Introduction   5.1
    5.2   Materials and Construction of Flat and V-Belts   5.2
    5.3   Geometric Relationship for Length of Belt   5.3
        5.3.1   Derivation of Equation of Belt Length   5.4
    5.4   Power Rating and Concept of Slip and Creep in Belts   5.6
        5.4.1   Power Rating   5.6
        5.4.2   Concept of Slip and Creep in Belts   5.6
    5.5   Analysis of Belt Forces and Belt Tensions   5.6
        5.5.1   Belt Tension Analysis for Flat Belt   5.6
        5.5.2   Belt Tension Analysis for V-belt   5.8
    5.6   Maximum Power Condition   5.11
    5.7   Selection of Flat and V Belts from Manufacturer's Catalogue   5.13
        5.7.1   Selection of Flat Belts   5.13
        5.7.2   Selection of V belts From Manufacturer's Catalogue   5.15
    5.8   Belt Tensioning Methods   5.18
    5.9   Construction and Applications of Timing Belts   5.19

WIRE ROPES

    5.10   Construction of Wire Ropes   5.20
    5.11   Lay of Wire Ropes   5.21
    5.12   Stresses in Wire Ropes   5.22
    5.13   Selection of Wire Ropes   5.24
    5.14   Rope Drum Construction and Design   5.24

CHAIN DRIVES

5.15	Introduction	5.26
5.16	Types of Power Transmission Chains	5.27
	5.16.1 Roller Chains	5.27
5.17	Chain Geometry	5.28
5.18	Polygonal effect in Chains	5.28
5.19	Modes of Failure for Chain	5.29
5.20	Lubrication of Chains	5.30
	• Solved Examples	5.31
	• Exercise	5.47

6. SLIDING CONTACT BEARINGS   **6.1 – 6.44**

6.1	Lubricating Oils	6.1
6.2	Properties of Lubricating Oils	6.1
6.3	Lubricating Oil Additives	6.4
6.4	Selection of Lubricating Oils	6.5
6.5	Properties and Selection of Bearing Materials	6.7
6.6	Hydrodynamic Lubrication	6.11
6.7	Theory of Hydrodynamic Lubrication	6.11
6.8	Mechanism of Pressure Development	6.13
6.9	Reynold's Equation	6.14
6.10	Raimondi and Boyd Method	6.20
	• Solved Examples	6.27
	• Exercise	6.43

Unit I

SPUR GEARS

GEAR DRIVES

1.1 INTRODUCTION

A positive drive, consisting of toothed wheels which by direct contact, transmits power and motion from one shaft to another, is called as gear drive. A gear drive in comparison with belt, rope and chain drives offers the following advantages.

- Velocity ratio is constant.
- It can transmit more power.
- Efficiency is more.
- It can be operated at very slow or very high speeds.
- It is a compact drive.

However there are some disadvantages such as:

- Lubrication is required to be ensured constantly.
- Initial as well as running cost is high.
- Exact centre distance has to be maintained.
- Manufacturing is difficult and hence costly.

1.2 CLASSIFICATION OF GEARS

Gears are classified as follows:

(a) According to the position of shaft axes:

(i) Parallel

(ii) Intersecting

(iii) Non-parallel and non-intersecting (Skew)

To transmit power between two parallel shafts, spur or helical gears are used. If teeth are cut parallel to the axis of rotation, it is known as spur gear [Refer Fig. 1.1 (a)]. If teeth are cut inclined with the axis of rotation it is known as helical gear [Refer Fig. 1.1 (b)].

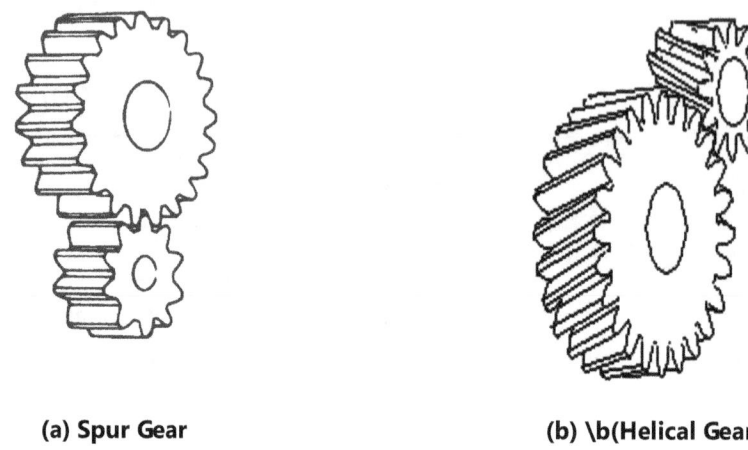

(a) Spur Gear **(b) \b(Helical Gear**

Fig. 1.1

If power is to be transmitted between two intersecting shafts, bevel gear is used. In bevel gears, the teeth are cut along the generator of frustum of cone. Such bevel gear is called as straight teeth bevel [Refer Fig. 1.1 (c)]. If teeth are cut with a curvature on the face of bevel, it is called spiral bevel gear.

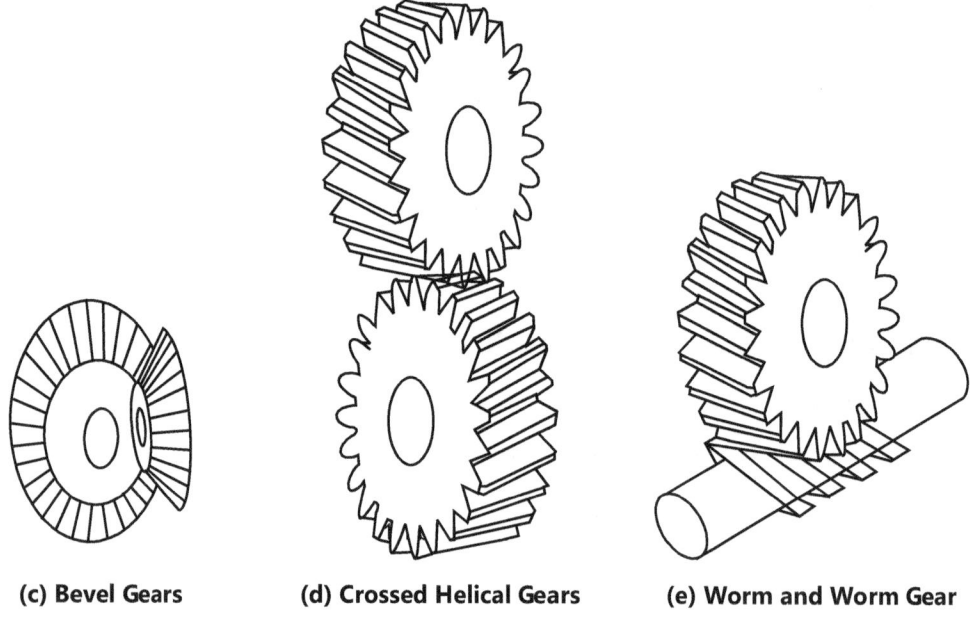

(c) Bevel Gears **(d) Crossed Helical Gears** **(e) Worm and Worm Gear**

Fig. 1.1

If power is to be transmitted between two non-parallel non-intersecting (skew) shafts, spiral gears are used. In this, two helical gears with same hand of helix or opposite hand with unequal helix angles are meshed giving skew arrangement of shafts. The angle between shaft axes is dependent on the hand of helix and value of the helix angle. If the power is to be transmitted at right angles with skew arrangement of shaft axes, we use worm and worm gear. In this drive, worm is a screw thread meshed with a helical gear. [Refer Fig. 1.1 (e)].

(b) According to pitch line velocity:

Gears are classified with this criterion as

- Low speed gears- pitch line velocity less than 3 m/s.
- Medium speed gears- pitch line velocity between 3 m/s to 15 m/s.
- High speed gears- pith line velocity more than 15 m/s.

(c) According to type of gearing:

- External gear
- Internal gear
- Rack and pinion

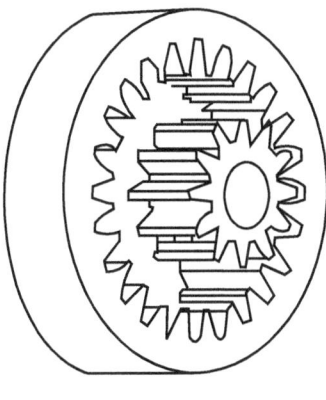 

(f) External - Internal Gear   (g) Rack and Pinion

Fig. 1.1

External gears are more popular because of ease of manufacture and ease of achieving the required precision. In this case, the direction of rotation of meshing gears is opposite to each other while for internal gears it is same. Rack and pinion is used to covert rotary motion into sliding motion.

1.3 GEAR TOOTH TERMINOLOGY

Following are the important terms to be used in this unit (Refer Fig. 1.2).

(i) **Pitch circle:** It is the imaginary circle which by pure rolling action would give the same motion as that of actual gear. Diameter of this circle is known as pitch circle diameter. This is the most important term which defines the profile of a gear tooth.

(ii) **Pitch point:** It is point of tangency between two pitch circles of meshing gears.

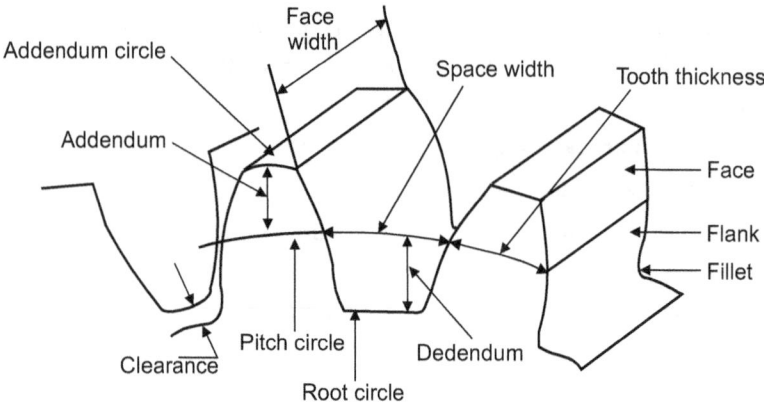

Fig. 1.2: Gear Tooth Terminology

(iii) **Pitch surface:** The rolling surface of two discs which has the diameter equal to pitch circle.

(iv) **Root circle:** It is the circle concentric with pitch circle above which the tooth profile starts. Base circle is the circle above which involute tooth profile starts. Hence, the root circle may or may not be same as the base circle. In case of involute profiles, the root and base circle are different and for cycloidal profiles they are same.

(v) **Pressure angle (ϕ):** It is the angle between common normal drawn at point of contact and common tangent to pitch circles. This angle determines the torque transmission.

(vi) **Face:** The portion of gear tooth above the pitch surface is called as face of a gear tooth.

(vii) **Flank:** The portion of the gear tooth below the pitch surface is called as flank.

(viii) **Addendum (h_a):** The radial height of the gear tooth above the pitch circle is called as addendum, and circle (concentric with pitch circle) passing through it is called addendum circle. It is the largest circle of the gear.

(ix) **Dedendum (h_f):** The radial depth of the gear tooth below pitch circle is called as Dedendum and the circle (concentric with pitch circle) passing through it is called dedendum circle. It is the smallest circle passing through the gear tooth profile.

(x) **Circular pitch (p_c):** It is the distance between the similar points of the successive teeth measured along the pitch circle. Mathematically, it is ratio of circumference of the pitch circle and the number of teeth on the gear. $p_c = \dfrac{\pi d}{z}$ where d is the diameter of the pitch circle and Z is the number of teeth.

(xi) **Diametral pitch (p_d):** It is the ratio of the number of teeth to the pitch circle diameter.

(xii) **Module (m):** It is the ratio of pitch circle diameter to the number of teeth. It is reciprocal of diametral pitch. This is the most important term as it decides the proportions of gear tooth profile and dimensions of gears. In the gear design once the module is known all other major dimensions can be known. Hence once the module is estimated by calculations, the list of standard modules is referred to finalize the value. Closest value of the calculated module will be chosen from the list. The standard modules list gives the information of available cutters. There are two series of standard modules namely module of first choice and second choice. As far as possible the module of first choice shall be chosen. Refer Table 1.1.

(xiii) **Clearance (C):** It is the radial distance between the top of tooth to the bottom of tooth, in a meshing gear.

(xiv) **Total depth:** It is sum of the addendum and dedendum.

(xv) **Working depth:** It is the sum of addendum of two meshing teeth.

(xvi) **Tooth thickness:** It is the width of the gear tooth measured along pitch circle.

(xvii) **Tooth Space:** It is the width of space between two successive teeth measured along the pitch circle.

(xviii) **Backlash:** It is the difference between the tooth space and tooth thickness measured along the pitch circle. Small backlash is desirable as it avoids jamming by accommodating the inaccuracies and also compensates for thermal expansion of the profile. The backlash may be obtained, either by setting the tool deeper into the gear blank or slight increase in the centre distance.

(xix) **Face width (b):** It is the width of gear tooth measured parallel to the axis of rotation.

(xx) **Fillet radius:** It is the radius connecting the tooth profile with root or base circle.

Table 1.1: List of Standard Modules

Module of first choice (mm)	1, 1.25, 1.5, 2, 2.5, 3, 4, 5, 6, 8, 10, 12, 16, 20, 25, 32, 40, 50
Module of second choice (mm)	1.125, 1.375, 1.75, 2.25, 2.75, 3.5, 4.5, 5.5, 7, 9, 11, 14, 18, 22, 28, 36, 45

1.4 LAW OF GEARING

It states that the common normal drawn at any point of contact must intersect the line joining centres of rotation giving always the same pitch points for all points of contact to get constant angular velocity ratio.

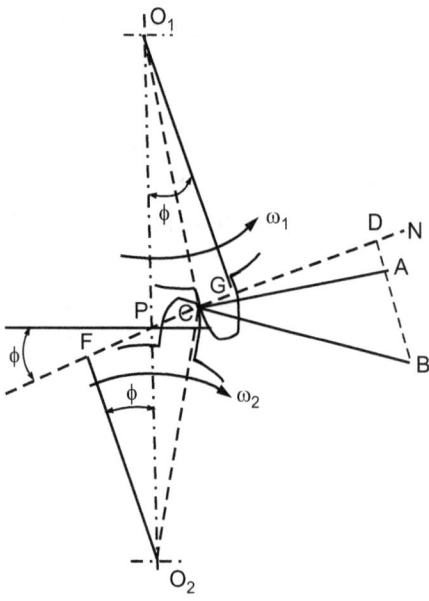

Fig. 1.3: Law of Gearing

In Fig. 1.3, Two profiles 1 and 2 are making contact at point C. A common normal drawn from this point C intersects line O_1O_2 at point P. For any other point of contact on these two profiles, the same intersection point between O_1O_2 and common normal (point P) should be obtained. CA and CB are the velocities of point C on gears 1 and 2 respectively. Their component CD along the common normal at C must be same if there is to be no slip. It can be shown mathematically that, the ratio of the angular velocities of the two profiles is inversely proportional to the ratio of distance between the pitch point and the centre of rotation.

$$\frac{\omega_2}{\omega_1} = \frac{O_1P}{O_2P} = \text{Constant}$$

If for any point of contact, the pitch point (point of intersection between common normal drawn at point of contact and the line joining centres of rotation) remains same, the ratio O_1P/O_2P will be constant or the ratio of angular velocities will be same. This is the law of gearing.

1.5 FORMS OF GEAR TOOTH PROFILE

The profiles which satisfy this condition are called conjugate profiles. For the standardization two profiles are generally used namely:

- Involute profiles.
- Cycloidal profiles.

The comparison of these two profiles is given below:

Sr. No.	Involute Profiles	Cycloidal Profiles
1.	It is defined as the locus of the end of a thread which is tightly wound on a cylinder and released. It gives a single curve known as involute.	It is a combination of two curves obtained by rolling a circle inside and outside of a pitch circle for one complete revolution without slipping. The two opposite curvatures obtained this way are known as hypo-cycloid and epicycloid respectively.
2.	Path of contact is a straight line and lies along the common normal	Path of contact is same as the arc of contact and it lies along the rolling circle.
3.	The pressure angle remains constant as all points of contact lie along same common normal.	Common normal changes the inclination with the common tangent to the pitch circles for different points of contact.
4.	For little variation in centre distance the velocity ratio is unaffected.	Exact centre distance has to be maintained else the velocity ratio will differ.
5.	Easy to manufacture and inspect.	Difficult to manufacture.
6.	As pressure angle remains constant, they are suitable for power transmission.	As the pressure angle varies as the point of contact, used for motion transmission.
7.	Interference occurs.	No interference as the exactly opposite curvatures makes contact.
8.	Due to interference there are limitations for minimum number of teeth.	No such limitations.
9.	Weaker due to radial flank.	Stronger because of wider base.

1.6 SELECTION OF TYPES OF GEARS

The table 1.2 gives broad guidelines for the selection of type of gear to be used for a given application.

Table 1.2: Guidelines for Selection of Gear Type

Type	Features	Application	Remarks
Spur	Parallel shafts, High speeds and loads, Maximum efficiency	Applicable to all types of trains and wide range of velocity ratios	Simplest tooth elements offering maximum precision First choice recommended for all gear meshes, except where very high speed or loads occur.
Helical	Parallel shafts, Very high load and speed, Efficiency slightly less than spur	Most applicable for very high speeds and high loads, Also applicable where spur is used	Equivalent quality to spur gears except the complication of helix angle. Recommended for all very high speed and load cases. Only the axial thrust should be accommodated.
Crossed helical	Skew shafts, Point contact, High sliding, low speeds, Light loads	Relatively low velocity ratio, low speeds and light loads only, Any angle skew shafts	To be avoided for precision meshes, Point contact limits capacity and precision, Suitable for right angle drives with less loads, Less expensive substitute for bevel gears, Good lubrication required due to point contact and high sliding.
Internal spur	Parallel shafts, high speed, high load	In case of high speed and high load, offers low sliding and high stress loading, good for high capacity and long life in planetary gear trains to produce large reduction ratios.	Not recommended for precision meshes, Because of design, fabrication and inspection limitations, should only be used if internal feature is necessary.

contd. ...

Bevel	Intersecting shafts, High speeds, high loads	Right angle shafts, intersecting shafts, high velocity ratios, high speeds and heavy loads, Low efficiency	Good choice for right angle ratios, particularly low ratios, however complicated tooth form and lubrication limits achievement of precision, should be located at one of the less critical meshes in the train.
Worm	Right-angles, Skew shafts, High velocity ratio, High speed and loads, low efficiency, Most designs non reversible	High velocity ratios, High loads, Angular meshes	Worm can be made with high precision, but worm gear has inherent limitations. To be considered for average precision cases but can be of high precision with care. Best choice for combination of right angle with higher velocity ratios. High sliding requires excellent lubrication.

1.6.1 Selection of Materials For Gears

Table 1.3 gives comparison of ferrous materials used for the gears based on strength and hardness.

Table 1.3: Gear Materials

Material	Minimum tensile strength, N/mm^2	IS Designations	BHN
Malleable Cast iron	280-320	WM280, BM320	217 core
Cast iron	200- 350	FG200	300 core
Cast steel	550	CS550	145 core
Plain carbon steel	500-800	50C4, 45C8, 50C8	143-248 core
Alloy steel	550-1550	55Cr70, 40Cr1, 27Mn2, 37Mn2, 45Mn2 Mo28, 35Mn2 Mo45, 40 Cr1 Mo28, 40Cr1 Mo60, 40Ni3, 30 Ni4 Cr1	200-500 core

1.7 STANDARD SYSTEMS OF GEAR TOOTH

There are four different standard gear tooth systems. These systems define the profile of the rack cutter (Refer Fig. 1.4) which is to be used for manufacturing the gears on large scale.

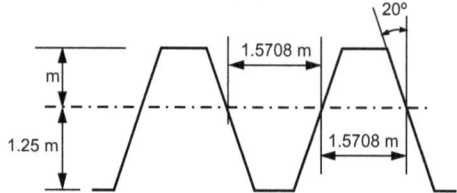

Fig. 1.4 (a): 20° Full Depth Involute Rack

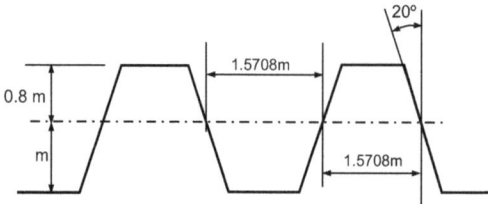

Fig. 1.4 (b): 20° Stub Involute Rack

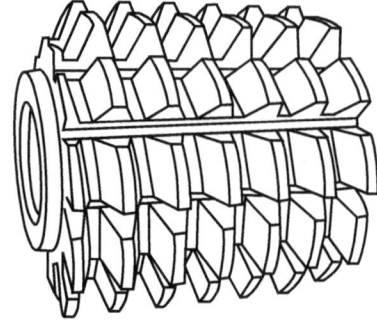

Fig. 1.4 (c): Hob cutter

(i) 14.5° composite system (consists of two curvatures one for cutting involute portion and other curve for cutting fillet).

(ii) 14.5° full depth involute system.

(iii) 20° full depth involute system.

(iv) 20° stub involute system.

The gears manufactured using the standard cutters are known as standard gears and have proportions of the profile in terms of module as given in Table 1.4.

Table 1.4: Proportions of Geometry for Various Standard Gear Tooth Systems

	14.5° Full Depth Involute System	20° Full Depth Involute System	20° Stub Involute System
Addendum	1 m	1 m	0.8 m
Dedendum	1.157 m	1.25 m	1 m
Working depth	2 m	2 m	1.60 m
Minimum total depth	2.157 m	2.25 m	1.8 m
Tooth thickness	1.5708 m	1.5708 m	1.5708 m
Minimum clearance	0.25 m	0.25 m	0.2 m
Fillet radius at root	0.4 m	0.4 m	0.4 m

Generally, 20° full depth involute system is preferred as it gives wider base in turn more stronger teeth. Also it helps in reduction of interference and longer path of contact.

1.8 ADDENDUM MODIFICATION OF GEARS

In case of gears with involute teeth, interference will occur when the number of teeth selected is less than minimum number of teeth required to avoid interference. In this phenomenon, the addendum part of the gear tooth will make contact with non-involute part of other meshing tooth in the region between the base circle and the dedendum circle. To avoid this contact, the addendum of one of the gears is reduced or modified. Practically, while manufacturing the gear, the rack cutter will be shifted by some distance away from the gear blank and for cutting the other meshing gear the rack cutter is shifted towards the centre of the gear blank by same distance. This process is also known as rack shift. (Fig 1.5). Variation in addendum modification coefficient is shown in figure as 'x'.

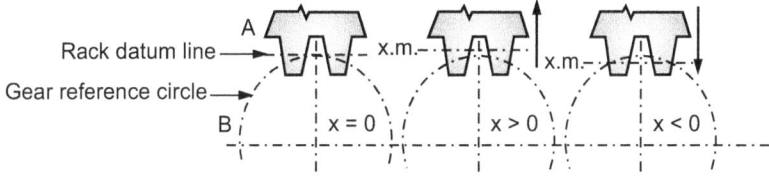

Fig. 1.5: Rack Shift Method

1.9 CROWNING OF GEAR TOOTH

Crowning is a method of strengthening a gear tooth in which uniform distribution of the load along the face width is ensured. When gears mesh with each other the force is transferred from driver to the driven gear along the common normal. The distribution of these forces on the gear tooth is assumed to be uniform. But due to the following reasons this distribution does not remain uniform.

- There are inaccuracies in the tooth profile due to manufacturing limitations and distortion of the profile may occur during heat treatment. These inaccuracies will redistribute the loads resulting in non-uniform loading of gear tooth.
- The elastic deformation of the shaft may also vary the load distribution.
- Also if positional accuracy of bearings and shafts is not up to the mark, the distribution of load will not be uniform.

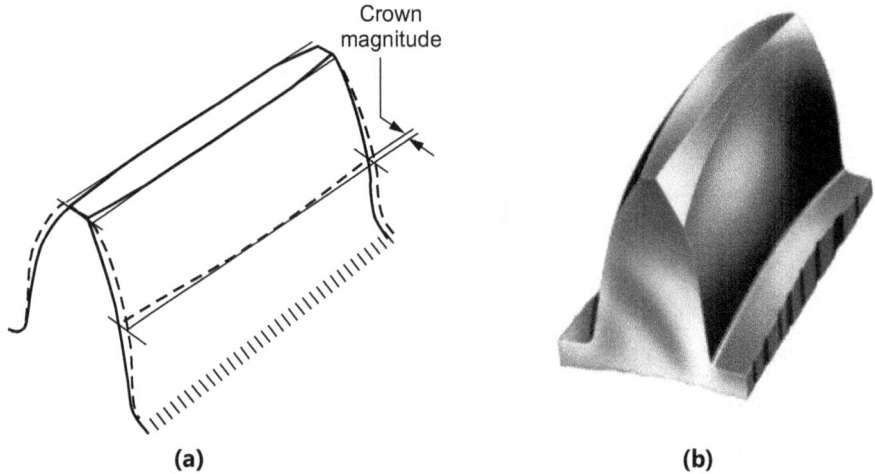

Fig. 1.6: Crowning of Tooth Profile

As a result of this, the maximum pressure gets shifted to the end of tooth along the face width. If at the end of gear tooth extra curvature is added, the maximum pressure will shift towards the central region. Practically, the crowning is done using gear shaving method. (Refer Fig. 1.6).

1.10 BASIC MODES OF GEAR TOOTH FAILURES

Basically, the gear tooth in mesh may break in bending due to excessive loading and as the profiles are in continuous contact it may fail by destruction of surfaces in contact.

(a) Bending or tooth breakage failure:

During meshing, the gear tooth is subjected to static and dynamic loadings. The normal force is resolved in different directions and if the dominant force component (tangential force) is considered, the tooth acts as a cantilever beam which starts bending due to this tangential force, and for a certain load it may break. In order to avoid this kind of failure, one may estimate the module that avoids this failure or select a higher grade material.

(b) Surface destruction:

There are various ways to cause the destruction of the profile surfaces as described below.

(i) **Abrasive wear:** In a gear box, lubricating oil is required in order to limit the temperature of gear box in desired range and reduce the friction. The foreign particles, wear debris or dirt present in the lubricant oil, comes in contact with the interacting profiles (as the oil is splashed) which destructs the interacting profiles. To avoid this kind of failure, oil filter should be used at the inlet port of the lubricating oil. Also the oil should be drained at a regular frequency such that the wear debris are driven out and then fresh oil should be poured.

(ii) **Corrosive wear:** This type of wear is characterized by chemical action of ingredients in the lubricant like high pressure additives. Presence of moisture, foreign materials in the lubricant may corrode the gear tooth profile. In order to avoid this kind of failure, proper lubricant should be chosen, entry to the foreign materials should be restricted and oil be replaced at regular frequency.

(iii) **Initial (corrosive) pitting:** The high spots in the profiles due to inaccuracies get worn out progressively and load is redistributed. Small pits are formed at these high spots after the wear. This is known as initial pitting. The initial pitting can be avoided by machining the gears accurately and ensuring positional accuracy such that the gear tooth is loaded uniformly across the face width.

(iv) **Destructive pitting:** This failure occurs when the stress induced in the surface exceeds the surface endurance strength. When gears are meshed, the radial load puts pressure at the interface and the stress is induced which is called as Hertz or contact stress in the interface. If this contact stress is more than the surface endurance strength, the material removal will start and small pits are formed which progressively develops a crack which continues propagating and fatigue failure occurs. Actually, gears require soft core for damping the shock loading but to improve the surface endurance strength gears need case hardening. In the subsurface region, another failure may occur called as spalling in which due to low subsurface strength, cracks are initiated and progressively develop and appear on the surface. To avoid this kind of failure the case depth of hardening should be increased. But if the case depth is increased, the gear will become more brittle. This failure can be avoided by improving the surface endurance strength by improving surface hardness.

(v) **Scoring:** This failure occurs if lubrication system fails. If sufficient quantity of lubricating oil doesn't reach at the contacting interface, the temperature of the gear tooth goes on increasing. At some moment even gear teeth may get welded. Due to supplied power, these welds get broken or teeth may break. This kind of failure is most likely in case the operating speed of gears is high, or the inaccurate profiles are meshed or heavy tooth load is applied. Remedies for this failure are:

- Ensure the presence of the lubricant with sufficient quantity. Using an oil level indicator or dip stick one can ensure the sufficient quantity of lubricant and also

to limit the operating speed. In some cases additional fins are required to cool the lubricant. If natural convection is not giving required temperature a fan is required additionally to cool the fins and in turn the lubricant.
- Surface finish of the gear tooth profiles should be good.
- Limit the sliding velocity.
- Apply safe load on the gear tooth.

1.11 GEAR LUBRICATION METHODS

Gear lubrication plays a very important role in successful working of a gear drive. Even a properly designed and mounted gear drive can fail with inadequate lubrication. Gears operating at lower pitch line velocities (in case of hand driven mechanisms) are grease lubricated. For medium range of pitch line velocities the gears are placed in an enclosure and dipped in oil. Rotation of the gears induces a splash which will reach the contacting teeth and bearings. The lubrication method in this case is splash lubrication. The type of lubricant used can be straight mineral oil or extreme-pressure lubricants. In some cases to improve the heat transfer a jet of oil is sprayed on the contacting surfaces using an oil pump. In both of these cases a special care has to be taken in order to avoid leakage of oil out of the gear box. Gasket at the mating parts of the gear box casing, oil seals on the shafts which are extruding out of the casing, oil inlet and drain plugs and oil level indicators have to be provided. Also an air breather which ensures the atmospheric pressure inside the casing is required.

SPUR GEARS

1.12 SPUR GEARS - NUMBER OF TEETH AND FACE WIDTH

1.12.1 Number of Teeth

In the design of gears, the important initial step is choosing number of teeth. As the number of teeth decides the operating speed and the torques on various shafts in the gear train or gear box, it becomes very much important to choose the appropriate number of teeth to satisfy the functional requirement of the gear train or gear box under design. Minimum number of teeth required to avoid interference for a standard full depth involute system is given by $Z_{min} = \dfrac{2}{\sin^2 \phi}$

where ϕ is the pressure angle.

Although, the primary step for selecting the number of teeth is based on the functional requirement, the second step which would be applied after this is inclusion of **hunting tooth** in the number of teeth finalized in first step.

Hunting Tooth:

Consider a gear pair in mesh, in which pinion has 'x' number of teeth and gear has '2x'. It means that for one complete revolution of gear, the pinion will rotate twice and same pair of teeth would mesh with each other always. If the number of teeth on gear is increased to '2x + 1', different teeth of pinion and gears would mesh in successive rotations and the uniform wear of all teeth will take place.

1.12.2 Face Width

In order to obtain uniform distribution of tangential tooth load over the face width of the gear, it is important to maintain optimum face width. If the face width is more the force distribution will not be uniform as there will be more load in the middle of the face width compared to the ends. And if the face width is very small, more wear would take place and the shock absorption capacity will be reduced. The face width is expressed in terms of module and usually face width is taken in the range 8 m to 12 m.

$$8\,m < b < 12\,m$$

1.13 DESIRABLE PROPERTIES AND SELECTION OF GEAR MATERIAL

Following properties should be possessed by the gear material:

- The gear material should have more yield strength in order to withstand heavy static and dynamic loading along with softer core to absorb the shocks.
- The coefficient of friction should be less to avoid wear and heat generation.
- The coefficient of thermal expansion should be more.
- It should be heat treatable as case hardening is required in order to avoid pitting failure.
- It should have better machinality as this would decide the precise profile cutting.
- It should possess fairly good corrosion resistance.

For selection of gear materials please refer Table 1.2.

1.14 CONSTRUCTIONAL DETAILS OF GEAR WHEEL

The gear construction is done on the basis of size and material of the gear. Based on size and method of manufacture the following gear constructions are usually used.

(i) Integral gear: The gear is made integral with the shaft if the root circle of the gear is slightly greater than the diameter of shaft with a difference in root circle diameter and the shaft diameter almost equal to the radius of shaft [Fig. 1.7 (a)]. In this case, key is not required. If gear fails, the shaft also needs to be replaced.

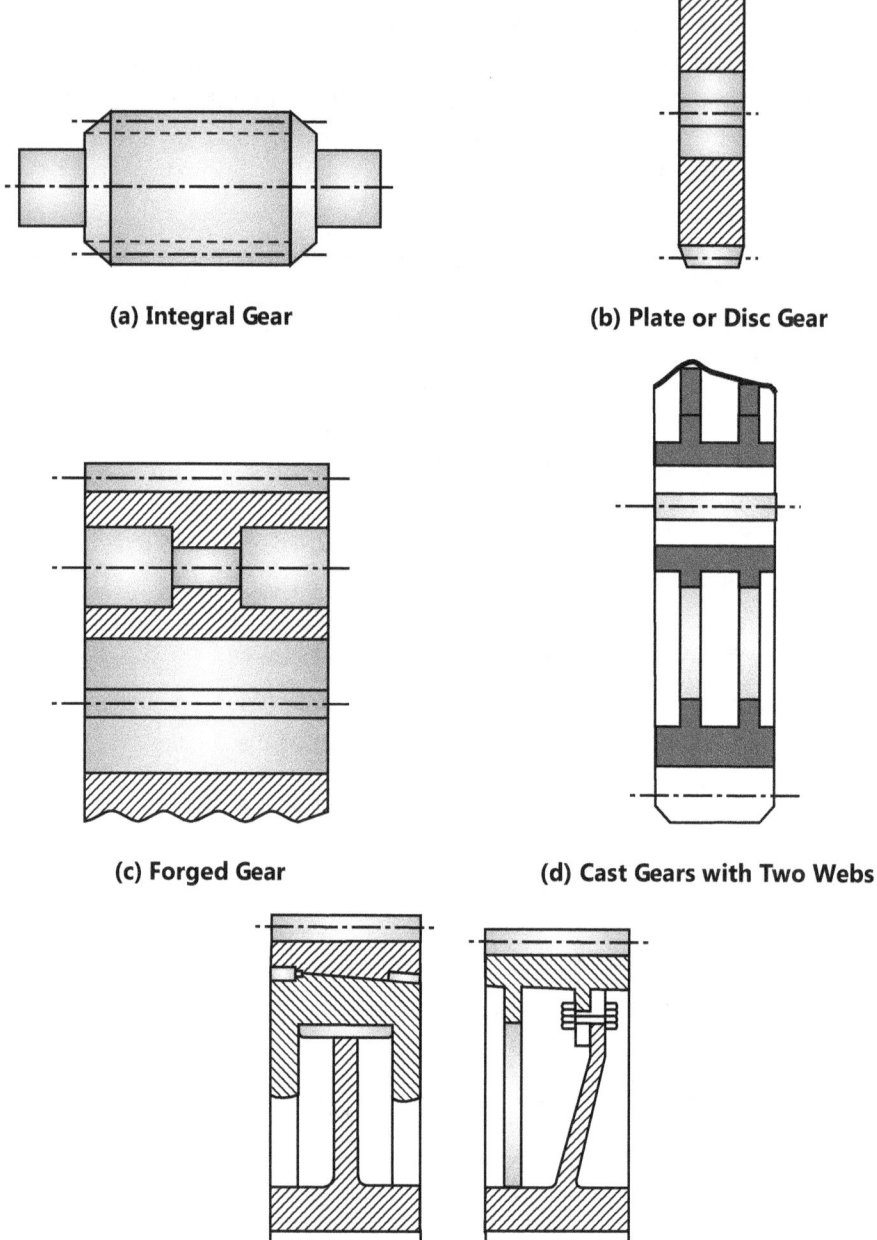

Fig. 1.7

(ii) Plate or disc type: If the gear blank radius is up to 75 mm gears are machined on rolled bars. The details of the construction are shown in Fig. 1.7 (b).

(iii) Forged gear: The gears with a radius of gear blank ranging from 75 mm to 200 mm are forged. The details of the construction are given in the Fig. 1.7 (c). The forged gear is strong and light in weight and low cost in case of mass scale manufacturing.

(iv) Cast gear: There are two different construction methods for the gears of this type. The cast gears will be solid cast with a web if a gear blank diameter is up to 900 mm and will be a rimmed gear with two webs will be preferred if the blank diameter is more than 1000 mm. [Refer Fig. 1.7 (d)].

(v) Cast iron hub connected with steel rim: Rimmed construction with arms or webs connecting the rim with hub is used if the gear blank diameter is more than 1000 mm. In such construction a steel ring on which gear teeth are cut is connected to cast iron rim either by using bolts or grub screws. The thickness of the rim is decided considering the cutting of teeth. [Refer Fig. 1.7 (e)]

1.15 FORCE ANALYSIS

When two gears mesh with each other and driving gear starts rotating, the driving force is exerted on the meshing driven gear along the line of action (common normal drawn at point of contact). Thus, the force transmission line is inclined with the line of motion transmission by an angle equal to pressure angle. This driving force (P_n) will be resolved along the line of motion (P_t) (i.e. common tangent to pitch circles) and along the line joining centers of rotation (P_r). The component along the line of motion is called as tangential force which is a desirable force producing the output torque and the component along the line joining centres of rotation is called as radial force which is undesirable as it tries to separate two meshing gears.

Torque supplied by the driving shaft is given by $T = \dfrac{60P \times 10^6}{2\pi N}$ N-mm

Torque transmitted is given by $T = P_t \times \dfrac{d_p}{2}$ N-mm.

where,
- P = Power supplied in kW
- N = Speed of driver in r.p.m.
- P_t = Tangential tooth force in N
- d_p = Pitch circle diameter of the driver in mm

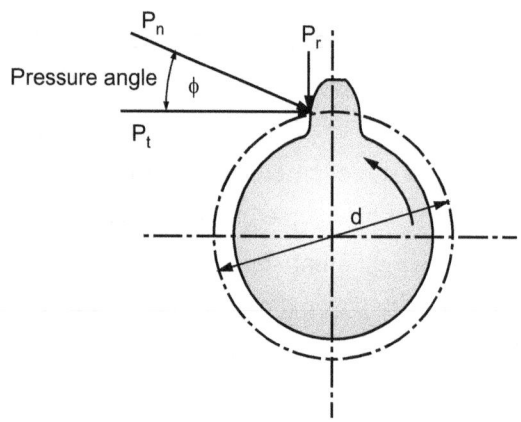

Fig. 1.8: Force Analysis

Direction of rotation of the driver as shown is anticlockwise. The normal force P_n is transmitted along the line of action, which is further resolved into two components. Refer Fig. 1.8.

Magnitude of tangential component in terms of normal force will be

$$P_t = P_n \cos \phi$$

and the radial tooth force is given by

$$P_r = P_n \sin \phi$$

The tangential force P_t can be determined from the known values of power, speed and p.c.d. of driver. Knowing P_t one can find the normal and radial force magnitudes using following equations

$$P_r = P_t \tan \phi$$

and

$$P_n = \frac{P_t}{\cos \phi}$$

This is an approximate method of determining the tooth forces. The exact method is much complex and is out of scope for this book. For the above analysis the following assumptions are considered.

- Only one pair of teeth takes the total load (while in actual case more than one pair shares the normal force transferred from driver to driven).
- The magnitude of the resultant load is considered to be constant.
- Static loading conditions are considered.

1.16 DESIGN CONSIDERATIONS

For design of gears the following important points should be considered:

- The gear tooth should be strong to withstand static and dynamic loading.
- The gear tooth must resist deflection, accelerations and stress concentration.
- The tooth should have good wear resistance ensuring long life.

- Economy of material and space constraint shall be considered.
- Interference shall be avoided using appropriate length of path of contact.
- Perfect alignment and elastic deformation of gears, shafts, supporting members shall be considered.
- Appropriate lubrication system to ensure better performance.

1.17 BEAM STRENGTH (LEWIS EQUATION)

In 1892 Wilfred Lewis developed an equation stating the bending strength of a gear tooth. Beam strength of a gear tooth is defined as the maximum tangential load that tooth can sustain without bending or tooth breakage. The analysis done by Lewis was based on the following assumptions.

- The tangential force is uniformly distributed over the face width of the gear.
- The effect of separating force (radial force) is neglected.
- Stress concentration effect is neglected.
- Only one pair of teeth is in contact which takes the total load at any time.

In the assumptions stated above the tangential load is considered to be uniformly distributed over the face width of the gear. The face width is expressed in terms of module and usually face width is taken in the range 8 m to 12 m.

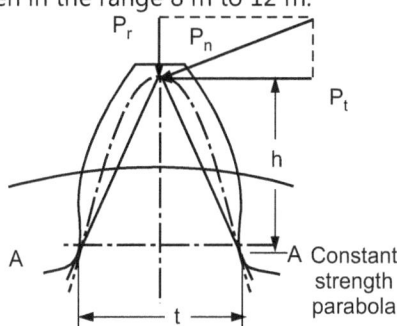

Fig. 1.9: Gear Tooth as Cantilever

Refer Fig. 1.9, which shows a gear tooth profile and an uniform strength parabola inscribed within the tooth profile. Except at base, the gear tooth profile is stronger than the parabola. At section 'AA' the profile and parabola have same strengths. Hence at this section,

Bending moment, $M = P_t \times h$

Moment of inertia of the section at AA, $I = bt^3/12$

And $Y = t/2$

Hence, bending stress at section AA is given by

$$\sigma_b = \frac{M}{\left(\frac{I}{Y}\right)} = \frac{P_t h \times 12 \times \left(\frac{t}{2}\right)}{bt^3} = P_t \left(\frac{6h}{bt^2}\right) \qquad \ldots (1.1)$$

Or $\quad P_t = mb\sigma_b \left(\dfrac{t^2}{6hm}\right)\quad$ ... (Multiplying and dividing by module m)

Let, $\quad Y = \left(\dfrac{t^2}{6hm}\right)$

$P_t = \sigma_b \cdot b \cdot Y \cdot m$

where,
- P_t = Tangential tooth load in N
- m = Module of the gear in mm
- b = Face width in mm (to be chosen between 8 m < b < 12 m)
- σ_b = Permissible bending stress in N/mm² (To be taken as $S_{ut}/3$)
- t = Tooth thickness at root in mm
- h = Height of gear tooth which is length of the cantilever in mm and
- Y = Lewis form factor

This equation gives a relationship between tangential tooth load and bending stress. If the tangential tooth load is varied, the induced bending stress also varies. Beam strength is the ultimate or maximum value of tangential load a gear tooth can sustain without breaking. Hence to get the beam strength of a given gear tooth the permissible value of the bending stress should be used. The tangential load thus obtained using permissible bending stress is considered as beam strength and will be denoted by S_b hence fourth.

$$S_b = \sigma_b \cdot b \cdot Y \cdot m \qquad \ldots (1.2)$$

The permissible value of bending stress for any gear material is taken as one third of ultimate tensile strength. This is done to consider the endurance strength of a gear tooth, as gear tooth is not subjected to static loading. The bending stress on an individual gear tooth is varying. Hence to find the corrected endurance strength considering all the factors such as size factor, shape factor, reliability factor, fatigue stress concentration factor and the approximate relation for the endurance strength of a standard specimen, the corrected endurance strength can be obtained as one third of ultimate tensile strength.

In the beam strength equation, Y is a Lewis form factor which can be obtained by empirical relations given below or the tables given in data books and standards may be used. In both the cases the value of Lewis form factor is based on the number of teeth. If the number of teeth is more, the Lewis form factor will be higher. Following empirical equations may be used for determining the Lewis form factor.

For 14.5° full depth involute and composite systems,

$$Y = 0.389 - \dfrac{2.148}{Z}$$

For 20° full depth involute systems,
$$Y = 0.484 - \frac{2.87}{Z}$$

For 20° stub involute systems,
$$Y = 0.55 - \frac{2.64}{Z}$$

1.18 VELOCITY FACTOR

The tangential load is a static load. In addition to this, because of the following reasons, dynamic load is induced between the meshing teeth.
- In accurate tooth profile
- Uneven tooth space
- Bearing misalignment
- Inertia of moving parts.

This dynamic load can be estimated by either approximate or exact analysis. While designing a gear pair in the initial stages it is recommended to use approximate method. And once the module is known the exact method can be used to check the design.

The approximate analysis was developed by Barth and he came out with empirical relations to find the velocity factor (also known as Barth factor) to consider the effect of dynamic load. This factor is used to find the magnitude of the maximum tangential load for design of gears.

(i) For ordinary and commercially cut gears made with form cutters and pitch line velocity less than 10 m/s.
$$C_v = \frac{3}{3 + v}$$

(ii) For generated teeth with pitch line velocity less than 20 m/s.
$$C_v = \frac{6}{6 + v}$$

(iii) For precise teeth shaved, ground and lapped and pitch line velocity more than 20 m/s.
$$C_v = \frac{5.6}{5.6 + \sqrt{v}}$$

In all the above relations, v is the pitch line velocity in m/s units.

1.19 SERVICE FACTOR

It is a load modifying factor used to find the maximum tangential load. While the forces on meshing gear teeth are analyzed, the effect of inertia and other resisting forces for acceleration or in the instant when the gears start rotating from rest condition are not considered. Hence to incorporate all such conditions in the analysis a simple way is to modify the magnitude of tangential load obtained using the mean torque. Hence, the service factor may be given by ratio of maximum tangential load actually applied to the tangential load obtained using mean torque value.

The service factor depends on type of prime mover and the type of driven machinery and can be obtained using the recommendations given in the Table 1.5. The service factor for a same application with different prime movers is different. (e.g.: If prime mover is a motor, the service factor would be smaller and for same driven machine if prime mover is I.C. Engine the service factor is higher.) If the type of prime mover is same and the driven machine is different, the service factor will be different. Depending on whether an electric motor starts on no load or full load, the starting torque of the motor is higher compared to its rated torque. This ratio also represents service factor.

The range of recommended service factor is from 1.10 to 2.25.

Let T be the mean torque obtained from equation $T = \dfrac{60P \times 10^6}{2\pi N}$

The tangential load would be found using equation $P_t = \dfrac{2T}{d}$

The tangential load will get modified using equation $= C_s P_t$.

Table 1.5: Cs (considering 8 hrs/day operation)

Power Source	Load on driven machine		
	Uniform	Moderate shock	Heavy shock
Uniform - Electric motor	1.00	1.25	1.75
Light shock - Multi cylinder engine	1.25	1.50	2.00
Heavy shock - Single cylinder engine	1.50	1.75	2.25

1.20 LOAD CONCENTRATION FACTOR (C_L)

In the Lewis beam strength equation it was assumed that the tangential tooth load is uniformly distributed over the face width. But practically because of misalignments in gears, bearings or errors, elastic deformation of gears or supporting elements like bearings, housings or casing the tangential tooth load gets concentrated at any position along the face width. To consider this effect load concentration factor is used to modify the tangential tooth load. The value of the load concentration factor can be chosen from the Table. The range of this factor varies from 1.3 to 2.2. The lower value is recommended in the precise mounting and the higher value corresponds to average accuracy in mounting the bearings.

1.21 EFFECTIVE LOAD ON GEAR (P_{eff})

For the design of the spur gear based on the beam strength, it is already discussed that the tangential load will be considered. Further the modifying factors for this tangential load were discussed. Considering all these modifying factors the effective load is obtained. It is assumed that the gear tooth is subjected to this effective load and the module will be obtained.

$$P_{eff} = \frac{C_s C_L P_t}{C_v} \quad \text{[To be used in the initial stages of the design]} \quad \ldots (1.3)$$

$$P_{eff} = C_s C_L P_t + P_d \quad \text{[To be used after knowing the module]} \quad \ldots (1.4)$$

Here, P_{eff} is the effective tooth load in N.
C_s is the service factor
C_L is the load concentration factor
C_v is the velocity factor
P_t is the tangential tooth load in N
P_d is the dynamic tooth load obtained by Buckingham's equation in N

Buckingham's Incremental Dynamic Tooth Load Equation

The effective load obtained using velocity factor is only an approximate estimate of the dynamic load. In practice it was observed that the dynamic load depends greatly on accuracy with which the gears are cut and gears are mounted. Elaborate experimentation led Buckingham to arrive at an equation which can estimate the incremental dynamic load. The incremental load is to be added to the maximum tangential load to obtain effective load.

$$P_d = \frac{21v \, (C \cdot b + C_s C_L P_t)}{21v + \sqrt{(C \cdot b + C_s C_L P_t)}} \quad \ldots (1.5)$$

This equation is also written as

$$P_d = \frac{21v \, (C \cdot b + P_{tmax})}{21v + \sqrt{(C_b + P_{tmax})}}$$

where, $P_{tmax} = C_s \cdot C_L \cdot P_t$
v = Pitch line velocity in m/s
b = The face width of gear in mm
C = Deformation factor in N/mm

$$C = e \cdot \frac{K}{\left[\dfrac{1}{E_p} + \dfrac{1}{E_g}\right]}$$

K = Factor depending upon tooth form
K = 0.107 for 14.5° full depth involute and composite systems.
 = 0.111 for 20° full depth involute teeth.
 = 0.115 for 20° stub involute systems.

E_p, E_g are the moduli of elasticity for pinon and gear materials respectively in N/mm^2.
e is the total tooth error in the pinion and the gear, mm.

With standard values of E_p, E_g for steel materials = 2.07×10^5 N/mm² and K for 20° pressure angle

$$C = 11500*e \quad \text{(N/mm) for Steel pinion with steel gear}$$
$$C = 10000*e \quad \text{(N/mm) for steel pinion on Cast Iron gear}$$
$$C = 8900*e \quad \text{(N/mm) for Cast Iron pinion with Cast Iron gear}$$

To find the tooth error, standards give one to twelve grades of the accuracy levels of gear cutting obtained by considering various manufacturing processes and the error equations related to them where e = 16.0 + 1.25ϕ, and ϕ is called tolerance factor and to be found using equation, $\phi = m + 0.25\sqrt{d}$. Refer Table 1.6 for error equations for various grades.

e.g. for a gear of grade 8, to find the error in pinion in microns, use e_p = 16.0 + 1.25 (m + 0.25 $\sqrt{d_p}$) with values of d_p and module m for the pinion. For error on gear use d_g in place of d_p. (Values of d_p or d_g should be in mm)

To find the total error, add the tooth error of pinion and gear. These equations give value of error in microns to be converted in mm.

Total tooth error: $e = e_p + e_g$

Table 1.6: Tooth Profile Error

Grade	Error in tooth profile (in micron)
1.	e = 0.80 + 0.06 ϕ
2.	e = 1.25 + 0.10 ϕ
3.	e = 2.00 + 0.16 ϕ
4.	e = 3.20 + 0.25 ϕ
5.	e = 5.00 + 0.40 ϕ
6.	e = 8.00 + 0.63 ϕ
7.	e = 11.0 + 0.90 ϕ
8.	e = 16.0 + 1.25 ϕ
9.	e = 22.0 + 1.80 ϕ
10.	e = 32.00 + 2.50 ϕ
11.	e = 45 + 3.55 ϕ
12.	e = 63.00 + 5.00 ϕ

1.22 WEAR STRENGTH (BUCKINGHAM'S EQUATION)

Gear tooth fails in pitting i.e. surface destruction if the induced contact stress at the surface exceeds the surface endurance strength of the material. To avoid this failure, the size and the surface hardness should be so chosen that the gear becomes capable of taking the effective tooth load. This theory was invented by Buckingham.

Refer Fig. 1.10 (a) in which two cylinders of diameters d_1 and d_2 and unit length (length = l) are making contact with each other. These cylinders are pressed against each other. The contact or Hertz stress is induced at the interface. It is given by

$$\sigma_c = \frac{2P}{\pi h l} \qquad \ldots (1.6)$$

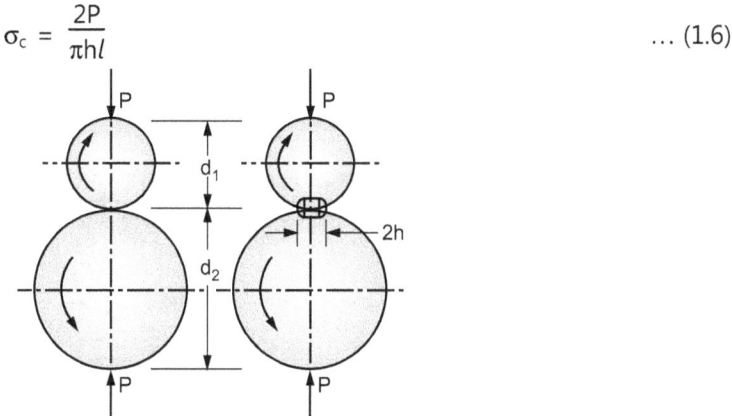

Fig. 1.10 (a): Cylinders Rolling on Each Other

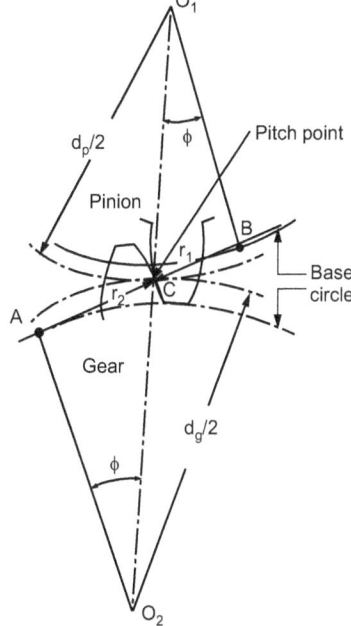

Fig. 1.10 (b): Gears in Mesh

Here,
$$h = \left[\dfrac{2P(1-v)^2\left[\dfrac{1}{E_1}+\dfrac{1}{E_2}\right]}{\pi l\left(\dfrac{1}{d_1}+\dfrac{1}{d_2}\right)}\right]^{\frac{1}{2}}$$

Where,

σ_c = The maximum compressive stress
P = Compressive force applied to press the cylinders
h = Half width of deformation
l = Axial length of cylinder
d_1, d_2 = Diameters of the cylinders
E_1, E_2 = Modulii of elasticity for cylinder materials
v = Poission's ratio.

The effect of compressive force P is to deform the cylinder in approximate elliptical shape with 2h as width and l as length. Substituting h in σ_c equation and squaring both sides,

$$\sigma_c^2 = \dfrac{1}{\pi(1-v^2)}\left(\dfrac{P}{l}\right)\left[\dfrac{\left(\dfrac{1}{r_1}+\dfrac{1}{r_2}\right)}{\left(\dfrac{1}{E_1}+\dfrac{1}{E_2}\right)}\right] \quad \ldots (1.7)$$

Where, r_1 and r_2 are the radii of the two cylinders rolling with a radial pressure. Considering Poisson's ratio as 0.3,

$$\sigma_c^2 = 0.35\left(\dfrac{P}{l}\right)\left[\dfrac{\left(\dfrac{1}{r_1}+\dfrac{1}{r_2}\right)}{\left(\dfrac{1}{E_1}+\dfrac{1}{E_2}\right)}\right]$$

The above equation gives the relation for the maximum compressive stress or Hertz stress for the cylinders rolling with radial pressure.

When only one pair of teeth takes the load, contact takes place at pitch point. Refer Fig. 1.22 (b). The analysis presented here is considering the contact takes place at the pitch point. Hence, the radius of curvature of the gear tooth is selected at pitch point. Also the dynamic load is imposed on the tooth near pitch line area and the wear on gear tooth usually occurs near the pitch line.

If same theory is to be applied to the gears, following substitutions shall be made.

$r_1 = O_1C \cdot \sin\phi = \dfrac{d_p \sin\phi}{2}$ and $r_2 = O_2C \cdot \sin\phi = \dfrac{d_g \sin\phi}{2}$ which are the radii of curvature of the tooth profiles. Length of cylinder would be replaced by the face width $l = b$.

$$\left(\dfrac{1}{r_r}+\dfrac{1}{r_2}\right) = \dfrac{2}{\sin\phi}\left[\dfrac{1}{d_p}+\dfrac{1}{d_2}\right] \quad \ldots (1.8)$$

If Q is considered as ratio factor given by $\dfrac{2Z_g}{Z_p + Z_g}$

Or
$$Q = \frac{2d_g}{d_p + d_g} \quad \text{... [as } d = mZ\text{]}$$

$$\left(\frac{1}{d_p} + \frac{1}{d_g}\right) = \frac{d_p + d_g}{d_p d_g} = \frac{2}{Q d_p} \quad \text{... (1.9)}$$

From equations (a) and (b),

$$\left(\frac{1}{r_1} + \frac{1}{r_2}\right) = \frac{4}{Q d_p \sin \phi}$$

The force along the pitch line is P_n which is $P_n = \dfrac{P_t}{\cos \phi}$.

Substituting all these values in the contact stress equation (1.7),

$$\sigma_c^2 = \frac{1.4 P_t}{b Q d_p \sin \phi \cos \phi \left(\dfrac{1}{E_p} + \dfrac{1}{E_g}\right)} \quad \text{... (1.10)}$$

Defining a load stress factor K as

$$K = \frac{\sigma_c^2 \sin \phi \cos \phi \left(\dfrac{1}{E_p} + \dfrac{1}{E_g}\right)}{1.4}$$

$$P_t = b Q d_p K$$

This equation gives the relation between the contact stress and the applied tangential load. If load increases the induced contact stress also increases. If the induced stress exceeds the endurance strength of gear surface, pitting failure occurs. Hence in order to avoid this failure, the maximum safe tangential force known as wear strength (S_w) can be estimated based on the permissible values of the endurance limit.

$$\therefore \quad S_w = b Q d_p K \quad \text{... (1.11)}$$

The load stress factor K can be calculated as follows:

For 20° pressure angle, steel as material for gears, the modulus of elasticity is 207000 N/mm², and the compressive stress according to Gustav Niemen,

$$\sigma_c = 0.27 \, BHN \, kgf/mm^2 = (0.27 \times 9.81) \, BHN \, N/mm^2$$

Considering the material of pinion and gear as steel, and substituting the value of contact stress, the load stress factor will be approximately

$$K = 0.16 \left(\frac{BHN}{100}\right)^2 \quad \text{... (for pinion and gear made of steel)}$$

$$K = 0.18 \left(\frac{BHN}{100}\right)^2 \quad \text{... (for steel pinion and cast iron gear)}$$

$$K = 0.21 \left(\frac{BHN}{100}\right)^2 \quad \text{... (for pinion and gear made of cast iron)}$$

With the following substitutions wear strength of a gear tooth in terms of module is estimated.

- b, the face width taken between 8 m to 10 m.
- Q, the ratio factor is evaluated by equation $\dfrac{2Z_g}{Z_p + Z_g}$
- d_p, the pitch circle diameter can be taken as $m \times Z_p$
- K, the load stress factor $K = 0.16 \left(\dfrac{BHN}{100}\right)^2$

1.23 GEAR DESIGN

Gear designer is mainly confronted with two situations.

- In the first situation, he is required to find the required module and thus design the gear pair for a given load and required speed.
- In the second situation, for a given gear drive designer is required to find factor of safety for transmitting certain power. He may face a situation where a given gear pair is reporting failure and is interested in knowing the theoretical factor of safety for transmitting that power.

The following procedure may be adopted for the estimation of the module.

Estimate load in terms of module:

- Find pitch line velocity $v = \dfrac{\pi \cdot d \cdot N_p}{60 \times 1000}$ ... m/sec. where ($d = Z_p \times m$) is in mm, and Z_p is known.
- Find tangential load, $P_t = \dfrac{\text{Power (kW)} \times 1000}{v}$ ... (N) in terms of module.
- Find velocity factor C_v using appropriate relationship in terms of module.
- Knowing factor C_s, C_L and C_v find, $P_{eff} = \dfrac{C_s C_L P_t}{C_v}$

Estimate Beam and Wear Strength in Terms of Module: For checking the beam strength, initially the weak element out of pinion and gear is identified using equation $S_b = \sigma_b \cdot b \cdot Y \cdot m$. If pinion and gear materials are same, pinion will always be weaker of the two since 'Y' for smaller value of Z will be smaller and other quantities are same for both. For different materials for pinion and gear, first calculate the product of permissible bending stress and the Lewis form factor $(\sigma_b Y)_{pinion}$, $(\sigma_b Y)_{gear}$ for pinion as well as gear. The weaker element will have this product smaller of the two. Considering b = 10 m, beam strength will be calculated in terms of module which is unknown at this stage. Smaller S_b controls the design for beam strength.

Wear strength (S_w) is estimated in terms of module and is estimated for a pair. The hardness estimated is applicable for both pinion and gear. However, since pinion will rotate more revolutions compared to gear, it will wear out more. Hence in practice gear is provided with the calculated value of hardness and pinion hardness may be increased by 25 to 30 BHN.

The module for the weaker element is found out based on either Beam strength or Wear strength. Determine the module based on the smallest value of the Beam or Wear strength.

Effective load and the strength can now be equated considering factor of safety as below.

$$\text{Smaller of } (S_b) \text{ or } (S_w) = P_{eff} \times (FS)$$

Unknown module can now be found out.

Procedure to find factor of Safety/Transmission Capacity for a given Gear Drive (Module Known):

- Find pitch line velocity, $v = \dfrac{\pi \cdot d \cdot N_p}{60 \times 1000}$ ... m/sec. where d is in mm

- Find tangential load, $\dfrac{\text{Power (kW)} \times 1000}{v}$ ... N

- Knowing factor C_s and C_L find, $P_{t\,max} = C_s \cdot C_L \cdot P_t$

- Designer decides the grade of gear cutting accuracy based on the technical requirements and its cost impact. Higher accuracies will result into lesser gear cutting errors. This will reduce dynamic loads and improve tangential load capacity. This however also increases the cost. Designer has to strike a balance. Once the accuracy grade is selected, permissible tooth errors on pinion (e_p) and on gears (e_g) can be estimated. Knowing pinion/gear materials and permissible error ($e = e_p + e_g$), deformation factor C can be found out.

- Find dynamic load P_d using: $P_d = \dfrac{21\,v\,(C \cdot b + P_{tmax})}{21\,v + \sqrt{(C_b + P_{tmax})}}$

- Find $P_{eff} = P_{t\,max} + P_d$

- Find the beam strength S_b and Wear Strength S_w as discussed above.

- Effective load and the strength can now be equated considering factor of safety as below.

$$\text{Smaller of } (S_b) \text{ or } (S_w) = P_{eff} \times (FS)$$

- The unknown either FS or $P_{t\,max}$ can be found out from above equation.

SOLVED EXAMPLES

Example 1.1: Design a spur gear pair with 20° involute teeth based on beam strength. The velocity factor is to be used to account for dynamic load. The pinion shaft is connected to a 12 kW, 1440 rpm motor. The reduction ratio is 4 : 1 and pinion has 18 teeth. Pinion as well as gear are made of 40 C8 (S_{ult} = 610 MPa). The factor of safety and service factors both can be taken as 1.5.

Specify the dimensions of gears and suggest suitable hardness for gear.

Given data: Input power = 12 kW, N_p = 1440 rpm, $\dfrac{Z_g}{Z_p}$ = 4, Z_p = 18, (S_{ult}) = 610 N/mm², C_s = FS = 1.5.

Solution: Effective load (Based on P_t, C_s, C_v). We first find tangential load on the pinion.

Torque on pinion:

$$T_p = \frac{60 \times P}{2\pi \cdot N} \times 10^6 \text{ N·mm}$$

$$= \frac{60 \times 12}{2\pi \times 1440} \times 10^6 = 79577.5 \text{ N·mm}$$

Tangential load P_t:

$$P_t = \frac{2 \cdot T}{m \cdot Z_p} = \frac{2 \times 79577.5}{m \times 18} = \frac{8842}{m}$$

Velocity factor C_v: (Assuming velocity to be less than 10 m/sec.)

$$C_v = \frac{3}{3 + v}$$

where,

$$v = \frac{\pi d_p \cdot N_p}{60 \times 1000} = \frac{\pi \times 18 \times m \times 1440}{60 \times 1000}$$

$$= 1.36 \text{ m}$$

$$C_v = \frac{3}{3 + 1.36 \text{ m}}$$

Effective load, P_{eff}:

$$P_{eff} = \frac{C_s}{C_v} \cdot P_t$$

$$= \frac{1.5}{\left[\dfrac{3}{(3 + 1.36 \text{ m})}\right]} \times \frac{8842}{m}$$

$$P_{eff} = \frac{13263 (1 + 0.453 \text{ m})}{m}$$

Beam strength:

Since pinion and gear are made from same material, pinion is weaker. Hence, here, we find beam strength for pinion.

$$S_b = \sigma_b \cdot b \cdot Y \cdot m$$

where,
$$\sigma_b = \frac{S_{ult}}{3} = \frac{610}{3}$$

$$b = 10 \cdot m$$

$$Y = 0.484 - \frac{2.87}{Z_p}$$

$$= 0.484 - \frac{2.87}{18} = 0.324$$

$$S_b = \frac{610}{3} \times (10\,m) \times 0.324 \times m$$

$$= 658.8\,m^2$$

S_w cannot be calculated as hardness is not known.

∴ Equating bending strength with P_{eff} considering FS.

$$S_b = FS \times P_{eff}$$

$$658.8\,m^2 = 1.5 \times \left[\frac{13263\,(1 + 0.453\,m)}{m}\right]$$

$$658.8\,m^3 = 19894.5 + 9012.2\,m$$

$$m^3 - 13.67\,m - 30.2 = 0$$

Solving, $m \simeq 4.5$ mm

Next preferred module value is 5 mm.

Hence, we select m = 5 mm (for both pinion and gear).

$$\text{Pinion width} = 10\,m = 50\,mm$$
$$\text{Pinion diameter} = m \cdot Z_p = 90\,mm$$
$$\text{Gear diameter} = m \cdot Z_g = 360\,mm$$

Exact value of effective load

$$P_{eff} = \frac{13263\,(1 + 0.453\,m)}{m}, \text{ with } m = 5\,mm$$

$$= 8661\,N$$

Wear strength : (In terms of BHN)

$$S_w = b \cdot Q \cdot d_p \cdot K$$

where,
$$Q = \frac{2Z_g}{Z_g + Z_p} = \frac{2 \times 72}{18 + 72} = 1.6$$

$$K = 0.16 \left(\frac{BHN}{100}\right)^2$$

$$S_w = (10 \times 5)(1.6)(90) \times 0.16 \left(\frac{BHN}{100}\right)^2 = 1152 \left(\frac{BHN}{100}\right)^2$$

Equating wear strength with effective load considering FS,

$$S_w = FS [P_{eff}]$$

$$1152 \left(\frac{BHN}{100}\right)^2 = 1.5 [8661]$$

$$BHN = 335.8 \simeq 336$$

Example 1.2: A pair of spur gears with a 20° pressure angle consists of a 25 teeth pinion with 60 teeth gear. The module is 5 mm while its face width is 50 mm. The pinion rotates at 600 rpm. The gears are made of steel and heat treated to a surface hardness of 250 BHN. Assume that the dynamic load is accounted by means of velocity factor. The service factor and factor of safety are 1.75 and 2.1 respectively. Calculate wear strength of the gear, the static load that gears can transmit without pitting and rated power that can be transmitted.

Assume $C_v = \dfrac{3}{3+v}$

Given data: $Z_p = 25$, $Z_g = 60$, $m = 5$ mm, $b = 50$ mm, $N_p = 600$, $BHN = 250$, $C_s = 1.75$, $FS = 2.1$.

Solution: Design in this case is based only on wear strength.

(a) Wear strength: ($b = 50$, $d_p = m \times Z_p = 125$)

$$S_w = b \cdot K \cdot Q \cdot d_p$$

$$K = 0.16 \left(\frac{BHN}{100}\right)^2 \text{ for steel on steel}$$

$$= 0.16 (2.5)^2 = 1.0$$

$$Q = \frac{2Z_g}{Z_g + Z_p} = 1.4117$$

$$S_w = 50 \times 1.0 \times 1.41 \times 125$$

$$= 8823 \text{ N}$$

(b) Effective load:

$$P_{eff} = \frac{C_s}{C_v} \cdot P_t$$

Pitch line velocity v

$$v = \frac{\pi d_p \cdot N_p}{60 \times 1000} = \frac{\pi \times 125 \times 600}{60 \times 1000} = 3.927 \text{ m/sec}$$

$$C_v = \frac{3}{3+v} = \frac{3}{3+3.927} = 0.433$$

$$\therefore P_{eff} = \frac{1.75}{0.433} \cdot P_t = 4.041 \cdot P_t$$

DESIGN OF MACHINE ELEMENTS - II   SPUR GEAR

Equating P_{eff} with wear strength considering factor of safety

$$S_w = FS \cdot (P_{eff})$$
$$8823 = 2.1 \times 4.041 \, P_t$$

∴ Static load capacity, $P_t = 1040$ N

(c) Rated power capacity $\left(\text{Torque} = P_t \times \dfrac{d_p}{2} = 65000 \text{ N·mm}\right)$

$$P = \frac{2\pi NT}{60 \times 10^6} = \frac{2\pi \times 600 \times 65000}{60 \times 10^6} = 4.08 \text{ kW}$$

Example 1.3: A pair of 20° full involute teeth spur gear is to transmit 35 kW at 750 rpm. The velocity ratio is ratio 3.5 : 1. The pinion is made of steel having allowable stress of 110 N/mm². The gear is made of cast iron having allowable stress of 60 N/mm².

The pinion has 16 teeth and the face width is 12 times the module. Determine the module, face width and pitch diameter of both pinion and gear from the standpoint of strength taking into consideration the velocity factor.

Tooth form factor is $Y = 0.484 - \dfrac{2.85}{Z}$

Velocity factor $C_v = \dfrac{5}{5+v}$

Assume service factor as 1.5 and load concentration factor as 1.3.
Consider factor of safety as 1.5.

Given data: 35 kW, $N_p = 750$ rpm, $\dfrac{Z_2}{Z_1} = 3.5$, $(\sigma_{all})_{pinion} = 110$ N/mm², $(\sigma_{all})_{gear} = 60$ N/mm², $Z_p = 16$, $Z_g = 56$, $b = 12$ m, $C_s = 1.5$, $C_L = 1.3$.

Solution:

Effective load:

$$\text{Tangential load} = \frac{\text{Power}}{\text{Pitch line velocity}} = \frac{35 \times 10^6}{\left(\dfrac{\pi \times 16 \, m \times 750}{60}\right)}$$

$$P_t = \frac{35 \times 10^3}{0.628 \, m} = \frac{55704}{m}$$

$$C_v = \frac{5}{5+v} = \frac{5}{(5 + 0.628 \, m)}$$

∴ $$P_{eff} = \left(\frac{C_s C_L}{C_v}\right) P_t = \frac{1.5 \times 1.3 \, (5 + 0.628 \, m)}{5} \times \frac{55704}{m}$$

$$P_{eff} = \frac{108622.8 \, (5 + 0.628 \, m)}{5 \, m}$$

Beam strength:

$$S_b = \sigma_b \cdot b \cdot Y \cdot m$$

Since pinion and gear materials are different, we need to find which one is weaker.

$$Y_p = 0.484 - \frac{2.85}{Z_p} = 0.484 - \frac{2.85}{16} = 0.306$$

$$Y_g = 0.484 - \frac{2.85}{Z_g} = 0.484 - \frac{2.85}{56} = 0.4331$$

$$(\sigma_b \cdot Y)_{pinion} = 110 \times 0.306 = 33.66$$

$$(\sigma_b \cdot Y)_{gear} = 60 \times 0.4331 = 25.986$$

Since, $(S_b \cdot Y)_{gear} < (S_b \cdot Y)_{pinion}$

Gear is weaker. Hence, beam strength will be calculated based on gear strength.

$$\therefore S_b = (\sigma_b \cdot Y)_{gear} \times b \times m$$
$$= 25.986 \times 12.m \times m = 311.84 \, m^2$$

Equating beam strength with P_{eff} considering factor of safety

$$S_b = (P_{eff}) \, FS$$

$$311.84 \, m^2 = \left[\frac{108622.8 \, (5 + 0.628 \, m)}{5m}\right] \times 1.5$$

$$m^3 = 104.49 \, (5 + 0.628 \, m)$$

$$m^3 - 65.625 \, m - 522.45 = 0$$

By trial and error method

$$m \simeq 10.7 \text{ mm}$$

Select next preferred module size = 12 mm

(a) Module $\simeq$ 12 mm
(b) Face width = 12 m = 144 mm
(c) Pinion pitch circle diameter = $m \times Z_p$ = 192 mm
    Gear pitch circle diameter = $m \times Z_g$ = 672 mm

Example 1.4: A pair of spur gear with 20° full depth involute consists of 20 teeth pinion meshing with 60 teeth on gear. The pinion rotates at 1000 rpm and receives 20 kW power through its shaft. The pinion as well as gear are made up of steel and the permissible bending stress is 260 N/mm². The gears are machined to grade 7. For this grade $e = 11 + 0.9 \, \phi$ where $\phi = (m + 0.25 \sqrt{d})$ where, m and d are the module and pcd respectively. Use Lewis form factor.

$$Y = 0.484 - \frac{2.85}{Z} \text{ and } C_v = \frac{6}{6 + v}$$

DESIGN OF MACHINE ELEMENTS - II — SPUR GEAR

Design the gears, specify their dimensions and find out the required value of surface hardness of gear. Take load concentration factor as 1.3, service factor as 1.25. Consider dynamic load by Buckingham's equation.
Required factor of safety is 1.5.
Deformation factor 'C' for gear spur is $11500 \cdot e$ N/mm.

Given data: $Z_p = 20$, $Z_q = 60$, $N_p = 1000$ rpm, Power = 20 kW, $(\sigma_b)_{all} = 260$ N/mm², $C_s = 1.25$, $C_L = 1.3$, FS = 1.5.

Solution:

$$\text{Pitch line velocity, } v = \frac{\pi d_p N_p}{60 \times 10^3} = \frac{\pi \times 20\, m \times 1000}{60 \times 10^3} = 1.047\, m$$

$$\text{Tangential force, } P_t = \frac{\text{Power}}{\text{Velocity}} = \frac{20 \times 10^3}{1.047\, m} = \frac{19102.2}{m}\, N$$

$$\text{Velocity factor, } C_v = \frac{6}{6+v} = \frac{6}{6+1.047\, m}$$

$$\text{Effective load, } P_{eff} = \left(\frac{C_s \cdot C_L}{C_v}\right) P_t = \frac{1.25 \times 1.3}{\left(\frac{6}{6+1.047\, m}\right)} \times \frac{19102.2}{m}\, N$$

$$P_{eff} = \frac{5173.5\,(6 + 1.047\, m)}{m}$$

Beam strength: ($\sigma_b = 260$ N/mm², $b = 10\, m$)

$$S_b = \sigma_b \cdot b \cdot Y \cdot m$$

Since pinion and gear materials are same, pinion is weaker. Hence, we obtain S_b for pinion.

$$\text{Lewis form factor, } Y_p = 0.484 - \frac{2.85}{20} = 0.3415$$

$$S_b = 260 \times 10\, m \times 0.3415 \times m$$
$$S_b = 888\, m^2$$

Finding module:

Equating bending strength to P_{eff} considering factor of safety

$$S_b = (P_{eff})(FS)$$

$$888\, m^2 = \frac{5173.5\,(6 + 1.047\, m)}{m} \times 1.5$$

$$888\, m^2 = \frac{7760.25\,(6 + 1.047\, m)}{m}$$

$$m^3 - 9.149\, m - 52.4 = 0$$

Solving $m \simeq 4.8$

Considering next preferred module and checking against dynamic load we select $m = 6$ mm.

Checking design for dynamic load by Buckingham's equation.

DESIGN OF MACHINE ELEMENTS - II — SPUR GEAR

Dynamic load:

$$P_d = \frac{21v\,(b \cdot C + C_s \cdot C_L \cdot P_t)}{21v + \sqrt{(b \cdot C + C_s \cdot C_L \cdot P_t)}}$$

With $b = 60$ mm, $d_p = 20 \times 6 = 120$ mm, $d_g = 60 \times 6 = 360$ mm.

Total tooth error e:

Error on pinion $\quad e_p = 11 + 0.9\,(m + 0.25\sqrt{d_p})$

$\qquad\qquad\qquad\quad = 11 + 0.9\,(6 + 0.25\sqrt{120}) = 18.86\ \mu m$

Error on gear $\quad e_g = 11 + 0.9\,(6 + 0.25\sqrt{360}) = 20.67\ \mu m$

Total tooth error $\quad e = e_p + e_g = 39.53\ \mu m = 0.03953$ mm

$\qquad\qquad\qquad v = 1.05 \times m = 6.3$ m/sec.

$$P_t = \frac{19102.2}{m} = 3184\ N$$

Deformation factor, $C = 11500 \times e = 454.6$ N/mm

$$\therefore\ P_d = \frac{21 \times 6.3\,(60 \times 454.6 + 1.25 \times 1.3 \times 3184)}{21 \times 6.3 + \sqrt{(60 \times 454.6 + 1.25 \times 1.3 \times 3184)}}$$

$$= \frac{132.3\,(32450)}{132.3 + \sqrt{32450}} = \frac{132.3 \times 32450}{132.3 + 180.2} = 13738\ N$$

Precise value of P_{eff}:

$$P_{eff} = (C_s \cdot C_L \cdot P_t + P_d)$$

$$= (1.25 \times 1.3 \times 3184 + 13738)$$

$$= 5174 + 13738 = 18912\ N$$

Factor of safety:

$$FS = \frac{\text{Beam strength}}{P_{eff}} = \frac{888\ m^2}{18912} = 1.69$$

Since this is higher than required value of 1.5, design is safe.

$$d_p = m \times Z_p = 6 \times 20 = 120\ mm$$

$$d_g = m \times Z_g = 6 \times 60 = 360\ mm$$

$$b = 10 \cdot m = 60\ mm$$

Centre diameter, $a = \dfrac{d_p + d_g}{2} = 240$ mm

Addendum, $h_a = 1\,m = 6$ mm

Dedendum, $h_f = 1.25\,m = 7.5$ mm

DESIGN OF MACHINE ELEMENTS - II — SPUR GEAR

Required surface hardness:

$$\text{Wear strength} = b \cdot Q \cdot K \cdot d_p$$

$$Q = \frac{2Z_g}{Z_g + Z_p} = \frac{2 \times 60}{60 + 20} = \frac{120}{80} = 1.5$$

To avoid pitting failure

$$b \cdot Q \cdot K \cdot d_p > (FS) \cdot P_{eff}$$

$$60 \times 1.5 \times K \times 120 > 1.5 \times 18912$$

$$K > 2.62$$

$$0.16 \left(\frac{BHN}{100}\right)^2 > 2.62$$

$$BHN > 404.6$$

Minimum required BHN is 405.

Example 1.5: Following data is given for a pair of spur gear with 20° fuel depth involute teeth. Number of teeth on pinion = 20, Number of teeth on gear = 50. Speed of pinion = 1200 rpm. Module = 4 mm. Service factor = 1.5. Face width = 32 mm. Both gears are made of steel with an ultimate strength of 600 N/mm². Using velocity factor to account for dynamic load, calculate beam strength and rated power that gears can transmit without bending failure. Factor of safety is 1.5. Use $C_v = \dfrac{3}{3 + v}$

Given data: $Z_p = 20$, $Z_g = 50$, $N_p = 1200$ rpm, $m = 4$ mm, $C_s = 1.5$, $b = 32$ mm, $(\sigma_b)_{all} = 600$ N/mm², FS = 1.5.

Solution: Since both pinion and gear are of same material, pinion is weaker. Hence, beam strength will be calculated based on pinion strength.

$$S_b = \sigma_b \cdot b \cdot Y \cdot m \quad \left(\sigma_b = \frac{600}{3}, b = 32 \text{ mm}, m = 4 \text{ mm}\right)$$

$$Y = 0.484 - \frac{2.87}{Z_p}$$

$$= 0.484 - \frac{2.87}{20} = 0.3405$$

$$\therefore \quad S_b = \frac{600}{3} \times 32 \times 0.3405 \times 4 = 8717 \text{ N}$$

$$\text{Velocity, } v = \frac{\pi \cdot d_p N_p}{60 \times 1000} = \frac{\pi \times (4 \times 20) \times 1200}{60 \times 1000} = 5.026 \text{ m/sec.}$$

$$C_v = \frac{3}{3 + v} = \frac{3}{3 + 5.026} = 0.374$$

DESIGN OF MACHINE ELEMENTS - II SPUR GEAR

Effective load on gear tooth

$$P_{eff} = \left[\frac{C_s \times C_L}{C_v}\right] P_t = \left(\frac{1.5 \times 1}{0.374}\right) P_t = 4.013\, P_t$$

Equating beam stress with P_{eff}. Considering factor of safety,

$$S_b = (P_{eff})\, FS$$
$$8717 = [4.013 \times P_t]\, 1.5$$
$$P_t = 1448.2\ N$$

$$\text{Torque transmitted} = \frac{P_t \times d_p}{2} = \frac{1448.2 \times 80}{2} = 57925\ N\cdot mm$$

Rated power transmitted

$$P = \frac{2\pi NT}{60 \times 10^6} = \frac{2\pi \times 1200 \times 57925}{60 \times 10^6} = 7.28\ kW$$

Example 1.6: The pinion shaft of a spur gear pair is connected to a 12 kW electric motion running at 1440 rpm. Gear tooth system is 20° full depth involute. Pinion has 18 teeth and the gear has 72 teeth. Module is 6 mm. Application factor is 1.25 and service factor 1.4. Face width of the gear is 60 mm. Gears are machined to grade 8. Deformation factor is to be obtained from the relation $C = \dfrac{K \cdot e}{\left[\dfrac{1}{E_p} + \dfrac{1}{E_g}\right]}$ with K = 0.11. Pinion and gear materials are alloy steel with S_{ult} = 800 MPa and E = 2.1 × 10^5 N/mm². Gears are heat treated to 360 BHN. Assuming the dynamic load to be accounted by Buckingham equation.

Find:
(a) Factor of safety against bending failure.
(b) Factor of safety against pitting failure.

Given data: 12 kW, 1440 rpm, Z_p = 18, Z_g = 72, m = 6 mm, C_L = 12.5, C_s = 1.4, b = 60 mm.

Solution:

Tangential load on pinion:

$$\text{Linear velocity at contact point, } v = \frac{\pi d_p \cdot N_p}{60 \times 1000} = \frac{\pi (18 \times 6) 1440}{60 \times 1000}$$

$$= 8.14\ m/sec$$

$$\text{Tooth load, } P_t = \frac{\text{Power}}{\text{Velocity}}$$

$$= \frac{12 \times 10^3}{8.14}$$

$$= 1474.2\ N$$

Tooth error for accuracy grade 8 is given by,

$$e = 16 + 1.25\ [m = 0.25\sqrt{d}]$$
$$e_p = 16 + 1.25\ [6 + 0.25\sqrt{6 \times 18}] = 26.75$$
$$e_g = 16 + 1.25\ [6 + 0.25\sqrt{6 \times 72}] = 29.99$$
$$\therefore\ e = e_p + e_g = 56.74\ \mu m = 0.05674\ mm$$

Deformation factor (E for steel: 2.1×10^5 N/mm^2)

$$C = \frac{K \cdot e}{\left[\dfrac{1}{E_p} + \dfrac{1}{E_g}\right]} = \frac{0.11 \times 0.05674}{\dfrac{1}{10^5}\left[\dfrac{1}{2.1} + \dfrac{1}{2.1}\right]} = 655.34\ N/mm$$

$$P_d = \frac{21 \cdot v\ (b \cdot C + C_s \cdot C_L \cdot P_t)}{21v + [\sqrt{b \cdot C + C_s \cdot C_L \cdot P_t}]}$$

$$= \frac{21 \times 8.14\ (60 \times 655.34 + 1.4 \times 1.25 \times 1474.2)}{21 \times 8.14 + [\sqrt{60 \times 655.34 + 1.4 \times 1.25 \times 1474.2}]}$$

$$P_d = \frac{21 \times 8.14\ (41900.25)}{21 \times 8.14 + \sqrt{41900 \cdot 25}} = \frac{7162428}{375.63} = 19068\ N$$

$$P_{eff} = C_s \cdot C_L \cdot P_t + P_d$$
$$= 1.4 \times 1.25 \times 1474.2 + 19068 = 2580 + 19068 = 21648\ N$$

Beam strength:

Since pinion and gear are of same material, beam strength will be calculated based on pinion which is weaker.

$$S_b = \sigma_b \cdot b \cdot Y \cdot m \quad \left(b = 60\ mm,\ m = 6\ mm,\ \sigma_b = \frac{800}{3}\ N/mm^2\right)$$

$$Y = 0.484 - \frac{2.87}{Z_p} = 0.484 - \frac{2.87}{18} = 0.3245$$

$$S_b = \frac{800}{3} \times 60 \times 0.3245 \times 6 = 31152\ N$$

Wear strength:

$$S_w = b \cdot Q \cdot d_p \cdot K \quad \left[b = 60,\ K = 0.16\left(\frac{BHN}{100}\right)^2,\ d_p = 108\right]$$

$$Q = \frac{2Z_g}{Z_g + Z_p} = \frac{2 \times 72}{72 + 18} = 1.6$$

$$K = 0.16\left(\frac{360}{100}\right)^2 = 2.07$$

$$S_w = 60 \times 1.6 \times 108 \times 2.074 = 21499\ N$$

Factor of safety:

$$S_b = [P_{eff}] \, FS \qquad \therefore FS = \frac{31152}{21648} = 1.44 \text{ (In bending)}$$

$$S_w = [P_{eff}] \, FS \qquad \therefore FS = \frac{21499}{21648} = 0.99 \text{ (In wear)}$$

Example 1.7: Three gears with idler arrangement are connected as shown below. Gear P is the driver with 18 teeth, Q is the idler with 54 teeth and R is the driven with 36 teeth. All gears are 20° full depth involute profiles and module is 4 mm. The driver P is transmitting 5 kW power at 1500 rpm. Assuming all gear are centrally mounted on their respective shafts. Find:
1. Torque transmitted by each shaft.
2. Forces acting on each gear and show their directions.
3. Radial force acting on each bearing holding shaft 'P'.

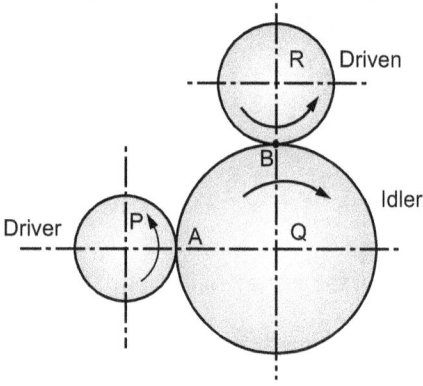

Fig. 1.11

Given data: Input power P = 5 kW at 1500 rpm.

Solution:

1. Torque on shaft P:

$$T_p = \frac{\text{Power} \times 60 \times 10^6}{2\pi N} = \frac{5 \times 60 \times 10^6}{2\pi \times 1500} = 31831 \text{ N·mm}$$

Gear R rotates at $\left(\dfrac{18}{36}\right)$ speed as 'P': 750 rpm.

Torque on shaft R: $\quad T_R = \dfrac{\text{Power} \times 60 \times 10^6}{2\pi N} \times \dfrac{5 \times 60 \times 10^6}{2\pi \times 750} = 63662 \text{ N·mm}$

Idler does not transmit any torque.

$\therefore$ Torque on shaft Q is zero.

2. Forces on gears 'P':

Tangential force on driver 'P':

$$(P_{tp}) = \frac{\text{Torque}}{d_p/2} = \frac{31831}{(m \cdot Z_p/2)} = \frac{31831}{(5 \times 18/2)} = 707.4 \text{ N}$$

Radial force on driver gear 'P':

$$(P_{rp}) = (P_{tp}) \times \tan \phi = 707.4 \tan 20° = 257.5 \text{ N}$$

Forces on Gear 'Q' and 'R':

- Tangential and radial forces on Q acting at contact point, 'A' will be same as above but opposite in direction.
- Thus, $(P_{tQ}) = (P_{tP})$ and $(P_{rQ}) = (P_{rP})$

Tangential forces between Q and R will again be of same magnitude since whatever torque is received at point A is transmitted further at point B. Further same will be the magnitude of forces transmitted on gear 'R' at point B.

Forces with their directions are shown in the Fig. 1.12.

Thus, $P_{tQ} = P_{tQ} = P_{tR} = 707.4$ N

and $P_{rp} = P_{rQ} = P_{rR} = 257.5$ N

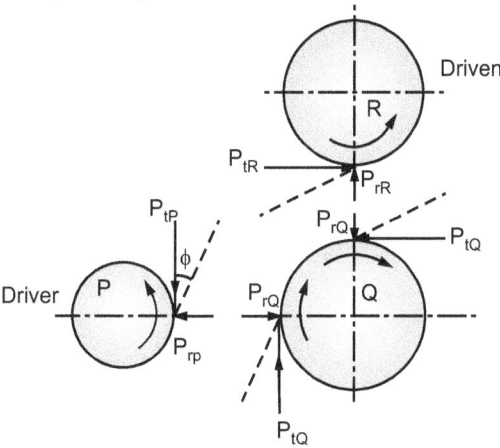

Fig. 1.12

Force directions:

Between P and Q: P is the driver and Q is the driven.

On the driver, tangential force direction is opposite to direction of motion. Hence, at point A force on 'P' is in the downward direction. On the driven, tangential force direction is in the same direction of motion. Hence, at point A force on 'Q' is in the upward direction.

Between Q and R: Q is the driver and R is driven.

Force directions between Q and R can be decibel on above lines.

DESIGN OF MACHINE ELEMENTS - II — SPUR GEAR

3. **Resultant radial force on shaft 'P':**

$$= \sqrt{P_{tP}^2 + P_{rP}^2} = \sqrt{(707.4)^2 + (257.5)^2} = 752.8 \text{ N}$$

Since gears are centrally mounted.

Radial force on each bearing $= \dfrac{752.8}{2} = 376.4$ N

Example 1.8: A pair of spur gears with 20° full depth involute teeth system consists of pinion with 21 teeth running at 720 rpm meshing with gear running at 378 rpm. Pinion is made of alloy steel with $S_{ult} = 620$ N/mm² and gear with plain carbon steel having $S_{ult} = 540$ N/mm². Gear pair is heat treated to 300 BHN. Face width is 10 times module. Service factor and factor of safety are 1.5 and 1.75 respectively. Gear pair is manufactured by hobbing process. Centre distance between pinion and gear shaft is 152.5 mm. Assuming velocity factor accounts for dynamic load, calculate.

  (i) Beam strength
  (ii) Wear strength
  (iii) Maximum static load that gear pair can transmit.
  (iv) Rated power that gear pair transmit. Take velocity factor, $C = \dfrac{6}{6+v}$

Given data: $Z_p = 21$, $N_p = 720$ rpm, $N_g = 378$ rpm, $(S_{ult})_{pinion} = 620$ N/mm², $(S_{ult})_{gear} = 540$ N/mm², BHN = 300, $C_s = 1.5$, FS = 1.85.

Solution: Centre distance $= \dfrac{d_p + d_g}{2} = 152.5$ mm, $Z_g = 21 \times \dfrac{720}{378} = 40$

$$d_p = m \cdot Z_p = 5 \times 21 = 105 \text{ mm}$$
$$d_g = m \cdot Z_g = 5 \times 40 = 200 \text{ mm}$$

Thus, $d_g = 200$ mm, $d_p = 105$ mm, Module = 5 mm

Beam strength:

Pinion and gear are of different materials. Hence, we must find which one is weaker.

$$(\sigma_b \cdot Y)_{Pinion} = \dfrac{S_{ult}}{3} \times \left(0.484 - \dfrac{2.87}{Z_p}\right) = \dfrac{620}{3} \times \left(0.484 - \dfrac{2.87}{21}\right) = 71.78$$

$$(\sigma_b \cdot Y)_{gear} = \dfrac{S_{ult}}{3} \times \left(0.484 - \dfrac{2.87}{Z_g}\right) = \dfrac{540}{3} \times \left(0.484 - \dfrac{2.87}{40}\right) = 74.2$$

Since, $(\sigma_b \cdot Y)_{Pinion} < (\sigma_b, Y)_{gear}$

Pinion is weaker.

Beam strength is to be calculated based on pinion strength.

Taking width = $10 \cdot m$

Beam strength $= \sigma_b \cdot b \cdot Y \cdot m$

$\phantom{\text{Beam strength}} = (71.78)(10\ m)$

$S_b = 717.8\ m^2 = 17945\ N$

Wear strength: $= b \cdot Q \cdot d_p \cdot K$ [With $b = 50$ mm, $d_p = 105$ mm]

$$Q = \frac{2Z_g}{Z_g + Z_p} = \frac{2 \times 40}{40 + 21} = 1.3115$$

$$K = 0.16 \left(\frac{BHN}{100}\right)^2 = 0.16\,(3)^2 = 1.44$$

$S_w = 50 \times 1.311 \times 105 \times 1.44$

$S_w = 9911\ N$

Static load capacity (P_t):

$$\text{Velocity factor } C_v = \frac{6}{6+v} = \frac{6}{\left(6 + \dfrac{\pi \times 105 \times 720}{60 \times 1000}\right)} = \frac{6}{6 + 3.958} = 0.602$$

$$P_{eff} = \left(\frac{C_s \cdot C_L}{C_v}\right) P_t = \left(\frac{1.5 \times 1}{0.602}\right) P_t$$

$\phantom{P_{eff}} = 2.492\ P_t$

Since wear strength < Beam strength,

Equating wear strength with effective load and considering factor of safety

$S_w = [P_{eff}]\ FS$

$9911 = [2.492\ P_t] \times 1.75$

$P_t = 2272\ N$

Static load capacity is 2272 N

Rated power transmitted:

$$\text{Power} = P_t \times v = \frac{2272 \times 3.958}{1000} = 8.99\ kW$$

Example 1.9: A spur gear pair is to transmit 8 kW power at 750 rpm to another machine at 300 rpm. Pinion and gear, both are made of same steel having ultimate tensile strength of 620 N/mm². Surface hardness is 330 BHN. Pinion has 20 teeth, the module is 5 mm and face width is 60 mm. Service factor is 1.5 and load concentration factor is 1.4.

Determine the factor of safety in bending and wear.

(a) By considering that velocity factor accounts for dynamic load.

(b) By considering dynamic load using Buckingham equation.

Use the following data:

$$\text{Barth factor, } C_v = \frac{3}{3+v}$$

Tooth profile error (e) = 0.05 mm

$$\text{Dynamic factor, } C = K \cdot e \left[\frac{E_p \cdot E_g}{E_p + E_g} \right]$$

Tooth form factor, K = 0.111

$$E = 2.1 \times 10^5 \text{ N/mm}^2 \text{ for both materials.}$$

Given data:

Power = 8 kW, N_p = 750 rpm, N_g = 300 rpm, 330 BHN, (S_{ult}) = 620 N/mm², Z_p = 20, m = 5, b = 60, C_s = 1.5, C_L = 1.4.

Solution: Factor of safety in bending and wear:

$$\text{Velocity at pitch point} = v = \frac{\pi d_p \cdot N_p}{60 \times 1000} = \frac{\pi (5 \times 20) \, 750}{60 \times 1000} = 3.93 \text{ m/sec.}$$

$$\text{Tangential force, } P_t = \frac{\text{Power}}{\text{Velocity}} = \frac{8 \times 1000}{3.93} = 2037.2 \text{ N}$$

$$\text{Velocity factor, } C_v = \frac{3}{3+v} = \frac{3}{3+3.93} = 0.433$$

$$P_{eff} = \left[\frac{C_s \cdot C_L}{C_v} \right] P_t = \left[\frac{1.5 \times 1.4}{0.433} \right] \times 2037.2 = 9880 \text{ N}$$

Beam strength S_b:

Since pinion and gear have same material, pinion is weaker.

$$(\sigma_b Y)_{pinion} = \left(\frac{S_{ult}}{3} \right)_{pinion} \times Y_p = \left(\frac{620}{3} \right) \times \left(0.484 - \frac{2.87}{20} \right) = 70.37$$

$$S_b = \sigma_b \cdot b \cdot Y \cdot m = 70.37 \times 60 \times 5 = 21111 \text{ N}$$

Wear strength S_w: b = 60 mm, d_p = 100 mm,

$$S_w = b \cdot Q \cdot d_p \cdot K$$

$$Q = \frac{2Z_g}{Z_g + Z_p} = \frac{2 \times 50}{50 + 20} = 1.428$$

$$k = 0.16 \left(\frac{BHN}{100} \right)^2 = 0.16 \left(\frac{330}{100} \right)^2 = 1.742$$

$$S_w = 60 \times 1.428 \times 100 \times 1.742 = 14929 \text{ N}$$

$$\text{Factor of safety in bending (based on velocity factor)} = \frac{21111}{7057.3} = 2.99$$

$$\text{Factor of safety in wear (based on velocity factor)} = \frac{14929}{7057.3} = 2.11$$

Factor of safety based on Buckingham equation:

$$\text{Dynamic load, } P_b = \frac{21 \cdot v (b \cdot C + P_{tmax})}{21 \cdot v + \sqrt{b \cdot C + P_{tmax}}}$$

$$P_{tmax} = C_s \cdot C_L \cdot P_t = 1.5 \times 1.4 \times 2037.2 = 4278 \text{ N}$$

$$C = K \cdot e \left[\frac{E_p \cdot E_g}{E_p + E_g} \right]$$

$$= 0.111 \times 0.05 \left[\frac{(2.1)^2 \times 10^{10}}{2 \times 2.1 \times 10^5} \right] = 582.75 \text{ N/mm}$$

$$P_d = \frac{21 \times 3.93 (60 \times 582.75 + 4278)}{21 \times 3.93 + \sqrt{(60 \times 582.75 + 4278)}} = \frac{21 \times 3.39 \times 39243}{21 \times 3.93 + 198.1}$$

$$= 11541 \text{ N}$$

$$P_{eff} = C_s \cdot C_L \cdot P_t + P_d = 4278 + 11541 = 15819 \text{ N}$$

$$\text{Factor of safety in bending} = \frac{S_b}{P_{eff}} = \frac{21111}{15819} = 1.33$$

$$\text{Factor of safety in wear} = \frac{S_b}{S_w} = \frac{14929}{15819} = 0.94 \quad \begin{pmatrix} \text{Design in inadequate} \\ \text{against wear strength} \end{pmatrix}$$

As a corrective action wear strength has to be increased or tooth pitch error should be reduced by going for more accurate tooth cutting and finishing.

Example 1.10: A spur gear pinion having 20 teeth made of plain carbon steel with S_{ult} = 540 N/mm² is to mesh with gear having 85 teeth made of gray cast iron FC 260. Pinion shaft is connected to 10 kW. 1440 rpm electric motor. Starting torque is twice rated torque. Tooth system is 20° full-depth involute. Face width is 10 times module for which load distribution factor is 1.4. Gears are machined to meet specifications of grade 7; for which deformation factor is 11500 e.

(a) If factor of safety against bending is 1.5, design gear pair by using velocity factor and Buckingham's equation for dynamic load.

(b) If factor of safety against pitting is 2.0 specify hardness.

Take   Velocity factor, $C_v = \dfrac{3}{3 + v}$

Deformation factor, $C = 11500 \text{ e}$

Lewis form factor, $y = 0.484 - \dfrac{2.87}{Z}$

Load stress factor, $K = 0.18 \left[\dfrac{BHN}{100} \right]^2$

DESIGN OF MACHINE ELEMENTS - II — SPUR GEAR

For grade 6:
$$e = 8 + 0.63\,[m + 0.25\sqrt{d}]$$

Given data: $Z_p = 20$, $Z_g = 85$, $(S_{ult})_{pinion} = 540$ N/mm², $(S_{ult})_{gear} = 260$ N/mm², Power = 10 kW, $N_p = 1440$ rpm, $C_s = 2$, $b = 10.m$, $C_L = 1.4$, FS = 1.5 in bending.

Solution: Effective load considering velocity factor:

$$\text{Pitch line velocity, } v = \frac{\pi d_p \cdot N_p}{60 \times 1000} = \frac{\pi(20 \cdot m)\,1440}{60 \times 1000} = (1.508 . m)\ \text{m/sec.}$$

$$\text{Tangential force, } P_t = \frac{\text{Power}}{v} = \frac{10 \times 10^3}{1.508} = \left(\frac{6631.3}{m}\right) \text{N}$$

$$\text{Velocity factor, } C_v = \frac{3}{3+v} = \frac{3}{(3 + 1.508\,m)}$$

$$P_{eff} = \left(\frac{C_s \cdot C_L}{C_v}\right) P_t = \frac{2 \times 1.4\,(3 + 1.508\,m)}{3} \times \left(\frac{6631.3}{m}\right)$$

$$P_{eff} = \frac{6189.2\,(3 + 1.508\,m)}{m}$$

Beam strength:

Since pinion and gear materials are different

$$(\sigma_b \cdot Y)_p = \frac{540}{3} \times \left(0.484 - \frac{2.87}{Z_p}\right) = \frac{540}{3} \times \left(0.484 - \frac{2.87}{20}\right) = 61.29$$

$$(\sigma_b \cdot Y)_g = \frac{260}{3} \times \left(0.484 - \frac{2.87}{Z_g}\right) = \frac{260}{3} \times \left(0.484 - \frac{2.87}{85}\right) = 39.02$$

Thus, gear is weaker and beam strength is calculated based on gear strength.

∴ Beam strength $S_b = (\sigma_b \cdot Y)\,b \cdot m = (39.02) \times 10\,m \times m = 390.2\,m^2$

Equating beam strength with effective load considering factor of safety

$$S_b = [P_{eff}]\,FS$$

$$390.2\,m^2 = \left[6189.2\,\frac{(3 + 1.508\,m)}{m}\right] \times 1.5$$

$390.2\,m^3 - 13999.97\,m - 27851.4 = 0$

$m^3 - 35.88\,m - 71.38 = 0$

Solving by trial and error, m = 6.9 mm

We select next preferred size of module = 8 mm.

Checking by considering Buckingham's equation:

$$\text{Dynamic load, } P_d = \frac{21 \, v \, (b \cdot C + F_t)}{21 \cdot v + \sqrt{b \cdot C + F_t}}$$

where, $(P_{t\,max}) = F_t = C_s \cdot C_L \, (P_t)$

$$= 2 \times 1.4 \left(\frac{6631.3}{8}\right)$$

$$= 2321 \text{ N}$$

Deformation factor, $C = 11500 \cdot e$

$e_p = 8 + 0.63 \, (m + 0.25 \sqrt{d_p}) = 8 + 0.63 \, (8 + 0.25 \sqrt{20 \times 8})$

$\quad = 15.03 \, \mu m$

$e_g = 8 + 0.63 \, (8 + 0.25 \sqrt{85 \times 8})$

$\quad = 17.14 \, \mu m$

$e = e_p + e_g$

$\quad = 32.17 \, \mu m$

$\quad = 0.03217 \text{ mm}$

Deformation constant, $C = 11500 \times 0.0321$

$\quad = 369.96$

$$P_d = \frac{21 \times (1.508 \times 8) \, (80 \times 369.96 + 2321)}{21 \times (1.508 \times 8) + \sqrt{80 \times 369.96 + 2321}}$$

$$P_d = \frac{21 \times 12.064 \, (31917.8)}{21 \times 12.064 + (178.6)}$$

$\quad = 18718 \text{ N}$

$P_{eff} = P_{tmax} + P_d$

$\quad = 2321 + 18717$

$\quad = 21039 \text{ N}$

$S_b = 390.2 \text{ m}^2$

$\quad = 390.2 \times 64$

$\quad = 24972.8 \text{ N}$

$$FS = \frac{24972.8}{21039}$$

$\quad = 1.186$

Since, the factor of safety < 1.5.

We need to redesign.

Trial 1: Consider module = 10 · mm

$$P_t = \left(\frac{6631.3}{m}\right) = \frac{6631.3}{m}$$

Velocity factor, $v = \dfrac{\pi d_p \cdot N_p}{60 \times 1000} = (1.508 \cdot m)$

$$P_{eff} = \frac{6189.2\,(3 + 1.508\,m)}{m}$$

$$= 11190 \text{ N}$$

Checking for dynamic load

$e_p = 8 + 0.63\,(m + 0.25\sqrt{d_p}) = 8 + 0.63\,(10 + 0.25\sqrt{20 \times 10}) = 16.52$ μm

$e_g = 8 + 0.63\,(m + 0.25\sqrt{d_g}) = 8 + 0.63\,(10 + 0.25\sqrt{85 \times 10}) = 18.89$ μm

$e = e_p + e_g = 35.41$ μm $= 0.03541$ mm

$C = 11500 \times e = 407.2$ N/mm

$$P_d = \frac{21 \cdot v\,(b \cdot C + F_t)}{21 \cdot v + \sqrt{b \cdot C + F_t}}$$

With $(P_{tmax}) = F_t = C_s \cdot C_L \cdot P_t$

$$= 2 \times 1.4 \times \left(\frac{6631.3}{10}\right) = 1856.77$$

$$P_d = \frac{21 \times 1.508 \times 10\,(100 \times 407.2 + 1856.77)}{21 \times 1.508 \times 10 + \sqrt{100 \times 407.2 + 1856.77}}$$

$$= \frac{316.68\,(40720 + 1856.77)}{316.68 + 206.3}$$

$$= \frac{316.68\,(42576.77)}{523.00}$$

$$= 25780 \text{ N}$$

$P_{eff} = P_{tmax} + P_d = 1856.77 + 25780 = 27637$ N

$S_{bmax} = 390.2\,m^2 = 39020$ N

$$FS = \frac{39020}{27637} = 1.41$$

Since FS < 1.5.

We need to take trial with m = 12 mm

Trial 2: $e_p = 8 + 0.63\,(m + 0.25\sqrt{d_p}) = 8 + 0.63\,(12 + 0.25\sqrt{20 \times 12}) = 18.00$ μm

$e_g = 8 + 0.63\,(12 + 0.25\sqrt{85 \times 12}) = 20.59$ μm

$e = e_p + e_g = 38.59$ μm $= 0.03859$ mm

$C = 11500 \times e = 443.785$ N/mm

$$P_{t\,max} = F_t = 2 \times 1.4 \times \left(\frac{6631.3}{m}\right)$$

$$= 1547.3 \text{ N}$$

$$P_d = \frac{21 \times 1.508 \times 12\,(120 \times 443.785 + 1547.3)}{21 \times (1.508 \times 12) + \sqrt{120 \times 443.785 + 1547.3}}$$

$$= \frac{20825446.8}{614.113}$$

$$= 33911 \text{ N}$$

$$P_{eff} = P_{tmax} + P_d$$

$$= 1547.3 + 33911$$

$$P_{eff} = 35458.3 \text{ N}$$

$$S_b = 390.2\, m^2 = 390.2\,(12)^2$$

$$= 56188.8 \text{ N}$$

$$\text{Factor of safety} = \frac{S_b}{P_{eff}}$$

$$\frac{56188.8}{35458.3} = 1.58$$

∴ We select module = 12 mm

Hardness required for factor of safety = 2.

(b) With module m = 12 mm.

$$P_{eff} = 35448.3 \text{ N}$$

For

$$S_w = 35458 \times 2 = 70916 \text{ N}$$

$$S_w = b \cdot Q \cdot d_p \cdot K \quad b = 10\,m = 120 \text{ mm}$$

$$d_p = m \cdot Z_p = 12 \times 20 = 240 \text{ mm}$$

$$Q = \frac{2Z_g}{Z_g + Z_p} = \frac{2 \times 85}{85 + 20} = 1.69$$

∴

$$K_{required} = \frac{70916}{120 \times 240 \times 1.69} = 1.456$$

$$K = 1.456 = 0.18\left(\frac{BHN}{100}\right)^2$$

$$BHN = 285$$

Material hardness required is 285 BHN.

EXERCISE

1. State and explain different types of gear tooth failures, their causes and remedies.
   (May 2012)
2. Explain the following terms: (a) Hunting tooth, (b) Crowning of gear tooth.
   (May 2013)
3. What is dynamic load on gears? State the factors on which the dynamic load depends and explain the methods of estimation of dynamic load on gear tooth.
   (April 2009)
4. Discuss the standard systems of gear tooth. **(April 2010)**
5. Explain why Involute profile is preferred over cycloidal profile for gear tooth.
   (April 2010)
6. Discuss lubrication of gears. **(April 2010)**
7. Write a note on gear lubrication. **(April 2012)**
8. What are the effects of decreasing the pressure angle in gear design? **(Oct. 2011)**
9. What is addendum modification in gears? State the advantages and limitations of it.
   (Oct. 2011)
10. Explain the selection of gear type for a given application.
11. What are various materials suitable for the gears?
12. Explain design considerations for the gears.
13. Discuss the desirable properties of gear material.
14. Explain in brief selection of number of teeth on the gears.
15. Explain the various assumptions in Lewis beam strength equation.
16. What are different types of gear tooth failures and there remedies?
17. Derive an expression for the beam strength of the gear.
18. Why the pinion is always weaker in pitting?
19. How the surface endurance strength is improved?

Unit II

HELICAL AND BEVEL GEARS

HELICAL GEARS

2.1 INTRODUCTION

In case of spur gear, teeth are cut parallel to the axis of the shaft. Due to this the contact between teeth in mesh occurs completely along the face width. This results in sudden impact of load from driving tooth onto the driven tooth which results in generation of noise, more so when gears rotate at high speed.

To overcome this limitation helical gears were introduced. In case of helical gears teeth are cut on a cylindrical blank at some angle with the axis of the shaft. Because of this, the contact between meshing teeth starts with a point contact on the edge and develops into line contact whose length of contact gradually increases. Thus, impact is less, resulting in a smooth and silent transmission of power. Another advantage of helical gears is since teeth are cut at an angle, contact ratio (i.e. number of pairs of teeth in contact) is more as compared to the spur gear with same number of teeth and gear width. Thus, helical gear will transmit more power compared to spur gear. Contact ratio being higher, helical gears can also permit lesser number of teeth compared to spur gear of same diameter and module. Helical gears would however introduce axial thrusts which is not present in spur gears and would demand higher shaft alignment accuracies. (Refer Fig. 2.1)

Axial thrust in helical gears can be eliminated by introducing double helical gears. These are called Herringbone gears. Teeth are cut along the width in two parts. One half is with LH helix and the other half with RH helix. The axial thrust produced on two parts opposes each other and the resultant is zero. Thus, these gears are able to eliminate axial thrust. Cost of manufacture and alignment requirements are more stringent thus increasing the cost.

The proper selection of type of gear is a combination of different requirements and their technical cost influence.

(a) Single Helical Gear   (b) Double Helical Gear

Fig. 2.1

To combine the advantages of low noise of helical gears and low cost of spur gears, in many applications involving multistage gear boxes, a helical gear pair is used in the first stage where speed are high and torque (and thus the tangential force and axial thrust) will be less. Helical gears can also be used to transmit power between two non-parallel and non-intersecting shafts. For transmitting power between two parallel shafts, the helix angle of the meshing gears has to be same and hand of helix must be opposite. In this chapter, we limit our discussions only to single helical gears transmitting power between two parallel shafts.

2.2 IMPORTANT TERMS FOR HELICAL GEARS

Helix Angle (ψ): It is the angle made by the axis of the tooth with axis of rotation.

Transverse Circular Pitch (P_c): It is the distance between two successive teeth measured along pitch circle in transverse plane.

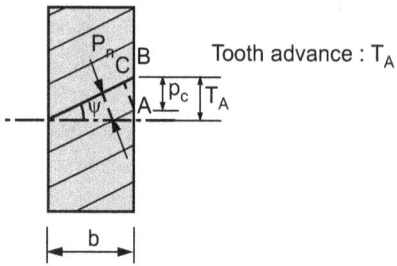

Fig. 2.2: Helical Gear

$$P_c = \frac{\pi \cdot d}{Z}$$

where, Z is the number of teeth.

Normal Circular Pitch (P_n): It is the distance between two successive teeth measured along pitch circle in the plane perpendicular to the axis of teeth.

Axial Pitch (P_a): It is the distance between two successive teeth measured along the axis of rotation.

From triangle ABC,

$$\frac{P_n}{P_c} = \frac{AC}{AB} = \cos \psi$$

$$P_n = P_c \cdot \cos \psi$$

Similarly, $\quad m_n = m \cdot \cos \psi$

where, m is the transverse module

m_n is the normal module.

In helical gears, normal module is treated as standard since the tooling is made accordingly.

Table 2.1 gives the values of normal module of first and second preference.

Table 2.1: List of standard Modules

Module of first choice (mm)	1, 1.25, 1.5, 2, 2.5, 3, 4, 5, 6, 8, 10, 12, 16, 20, 25, 32, 40, 50
Module of second choice (mm)	1.125, 1.375, 1.75, 2.25, 2.75, 3.5, 4.5, 5.5, 7, 9, 11, 14, 18, 22, 28, 36, 45

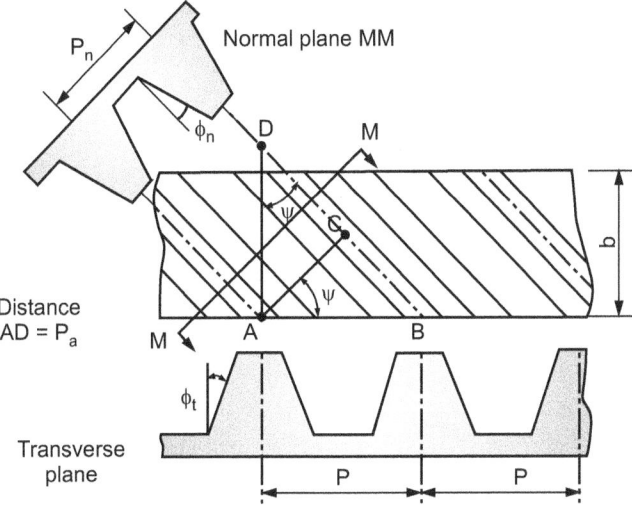

Fig. 2.3: Terminology of Helical Gears

From triangle ABD (Refer Fig. 2.3),

$$P_a = \frac{P_c}{\tan \psi}$$

Transverse Pressure Angle (ϕ_t): Pressure angle is the angle between tangent to the pitch circles and common normal drawn at point of contact measured in transverse (plane of rotation) plane.

Normal Pressure Angle (ϕ_n): This is the pressure angle measured in the normal plane (Plane perpendicular to the teeth). Standard normal pressure angles are 14.5°, 20°, 25°.

It can be seen $\tan \phi_t = \dfrac{\tan \phi_n}{\cos \psi}$

Formative Number of Teeth:

In the previous chapter, we have analysed spur gear. In order to simplify the analysis of helical gear, an imaginary spur gear (also called as formative spur gear or equivalent spur gear) is considered and on this spur gear number of teeth are found, which are called virtual number of teeth or formative number of teeth.

Consider a helical gear cut by a plane A-A, normal to the tooth axis and passing through its center. (Refer Fig. 2.4). The cross section along plane A-A will appear as an ellipse with its semi major axis (a) as $\left(\dfrac{d}{2\cos\psi}\right)$ and semi minor axis (b) as $\left(\dfrac{d}{2}\right)$.

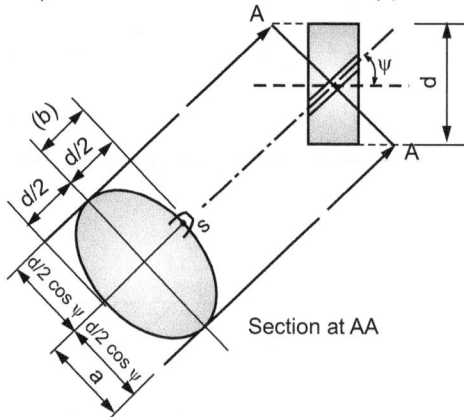

Fig. 2.4

The radius of curvature r' at point 'S' is given by coordinate geometry as

$$r' = \dfrac{a^2}{b} = \dfrac{\left(\dfrac{d}{2\cos\psi}\right)^2}{(d/2)}$$

$$= \dfrac{d}{2\cos^2\psi}$$

So, the imaginary spur gear, in the plane AA has pitch circle radius r' (diameter d') and module m_n. Formative number of teeth for a helical gear are the number of teeth that can be generated on the surface of a cylinder having a radius equal to the radius of curvature at a point at the tip of the minor axis of an ellipse (radius at point 'S' in the Fig. 2.4) obtained as above.

The pitch circle diameter of the equivalent spur gear will be d'.

Thus, $\quad d' = 2r' = \dfrac{d}{\cos^2\psi}$

Number of teeth on this imaginary spur gear are

$$z' = \dfrac{d'}{m_n} = \dfrac{d}{m_n \cos^2\psi}$$

Since, $\quad d = Z \times m = \dfrac{Zm_n}{\cos\psi}$

∴ $\quad Z' = \dfrac{Z}{\cos^3\psi}$

where, $\quad Z'$ = Virtual or formative number of teeth
$\quad\quad\quad\; Z$ = Actual number of teeth

The virtual number of teeth being larger than the actual number of teeth, Lewis form factor gives higher values and the gear has better strength compared to spur gears with same number of teeth.

Dimensions and Proportions of Helical Gear:

Addendum: $h_a = m_n$

Dedeundum: $h_f = 1.25\, m_n$

Clearance: $0.25\, m_n$

Addendum circle diameter: d_a

$$d_a = d + 2h_a = \frac{Z \cdot m_n}{\cos \psi} + 2m_n$$

$$d_a = m_n \left[\frac{Z}{\cos \psi} + 2 \right]$$

Dedendum circle diameter: $\quad d_f = m_n \left[\dfrac{Z}{\cos \psi} - 2.5 \right]$

Helix angle normally varies from 15 to 25°.

Face Width (b):

For smooth operation of helical gears and to ensure contact ratio more than one, the distance between the leading edge of the tooth and the trailing edge of the same tooth (T_A) must be more than the circular pitch.

Thus, the width of a gear and its helix angle are interrelated.

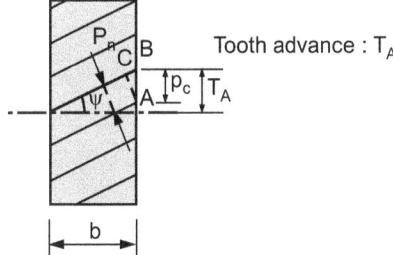

Fig. 2.5

Contact ratio = Tooth Advance (T_A)/ Circular pitch (P_c) ... should be greater than 1.

From Fig. 2.5, $\quad T_A = b \cdot \tan \psi$

Therefore, $\quad b > \dfrac{P_c}{\tan \psi} = \dfrac{\pi \cdot m}{\tan \psi} = \dfrac{\pi \cdot m_n}{\cos \psi \cdot \tan \psi} = \dfrac{\pi \cdot m_n}{\sin \psi}$

Thus, $\quad b_{min} = \dfrac{\pi \cdot m_n}{\sin \psi}$

In practice 'b' should be at least $= 1.15\, b_{min}$

Satisfying this condition usual values selected are between (9 to 12) m_n.

2.3 FORCE ANALYSIS

Fig. 2.6 shows pitch cylinder of a driven gear. The direction of rotation of the gear is clockwise as shown. Therefore, the direction of tangential force will be in the same direction as the direction of rotation i.e. P_t will assist the motion at the contact point. Let P_n be the normal force transferred from the driving tooth on the driven gear tooth along the common normal drawn at point of contact. This force is inclined to the axis of rotation by helix angle ψ. The force P_n is resolved in three perpendicular directions which align with

Tangential force: P_t
Radial force: P_r and
Axial force: P_a

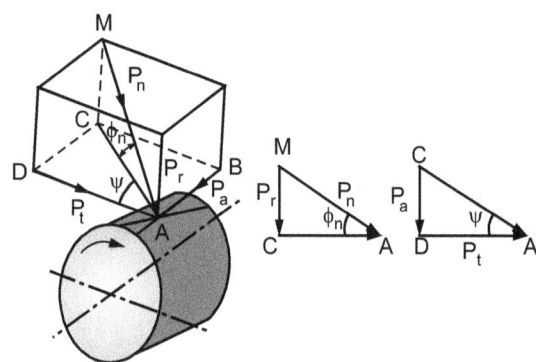

Fig. 2.6

Referring Fig 2.6

Radial component: $\quad P_r = P_n \cdot \sin \phi_n \quad$ ...(2.1)

Component along AC (X): $\quad X = P_n \cdot \cos \phi_n \quad$ ...(2.2)

Further $\quad P_a = X \cdot \sin \psi = P_n \cdot \cos \phi_n \cdot \sin \psi \quad$ ...(2.3)

$\quad P_t = X \cdot \cos \psi = P_n \cdot \cos \phi_n \cdot \cos \psi \quad$ ...(2.4)

From equations (2.3) and (2.4),

$$P_a = P_t \cdot \tan \psi \quad ...(2.5)$$

From equations (2.1) and (2.4),

$$P_r = P_t \left(\frac{\tan \phi_n}{\cos \psi} \right) \quad ...(2.6)$$

In practice, P_t can be found out by knowing the power to be transmitted.

and $\quad P_t = \dfrac{P}{v} = \dfrac{60 \times 10^6 \, P}{\pi d \times N}$

where,
$\quad P$ = Power in kW
$\quad v$ = Pitch line velocity in m/s
$\quad d$ = Pitch circle diameter in mm
$\quad N$ = Speed r.p.m.

Once the tangential force P_t is found out, P_r and P_a can be estimated by using the equations 2.5 and 2.6 above. These forces will ultimately be transferred to the shaft and the bearings. The directions of these forces on driving and driven gears can be found using following guidelines.
- The direction of tangential force on the driven gear tooth will be in the same direction as the motion at the point contact.
- Radial force is always a separating force and acts in a direction such that it will try to increase the center distance.
- The direction of axial force can be decided as below.
- Identify which one is a driving gear and find hand of helix on it.
    (a) For this RH/ LH thumb rule can be applied. Care should be taken to ensure that thumb is along the axis of rotation.

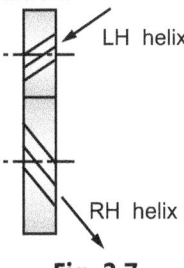

Fig. 2.7

(b) Alternately for a horizontal shaft helical gear, trace a downward arrow along the tooth axis (Refer Fig. 2.7). If the arrow points towards left side, gear helix is LH or if it points to right side, gear is a RH gear.

To find the direction of axial component of load.
- On the driving gear use left hand for LH helix and right hand for RH helix.

Align fingers in direction of rotation. The thumb indicates direction of axial component for driving gear. For driven gear the thrust direction will be opposite to that on driving gear.

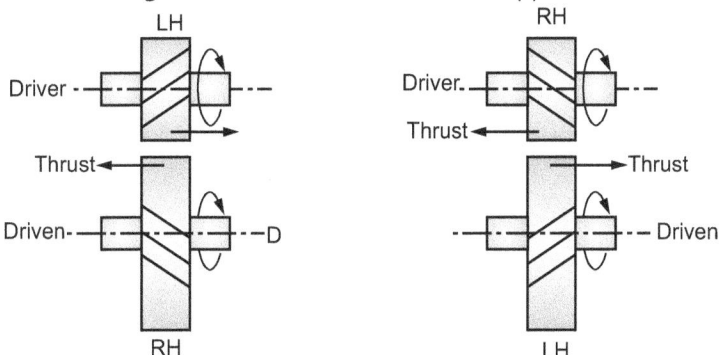

Fig. 2.8: Helical Gear: Axial Thrust Direction

Axial thrust directions for two configurations are shown in Fig 2.8.

2.4 BEAM STRENGTH OF HELICAL GEAR (LEWIS EQUATION)

The analysis of beam strength for a helical gear is performed on the similar lines as that of spur gear by considering equivalent spur gear for a given helical gear. This equivalent spur gear has pitch circle diameter as d', module as m_n and number of teeth as Z'.

Beam strength for a spur gear is: $S_b = \sigma_b \cdot b \cdot Y \cdot m$

When applied to the equivalent spur gear equation will be

$$S_{bn} = \sigma_b \cdot b' \cdot Y' \cdot m_n$$

Thus,
$$S_{bn} = \sigma_b \cdot \left(\frac{b}{\cos \psi}\right) \cdot Y' \cdot m_n$$

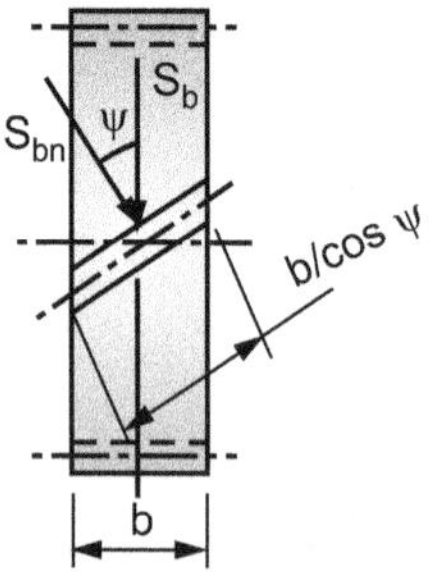

Fig. 2.9: Beam Strength for Helical Gear

'S_b' for the spur gear gets converted to S_{bn}. (Fig 2.9). This is because, the force considered for a spur gear beam strength is its capacity to withstand a force perpendicular to tooth axis. S_{bn} is perpendicular to tooth axis. However its component S_b (= $S_{bn} \cdot \cos \psi$) only is useful for torque transmission.

$$S_b = S_{bn} \times \cos \psi$$

Therefore,
$$S_b = \frac{\sigma_b \cdot b \cdot Y' \cdot m_n}{\cos \psi} \times \cos \psi$$

Thus,
$$S_b = \sigma_b \cdot b \cdot Y' \cdot m_n \qquad \ldots (2.7)$$

Where, Y' is Lewis form factor based on formative number of teeth.

For 14.5° full depth involute and composite systems,

$$Y' = 0.389 - \frac{2.148}{Z'}$$

For 20° full depth involute systems,

$$Y' = 0.484 - \frac{2.87}{Z'}$$

Equation (2.7) is the beam strength equation for helical gear. In order to avoid bending of tooth beam strength has to be more than effective load on gear tooth.

Denoting factor of safety as FS

$$S_b > P_{eff}$$
$$S_b = (FS) \, P_{eff}$$

2.5 WEAR STRENGTH OF HELICAL GEAR

Wear strength of helical gear can be found out by modifying the wear strength equation of the spur gear. To do this an equivalent (formative or imaginary) spur gear is considered having pitch circle diameter as d', module as m_n and number of teeth as Z'.

Wear strength of spur gear is given by

$$\therefore \quad S_w = bQd_pK$$

Wear strength of equivalent spur gear will be

$$S_{wn} = \left(\frac{b}{\cos \psi}\right) \cdot Q' \cdot \left(\frac{d_p}{\cos^2 \psi}\right) K$$

Since,

$$Q' = \frac{2Z_g'}{Z_g' + Z_p'} = \frac{2Z_g}{Z_g + Z_p} = Q$$

$$\therefore \quad S_{wn} = \frac{b \cdot Q \cdot d_p \cdot K}{\cos^3 \psi}$$

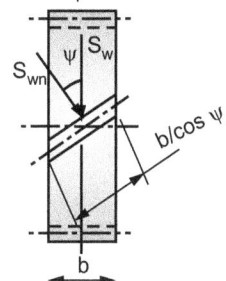

Fig. 2.10: Wear Strength for Helical Gear

With the same comments applicable as for the beam strength equation (Refer Fig. 2.10), wear strength equation reduces to

$$S_w = S_{wn} \cdot \cos \psi = \frac{b \cdot Q \cdot d_p \cdot K}{\cos^2 \psi} \qquad \ldots (2.8)$$

Values of K can be similarly obtained as in case of spur gear.

$$K = 0.16 \left(\frac{BHN}{100}\right)^2 \quad \ldots \text{(for pinion and gear made of steel)}$$

$$K = 0.18 \left(\frac{BHN}{100}\right)^2 \quad \ldots \text{(for steel pinion and cast iron gear)}$$

$$K = 0.21 \left(\frac{BHN}{100}\right)^2 \quad \ldots \text{(for pinion and gear made of cast iron)}$$

Equation (2.8) is the wear strength equation. To avoid pitting failure wear strength should be greater than the effective load on meshing teeth.

$$S_w > P_{eff}$$

Denoting factor of safety as FS

$$S_w = (FS) P_{eff}$$

2.6 EFFECTIVE LOAD

Similar to spur gear, in the preliminary stage, approximate approach is selected to account for dynamic load.

$$P_{eff} = \frac{C_L C_s P_t}{C_v}$$

where,
C_L = Load concentration factor
C_s = Service factor
C_v = Velocity factor

- The velocity factor for helical gears depends on pitch line velocity, gear cutting accuracy and accuracy of gear mounting. Typical value could be $C_v = 6/(6 + V)$.
- Values of load concentration factor and service factors are based on experience on previous equipments. In absence of such data, guide line values can be referred from design data handbooks.
- Once the value of module is estimated based on preliminary calculations, gear dimensions are known, manufacturing methods can be finalized and then Buckingham's equation can be used to have more precise estimation of the dynamic load. Thus, dynamic load is calculated from Buckingham's incremental dynamic tooth load equation.

Incremental dynamic tooth load is given by

$$P_d = \frac{21 \cdot V \, (b \cdot C \cos^2 \psi + P_{tmax}) \cos \psi}{21 \cdot V + \sqrt{b \cdot C \cdot \cos^2 \psi + P_{tmax}}}$$

where,
$P_{tmax} = (C_s \cdot C_l) \cdot P_t$

C is the deformation constant (N/mm)

With standard values of E_p, E_g for steel materials = 2.07×10^5 N/mm² and K for 20° pressure angle.

$C = 11500 \times e$ (N/mm) for Steel pinion with steel gear

$C = 10000 \times e$ (N/mm) for Steel pinion on Cast Iron gear

$C = 8900 \times e$ (N/mm) for Cast Iron pinion with Cast Iron gear

Tooth error for grade 8 pinion and gear is given by

$$e_p = 16.0 + 1.25 \left(m + 0.25 \sqrt{d_p}\right)$$

and

$$e_g = 16.0 + 1.25 \left(m + 0.25 \sqrt{d_g}\right)$$

Table 2.2: Tooth Profile Error

Grade	Error in Tooth Profile (in micron)
1.	$e = 0.80 + 0.06\phi$
2.	$e = 1.25 + 0.10\phi$
3.	$e = 2.00 + 0.16\phi$
4.	$e = 3.20 + 0.25\phi$
5.	$e = 5.00 + 0.40\phi$
6.	$e = 8.00 + 0.63\phi$
7.	$e = 11.00 + 0.90\phi$
8.	$e = 16.00 + 1.25\phi$
9.	$e = 22.00 + 1.80\phi$
10.	$e = 32.00 + 2.50\phi$
11.	$e = 45.00 + 3.55\phi$
12	$e = 63.00 + 5.00\phi$

Precise estimation of effective load can now be obtained as

$$P_{eff} = C_s \cdot C_L \cdot P_t + P_d$$

2.7 HELICAL GEAR DESIGN PROCEDURE

Design procedure for helical gears is similar to that for spur gears. However, it is important to note following points.

- Center distance: (a) can be obtained as below:

$$a = \frac{d_p}{2} + \frac{d_g}{2} = \frac{m \cdot Z_p}{2} + \frac{m \cdot Z_g}{2} = m \cdot \left(\frac{Z_p + Z_g}{2}\right)$$

Thus,
$$a = m \left(\frac{Z_p + Z_g}{2}\right) = \frac{m_n}{\cos \lambda} \left(\frac{Z_p + Z_g}{2}\right)$$

where, m_n is the standard value of module to be selected from preferred values.

- Beam strength equation and wear strength equations get modified as explained above.
- In case of spur gears, only radial loads are passed on to the shaft because of (tangential + radial) load on the gear. For helical gears forces on gears will be tangential + radial + axial. Loads transferred to the shaft will be radial + axial.

SOLVED EXAMPLES

Example 2.1: A pair of helical gear consists of 24 teeth pinion meshing with 120 teeth gear. The pinion rotates at 720 rpm. The normal pressure angle is 20° while helix angle is 25°. The face width is 40 mm and the normal module is 4 mm. The pinion as well as gear are made of steel 40 C_8 (S_{ult} = 600 N/mm²) with surface hardness of 350 BHN. The service factor and the factor of safety are 1.5 and 2 respectively. Assuming that velocity factor accounts for the dynamic load, calculate the power transmitting capacity of gears. Use $C_v = \dfrac{5.6}{5.6 + \sqrt{v}}$.

Given data: Z_p = 24, Z_g = 120, ϕ_n = 20°, ψ = 25°, N_p = 720 rpm, b = 40 mm, m_n = 4 mm, S_{ult} = 600 N/mm², C_s = 1.5, FS = 2.

Solution: Virtual number of teeth, $Z'_p = \dfrac{Z_p}{\cos^3 \psi} = \dfrac{24}{\cos^3 25} = 32.239$

As material for pinion and gear is same, pinion is weaker. Hence beam strength is found for the pinion. Lewis form factor for virtual number of teeth on pinion.

$$Y'_p = 0.484 - \dfrac{2.87}{Z'_p} = 0.484 - \dfrac{2.87}{32.239} = 0.3949$$

Beam strength of pinion material:

$$S_b = \sigma_b \cdot b \cdot Y' \cdot m_n$$
$$= \dfrac{600}{3} \times 40 \times 0.3949 \times 4 = 12636.8 \text{ N}$$

Wear strength is given by

$$S_w = \dfrac{b \cdot Q \cdot d_p \cdot K}{\cos^2 \psi}$$

where, $d_p = \dfrac{m_n \cdot Z_p}{\cos \psi} = \dfrac{4 \times 24}{\cos 25} = 105.924$ mm

and Ratio factor, $Q = \dfrac{2 \cdot Z_g}{Z_g + Z_p} = \dfrac{2 \times 120}{120 + 24} = 1.667$

$$K = 0.16 \left(\dfrac{BHN}{100}\right)^2 = 1.96$$

∴ $$S_w = \dfrac{40 \times 1.667 \times 105.924 \times 1.96}{\cos^2 25}$$

$$S_w = 16853 \text{ N}$$

Since, $S_b < S_w$, load capacity will be based on beam strength (S_b).

Velocity factor C_v is given as

$$C_v = \frac{5.6}{5.6 + \sqrt{v}}$$

where, $\quad v = \dfrac{\pi d_p \times N_p}{60 \times 1000} = \dfrac{\pi \times 105.924 \times 720}{60 \times 1000} = 3.993$ m/sec.

$$C_v = \frac{5.6}{5.6 + \sqrt{3.993}} = 0.737$$

Effective load, $\quad P_{eff} = \left(\dfrac{C_s \times C_L}{C_v}\right) P_t$

$$= \left(\frac{1.5 \times 1}{0.737}\right) P_t = 2.035\, P_t$$

Equating S_b with P_{eff} considering factor of safety

$$S_b = [P_{eff}]\, FS$$
$$12636.8 = [2.035 \cdot P_t]\, 2$$
$$\therefore \quad P_t = 3104.86\ N$$

Power transmitting capacity

$$\text{Power} = P_t \times v = 3104.86 \times 3.993$$
$$= 12397.7\ \text{Watts}$$
$$\text{Power} = 12.4\ \text{kW}$$

Example 2.2: A pair of helical gears consists of 18 teeth pinion with 45 teeth gear having 20° normal pressure angle. Pinion receives 7.5 kW power at 2000 rpm. Determine the module and face width of gear to avoid bending failure. Assume the following data.

(a) Helix angle = 23°, (b) Safe stress for pinion and gears: 150 N/mm², (c) Factor of safety = 2 and service factor = 1.25.

Determine the tangential, axial and radial components of the resultant tooth force.

Use $C_v = \dfrac{5.6}{5.6 + \sqrt{v}}$.

Given data: $\phi_n = 20°$, $\psi = 23°$, $Z_p = 18$, $Z_g = 45$, Power = 7.5 kW, $N_p = 2000$ rpm, $(\sigma_b)_{all} = 150$ N/mm², FS = 2, $C_s = 1.25$.

Solution: Effective force based on velocity factor:

Pitch line velocity, $\quad v = \dfrac{\pi d_p \cdot N_p}{60 \times 1000} = \pi \cdot \left(\dfrac{m_n \cdot Z_p}{\cos \psi}\right) \cdot \dfrac{N_p}{60 \times 1000}$

$$= \frac{\pi \times m_n \cdot 18}{0.9205} \times \frac{2000}{60 \times 1000} = (2.0478 \cdot m_n)\ \text{m/sec}$$

Tangential force, $P_t = \dfrac{\text{Power}}{\text{Velocity}} = \dfrac{7.5 \times 10^3}{2.0478 \times m_n} = \left(\dfrac{3662.46}{m_n}\right)$ N

$$C_v = \dfrac{5.6}{5.6 + \sqrt{v}} = \dfrac{5.6}{5.6 + \sqrt{2.0478\, m_n}}$$

Effective force, (Assuming $C_L = 1$, since not given)

$$P_{eff} = \left(\dfrac{C_s \cdot C_L}{C_v}\right) \cdot P_t = (1.25) \times \left(\dfrac{3662.46}{m_n}\right) \times \dfrac{5.6 + \sqrt{2.0478\, m_n}}{5.6}$$

$$P_{eff} = \dfrac{817.5}{m_n}\left(5.6 + \sqrt{2.0478\, m_n}\right)$$

Beam strength:

Since pinion and gear materials are same, pinion is weaker. Hence beam strength is found for pinion.

$$Z'_p = \dfrac{Z_p}{\cos^3 \psi} = \dfrac{18}{\cos^3 23} = 23.078$$

Lewis form factor

$$Y'_p = 0.484 - \dfrac{2.87}{Z'_p} = 0.484 - \dfrac{2.87}{23.078} = 0.3596$$

Pinion beam strength:

$$S_b = \sigma_b \cdot b \cdot Y'_p \cdot m_n$$
$$= 150 \times 10 \cdot m_n \times 0.3596 \times m_n$$
$$= 539.4\, m_n^2$$

To avoid bending failure, equating beam strength to P_{eff}, considering factor of safety.

$$S_b = (P_{eff}) \cdot FS$$
$$539.4\, m_n^2 = \left[\dfrac{817.5}{m_n}\left(5.6 + \sqrt{2.0478\, m_n}\right)\right] \times 2$$

Simplifying,

$$m_n^3 - 4.335\sqrt{m_n} - 16.97 = 0$$

Solving by trial and error, $m_n = 2.9$ mm

We select next higher standard module, $m_n = 3$.

Gear face width will be $b = 10 \times m_n = 30$ mm.

$$S_b = 539.4\, m_n^2 = 4854.6 \text{ N}$$
$$P_{eff} = 2201.0 \text{ N}$$

DESIGN OF MACHINE ELEMENTS - II   HELICAL GEARS AND BEVEL GEARS

Forces on gears:

(1) Tangential force, $P_t = \dfrac{3662.46}{m_n} = 1220.8$ N

(2) Radial force, $P_r = \left(\dfrac{\tan \phi_n}{\cos \psi}\right) \cdot P_t = 618.4$ N

(3) Axial force, $P_a = (\tan \psi) \cdot P_t = 518.2$ N

Assuming pinion having LH helix and rotating in clockwise direction as viewed left side, forces are as shown in Fig. 2.11.

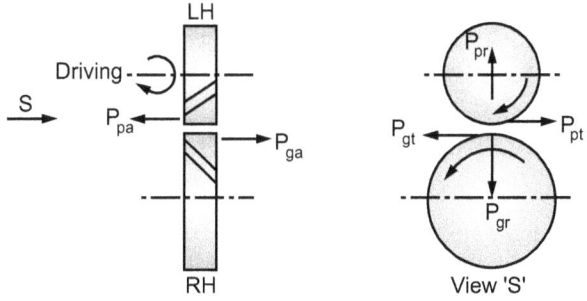

Fig. 2.11

Example 2.3: Following data is given for a helical gear pair hardened to 350 BHN (20° full depth involute) transmitting 15 kW power from an electric motor at 720 rpm to a machine running at 360 rpm.

Number of teeth on pinion = 18

Centre distance = 180 mm

Helix angle = 26°

Helix angle = 12 × Normal module

Permissible bending stress = 150 N/mm² (for both)

Service factor = 1.1.

Combined tooth error = 40 microns

Deformation factor = (11600 × Error) N/mm

Find FS in bending and pitting. Use

$$F_d = \dfrac{21 \cdot V (b \cdot C \cos^2 \psi + F_{tmax}) \cos \alpha}{21 \cdot V + \sqrt{b \cdot C \cdot \cos^2 \psi + P_{tmax}}}, \quad Y = 0.484 - \dfrac{2.87}{Z'}$$

Given data: $\phi_n = 20°$, Power = 15 kW, $N_p = 720$ rpm, $N_q = 360$ rpm, $Z_p = 18$, C.D. = 180 mm, $\psi = 26°$, $b = 12 \times m_n$, $(\sigma_b)_{all} = 150$ N/mm², $C_s = 1.1$, $e = 40$ μm, $C = 11600 \times e$.

Solution: $Z_p = 18$, $d_p = \dfrac{m_n \cdot Z_p}{\cos \psi}$, $d_g = \dfrac{m_n \cdot Z_g}{\cos \psi}$

Centre distance, $a = 180 = \dfrac{d_p + d_g}{2} = \dfrac{m_n}{2\cos\psi}(Z_p + Z_g)$

$\therefore \quad 180 = \dfrac{m_n(18+36)}{2 \times \cos 26}$, $m_n = 5.992 \approx 6$ mm

Thus, gears have normal module $m_n = 6$ mm.

Pitch line velocity, $v = \dfrac{\pi \cdot d_p \cdot N_p}{60 \times 1000} = \pi \left(\dfrac{m_n \cdot Z_p}{\cos\psi}\right) \dfrac{720}{60 \times 1000} = 4.53$ m/sec

Tangential force, $P_t = \dfrac{\text{Power}}{\text{Velocity}} = \dfrac{15 \times 10^3}{4.53} = 3311.3$ N

$P_{tmax} = P_t \times C_s \times C_L = 3311.3 \times 1.1 \times 1 = 3643$ N

Deformation factor, $C = 11600 \times e = 11600 \times 0.04 = 464$ N/mm

Dynamic load, $P_d = \dfrac{21 \cdot V (b \cdot C \cos^2\psi + P_{tmax}) \cos\psi}{21 \cdot V + \sqrt{b \cdot C \cdot \cos^2\psi + P_{tmax}}}$

$= \dfrac{21 \times 4.53 (72 \times 464 \times \cos^2 26 + 3643) \cos 26}{21 \times 4.53 + \sqrt{(72 \times 464 \times \cos^2 26 + 3643)}}$

$P_d = 9694.63$ N

Equivalent load considering dynamic load by Buckingham's equation

$P_{eff} = P_{tmax} + P_d$

$P_{eff} = 3643 + 9694.63 = 13338$ N

Bending Strength:

Since pinion and gear have same material, pinion is weaker.

$\therefore$ Beam strength is found for pinion

$S_b = \sigma_b \cdot b \cdot Y_p' \cdot m_n$

$Z_p' = \dfrac{Z_p}{\cos^3\psi} = \dfrac{18}{\cos^3 26} = 24.79$

$Y_p' = 0.484 - \dfrac{2.87}{Z_p'} = 0.484 - \dfrac{2.87}{24.79} = 0.368$

$S_b = (150) \times 72 \times 0.368 \times 6 = 23846.4$ N

Wear Strength:

$S_w = \dfrac{b \cdot Q \cdot d_p \cdot K}{\cos^2\psi}$

$d_p = \dfrac{m_n \cdot Z_p}{\cos\psi} = \dfrac{6 \times 18}{\cos 26} = 120.161$ mm

$$K = 0.16\left(\frac{350}{100}\right)^2 = 1.96$$

$$Q = \frac{2Z_g}{Z_g + Z_p} = \frac{2 \times 36}{18 + 36} = 1.333$$

$$S_w = \frac{72 \times 1.333 \times 120.161 \times 1.96}{\cos^2 26} = 27981 \text{ N}$$

$$(FS)_{bending} = \frac{S_b}{P_{eff}} = \frac{23846.4}{13338} = 1.788$$

$$(FS)_{wear} = \frac{S_w}{P_{eff}} = \frac{27981}{13338} = 2.1$$

Example 2.4: A pair of parallel helical gears consists of 18 teeth pinion rotating at 6000 rpm and supplying 2.5 kW power to gear. The speed reduction is 4 : 1. Normal pressure angle and helix angles are 20° and 23° respectively. Both gears are made of hardened steel (S_{ult} = 600 N/mm²). Motor starting torque is 150% of the rated torque and required factor of safety is 1.8. Gears are manufactured to grade 6 for which error may be taken as e = 8 + 0.63 ϕ where, ϕ = m_n + 0.25 $\sqrt{d}$. Gears are hardened to 250 BHN.

Estimate the normal module by considering velocity factor. $C_v = \dfrac{5.6}{5.6 + \sqrt{v}}$. Determine dynamic load by considering Buckingham's equation. Take deformation factor as C = 11500 · e.

Given data: Z_p = 18, N_p = 6000 rpm, Speed ratio = 4, ϕ_n = 20°, ψ = 23°, S_{ult} = 600 N/mm², C_s = 1.5, FS = 1.8, BHN = 250.

Solution: Effective load based on velocity factor:

$$d_p = \frac{m_n \cdot Z_p}{\cos \psi} = \frac{18 \times m_n}{\cos 23} = 19.555 \, m_n$$

$$v = \text{Pitch line velocity} = \frac{\pi \cdot d_p \cdot n_p}{60 \times 1000} = \frac{\pi \times 19.555 \times m_n \times 6000}{60 \times 1000} = 6.143 \, m_n$$

$$\text{Tangential force, } P_t = \frac{\text{Power}}{\text{Velocity}} = \frac{2.5 \times 10^3}{6.143 \, m_n} = \frac{407}{m_n}$$

$$\text{Velocity factor, } C_v = \frac{5.6}{5.6 + \sqrt{v}} = \frac{5.6}{5.6 + \sqrt{6.143 \, m_n}}$$

$$\text{Effective force, } P_{eff} = \left(\frac{C_s \cdot C_L}{C_v}\right) P_t = 1.5 \times 1 \times \left(\frac{5.6 + \sqrt{6.143 \, m_n}}{5.6}\right) \frac{407}{m_n}$$

$$= \frac{109}{m_n}\left(5.6 + \sqrt{6.143 \, m_n}\right)$$

Beam strength:

Pinion is weaker since material is same for pinion and gear. Hence beam strength is calculated for pinion.

$$S_b = \sigma_b \cdot b \cdot Y' \cdot m_n$$

$$Z'_p = \frac{Z_p}{\cos^3 \psi}$$

$$= \frac{18}{\cos^3 23} = 23.08$$

$$Y'_p = 0.484 - \frac{2.87}{Z'_p} = 0.3596$$

$$S_b = \left(\frac{600}{3}\right) \times 10 \cdot m_n \times 0.3596 \times m_n$$

$$S_b = 719.2 \, m_n^2$$

Wear strength:

$$S_w = \frac{b \cdot Q \cdot d_p \cdot K}{\cos^2 \psi}$$

where,

$$Q = \frac{2Z_g}{Z_g + Z_p} = \frac{2 \times 72}{18 + 72} = 1.6$$

$$K = 0.16 \left(\frac{BHN}{100}\right)^2$$

$$= 0.16 \left(\frac{250}{100}\right)^2 = 1$$

$$S_w = \frac{10 \times m_n \times 1.6 \times 19.555 \, m_n \times 1}{\cos^2 23}$$

$$= 369.25 \, m_n^2$$

As $S_w < S_b$, wear strength will govern the design.

Equating S_w with P_{eff} considering factor of safety.

$$S_w = [P_{eff}] \, FS$$

$$369.25 \, m_n^2 = \frac{109}{m_n} \left(5.6 + \sqrt{6.143 \, m_n}\right)$$

$$m_n^3 - 0.732 \sqrt{m_n} - 1.65 = 0$$

$$m_n \simeq 1.4 \, mm$$

We select $m_n = 2$ mm

For checking the design by considering dynamic load using Buckingham equation.

Dynamic load:

$$d_p = 19.555 \times m_n, \quad d_g = \frac{72 \times m_n}{\cos 23} = 156.43 \text{ mm}$$

Tooth error, $e = 8 + 0.63(m_n + 0.25\sqrt{d})$

$$e_p = 8 + 0.63(2 + 0.25\sqrt{19.555 \times 2}) = 10.166 \text{ μm}$$

$$e_g = 8 + 0.63(2 + 0.25\sqrt{156.43}) = 11.23 \text{ μm}$$

$$e = e_p + e_g = 21.396 \text{ μm} = 0.021396 \text{ mm}$$

$$C = 11500 \times e = 246 \text{ N/mm}$$

$$P_d = \frac{21 \cdot v \,(b \cdot C \cdot \cos^2 \psi + P_{tmax}) \cos \psi}{21 \cdot v + \sqrt{b \cdot C \cos^2 \psi + P_{tmax}}}$$

With $v = 6.143 \times m_n = 12.286$ m/sec.

and $P_{tmax} = (C_s \cdot C_L) P_t$

$$= (1.5 \times 1)\frac{407}{2}$$

$$= 305.3 \text{ N}$$

$$P_d = \frac{21 \times 12.286 \,(20 \times 246 \cos^2 23 + 305.3) \cos 23}{21 \times 12.286 + \sqrt{20 \times 246 \cos^2 23 + 305.3}}$$

$$P_d = 3270.5 \text{ N}$$

$$P_{eff} = P_{tmax} + P_d = 3270.5 + 305.3 = 3575.8 \text{ N}$$

Beam strength $\quad S_b = 719.2 \, m_n^2 = 2877 \text{ N} \quad \therefore FS = \left(\frac{2877}{3575}\right) = 0.8$

Wear strength $\quad S_w = 369.25 \, m_n^2 = 1476 \text{ N} \quad \therefore FS = \left(\frac{1476}{3575}\right) = 0.4$

Trial 1: Since FS is even less than 1 and we require FS = 2.

Let us select $m_n = 4$.

$$e_p = 8 + 0.63(4 + 0.25\sqrt{19.555 \cdot m_n}) = 11.91 \text{ μm}$$

$$e_g = 8 + 0.63[4 + 0.25\sqrt{(19.555 \, m_n \times 4)}] = 13.3 \text{ μm}$$

$$e = e_p + e_g = 25.21 \text{ μm} = 0.02521 \text{ mm}$$

$\therefore$ Deformation constant, $C = 11500 \times e = 289.9$ N/mm

$$b = 10 \cdot m_n = 40 \text{ mm}$$

$$v = 6.143 \times m_n = 24.572 \text{ m/sec.}$$

$$P_t = \frac{407}{m_n} = \frac{407}{4} = 101.75$$

$$P_{tmax} = \left(\frac{C_s \cdot C_L}{1}\right) P_t = 1.5 \times 1.0 \times 101.75 = 156.62 \text{ N}$$

By Buckingham equation

$$P_d = \frac{21 \times 24.572 \,(40 \times 289.9 \times \cos^2 23 + 156.62) \cos 23}{21 \times 24.572 + \sqrt{40 \times 289.9 \cos^2 23 + 156.72}}$$

$$= 7847.6 \text{ N}$$

$P_{eff} = P_{tmax} + P_d = 152.62 + 7695 = 7847.6 \text{ N}$

Beam strength, $S_b = 719.2\, m_n^2 = 11508 \text{ N}$ ∴ FS = 1.47

Wear strength, $S_w = 369.25\, m_n^2 = 5907 \text{ N}$ ∴ FS = 0.75

Thus, we see that results are better than original but still inadequate since factor of safety required in bending as well as wear should be two.

Trial 2:

We select module = 6 mm. Further, since $S_w \ll S_b$. We increase material hardness to 350 BHN so that S_w will be improved.

We conduct above steps again and also find new value of S_w.

$$e_p = 8 + 0.633\,(4 + 0.25\sqrt{19.555 \times 6}) = 12.23 \text{ μm}$$

$$e_g = 8 + 0.63\,(4 + 0.25\sqrt{19.555 \times 4 \times 6}) = 13.93 \text{ μm}$$

$$e = e_p + e_g = 26.16 \text{ μm} = 0.02616 \text{ mm}$$

Thus, $C = 11500 \times e = 300.8 \text{ N/mm}$

Width, $b = 10 \times m_n = 60 \text{ mm}$

$v = 6.143 \times m_n = 36.858 \text{ m/sec}$

$$P_t = \frac{407}{m_n} = 67.8 \text{ N}$$

$P_{tmax} = 1.5 \times 1 \times 67.8 = 101.7 \text{ N}$

By Buckingham Equation

$$P_d = \frac{21 \times 36.858 \,(60 \times 300.8 \times \cos^2 23 + 101.7) \cos 23}{21 \times 36.858 + \sqrt{60 \times 300.8 \cos^2 23 + 101.7}}$$

$P_d = 12931 \text{ N}$

$P_{tmax} = 101.7 \text{ N}$

$P_{eff} = P_{tmax} + P_d = 13033 \text{ N}$

Beam strength $= 719.2\, m_n^2 = 25893 \text{ N}$

$$\text{Wear strength} = \frac{b \cdot Q \cdot d_p \cdot K}{\cos^2 \psi}$$

$$= \frac{60 \times 1.6 \times (19.555 \times 6) \times 0.16 \left(\dfrac{350}{100}\right)^2}{\cos^2 23} = 26054 \text{ N}$$

$$\text{FS in bending} = \frac{S_b}{P_{eff}} = \frac{25893}{13033} = 1.987$$

$$\text{FS in wear} = \frac{S_w}{P_{eff}} = \frac{26054}{13033} = 1.999$$

Thus, the requirements are almost satisfied and we can select module = 6 mm with increased hardness for the surfaces to be 350 BHN.

Example 2.5: A steel helical pinion (S_{ult} = 800 N/mm^2) having 16 teeth meshes with a steel gear (S_{ult} = 720 N/mm^2). The pair transmits 20 kW power from 720 rpm motor to a 144 rpm machine. The application factor is 1.2 and load concentration factor is 1.1. Required factor of safety is 1.5. The face width is 10 times the normal module. The tooth system is 20° full depth involute while the helix angle is 25°. The gear is machined to grade. Deformation factor for the gear pair is 11000 · e N/mm. Design the gear pair by using the velocity factor and Buckingham's equation for dynamic load. Suggest the surface hardness for gear pair.

Use the following data:

$$Y = 0.484 - \frac{2.87}{Z'}$$

$$C_v = \frac{5.6}{5.6 + \sqrt{v}} \qquad e = 11 + 0.9(m_n + 0.25\sqrt{d})$$

$$\text{Load stress factor, } K = 0.16\left(\frac{BHN}{100}\right)^2 \qquad P_d = \frac{21 \cdot v\,(b \cdot C \cdot \cos^2\psi + P_{tmax})\cos\psi}{21 \cdot v + \sqrt{b \cdot C \cos^2\psi + P_{tmax}}}$$

Given data: Z_p = 16, Z_g = 80, Power = 20 kW, $(S_{ult})_{pinion}$ = 800 N/mm^2, $(S_{ult})_{gear}$ = 720 N/mm^2, C_s = 1.2, C_L = 1.1, FS = 1.5, $b = 10 \cdot m_n$, ϕ_n = 20°, ψ = 25°.

Solution:

Effective force:

$$\text{Pinion diameter } d_p = \frac{m_n \cdot Z_p}{\cos \psi} = \frac{m_n \cdot 16}{\cos 25} = 17.65\, m_n$$

$$\text{Pitch line velocity, } v = \frac{\pi \cdot d_p \cdot N_p}{60 \times 1000} = \frac{\pi \times 17.65 \cdot m_n \times 720}{60 \times 1000} = 0.665\, m_n$$

$$\text{Tangential force, } P_t = \frac{\text{Power}}{v} = \frac{20 \times 10^3}{0.665\, m_n} = \frac{30075.2}{m_n}$$

$$\text{Effective force, } P_{eff} = \left(\frac{C_s \cdot C_L}{C_v}\right) \cdot P_t = \frac{1.2 \times 1.1\,(5.6 + \sqrt{0.665\, m_n})}{(5.6)} \times \frac{30075}{m_n}$$

$$P_{eff} = \frac{7089.1}{m_n}[5.6 + \sqrt{0.665\, m_n}]$$

Beam strength:

$$S_b = \sigma_b \cdot b \cdot Y' \cdot m_n$$

$$Y'_p = 0.484 - \frac{2.87}{(Z_p/\cos^3 \psi)} = 0.35$$

$$Y'_g = 0.484 - \frac{2.87}{(80/\cos^3 \psi)} = 0.457$$

$$(\sigma_b \cdot Y'_p) = \frac{800}{3} \times 0.35 = 93.3 \qquad (\sigma_b \cdot Y'_g) = \frac{720}{3} \times 0.457 = 109.68$$

Since $(\sigma_b Y'_p)$ is smaller than $(\sigma_b Y'_g)$

Pinion is weaker. Hence beam strength is found for the pinion.

Beam strength:

$$S_b = \sigma_b \cdot b \cdot Y' \cdot m_n = 93.3 \times 10 \cdot m_n \times m_n = 933\, m_n^2$$

Equating beam strength with P_{eff} considering factor of safety

$$S_b = FS\,(P_{eff})$$

$$933\, m_n^2 = 1.5 \left[\frac{7089.1}{m} \cdot \left(5.6 + \sqrt{0.665\, m_n}\right) \right]$$

$$m_n^3 - 9.29 \sqrt{m_n} - 63.8 = 0$$

Solving by trial and error, $m_n = 4.4$

We select module = 5 mm.

Dynamic Load using Buckingham Equation:

$V = 0.665\, m_n = 3.325$ m/sec, $b = 10 \times m_n = 50$ mm

$$P_{tmax} = P_t \times C_s \cdot C_L = \frac{30075}{m_n} \times 1.2 \times 1.1 = 7939\ N$$

$$d_p = \frac{m_n \cdot Z_p}{\cos \psi} = \frac{5 \times 16}{\cos 25} = 88.27\text{ mm} \qquad d_g = \frac{m_n \cdot Z_g}{\cos \psi} = \frac{5 \times 80}{\cos \psi} = 441.35\text{ mm}$$

$$e_p = 11 + 0.9\,(m_n + 0.25\sqrt{d_p}) = 17.61\ \mu m$$
$$e_g = 11 + 0.9\,(m_n + 0.25\sqrt{441.35}) = 20.22\ \mu m$$
$$e = e_p + e_g = 37.83\ \mu m = 0.03783\text{ mm} \qquad C = 11000 \times 0.03783 = 416\ N/mm$$

$$P_d = \frac{21 \cdot v\,(b \cdot C \cos^2 \psi + P_{tmax})\cos \psi}{21 \cdot v + \sqrt{b \cdot C \cos^2 \psi + P_{tmax}}}$$

$$= 6948\ N$$

$$P_{eff} = P_{tmax} + P_d = 7939 + 6948 = 14887\ N$$

Beam strength, $S_b = 933\, m_n^2 = 23325\ N$

$$FS = \frac{S_b}{P_{eff}} = \frac{23325}{14887} = 1.56$$

Surface Hardness for Gear:

Wear strength is given by

$$F_w = \frac{b \cdot Q \cdot d_p \cdot K}{\cos^2 \psi}$$

$b = 50$ mm, $d_p = 88.27$ mm; $Q = \dfrac{2Z_g}{Z_g + Z_p} = \dfrac{2 \times 80}{16 + 80} = 1.667$

$$K = 0.16 \left(\frac{BHN}{100}\right)^2$$

$$F_w = \frac{50 \times 1.667 \times 88.27 \times 0.16}{\cos^2 \psi}\left(\frac{BHN}{100}\right)^2 = 1433.13 \left(\frac{BHN}{100}\right)^2$$

Equating wear strength with P_{eff} considering factor of safety

$$F_w = FS(P_{eff})$$

$$1433.13 \left(\frac{BHN}{100}\right)^2 = 1.5\,(14887)$$

Solving required value of hardness = 395 BHN.

Example 2.6: A pair of helical gears consists of 26 teeth pinion meshing with a 52 teeth gear. The normal module is 4 mm and normal pressure angle is 20°. Find the required value of helix angle if centre distance is to be maintained exactly 170 mm. The pinion transmits 5 kW power at 1500 rpm. Pinion has right hand helix and rotates clockwise when seen from the right side. Show the forces on pinion and gear.

Solution: $Z_p = 26$, $Z_g = 52$, $m_n = 4$ mm

$$\text{Centre distance, CD} = \frac{d_p}{2} + \frac{d_g}{2}$$

$$170 = \frac{m_n \cdot Z_p}{2 \cdot \cos \psi} + \frac{m_n \cdot Z_g}{2 \cdot \cos \psi}$$

$$= \frac{1}{\cos \psi}\left(\frac{4 \times 26}{2} + \frac{4 \times 52}{2}\right)$$

$\cos \psi = 0.9176$

Helix angle, $\psi = 23.42°$

$$\text{Torque on pinion 'A'} = \frac{(\text{Power})_{kW} \times 60 \times 10^6}{2\pi N} = \frac{5 \times 60 \times 10^6}{2\pi \times 1500}$$

$= 31830$ N·mm

$$\text{Tangential force on pinion} = \frac{31830}{\left(\dfrac{d_p}{2}\right)} = \frac{31830}{\left(\dfrac{m_n \times Z_p}{2 \times \cos \psi}\right)} = 561 \text{ N} = P_t$$

Axial force on pinion = $P_a = P_t \times \tan \psi = 243$ N = P_a

Radial force on pinion = $P_t \times \dfrac{\tan \phi_n}{\cos \psi} = 561 \times \dfrac{\tan 20°}{\cos 23.41°} = 223$ N = P_r

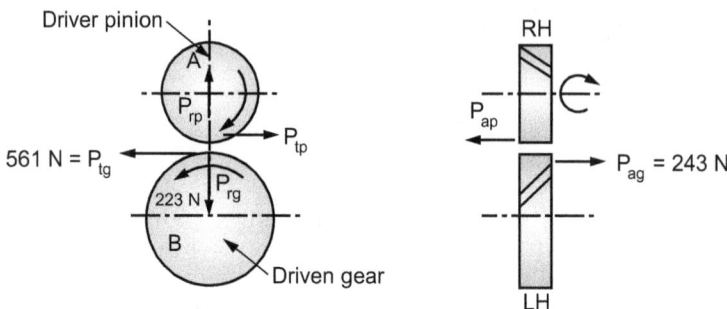

Fig. 2.12

Example 2.7: A pair of helical gears with 18 teeth on pinion and 54 teeth on gear transmits 10 kW power at 1500 rpm. Both gears are made of case hardened steel (S_{ult} = 720 N/mm²). Normal pressure angle is 20° and the helix angle is 24°. Motor starting torque is double the rated torque and load concentration factor is 1.1. Gears are finished to grade 6 and desired factor of safety is 1.6.

1. Estimate normal module considering dynamic load by velocity factor. Select standard module.
2. Determine dynamic load using Buckingham's equation and factor of safety in bending.
3. Recommend suitable hardness for gears.

For grade 6: $\quad e = 8 + 0.63(m + 0.25\sqrt{d})$

Deformation factor, $C = 11500 \times e$

$$C_v = \frac{5.6}{5.6 + \sqrt{v}} \qquad P_d = \frac{21 \cdot v(b \cdot C \cdot \cos^2\psi + P_{tmax})\cos\psi}{21 \cdot v + \sqrt{b \cdot C \cos^2\psi + P_{tmax}}}$$

Given data: $Z_p = 18$, $Z_g = 54$, Power = 10 kW, N_p = 1500 rpm, S_{ult} = 720 N/mm², $\phi_n = 20°$, $\psi = 24°$, $C_s = 2.0$, $C_L = 1.1$.

Solution: Effective force:

$$d_p = \frac{m_n \cdot Z_p}{\cos\psi} = \frac{18 \cdot m_n}{\cos 24} = 19.7\, m_n$$

$$v = \text{Pitch line velocity} = \frac{\pi \cdot d_p \cdot N_p}{60 \times 1000}$$

$$= \frac{\pi \times 19.7\, m_n \times 1500}{60 \times 1000} = 1.547\, m_n$$

$$\text{Tangential force, } P_t = \frac{\text{Power}}{\text{Velocity}} = \frac{10.0 \times 10^3}{1.547\, m_n} = \frac{6464.12}{m_n}\, N$$

$$\text{Velocity factor, } C_v = \frac{5.6}{5.6 + \sqrt{1.547\, m_n}}$$

Effective force, $P_{eff} = \left(\dfrac{C_s \cdot C_L}{C_v}\right) P_t$

$= \dfrac{2.0 \times 1.1 \times (5.6 + \sqrt{1.547\, m_n})}{5.6} \times \dfrac{6464.12}{m_n}$

$P_{eff} = \dfrac{2540\,(5.6 + \sqrt{1547\, m_n})}{m_n}$

Beam strength:

Pinion is weaker since material is same for pinion and gear.

∴ Beam strength for pinion: $S_b = \sigma_b \cdot b \cdot Y' \, m_n$

Lewis form factor, $Y'_p = 0.484 - \dfrac{2.87}{Z'_p}$

where, $Z'_p = \dfrac{Z_p}{\cos^3 \psi} = \dfrac{18}{\cos^3 24} = 23.61$

$Y'_p = 0.484 - \dfrac{2.87}{23.61} = 0.3624$

Beam strength:

$S_b = \sigma_b \cdot b \cdot Y' \cdot m_n = \dfrac{720}{3} \cdot (10\, m_n) \times 0.3624 \times m_n$

$S_b = 869.76\, m_n^2$

Equating beam strength with effective load considering factor of safety

$S_b = [P_{eff}]\, FS$

$869.76\, m_n^2 = \left[2540 \dfrac{(5.6 + \sqrt{1.547\, m_n})}{m_n} \right] 1.6$

$m_n^3 - 5.58\sqrt{m_n} - 26.16 = 0$

Solving by trial and error, $m_n = 3.4$ mm. We select $m_n = 4$ mm.

Check for dynamic load:

$e_p = 8 + 0.63\,(m_n + 0.25\sqrt{d_p}) = 8 + 0.63\,(4 + 0.25\sqrt{78.8}) = 11.92\, \mu m$

$e_g = 8 + 0.63\,(m_n + 0.25\sqrt{d_g}) = 8 + 0.63\,(4 + 0.25\sqrt{236.4}) = 12.94\, \mu m$

$e = e_p + e_g = 24.86\, \mu m$

Deformation factor, $C = 11500 \times e = 11500 \times 0.02486 = 285.89$ N/mm

$v = 1.547\, m_n = 6.188$ m/sec.

$P_{tmax} = \dfrac{6464.12}{m_n} = 1616$ N

$P_{tmax} = (C_s \cdot C_L)\, P_t = 2 \times 1.1 \times 1616 = 3555$ N

$$P_d = \frac{21 \cdot v \,(b \cdot C \cdot \cos^2 \psi + P_{tmax}) \cos \psi}{21 \cdot v + \sqrt{b \cdot C \cos \psi + P_{tmax}}}$$

$$= \frac{21 \times 6.188 \,(40 \times 285.89 \times \cos^2 24 + 3555) \cos 24}{21 \times 6.188 + \sqrt{(40 \times 285.89 \cos^2 24 + 3555)}}$$

$$P_d = 6363.2 \text{ N}$$

$$P_{eff} = P_{tmax} + P_d = 3555 + 6363.2 = 9918.2 \text{ N}$$

Factor of safety in bending $= \dfrac{S_b}{P_{eff}} = \dfrac{869.76 \, m_n^2}{P_{eff}} = 1.4$

Deciding hardness:

Wear strength should be $S_b = 13917$ N

$$S_w = \frac{b \cdot Q \cdot d_p \cdot K}{\cos^2 \psi}$$

where,

$$Q = \frac{2Z_g}{Z_g + Z_p} = \frac{2 \times 54}{18 + 54} = 1.5.$$

$\therefore$

$$K_{reqd.} = \frac{13917 \times \cos^2 24}{40 \times 1.5 \times (19.7 \times 4)} = 2.456$$

$$K = 2.456 = 0.16 \left(\frac{BHN}{100}\right)^2$$

$\therefore$ Required hardness, BHN = 392

BEVEL GEARS

2.8 INTRODUCTION

When power is to be transmitted between two intersecting shafts, bevel gears are used. In bevel gears, teeth are cut on a frustum of a cone. Bevel gears are of two types, straight teeth bevel and curved or spiral teeth bevel. In case of straight teeth bevel, the teeth are cut along the generators of the cone and if the teeth are extended they intersect with the axis of rotation [refer Fig. 2.13 (a)]. If curved teeth are cut on the frustum of cone the gear is called spiral teeth bevel [refer Fig. 2.13 (b)]. The point of intersection is known as apex point which is common for both, driving and driven bevel gears. Straight teeth bevel gears are easy to manufacture, easy to maintain while the spiral bevel, because of complicated shape of tooth requires special purpose machines. Because of this they are costlier compared with straight tooth bevel. The straight bevel gears create noise if operated at higher speeds while because of curved teeth, the contact between two meshing spiral gears take place gradually and results in quiet operation. Hence, they are suitable for high speed applications.

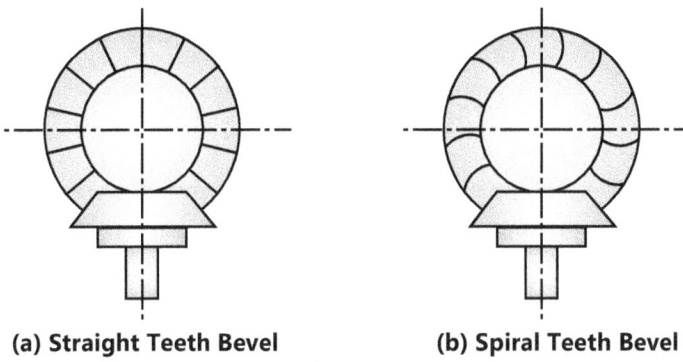

(a) Straight Teeth Bevel   (b) Spiral Teeth Bevel

Fig. 2.13

The bevel gear and pinion are designed in pairs. Hence, they are replaced together in pair. Although bevel gears can be used for almost any angle between shaft axes, they are most commonly used to connect shafts at right angles which are intersecting. In this chapter, only straight tooth bevel gears transmitting power at right angles will be discussed.

2.9 TERMINOLOGIES OF BEVEL GEARS

The terminologies of bevel gears are given below. (Refer Fig. 2.14)

(i) **Pitch Cone:** The tooth axes (pitch line) if extended, intersect the centre of rotation at apex point 'O'. The cone formed by extending the tooth axes is called as pitch cone.

(ii) **Pitch Cone Angle (γ):** The angle contained in the pitch line and the axis of rotation is called as pitch cone angle.

(iii) **Cone Distance (A_0):** It is the slant height of the pitch cone.

(iv) **Pitch Circle Diameter (d):** It is the diameter of the pitch circle at the larger end of bevel gear.

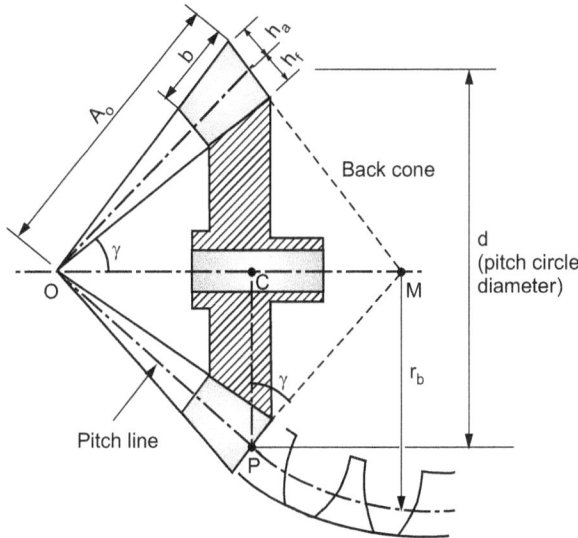

Fig. 2.14: Bevel Gear Terminology

(v) **Addendum (h_a):** It is the height of gear tooth above pitch circle measured at larger end of the gear.

(vi) **Dedendum (h_f):** It is the depth of gear tooth below the pitch circle measured at larger end of the gear.

(vii) **Back Cone:** It is the imaginary cone formed by drawing perpendiculars to the tooth axes (pitch line) on the opposite side of the pitch cone.

(viii) **Back Cone Radius (r_b):** It is the slant height of the back cone.

2.10 VIRTUAL NUMBER OF TEETH (Z')

For simplifying the analysis of bevel gears, an imaginary spur gear is considered which has pitch circle radius as back cone radius of the bevel gear and number of teeth as Z'. These teeth on imaginary spur gear are known as formative or virtual number of teeth. Referring to the Fig. 2.15.

For the back cone,

$$\text{Diameter} = 2r_b = Z' \times m$$

$$Z' = \frac{2r_b}{m} \quad \ldots (2.9)$$

Where m is the module at large end.

For the pitch cone, $\quad Z = \dfrac{d}{m} \quad \ldots (2.10)$

Dividing equation (2.9) by (2.10),

$$\frac{Z'}{Z} = \left(\frac{2r_b/m}{d/m}\right) = \frac{2r_b}{d}$$

In triangle PCM,

$$\sin(90° - \gamma) = \frac{d/2}{r_b}$$

or

$$\cos \gamma = \frac{d}{2r_b}$$

Hence,

$$\frac{Z'}{Z} = \frac{1}{\cos \gamma}$$

$$Z' = \frac{Z}{\cos \gamma} \quad \ldots (2.11)$$

Equation (2.11) is very important which shall be used in the design of bevel gears.

Geometric Relationships and Cone Distance (A_0):

Refer Fig. 2.15 which shows bevel gears in mesh.

Let $\quad \gamma_p, \gamma_g$ = Pitch cone angles of pinion and gear respectively.

$\quad d_p, d_g$ = Pitch circle diameters of pinion and gear measured at the large end.

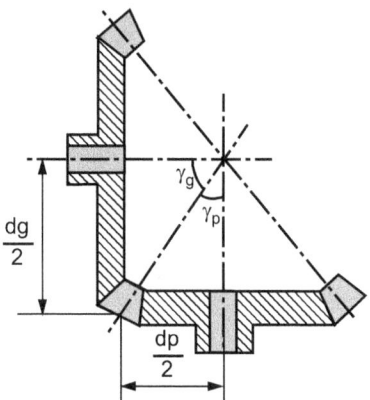

Fig. 2.15 Bevel Gears in Mesh

$$\tan \gamma_p = \frac{d_p/2}{d_g/2} = \frac{d_p}{d_g} = \frac{mZ_p}{mZ_g} = \frac{Z_p}{Z_g} \qquad \ldots (2.12)$$

$$\tan \gamma_g = \frac{d_g/2}{d_p/2} = \frac{d_g}{d_p} = \frac{mZ_g}{mZ_p} = \frac{Z_g}{Z_p} \qquad \ldots (2.13)$$

Considering that the two shafts are at right angles

$$\gamma_p + \gamma_g = 90°$$

Cone distance (slant height) is given by

$$A_o = \sqrt{\left(\frac{d_p}{2}\right)^2 + \left(\frac{d_g}{2}\right)^2}$$

2.11 FORCE ANALYSIS

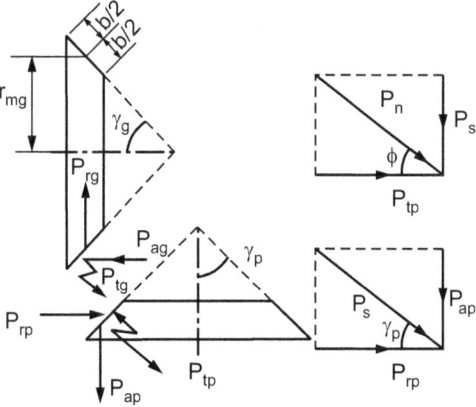

Fig. 2.16: Bevel Gear Pair in Contact

The Fig. 2.16 shows the various forces on the pinion and gear teeth. For the purpose of force analysis these forces are assumed to act at the midpoint of the face width along the pitch line.

Let

P_n - Resultant tooth force acting along common normal drawn at point of contact.

r_{mp}, r_{mg} - Radius of bevel pinion and gear at midpoint of face width

P_{tp}, P_{tg} - Tangential tooth forces on pinion and gear

P_{rp}, P_{rg} - Radial tooth forces on pinion and gear

P_{ap}, P_{ag} - Axial tooth forces on pinion and gear

ϕ - Pressure angle

From Fig. 2.16.

$$r_{mp} = \left[\frac{d_p}{2} - \frac{b \sin \gamma_p}{2}\right] \qquad \ldots (2.15)$$

$$r_{mg} = \left[\frac{d_p}{2} - \frac{b \sin \gamma_p}{2}\right] = \left[\frac{d_g}{2} - \frac{b \sin(90-\gamma_p)}{2}\right] = \left[\frac{d_g}{2} - \frac{b \cos \gamma_p}{2}\right] \qquad \ldots (2.16)$$

Refer Fig. 2.16.

At the midpoint of the face width, the resultant force (P_n) is resolved into two components, tangential (P_t) and the other separating force (P_s). The separating force (P_s) is further resolved into two components as radial (P_{rp}) and axial force (P_{ap}). The magnitudes of the forces on the pinion teeth can be obtained as below.

If T_p is the torque on the pinion, tangential force (P_{tp}) on the pinion is given by

$$P_{tp} = \frac{T}{r_{mp}} \qquad \ldots (2.17)$$

Knowing (P_{tp}), normal and separating force on the pinion is obtained as

$$P_n = P_{tp} \cos \phi \qquad \ldots (2.18)$$
$$P_s = P_{tp} \tan \phi \qquad \ldots (2.19)$$

Separating forces are further resolved into radial and axial (thrust) forces on the pinion.

$$P_{rp} = P_s \cos \gamma_p = P_{tp} \tan \phi \cos \gamma_p, \text{ and} \qquad \ldots (2.20)$$
$$P_{ap} = P_s \sin \gamma_p = P_{tp} \tan \phi \sin \gamma_p \qquad \ldots (2.21)$$

Once the forces on the pinion are found using above equations, the forces on gear tooth can be found out using following relations (Refer Fig. 2.16).

$$P_{tp} = P_{tg}, P_{rg} = P_{ap} \text{ and } P_{ag} = P_{rp} \qquad \ldots (2.22)$$

Force Directions on Pinion and Gear:

The direction of tangential force on pinion and gear is found by same method adopted for spur gear. On the driving gear direction of tangential force is opposite to motion and on the driven gear, the direction of force is same as direction of motion at the contact point. Radial and axial forces on pinion and gear are separating in nature. Hence, radial and axial force directions are easy to establish since both will act in such a direction as to separate pinion and gear.

2.12 BEAM STRENGTH OF BEVEL GEAR

To find the beam strength of bevel gear an imaginary spur gear is considered having number of teeth equal to virtual number of teeth. Considering an element of thickness dx situated at a distance x from the apex O and radius as r_x. Beam strength for this element with virtual number of teeth will be

$$S_{bx} = \sigma_b \cdot b_{x'} \cdot Y' \cdot m_x \qquad \ldots (2.23)$$

Where,

S_{bx} Beam strength of the element
b_x Face width of the element
σ_b Allowable bending stress
Y' Lewis form factor based on the virtual number of teeth
m_x Module for the element (Module for the bevel gear will not be constant along the width since the gear radius varies along its width)

From Fig. 2.17,

$$\frac{r_x}{R} = \frac{x}{A_0} \quad \text{OR} \quad r_x = \frac{xR}{A_0}$$

Considering the elemental section

$$m_x = \frac{2r_x}{Z} = \frac{2xR}{ZA_0}$$

Since,

$$m = \frac{2R}{Z}$$

$$m_x = m\left(\frac{x}{A_0}\right) \qquad \ldots (2.24)$$

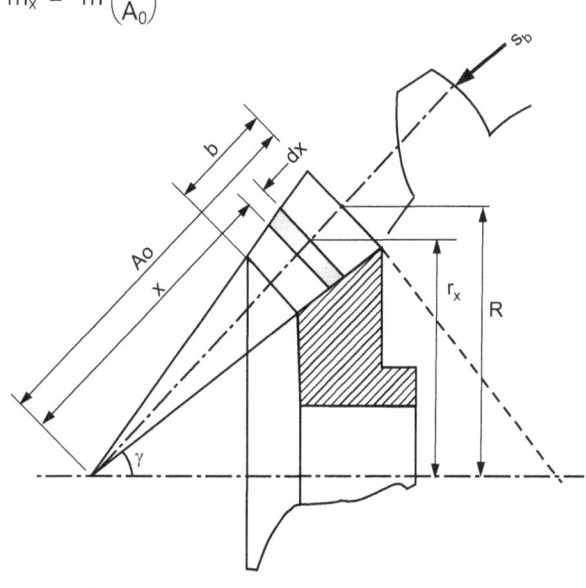

Fig. 2.17: Beam Strength of Bevel Gear

$$S = \sigma_b dx Y'\left(\frac{mx}{A_0}\right) = \frac{\sigma_b \cdot Y' \cdot m \cdot m dx}{A_0} \quad \ldots (2.25)$$

Torque on pinion shaft due to tangential force S_b on this element will be

$$T_x = S_{bx} \times r_x = \frac{\sigma_b \cdot Y' \cdot m \cdot R \cdot x^2 \, dx}{A_0^2} \quad \ldots (2.26)$$

Total torque on pinion shaft will be obtained by integrating the torque due to element within the range (A_0-b) to A_0

$$T = \int T_x \, dx = \int_{A_0-b}^{A_0} \frac{\sigma_b \cdot Y' \cdot m \cdot x^2 \cdot R}{A_0^2} \, dx = \left(\frac{\sigma_b Y' mR}{A_0^2}\right) \int_{A_0-b}^{A_0} x^2 \, dx$$

$$= \left(\frac{\sigma_b Y' mR}{A_0^2}\right)\left[\frac{x^3}{3}\right]_{A_0-b}^{A_0} = \sigma_b bY' mR\left[1 - \frac{b}{A_0} + \frac{b^2}{3A_0^2}\right] \quad \ldots (2.27)$$

Assuming S_b (tangential force) to be acting at the large end,

$$T = S_b \times R \quad \ldots (2.28)$$

Equating equations (2.27) and (2.28)

$$S_b = \sigma_b bY'm\left[1 - \frac{b}{A_0} + \frac{b^2}{3A_0^2}\right] \quad \ldots (2.29)$$

In the above equation since $\leq \frac{1}{3} A_0$, the term $\left(\frac{b^2}{3A_0^2}\right)$ is neglected being very small.

Hence, beam strength of a bevel gear is given by

$$S_b = \sigma_b bY'm\left[1 - \frac{b}{A_0}\right] \quad \ldots (2.30)$$

Where,

- S_b — Beam strength in N
- m — Module in mm
- b — Face width 10 m or $\frac{A_0}{3}$ (whichever is small)
- σ_b — Permissible bending stress $\sigma_b = \frac{S_{ut}}{3}$
- Y' — Lewis form factor based on virtual number of teeth

    $Y' = 0.484 - \frac{2.87}{Z'}$ for 20° full depth involute system

- A_0 — Cone distance

To avoid bending failure, the beam strength should be greater than the effective load.

2.13 WEAR STRENGTH

For the straight tooth bevel, the contact between the meshing teeth is line contact. This is similar to the spur gear pair in mesh. Hence for the equivalent spur gear with number of teeth equal to the virtual number of teeth, the wear strength equation can be written as:

$$S_w = b \cdot Q' \cdot K \cdot d_p' \qquad \ldots (2.31)$$

where,

  b — Face width of bevel gear (10 m or $A_0/3$ whichever smaller)

  Q' — Ratio factor given by equation $Q' = \dfrac{2Z_g'}{Z_g' + Z_p'} \qquad \ldots (2.32)$

Q' is the ratio factor for the equivalent spur gear pair.

For 90° angle between pinion and gear shaft we have

$$Z_p' = \frac{Z_p}{\cos \gamma_p} \quad \text{and} \quad Z_g' = \frac{Z_g}{\sin \gamma_p}$$

Substituting in the equation (2.32)

$$Q' = \frac{2Z_g}{Z_g + Z_p \cdot \tan \gamma_p}$$

  K — Load stress factor

$$K = 0.16 \left(\frac{BHN}{100}\right)^2 \ldots \text{for steel pinion meshing with steel gear}$$

$$K = 0.18 \left(\frac{BHN}{100}\right)^2 \ldots \text{for steel pinion meshing with cast iron gear}$$

$$K = 0.21 \left(\frac{BHN}{100}\right)^2 \ldots \text{for cast iron pinion meshing with cast iron gear}$$

  d_p' — Pitch circle diameter of equivalent spur gear. $d_p' = \dfrac{d_p}{\cos \gamma_p}$

$$S_w = \frac{bQ' K d_p}{\cos \gamma_p} \qquad \ldots (2.33)$$

In usual practice one of the bevel gears is fitted on a shaft with overhang (i.e. at the end of shaft). Due to this there may be excessive deflection of the shaft. The load between pinion and gear teeth is therefore not uniformly distributed along the width and gear pair does not transmits the forces to its capacity. Hence, the force transmission is considered to be 25% less than its full load capacities. **Buckingham's wear strength equation is expressed as**

$$S_w = \frac{0.75\, bQ' K d_p}{\cos \gamma_p} \qquad \ldots (2.34)$$

2.14 EFFECTIVE LOAD

For the design of the gears based on the beam or wear strength, it is already discussed that the effective tangential load is obtained by considering the tangential load with all the modifying factors such as service factor, load concentration factor and velocity factor. It is assumed that the gear tooth is subjected to this effective load. Equating effective load with the beam and wear strength considering appropriate factor of safety, the module will be obtained.

Like spur gears, in the initial stages of gear design, the dynamic load effect for the bevel gears is considered using approximate approach by using Barth or velocity factor.

$$P_{eff} = \frac{C_s C_L P_t}{C_v} \qquad \ldots (2.35)$$

[To be used in the initial stages of the design when module is unknown]

To determine the actual (available) factor of safety when module is known, the exact dynamic load using Buckingham's equation should be found. The effective load will be found based on exact dynamic load.

$$P_{eff} = C_s C_L P_t + P_d \text{ [To be used after knowing the module]}$$

Here, P_{eff} - Effective tooth load in N
C_s - Service factor
C_L - Load concentration factor
C_v - Velocity factor
P_t - Tangential tooth load in N
P_d - Dynamic tooth load obtained by Buckingham's equation in N

Velocity or Barth factor in case of bevel gears may be considered using either of the two equations given below:

$$C_v = \frac{6}{6+v} \quad \text{or} \quad C_v = \frac{5.6}{5.6+\sqrt{v}}$$

Buckingham's incremental dynamic tooth load equation is used to determine dynamic load.

$$P_d = \frac{21v\,(bC + C_s C_L P_t)}{21v + \sqrt{(bC + C_s C_L P_t)}} \qquad \ldots (2.36)$$

Here, V - Pitch line velocity in m/s
b - Face width of gear in mm
C - Deformation factor in N/mm

$$C = \frac{Ke}{\left[\dfrac{1}{E_p} + \dfrac{1}{E_g}\right]}$$

K is factor depending upon tooth form

K = 0.107 for 14.5° full depth involute and composite systems.

   = 0.111 for 20° full depth involute teeth.

   = 0.115 for 20° stub involute systems.

E_p, E_g are the moduli of elasticity for pinon and gear materials respectively in N/mm².

e is the total tooth error in the pinion and the gear, (= e_p + e_g) mm.

Procedure for obtaining tooth error 'e' is same as in case of spur gear and helical gears.

2.15 DESIGN OF STRAIGHT TEETH BEVEL GEARS

The design of straight teeth bevel gears is almost similar to the spur gears.

Following is the procedure for the design:

1. Calculate the pitch line velocity in terms of module from the given data.
2. Find the tangential load in terms of module using relation $P_t = \dfrac{P}{v}$. In this relation, the power should be considered in watts and the pitch line velocity in m/s.
3. Calculate C_v in terms of module.
4. Calculate P_{eff} in terms of module.
5. Determine the beam strength of the weaker element (pinion or gear) in terms of module using equation (2.30).
   - Determine the pitch cone angles for the pinion and gear using equations (2.14) and (2.13).
   - Determine the virtual (formative) number of teeth for pinion and gear using equation (2.11).
   - Determine the Lewis form factor based on virtual number of teeth on pinion and gear.
   - Obtain the product of bending stress and Lewis form factor for pinion and gear. Select the smaller of the two to obtain the beam strength.
   - Determine A_0 using equation (2.14) and $A_0/3$ and decide the face width. (10 m or $A_0/3$, smaller of the two).
6. Determine the wear strength of the pair (considering smaller of the hardness values for pinion and gear) in terms of module using equation (2.34).
   - Determine the ratio factor Q' based on the virtual number of teeth on pinion and gear.
   - Calculate load stress factor K.
7. Compare the beam strength and wear strength and identify the smaller of the two.

DESIGN OF MACHINE ELEMENTS - II   HELICAL GEARS AND BEVEL GEARS

8. Equate the smaller of beam and wear strength with effective load considering factor of safety to obtain the module.
9. Select the standard module and calculate, face width, pitch circle diameters of pinion and gear.
10. Calculate pitch line velocity, tangential load, tooth error and deformation factor.
11. Calculate the exact dynamic load using Buckingham's equation and new effective load based on exact dynamic load.
12. Calculate the beam and wear strength values and obtain the actual (available) factor of safety.
13. If the actual factor of safety is more than the initially taken, the gear design is safe. Else go for a new iteration with higher module and repeat the steps from 10 to 13 till the actual factor of safety is larger than the initially taken.

SOLVED EXAMPLES

Example 2.8: A pair of straight bevel gears, intersecting at right angles, consists of 20 teeth pinion meshing with 44 teeth gear. Pinion and gear are made of case hardened steel (UTS = 680 N/mm^2) and gear (UTS = 600 N/mm^2). Pinion transmits 12 kW power at 1500 rpm. Service factor is 1.75. Assuming that velocity factor accounts for dynamic load, design the gear pair for a factor of safety of 1.5. Assume surface hardness of 380 BHN for the gear pair. Use $C_v = \dfrac{5.6}{5.6 + \sqrt{v}}$.

Given: $Z_p = 20$, $Z_q = 44$, $(S_{ult})_{pinion} = 680$ N/mm^2, $(S_{ult})_{gear} = 600$ N/mm^2, Power = 12 kW, $N_p = 1500$ rpm, $C_s = 1.75$, FS = 1.5, BHN = 380.

Solution: Effective load:

$$d_p = m \cdot Z_p = 20 \cdot m$$

$$v = \text{Pitch line velocity} = \frac{\pi \cdot d_p \cdot N_p}{60 \times 1000} = \frac{\pi \times 20\, m \times 1500}{60 \times 1000} = 1.5708\, m \text{ (m/min)}$$

$$\text{Tangential force, } P_t = \frac{\text{Power}}{\text{Velocity}} = \frac{12 \times 10^3}{1.5708}$$

$$= \frac{7639.4}{m}$$

$$\text{Velocity factor} = \frac{5.6}{5.6 + \sqrt{v}} = \frac{5.6}{5.6 + \sqrt{1.5708\, m}}$$

$$P_{eff} = \left(\frac{C_s \cdot C_L}{C_v}\right) P_t = \frac{1.75 \times 1 \times (5.6 + \sqrt{1.5708\, m})}{5.6} \times \frac{7639.4}{m}$$

$$P_{eff} = \frac{2387.3\, (5.6 + \sqrt{1.5708\, m})}{m}$$

Beam strength:

$$S_b = \sigma_b \cdot b \cdot Y' \cdot m \left[1 - \frac{b}{A_o}\right]$$

$$\tan \gamma_p = \frac{Z_p}{Z_g} = \frac{20}{44} = 0.4545, \; \gamma_p = 24.44, \; \gamma_g = 65.56°$$

$$Z'_p = \frac{Z_p}{\cos \gamma_p} = \frac{20}{0.910} = 21.97 \qquad Y'_p = 0.484 - \frac{2.87}{Z'_p} = 0.353$$

$$Z'_g = \frac{Z_g}{\cos \gamma_g} = \frac{44}{0.413} = 106.35 \qquad Y'_g = 0.484 - \frac{2.87}{Z'_g} = 0.457$$

$$(\sigma_b \cdot Y'_p)_p = \frac{680}{3} \times 0.353 = 80.01$$

$$(\sigma_b \cdot Y'_g)_g = \frac{600}{3} \times 0.457 = 91.4$$

Since $(\sigma_b \cdot Y'_p) < (\sigma_b \cdot Y'_g)$, pinion is weaker. Beam strength will be based on pinion strength.

$$d_p = m \cdot Z_p = 20 \cdot m, \quad d_g = m \cdot Z_g = 44 \cdot m$$

Cone distance, $A_o = \sqrt{\left(\frac{d_p}{2}\right)^2 + \left(\frac{d_g}{2}\right)^2} = \sqrt{100\,m^2 + 484\,m^2} = 24.18\,(m)$

Now, $\quad b = \frac{1}{3} A_o = 8.055\,m$ or $10\,m$ (whichever is smaller)

∴ Width, $b = 8.055 = 8.1\,m$

Beam strength: S_b

$$S_b = (\sigma_b \cdot Y'_p)_p \cdot b \cdot m \left[1 - \frac{b}{A_o}\right] = 80.01 \times 8.1\,m \times m \left[1 - \frac{8.1}{24.17}\right] = 430.9\,m^2$$

Wear strength S_w:

$$\text{Ratio factor } Q' = \frac{2 \cdot Z'_g}{Z'_g + Z'_p} = \frac{2 \times 106.35}{106.35 + 21.97} = 1.658$$

$$K = 0.16 \left(\frac{BHN}{100}\right)^2 = 0.16 \left(\frac{380}{100}\right)^2 = 2.31$$

$$S_w = \frac{0.75\,b \cdot Q' \cdot d_p \cdot K}{\cos \gamma_p}$$

$$S_w = \frac{0.75 \times 8.1\,m \times 1.658 \times 20\,m \times 2.31}{0.91}$$

$$= 511.4\,m^2$$

Since, $S_b < S_w$, the gear pair is weaker in beam strength, hence check should be against S_b.

Equating S_b with effective force P_{eff} considering desired factor of safety.

$$S_b = (P_{eff})\, FS$$

$$430.9\, m^2 = \frac{2387.3\,(5.6 + \sqrt{1.5708\, m})}{m} \times 1.5$$

Simplifying,

$$m^3 - 10.41\sqrt{m} - 46.5 = 0$$

Solving trial and error, $\quad m \simeq 4.1$

We select next higher standard module, m = 5.

Hence,
$$m = 5 \text{ mm}$$
$$d_p = 20\, m = 100 \text{ mm}$$
$$d_g = 44 \text{ mm} = 220 \text{ mm}$$
$$\text{Addendum} = 1\, m = 5 \text{ mm}$$

Example 2.9: Straight bevel gears with 20 and 32 teeth are in mesh with their axes intersecting at right angles. Electric motor developing 10 kW power at 1500 rpm is connected to the pinion shaft. The load distribution factor is 1.2 and starting torque on motor is 150% of the rated torque. Both pinion and gear made of alloy steel having ultimate tensile strength (UTS) of 1000 N/mm^2 and are heat treated to a surface hardness of 400 BHN. Module and face width are 5 mm and 45 mm respectively. Gears are machined to grade 7. Take deformation factor as 11600 · e N/mm. Assuming that dynamic load is accounted by Buckingham's equation. Find:

1. Factor of safety in bending.
2. Factor of safety against pitting.

Tooth system used is 20° full depth involute.

$$e = 11 + 0.9\,(m + 0.25\sqrt{d_m})$$

Given data: $Z_p = 20$, $Z_g = 32$, Power = 10 kW, $N_p = 1500$ rpm, $C_l = 1.2$, $C_s = 1.5$, $S_{ult} = 1000$ N/mm^2, BHN = 400, m = 5 mm, b = 45 mm.

Solution: $\quad d_p = m \cdot Z_p = 100$ mm

$\tan \gamma_p = \dfrac{Z_p}{Z_g} = 0.625$, $\gamma_p = 32°$, $\gamma_g = 58°$, $D_g = m \cdot Z_g = 160$ mm.

$$\text{Pitch line velocity, } v = \frac{\pi \cdot d_p \cdot N_p}{60 \times 1000} = 7.854 \text{ m/sec}$$

$$\text{Tangential force, } P_t = \frac{\text{Power}}{\text{Velocity}} = \frac{10 \times 10^3}{7.854} = 1273.2 \text{ N}$$

Maximum tangential force, $P_{tmax} = (C_s \cdot C_l)\, P_t = 1.5 \times 1.2 \times P_t = 2291.8$ N

Tooth error e:

$$d_{mp} = d_p - b \sin \gamma_p = 100 - 45 \sin 32 = 76.15 \text{ mm}$$

$$d_{mg} = d_g - b \sin \gamma_g = 160 - 45 \sin 58 = 121.84 \text{ mm}$$

$$e_p = 11 + 0.9\,(5 + 0.25\sqrt{76.15}) = 17.46\ \mu \cdot m$$

$$e_g = 11 + 0.9\,(5 + 0.25\sqrt{121.84}) = 17.98\ \mu \cdot m$$

$$e = 35.44\ \mu m = 0.03544 \text{ mm}$$

$$C = 11600 \times 0.03544 = 411.18 \text{ N/mm}$$

Incremental dynamic load

$$P_d = \frac{21 \cdot v\,(b \cdot C + P_{tmax})}{21 \cdot v + \sqrt{b \cdot C + P_{tmax}}}$$

$$= \frac{21 \times 7.854\,(45 \times 411.7 + 2291.8)}{21 \times 7.854 + \sqrt{45 \times 411.18 + 2291.8}}$$

$$= 11094.8 \text{ N}$$

$$P_{eff} = P_{tmax} + P_d = 2291.8 + 11094.8 = 13386.6 \text{ N}$$

Beam strength:

Since pinion and gear materials are same, pinion is weaker.

Therefore, beam strength is calculated based on pinion strength.

$$S_b = \sigma_b \cdot b \cdot Y' \cdot m \left[1 - \frac{b}{A_o}\right]$$

$$\sigma_b = \frac{1}{3} \times 1000 = 333.3 \text{ N/mm}^2, \quad b = 45 \text{ mm}$$

$$Y' = 0.484 - \frac{2.87}{Z'_p} = 0.484 - \frac{2.87}{(Z_p/\cos \gamma_p)} = 0.484 - \frac{2.87}{23.58} = 0.362$$

$$A_o = \sqrt{\left(\frac{d_p}{2}\right)^2 + \left(\frac{d_g}{2}\right)^2} = \frac{1}{2}\sqrt{(100)^2 + (160)^2} = 94.34 \text{ mm}$$

$$S_b = 333.33 \times 45 \times 0.362 \times 5 \left[1 - \frac{45}{94.34}\right] = 14200 \text{ N}$$

Wear strength:

$$S_w = \frac{0.75 \, b \cdot Q' \cdot d_p \cdot K}{\cos \gamma_p};$$

$$Z'_p = \frac{Z_p}{\cos \gamma_p} = 23.58, \quad Z'_g = \frac{Z_g}{\cos \gamma_g} = 60.38$$

$$Q' = \frac{2Z'_g}{Z'_g + Z'_p} = \frac{2 \times 60.38}{23.58 + 60.38} = 1.438$$

$$K = 0.16 \left(\frac{BHN}{100}\right)^2 = 0.16 \left(\frac{400}{100}\right)^2 = 2.56$$

$$S_w = \frac{0.75 \times 45 \times 1.438 \times 100 \times 2.56}{0.848} = 14653.4 \, N$$

$$\text{Factor of safety in bending} = \frac{\text{Beam strength}}{P_{eff}} = \frac{14200}{13386.6} = 1.06$$

$$\text{Factor of safety in wear} = \frac{\text{Wear strength}}{P_{eff}} = \frac{14653.4}{13386.6} = 1.095$$

Example 2.10: A straight bevel pinion with 24 number of teeth meshes with a 56 teeth gear. The pinion transmits 10 kW power while rotating at 1500 rpm. Motor starting torque is 40% more than the rated torque and load concentration factor is 1.3. Pinion and gear both are made of alloy steel with their UTS values 820 and 680 N/mm² respectively. Hardness for pinion and gear is 400 and 380 respectively. Deformation factor may be taken as $11500 \cdot e$ N/mm with error 'e' given by $e = 8 + 0.63 \left[m + 0.25 \sqrt{d_m}\right]$. Design the gear for a factor of safety 1.2.

Use the following relation.

$$C_v = \frac{6}{6+v}; \quad Y = 0.484 - \frac{2.87}{Z'}$$

$$F_d = \frac{21 \cdot v \, (b \cdot C + F_{tmax})}{21 \cdot v + \sqrt{b \cdot C + F_{tmax}}}$$

Given data: $Z_p = 24$, $Z_g = 56$, Power = 10 kW, $N_p = 1500$ rpm, $C_s = 1.4$, $C_l = 1.3$, $(S_{ult})_{pinion} = 820$ N/mm², $(S_{ult})_{gear} = 680$ N/mm², BHN: 400/380, FS = 1.2.

Solution: Effective load: $d_p = m \cdot Z_p = 24 \cdot m$

$$v = \frac{\pi \, d_p \, N_p}{60 \times 1000} = 1.885 \, m$$

$$\text{Tangential force, } P_t = \frac{\text{Power}}{v} = \frac{10 \times 10^3}{1.885 \, m} = \frac{5305}{m}$$

$$C_v = \frac{6}{6+v} = \frac{6}{6+1.885\,m}$$

$$P_{eff} = \frac{C_s \cdot C_l}{C_v} \times P_t = \frac{1.4 \times 1.3\,(6+1.885\,m)}{6} \times \frac{5305}{m}$$

$$= \frac{1609\,(6+1.885\,m)}{m}$$

Beam strength:

$$S_b = \sigma_b \cdot b \cdot Y' \cdot m \left[1 - \frac{b}{A_o}\right]$$

$$\tan \gamma_p = \frac{Z_p}{Z_g} = \frac{24}{56} = 0.428;\ \gamma_p = 23.2°,\quad \gamma_g = 66.8°$$

$$Z'_p = \frac{Z_p}{\cos \gamma_p} = \frac{24}{\cos 23.2} = 26.11;\quad Y'_p = 0.484 - \frac{2.87}{Z'_p} = 0.374$$

$$Z'_g = \frac{Z_g}{\cos \gamma_g} = \frac{56}{\cos 66.8} = 142.15;\quad Y'_g = 0.484 - \frac{2.87}{Z'_g} = 0.464$$

$$(\sigma_b Y'_p)_p = \frac{820}{3} \times 0.374 = 102.2$$

$$(\sigma_b Y'_g)_g = \frac{680}{3} \times 0.464 = 105.63$$

Since $(\sigma_b Y'_p) < (\sigma_b Y'_g)$, pinion is weaker.

Beam strength will be calculated based on pinion.

$$d_p = m \cdot Z_p = 24\,m \qquad d_g = m \cdot Z_g = 56 \cdot m$$

$$\text{Cone distance, } A_o = \sqrt{\left(\frac{d_p}{2}\right)^2 + \left(\frac{d_g}{2}\right)^2} = \sqrt{144\,m^2 + 784\,m^2} = 30.46\,m$$

Now, $\quad b = \frac{1}{3} A_o = 10.15\,m$ or $10 \cdot m$ whichever is smaller.

∴ $\quad b = 10 \cdot m$

Beam strength $S_b = (\sigma_b \cdot Y'_p) \times b \cdot m \left[1 - \frac{b}{A_o}\right] = 102.2 \times 10 \cdot m \times m \left(1 - \frac{10.0}{30.46}\right) = 686.4\,m^2$

Wear strength:

$$\text{Ratio factor, } Q' = \frac{2 \cdot Z'_g}{Z'_g + Z'_p} = \frac{2 \times 142.15}{142.15 + 26.11} = 1.69$$

$$K = 0.16 \left[\frac{BHN}{100}\right]^2 = 0.16(3.8)^2 = 2.31$$

$$S_w = \frac{0.75 \cdot b \cdot Q' \cdot d_p \cdot K}{\cos \gamma_p}$$

$$= \frac{0.75 \times 10 \cdot m \times 1.69 \times 24\, m \times 2.31}{\cos 23.2} = 764.6\, m^2$$

Since $S_b < S_w$, design will be based on beam strength. Equating beam strength with effective load considering factor of safety

$$686.4\, m^2 = [P_{eff}]\, FS$$

$$686.4\, m^2 = \frac{1609\,(6 + 1.885\, m)}{m}$$

$$m^3 - 4.419\, m - 14 = 0$$

Solving, $m \simeq 3.1$

We select $m = 4$. Further, we check for dynamic load.

Check with m = 4:

$$\text{Tangential load, } P_t = \frac{5305}{m} = \frac{3505}{4} = 1326.3\, N$$

$$(P_t)_{max} = (C_s \cdot C_l)\, P_t = 1.4 \times 1.3 \times 1326.3$$

$$= \mathbf{2413.7\, N}$$

Dynamic load P_d:

$$d_{mp} = d_p - b \cdot \sin \theta_p = 4 \times 24 - 40 \times \sin 23.2 = 80.24\, mm$$

$$d_{mg} = d_g - b \sin \theta_g = 4 \times 56 - 40 \times \sin 66.8 = 187.23\, mm$$

$$e_p = 8 + 0.63\,(m + 0.25\,\sqrt{d_m})$$

$$= 8 + 0.63\,(4 + 0.25\,\sqrt{80.24}) = 11.93\, \mu m$$

$$e_g = 8 + 0.63\,(4 + 0.25\,\sqrt{187.23}) = 12.67\, \mu m$$

$$e = e_p + e_g = 0.0246\, mm$$

$$\therefore \quad C = 11500 \times 0.0246 = 282.9\, N/mm$$

$$v = 1.885\, m = 7.54\, m/sec.$$

$$P_d = \frac{21 \cdot v\,(b \cdot C + P_{tmax})}{21 \cdot v + \sqrt{b \cdot C + P_{tmax}}} = \frac{21 \times 7.54\,(40 \times 282.9 + 2413.7)}{158.34 + 117.174}$$

$$P_d = 7890\, N$$

$$\therefore \quad P_{eff} = P_{tmax} + P_d = 2413 + 7890 = 10303.7\, N$$

$$\text{Beam strength} = 686.4\, m^2 = 10982\, N \quad FS = \frac{S_b}{P_{eff}} = \frac{10982}{10303.7} = 1.06$$

$$\text{Wear strength} = 764.6\, m^2 = 12236\, N \quad FS = \frac{S_w}{P_{eff}} = \frac{12233.6}{10303.7} = 1.18$$

This is smaller than required factor of safety of 1.2. Hence, we take Trial 2 with $m = 5\, mm$.

Trial 2:

$$\text{Tangential load, } P_t = \frac{5305}{5}$$
$$= 1061 \text{ N}$$
$$P_{tmax} = (C_s \cdot C_l) P_t = 1.4 \times 1.3 \times 1061$$
$$= 1931 \text{ N}$$

Tooth error:

$$d_{mp} = d_p - b \sin \theta_p = 5 \times 24 - 50 \sin 23.2 = 100.3 \text{ mm}$$
$$d_{mg} = d_g - b \sin \theta_g = 5 \times 56 - 50 \sin 66.8 = 234.04 \text{ mm}$$
$$e_p = 8 + 0.63 \left(5 + 0.25 \sqrt{104.24}\right)$$
$$= 12.73 \text{ μm}$$
$$e_g = 8 + 0.63 \left(5 + 0.25 \sqrt{243.23}\right)$$
$$= 13.56 \text{ μm}$$
$$e = e_p + e_g = 0.02628 \text{ mm}$$
$$\therefore C = 11500 \times e$$
$$= 303 \text{ N/mm}$$
$$v = 1.885 \text{ m}$$
$$= 9.425 \text{ m/sec}$$
$$P_d = \frac{21 \cdot v (b \cdot C + P_{tmax})}{21 \cdot v + \sqrt{b \cdot C + P_{tmax}}}$$
$$= \frac{21 \times 9.425 (50 \times 303 + 1931)}{21 \times 9.425 + \sqrt{50 \times 303 + 1931}}$$
$$= 10287 \text{ N}$$
$$P_{eff} = 1931 + 10287 = 12218 \text{ N}$$

Beam strength $= 686.4 \, m^2 = 17160$ N $\quad FS = \dfrac{17160}{12218} = 1.4$

Wear strength $= 764.6 \, m^2 = 19115$ N $\quad FS = \dfrac{19115}{12218} = 1.56$ ∴ Safe.

Example 2.11: A straight bevel gear pair has 24 teeth pinion meshing with 60 teeth gear. Teeth are cut to 20° pressure angle full involute and the module is 4 mm. Two kW power is transmitted at 1000 rpm. The arrangement is as shown in Fig. 2.18.

Find: (a) Tangential, (b) Axial and (c) Radial forces acting on pinion and gear. Assuming suitable direction of rotation, indicate directions of forces.

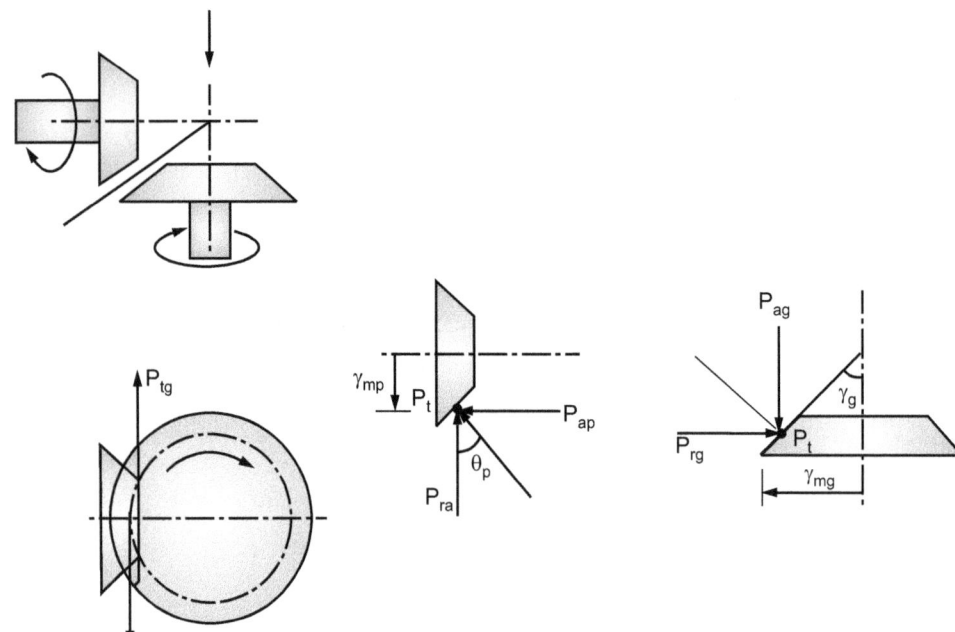

Fig. 2.18

Solution: $\tan \gamma_p = \dfrac{Z_p}{Z_g} = \dfrac{24}{60} = 0.4$, $\gamma_p = 21.8°$

Torque on pinion, $T_p = \dfrac{\text{Power} \times 60 \times 1000}{2\pi \cdot N_p} = 19.1$ Nm

Tangential force on pinion, $P_{tp} = \dfrac{T_p}{\left(\dfrac{d_{mp}}{2}\right)} = \dfrac{19100}{\left(\dfrac{d_{mp}}{2}\right)}$

Taking gear width $= 10\,m = 40$ mm

$d_{mp} = d_p - b \cdot \sin\theta_p = 96 - 40 \cdot \sin 21.8 = 81.14$ mm

$d_{mg} = d_g - b \cdot \sin\theta_g = 240 - 40 \sin 68.2 = 202.86$ mm

$\therefore \quad P_{tp} = \dfrac{T_p}{\left(\dfrac{d_{mp}}{2}\right)} = \dfrac{19100}{\left(\dfrac{81.14}{2}\right)} = 470.8$ N

$P_{tp} = P_{tg} = 470.8$ N

$P_{ap} = P_t \cdot \tan\phi \cdot \sin\gamma_p = 470.8 \times \tan 20 \cdot \sin 21.8 = 63.6$ N

$P_{rp} = P_t \cdot \tan\phi \cdot \cos\gamma_p = 470.8 \times \tan 20 \cos 21.8 = 159.1$ N

$P_{ag} = P_{r\,\text{pinion}} = 63.6$ N

$P_{rg} = P_{ap} = 159.1$ N

Example 2.12: A pair of bevel gears having 16 and 72 teeth has a module of 6 mm at the outer diameter. Pinion is made of alloy steel with a UTS of 700 N/mm² and surface hardness 260 BHN. Gears are made of cast iron with a UTS of 280 N/mm² and hardness 210 BHN. Assume velocity factor accounts for dynamic loads. The pinion rotates at 720 rpm and gears are 20° full involute.

1. Find: (a) Beam strength, (b) Wear strength and (c) Power transmission capacity of the gears.
2. Find forces on pinion.

Consider service factor of 1.5 and factor of safety 2.

Use the following relations: $b = \frac{1}{3} A_o$ or $10 \cdot m$ whichever is smaller.

$$Y' = 0.484 - \frac{2.87}{Z'}; \quad C_v = \frac{5.6}{5.6 + \sqrt{v}}; \quad K = 0.18 \left(\frac{BHN}{100}\right)^2$$

Given data: $Z_p = 16$, $Z_g = 72$, $m = 6$ mm, $(S_{ult})_p = 700$ N/mm², $(S_{ult})_{gear} = 280$ N/mm², BHN: 260/210, $C_s = 1.5$, FS = 2, $N_p = 720$ rpm, $\phi = 20°$.

Solution: Effective load: $d_p = m \cdot Z_p = 6 \times 16 = 96$ mm

$$v = \text{Pitch line velocity} = \frac{\pi \cdot d_p \cdot N_p}{60 \times 1000} = \frac{\pi \times 96 \times 720}{60 \times 1000} = 3.619 \text{ m/sec}$$

Tangential force $= P_t$

$$\text{Velocity factor} = \frac{5.6}{5.6 + \sqrt{v}} = 0.746$$

$$\text{Effective load, } P_{eff} = \left(\frac{C_s \cdot C_l}{C_v}\right) P_t = \frac{1.5 \times 1}{0.746} \cdot P_t = 2.01 \, P_t$$

Beam strength:

$$S_b = \sigma_b \cdot b \cdot Y' \, m \left[1 - \frac{b}{A_o}\right]$$

$$\tan \gamma_p = \frac{Z_p}{Z_g} = \frac{16}{72} = 0.222, \quad \gamma_p = 12.53°, \quad \gamma_g = 77.47°$$

$$Z'_p = \frac{Z_p}{\cos \gamma_p} = \frac{16}{\cos 12.53} = 16.39 \qquad Y'_p = 0.484 - \frac{2.87}{Z'_p} = 0.3088$$

$$Z'_g = \frac{Z_p}{\cos \gamma_g} = \frac{72}{\cos 77.47} = 331.9 \qquad Y'_g = 0.484 - \frac{2.87}{Z'_g} = 0.475$$

$$(\sigma_b \cdot Y')_p = \frac{700}{3} \times 0.3088 = 72.05$$

$$(\sigma_b \, Y')_g = \frac{280}{3} \times 0.475 = 44.33$$

Since $(\sigma_b Y')_g < (\sigma_b Y')_p$, gear is weaker and beam strength will be calculated for gear.

$$d_p = m \cdot Z_p = 6 \times 16 = 96 \text{ mm} \qquad d_g = 6 \times 72 = 432 \text{ mm}$$

$$\text{Cone distance, } A_o = \sqrt{\left(\frac{d_p}{2}\right)^2 + \left(\frac{d_g}{2}\right)^2} = 221.26$$

$b = \frac{1}{3} A_o = 73.75$ or $10\,m = 60$ mm whichever is smaller. Hence, $b = 60$ mm

Beam strength:

$$S_b = (\sigma_b \cdot Y)_g \, b \cdot m \left[1 - \frac{b}{A_o}\right] = 44.36 \times 60 \times 6 \left[1 - \frac{60}{221.26}\right] = 11631 \text{ N}$$

Wear strength:

$$S_w = \frac{0.75 \, d_p \cdot b \, Q' \cdot K}{\cos \gamma_p}$$

$$Q' = \frac{2 \cdot Z_g'}{Z_g' + Z_p'} = \frac{2 \times 331.9}{331.9 + 16.39} = 1.906$$

$$K = 0.18 \left(\frac{BHN}{100}\right)^2 = 0.18 \left(\frac{210}{100}\right)^2 = 0.794$$

$$S_w = \frac{0.75 \times 96 \times 60 \times 1.906 \times 0.794}{0.9762} = 6697.1 \text{ N}$$

Power transmission capacity:

Since $S_w < S_b$, wear strength will govern the capacity. Equating wear strength with effective load considering factor of safety,

$$S_w = (P_{eff}) \, FS$$
$$6697.1 = (2.01 \, P_t) \, 2$$
$$\therefore \qquad P_t = 1666 \text{ N (Tangential load)}$$

Power that can be transmitted will be

$$\text{Power} = \frac{2\pi \, N_p \times \left(P_t \times \frac{d_p}{2}\right)}{60 \times 1000 \times 10^3} = \frac{2\pi \times 720 \times (1666 \times 48)}{60 \times 1000 \times 10^3}$$

$$= 6.03 \text{ kW}$$

Forces on pinion: (At rated torque/power)

$$P_t = 1666 \text{ N}$$
$$P_a = P_t \cdot \cos \phi \cdot \sin \gamma_p = 1666 \cos 20 \sin 12.53 = 339.6 \text{ N}$$
$$P_r = P_t \cdot \cos \phi \cdot \cos \gamma_p = 1666 \cos 20 \cos 12.53 = 1528.2 \text{ N}$$

DESIGN OF MACHINE ELEMENTS - II

HELICAL GEARS AND BEVEL GEARS

Example 2.13: The pinion of a bevel gear pair is connected to 5 kW electric motor running at 1440 rpm. Reduction in speed is 3 : 1 from pinion to gear. Pinion has 18 teeth and is made from steel having UTS of 520 N/mm² and surface hardness of 300 BHN. Gear is made from cast iron having UTS of 300 N/mm² and hardness 300 BHN. Pressure angles for the gears is 20° and service factor is 1.2. Deformation factor 'C' may be taken as 116 N/mm.

Design the gears for a factor of safety of 1.25.

Take $C_v = \dfrac{6}{6+v}$, $K = 0.18\left(\dfrac{BHN}{100}\right)^2$.

Given data: Reduction 3 : 1, $Z_p = 18$, $Z_q = 54$, Power = 5 kW, $N_p = 1440$ rpm, $(S_{ult})_p = 520$ N/mm², $(S_{ult})_g = 300$ N/mm², $C_s = 1.2$, FS = 1.25, BHN = 300, C = 116 N/mm.

Solution: Effective load: $d_p = m \cdot Z_p = 18\,m$

$$v = \frac{\pi (18\,m) \times 1440}{60 \times 1000} = (1.357\,m)\ \text{m/sec}$$

Tangential load, $P_t = \dfrac{\text{Power}}{\text{Velocity}} = \dfrac{5 \times 10^3}{1.357\,m} = \dfrac{3684.6}{m}\ \text{N}$

$$P_{eff} = \left(\frac{C_s \cdot C_l}{C_v}\right) P_t = \frac{1.2 \times 1}{\left(\dfrac{6}{6+1.357\,m}\right)} \times \frac{3684.6}{m}$$

$$P_{eff} = \frac{736.92 \times (6 + 1.357\,m)}{m}$$

Beam Strength:

$\tan \gamma_p = \dfrac{Z_p}{Z_g} = \dfrac{1}{3}$, $\gamma_p = 18.435°$, $\gamma_g = 71.565°$

$$Z'_p = \frac{Z_p}{\cos \gamma_p} = \frac{18}{\cos 18.435} = 18.974, \qquad Z'_g = \frac{Z_q}{\cos \gamma_g} = 170.76$$

$$Y'_p = 0.484 - \frac{2.87}{Z'_p} = 0.3327$$

$$Y'_g = 0.484 - \frac{2.87}{Z'_g} = 0.4672$$

$$(\sigma_b \cdot Y')_p = \frac{520}{3} \times 0.3327 = 57.67$$

$$(\sigma_b \cdot Y')_g = \frac{300}{3} \times 0.4672 = 46.72$$

Since $(\sigma_b Y')_g < (\sigma_b \cdot Y')_p$, gear is weaker.

Beam strength will be based on gear capacity.

Beam strength:

$$S_b = (\sigma_b \cdot Y)_g \, b \cdot m \left[1 - \frac{b}{A_o}\right]$$

$$\text{Cone distance, } A_o = \sqrt{\left(\frac{d_p}{2}\right)^2 + \left(\frac{d_g}{2}\right)^2} = m\sqrt{\left(\frac{18}{2}\right)^2 + \left(\frac{54}{2}\right)^2} = 28.46 \, m$$

$$b = \frac{1}{3} A_o = 9.5 \, m \text{ or } 10 \, m \text{ whichever is smaller}$$

$\therefore \quad b = 9.5 \, m$

$$S_b = (46.72) \, 9.5 \, m \cdot m \left[1 - \frac{1}{3}\right] = 295.5 \, m^2$$

$$S_b = 295.5 \, m^2$$

Wear strength:

$$S_w = \frac{0.75 \, d_p \cdot b \cdot Q' \cdot K}{\cos \gamma_p}$$

$$Q' = \frac{2Z'_g}{Z'_g + Z'_p} = \frac{2 \times 170.76}{170.76 + 18.974} = 1.799$$

$$K = 0.18 \left(\frac{BHN}{100}\right)^2 = 1.62$$

$$S_w = \frac{0.75 \times 18 \, m \times 9.5 \, m \times 1.799 \times 1.62}{\cos 18.435} = 394 \, m^2$$

Since $S_b < S_w$

Beam strength will govern the design.

Equating beam strength with P_{eff}, considering factor of safety.

$$S_b = [P_{eff}] \, FS$$

$$295.5 \, m^2 = \frac{736.92 \, (6 + 1.357 \, m)}{m} \times 1.25$$

Simplifying,

$$m^3 - 4.23 \, m - 18.7 = 0$$

Solving by the trial and error $m \simeq 3.2$

We select next higher standard module = 4 mm.

Checking dynamic load by Buckingham's equation

Velocity, $v = 1.357 \, m = 5.428 \, m/sec$

$C = 116 \, N/m$

$b = 9.5 \, m = 38 \, mm$

$$P_{tmax} = P_t \, (C_s \cdot C_l) = 1.2 \times \frac{3684.6}{m}$$

$$= 1105.4 \, N$$

Check for Dynamic Load: (Buckingham's Equation)

$$P_d = \frac{21 \cdot v \, (b \cdot C + P_{tmax})}{21 \cdot v + \sqrt{b \cdot C + P_{tmax}}}$$

$$= \frac{21 \times 5.428 \, (38 \times 116 + 1105.4)}{21 \times 5.428 + \sqrt{38 \times 116 + 1105.4}}$$

$$= 3339.3 \text{ N}$$

$\therefore \quad P_{eff} = P_{tmax} + P_d = 1105.4 + 3339.3 = 4444.7 \text{ N}$

Factor of safety based on

Beam strength FS: $\dfrac{S_b}{P_{eff}} = \dfrac{295.5 \, m^2}{4444.7} = \dfrac{4728}{4444.7} = 1.06$

Based on wear strength FS $= \dfrac{S_w}{P_{eff}} = \dfrac{394 \, m^2}{4444.7} = \dfrac{6304}{4444.7} = 1.42$

Since factor of safety based on beam strength is < 1.25 design is not safe.

Hence, we need to increase module to next standard size.

Trial 1: We select module m = 5 mm.

$$D_p = m \cdot Z_p = 90 \text{ mm}$$
$$D_g = m \cdot Z_g = 270 \text{ mm}$$
$$v = 1.357 \times m = 6.785 \text{ m/sec}$$
$$A_o = 28.46 \times m = 142.3 \text{ mm}$$
$$b = 9.5 \, m = 47.5 \text{ mm} \simeq 48 \text{ mm}$$
$$P_t = \frac{3684.6}{m} = \frac{3684.6}{5} = 737 \text{ N}$$
$$P_{tmax} = (C_s \cdot C_l) \, P_t = (1.2 \times 1) \, 737 = 884.4 \text{ N}$$

Dynamic load:

$$P_d = \frac{21 \cdot v \, (b \cdot C + P_{tmax})}{21 \cdot v + \sqrt{b \cdot C + P_{tmax}}}$$

$$= \frac{21 \times 6.785 \, (48 \times 116 + 884.4)}{21 \times 6.785 + \sqrt{48 \times 116 + 884.4}}$$

$$P_d = 4126.1 \text{ N}$$

$\therefore \quad P_{eff} = P_{tmax} + P_d = 884.4 + 4126.1 = 5010.5 \text{ N}$

Factor of safety based on

Beam strength FS $= \dfrac{S_b}{P_{eff}} = \dfrac{295.5 \, m^2}{5010.5} = \dfrac{7387.5}{5010.5} = 1.47$

Wear strength FS $= \dfrac{S_w}{P_{eff}} = \dfrac{394 \, m^2}{5010.5} = \dfrac{9850}{5010.5} = 1.96$

This satisfies the requirements.

Hence, we select module m = 5 mm.

Example 2.14: A pair of straight bevel gears mounted on shafts that are intersecting at right angles, consists of a 20 teeth pinion meshing with a 32 teeth gear. The pinion shaft is connected to an electric motor developing 8.0 kW rated power at 1440 rpm. The starting torque of the motor is 150% of the rated torque. The pressure angle is 20°. Both gears are made of case hardened steel (σ_{ut} = 680 N/mm²). The teeth on gears are generated and finished by grinding and lapping processes to meet the requirements of class-3 grade. The factor of safety in preliminary stages of gear design is 2.

(i) In the initial stages of gear design, assume that velocity factor accounts for the dynamic load and that the pitch line velocity is 7.5 m/s. Estimate the module based on beam strength. Select the first preference value of module and calculate the main dimensions of the gears.

(ii) Determine the dynamic load using Buckingham's equation and find out the effective load for above dimensions. What is the correct factor of safety for bending?

(iii) Specify the surface hardness for the gears assuming a factor of safety of 2.

Use the following data:

- Velocity factor, $C_v = \dfrac{5.6}{5.6 + \sqrt{v}}$
- Determination factor, $C = 11400 \times e$ N/mm
- Buckingham's equation, $F_d = \dfrac{21 \cdot v \,(C \cdot b + F_t)}{21 \cdot v + \sqrt{C \cdot b + F_1}}$
- Maximum expected error between two meshing teeth (mm)

Module (mm)	upto 4	5	6	7	8
Class – 3 (e – mm)	0.0125	0.0125	0.0150	0.0170	0.0190

Given data: Z_p = 20, Z_q = 32, Power = 8 kW at 1440 rpm, C_s = 1.5, S_{ult} = 680 N/mm², FS = 2, v = 7.5 m/sec.

Solution:

(i) Effective force:

$$\text{Velocity} = \dfrac{\pi \,(m \cdot Z_p)\, 1440}{60 \times 1000} = 1.508 \, m$$

$$P_t = \dfrac{\text{Power}}{\text{Velocity}} \times \dfrac{8 \times 10^3}{1.508 \, m} = \dfrac{5305.2}{m} \, \text{m/sec}$$

$$\text{Velocity factor, } C_v = \dfrac{5.6}{5.6 + \sqrt{7.5}} = 0.6716$$

$$P_{eff} = \left(\dfrac{C_s \cdot C_l}{C_v}\right) = \dfrac{5305.2}{m} = \left(\dfrac{1.5 \times 1}{0.6716}\right) \dfrac{5305.2}{m} = \dfrac{11849}{m} \, N$$

$$\tan \gamma_p = \dfrac{Z_p}{Z_g} = \dfrac{20}{32} = 0.625, \quad \gamma_p = 32°, \quad \gamma_g = 58°$$

Beam strength:

$$S_b = \sigma_b \cdot Y' \cdot b \cdot m \left[1 - \frac{b}{A_o}\right]$$

Since material is same for pinion and gear, pinion is weaker.

$$Z'_p = \frac{Z_p}{\cos \gamma_p} = \frac{20}{0.848} = 23.58$$

$$Z'_g = \frac{32}{\cos \gamma_g} = \frac{32}{0.5299} = 60.386$$

$$Y'_p = 0.484 - \frac{2.87}{Z'_p} = 0.3623$$

$$A_o = \sqrt{\left(\frac{d_p}{2}\right)^2 + \left(\frac{d_g}{2}\right)^2}$$

$$= m\sqrt{\left(\frac{Z_p}{2}\right)^2 + \left(\frac{Z_g}{2}\right)^2} = m\sqrt{10^2 + 16^2}$$

$$= 18.87\ m$$

$$b = \frac{1}{3} A_o = 6.3\ m\ \text{or}\ 10\ m\ \text{whichever is smaller}$$

∴ We take b = 7 m

$$S_b = \left(\frac{680}{3}\right) \times 0.3623 \times 7m \cdot m \left[1 - \frac{7\ m}{18.87\ m}\right] = 361.6\ m^2$$

Equating beam strength with effective force considering factor of safety

$$S_b = (P_{eff})\ FS$$

$$361.6\ m^2 = \frac{11849}{m} \times 2$$

$$m^3 = 65.53$$

$$m = 4.03\ mm$$

∴ We select next higher standard module = 5 mm

Main gear dimensions will be

$$d_p = 20 \times 5 = 100\ mm$$
$$d_g = 32 \times 5 = 160\ mm$$
$$b = 7 \cdot m = 35\ mm$$
$$h_a = 1 \cdot m = 5\ mm$$
$$h_f = 1.25 \cdot m = 6.25\ mm$$

(ii) Dynamic load by Buckingham's equation:

$$P_d = \frac{21 \cdot v (C \cdot b + P_{tmax})}{21 \cdot v + \sqrt{C \cdot b + P_{t\,max}}}$$

$$v = \frac{\pi \times d_p \cdot N_p}{60 \times 1000}$$

$$= \frac{\pi \times 100 \times 1440}{60 \times 1000} = 7.54 \text{ m/sec}$$

$$P_t = \frac{5305.2}{m} = 1061 \text{ N}$$

$$P_{tmax} = (C_s \cdot C_l) P_t = 1.5 \times 1061 = 1591.5 \text{ N}$$

$$b = 7\,m = 35 \text{ mm}$$

$$C = 11400 \times e \quad\quad (e = 0.0125 \text{ mm from table})$$

$$= 11400 \times 0.0125 = 142.5 \text{ N/mm}$$

$$P_d = \frac{21 \times 7.54\,(142.5 \times 35 + 1591.5)}{21 \times 7.54 + \sqrt{142.5 \times 35 + 1591.5}}$$

$$= 4350.5 \text{ N}$$

$$P_{eff} = P_{tmax} + P_d$$

$$= 1591.5 + 4350.5 = 5942 \text{ N}$$

$$\text{Beam strength} = 361.6\,m^2 = 9040 \text{ N}$$

$$\therefore \text{Factor of safety} = \frac{9040}{5942} = 1.52$$

(iii) Surface hardness:

Wear strength required considering factor of safety = 2.

$$S_w = 2\,(P_{eff}) = 2 \times 5942 = 11884 \text{ N}$$

$$S_w = \frac{0.75\,d_p \cdot b\,Q'\,K}{\cos \gamma_p}$$

$$Q' = \frac{2Z'_g}{Z'_g + Z'_p} = \frac{2 \times 60.386}{60.386 + 23.58} = 1.439$$

$$K = 0.16 \left(\frac{BHN}{100}\right)^2$$

Thus,

$$11884 = \frac{0.75 \times 100 \times 35 \times 1.439 \times 0.16}{\cos 32°} \left(\frac{BHN}{100}\right)^2$$

$$BHN = 408$$

Example 2.15: A pair of cast iron bevel gears connects two shafts at right angles. Pinion and gear diameters are required to be 80 and 100 mm respectively. The tooth profiles of the gears are $14\frac{1}{2}°$ composite form and both materials have tensile strength of 240 N/mm². Pinion transmits 3 kW power at 1440 rpm. Considering that velocity factor accounts for dynamic load and taking gear with $b = \frac{1}{3}$ cone distance (slanting height). Service factor is 1.2. Take Lewis form factor $Y' = 0.039 - \frac{2.15}{Z'}$, $K = 0.21 \left(\frac{BHN}{100}\right)^2$. Use $C_v = \frac{6}{6+v}$. Take surface hardness as 280 to pinion and gear. Required minimum factor of safety is 1.2.

(a) Find the module and number of teeth on each gear considering bending failure.
(b) Check the design for wear.

Given data: $d_p = 80$ mm, $d_g = 100$ mm, $S_{ult} = 240$ N/mm², Power = 3 kW, $N_p = 1440$ rpm, $b = \frac{1}{3} A_o$

Solution:

$$\tan \gamma_p = \frac{Z_p}{Z_g} = \frac{d_p}{d_g}$$

$$= \frac{80}{100}; \gamma_p = 38.66°, \gamma_g = 51.34°$$

(a) Equivalent tangential force:

Pitch line velocity, $v = \frac{\pi d_p N_p}{60 \times 1000} = 6.0318$ m/sec

Tangential load, $P_t = \frac{Power}{Velocity}$

$$= \frac{3 \times 10^3}{6.0318}$$

$$= 497.4 \text{ N}$$

Velocity factor, $C_v = \frac{6}{6+v}$

$$= \frac{6}{6 + 6.0318}$$

$$= 0.4987$$

Effective load, $P_{eff} = \left(\frac{C_s \cdot C_l}{C_v}\right) P_t$

$$P_{eff} = \left(\frac{1.2 \times 1}{0.4987}\right) 497.4$$

$$= 1196.9 \text{ N}$$

DESIGN OF MACHINE ELEMENTS - II HELICAL GEARS AND BEVEL GEARS

Beam strength:

Since pinion and gear materials are same, pinion is weaker.

Beam strength of pinion is the deciding factor.

$$Z'_p = \frac{Z_p}{\cos \gamma_p} = \frac{\left(\frac{d_p}{m}\right)}{\cos \gamma_p} = \frac{80}{m \cos \gamma_p} = \frac{102.4}{m}$$

$$Z'_g = \frac{Z_g}{\cos \gamma_g} = \frac{\frac{d_g}{m}}{\cos \gamma_g} = \frac{100}{m \cos \gamma_g} = \frac{160}{m}$$

Lewis form factor, $Y'_p = 0.39 - \frac{2.12}{Z'_p} = 0.39 - \frac{(2.12)\,m}{102.4}$

$$= (0.39 - 0.0207\,m)$$

Slanting height, $A_o = \sqrt{\left(\frac{d_p}{2}\right)^2 + \left(\frac{d_g}{2}\right)^2} = \sqrt{40^2 + 50^2} = 64\text{ mm}$

Beam strength: S_b

Considering width $\quad b = \frac{1}{3} A_o$

$$S_b = \sigma_b \cdot b \, Y' \cdot m \cdot \left[1 - \frac{b}{A_o}\right]$$

$$= \left(\frac{240}{3}\right)\left(\frac{64}{3}\right)(0.39 - 0.0207\,m) \cdot m \left[1 - \frac{1}{3}\right]$$

$$= 1137.78\,(0.39 - 0.0207\,m)\,m = 443.7\,m - 23.55\,m^2$$

Equating effective loads and beam strength, considering factor of safety

$$S_b = (P_{eff})\,FS$$

$$(443.7\,m - 23.55\,m^2) = (1196.9) \times 1.2 = 1436.3$$

Simplifying,

$$m^2 - 18.8\,m + 61 = 0$$

Solving $\quad m = 4.2$

We select next higher preferred size m = 5 mm.

$$Z_p = \frac{d_p}{m} = \frac{30}{5} = 16 \qquad Z_g = \frac{100}{m} = 20$$

Checking for wear strength:

$$S_w = \frac{d_p \cdot b \cdot Q' \cdot K}{\cos \gamma_p}$$

$$Z'_p = \frac{102.4}{m} = 20.48 \qquad Z'_g = \frac{160}{m} = 32$$

$$Q' = \frac{2Z'_g}{Z'_g + Z'_p} = \frac{2 \times 32}{32 + 20.48} = 1.2195$$

$$K = 0.21 \left(\frac{BHN}{100}\right)^2 = 1.646$$

$$S_w = \frac{80 \times 22 \times 1.2195 \times 1.646}{\cos 38.66} = 4524 \text{ N}$$

With this factor of safety available is

$$FS = \frac{\text{Wear strength } (S_w)}{P_{eff}} = \frac{4524}{1196.2} = 3.78$$

Thus, design is safe in wear also.

EXERCISE

1. What are the advantages and disadvantages of straight bevel gears and spiral bevel gears. **(May 2011)**
2. Compare straight bevel, spiral bevel, hypoid bevel gear with sketch. **(Nov. 2011)**
3. What is formative number of teeth in helical gears? Derive the expression for formative number of teeth in helical gears. **(May 2012)**
4. Derive an expression for beam strength of straight bevel gears. **(May 2012)**
5. With neat sketch discuss force analysis of bevel gears. **(May 2013)**
6. Obtain an expression for beam strength of bevel gear in the following form.

$$S_b = mb\sigma_b Y \left[1 - \frac{b}{A_o} + \frac{b^2}{3A_o^2}\right]$$ **(May 2013)**

7. Derive an expression for beam strength of straight bevel gear tooth. **(April 2009)**
8. Derive a relation for virtual number of teeth for a helical gear. **(April 2010)**
9. Explain formative number of teeth for bevel gears. **(April 2010)**
10. With neat sketch explain components of forces acting on straight bevel gear. **(April 2012)**

11. What is the relationship between transverse and normal pressure angle and helix angle?
12. State two advantages and disadvantages of herringbone and double helical gear, also draw the sketches. **(April 2012)**
13. What are the different methods of mounting of bevel gear? Explain any one with sketch. **(April 2012)**
14. Compare straight bevel, spiral bevel hypoid bevel gear with sketch.

(October 2012)
15. Explain the bevel gear terminology.
16. Obtain an expression for the formative number of teeth.
17. Derive an expression for the beam strength of a bevel gear
18. Compare straight teeth and spiral teeth bevel.
19. Why the wear strength of the bevel gear is 25% less than its full load capacity?

✸✸✸

Unit III

ROLLING CONTACT BEARINGS

3.1 INTRODUCTION

For a mechanical engineer, power transmission or conversion of motion from one form into another is of prime concern. This process of power transfer or power generation is generally a noisy operation due to the complexity of the mechanisms and involves loss of power in friction and heat. The root cause of noise or wear of component is friction between the mating components. The term rolling contact bearing (or antifriction bearing), means a mechanical component that transfers or allows transfer of power or relative motion with minimum friction. Presence of bearing in assembly ensures free rotation of shaft or axle with minimum or less friction. Bearings in addition to providing supports for shafting and axles, also take forces that are acting on them and transfer them to the foundation or frames. Classification of bearings is done in two ways;

1. Direction of force that is acting on the bearing.
2. Type of friction between the shaft and bearing surfaces.

Depending on the direction of force acting, the bearing could be:
(a) Radial bearing
(b) Thrust bearing

Depending on the type of friction between the bearing surfaces, bearings could be:
(a) Sliding contact bearings
(b) Rolling contact bearings

In this chapter, we restrict our discussion to rolling contact bearings. These type of bearings are commonly used in variety of equipments such as machine tools, different machinaries, automobiles etc. They are easy to assemble, available as a standard unit and require relatively low maintenance and are suitable for applications involving frequent starts and stops.

Components and Nomenclature of Rolling Contact Bearing:

Rolling contact bearings (Fig. 3.1) consist of four essential parts viz., the outer ring, inner ring, (inner and outer races), balls or rolling elements and the separator (retainer or cage). Balls are hardened to carry heavy loads and withstand wear within acceptable limits.

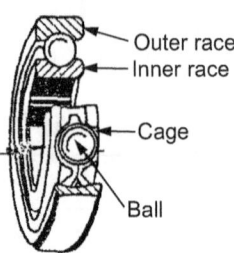

Fig. 3.1: Ball Bearing - Components

Depending on the type of rolling element (i.e. ball, cylindrical roller or taper roller) and on the direction of load with respect to the axis of rotation (radial or axial) there are various types of rolling contact bearings. Selection of proper type of bearing is very crucial for satisfactory functioning of any equipment.

3.2 TYPES OF ROLLING CONTACT BEARINGS

Some of the different types of rolling contact bearings are as under:

3.2.1 Deep Groove Ball Bearing

In deep groove ball bearing (Fig. 3.2), the balls are inserted into the grooves by moving the inner ring to an eccentric position. For this insertion purpose, the size of the ball is slightly less than radius of curvature of the grooves in the races.

Fig. 3.2: Single Row Deep Groove Ball-bearing

It is because of this arrangement, the balls and races roll without sliding. The relative motion in a ball bearing takes place only between the ball and race. The advantages and limitations of the deep groove ball bearing are summarized as under;

Advantages of Deep Groove Ball Bearings:

- Deep groove ball bearings have high load carrying capacity. Large ball sizes used in higher series increase its load carrying capacity.
- The construction of deep groove ball bearing is such that it is able to withstand radial and axial loads.

- It can tolerate some amount of angular misalignment.
- Less frictional losses and wear due to point contact between the balls and the races and is used in high-speed applications.
- Less operational noise due to point contact.
- They are available in wide range of sizes and are used as standard parts.
- Factory grease packed bearings are available that can be used without further lubrication in service.

Disadvantages of Deep Groove Ball Bearing:
- These ball bearings demand proper alignment for bearing mounting.
- Due to point contact it is less rigid and cannot used in machine tool applications where rigidity is of prime concern.
- Load carrying capacity is limited due to point contact.

3.2.2 Cylindrical Roller Bearing

In this type of (Fig. 3.3) bearing, there is line contact between the roller and bearing races. This enhances the load carrying capacity of the bearing. Such bearings offer following advantages and disadvantages.

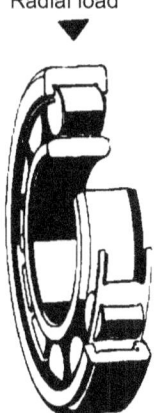

Fig. 3.3: Cylindrical Roller Bearing

Advantages of Cylindrical Roller Bearing:
- Load carrying capacity is high as compared with deep groove ball bearing due to line contact.
- This type of bearing possesses more rigidity than deep groove ball bearings.
- Line contact gives low coefficient of friction and hence low frictional losses.

Disadvantages of Cylindrical Roller Bearing:
- Unable to bear thrust load.
- Needs precise alignment between the axes of shaft and the bore as it is not self-aligning.
- Due to line contact its operation is noisy.

3.2.3 Angular Contact Bearings

The peculiarity of angular contact bearings is that the line of reaction at contact between the balls and races makes an angle with the axis of bearing (Fig. 3.4). This angle of contact depends upon the shape and size of grooves in inner and outer races. As the reaction possesses two components viz radial and axial; this bearing is capable of taking both radial and thrust loads.

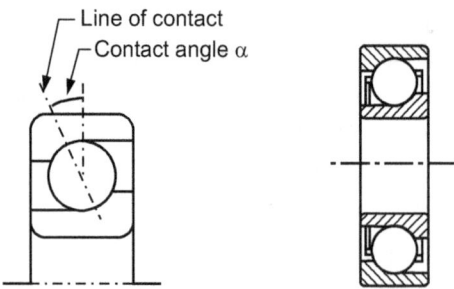

Fig. 3.4: Angular Contact Bearing

However, these bearings can take thrust load only in one direction. Therefore, these bearings are used in pairs. The pairs are kept side by side or at the opposite ends of the shaft. These bearings are assembled with a certain magnitude of preload on them. Relative advantages and disadvantages are summarized as under;

Advantages of Angular Contact Bearing:
- Capable of withstanding both radial and axial loads.
- Capable of withstanding large axial loads than deep groove ball bearings.

Disadvantages of Angular Contact Bearing:
- In order to withstand thrust load; there is requirement of two bearings in two directions.
- This type of bearing is required to be mounted with initial amount of axial play.
- It requires pre-loading.

3.2.4 Self-Aligning Bearings

In applications where field installation is required such as large conveyors or applications like agricultural machineries, railway axle etc., there is possibility of misalignment of power transmitting shaft with the bearing axis due to the high magnitudes of load variations involved. This action may damage the bearing oil film or surface which results into wear and breakdown. Provision is required to counter the effect of misalignment on the bearing and shaft assembly.

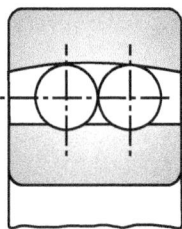

Fig. 3.5: Self Aligning Ball Bearing - Section

This is done with the use of self aligning bearings (Fig. 3.5). In self aligning bearing the surface of outer ring is made spherical such that its centre coincides with the centre of the bearing. It is due to this arrangement that the balls along with the inner race roll freely in the seat and can carry misalignment. These self aligning bearings are of two types viz; self aligning ball bearing and spherical roller bearing. In ball bearings there are two rows of balls that are in contact with the common spherical surface while in spherical roller bearings these balls are replaced by two rows of spherical rollers that run on a common spherical surface.

3.2.5 Taper Roller Bearings

These type of bearings include rolling elements that are in the form of frustum of a cone, arranged in such as way that the axes of individual rolling elements intersect with the common apex point on the axis of bearing. Due to this arrangement, pure rolling motion between the contacting surfaces is possible. The taper roller bearings (Fig. 3.6) can take radial and axial loads. Here also the line of resultant reaction of rolling element makes an angle with the axis of bearing as in angular contact bearings. Thus, even when bearing takes pure radial loads, axial load is also acting on the bearing and vice-versa. Therefore, the taper roller bearings are used in pairs to balance the thrust component. In taper roller bearings, the outer ring or cup can be separated from the rest elements. Inner ring is called cone. More common applications of these taper roller bearings include automobile cars, trucks, differential gear boxes, propeller shafts, rail road axle-boxes, rolling mills, etc. Advantages and disadvantages of this bearing are summarized as under:

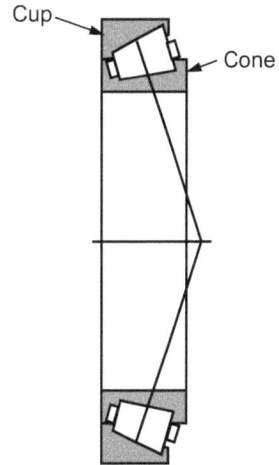

Fig. 3.6: Taper Roller Bearing

Advantages of Taper Roller Bearing:
- Due to cup and cone arrangement this type of bearing is able to withstand the heavy axial and radial loads.
- These bearings have more rigidity.
- As this bearing has separable construction, it allows easy assemblage and dismantling of the bearing parts.

Disadvantages of Taper Roller Bearing:
- These bearings are to be used in pairs in order to balance the axial force.
- In order to coincide the apex of cone with the apex of rolling element, it is necessary to adjust the axial location of the bearing with some pre-load.
- It cannot tolerate misalignment between shaft and housing axes.
- More costly due to versatile construction.

3.2.6 Thrust Ball Bearings

As the name indicates this bearing is capable of withstanding thrust load in one direction. It consists of balls that run between shaft and housing rings (Fig. 3.7). This bearing can take thrust loads only and is unable to carry radial loads. In its construction, large numbers of balls are used in compact space and this results into large thrust load carrying capacity. These bearings are used in applications which involve large thrust loads e.g. crane hooks.

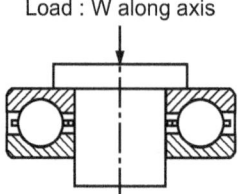

Fig. 3.7: Thrust Ball Bearing

Limitations of Thrust Ball Bearings:
- Unable to carry radial loads.
- Cannot tolerate misalignment and is not self aligning.
- Cannot operate at high speeds due to centrifugal forces and gyroscopic action generated.
- Cannot be used for horizontal shaftings.

Single Row Deep Grove (SRDG) ball bearing is the most popular type of bearing which is very commonly used in industry. It has high load carrying capacity, can take radial as well as axial load, can take misalignment and they are available in the sealed condition. Discussion here will be mainly focused on single row deep groove bearing.

Bearing Dimensions: A typical SRDG bearing size is described as $25 \times 47 \times 12$. Here 25 is the bore diameter, 47 is the outer diameter and 12 is the width. Bore diameter is same as the shaft diameter. For a given bore diameter, bearings are available in various sizes such as $(25 \times 52 \times 15)$, $(25 \times 62 \times 17)$, $(25 \times 80 \times 21)$. These bearings belong to different dimensional series and have higher load carrying capacities for the same bore diameter.

Bearing Designation: Bearings are designated (Table 3.1) by a 4 or 5 digit number. For example.

6308: Single row deep groove, medium series, bore 40 mm.

31306: Taper roller Bearing, medium series, bore 30 mm.

Table 3.1

Digit	CODE	Defines	Example
First OR First two	6 (2,31)	Type of bearing.	6: for SRDG 2: self aligning 31: taper roller bearing
Next	3 (0, 2, 4)	Dimension Series (Width series)	3: Medium series 0: Extra Light series 2: Light series 4: Heavy series
Last two	08 (00, 01, 02, 03.......)	Inner diameter (Bore code)	Bore = 08 × 5 = 40 mm For 00 = 10 mm, 01 = 12 mm, 02 = 15 mm, 03 = 17 mm [(From 04 onwards multiply last two digits by 05 to get diameter. For 04, Bore = 04 × 5 = 20]

3.3 STATIC AND DYNAMIC LOAD CARRYING CAPACITIES

3.3.1 Static Load Carrying Capacity: Static Load [C_o]

This is the load which acts on the bearing when the shaft is in stationery condition. Depending upon the self weight of the shaft, its mountings and the static load acting, a permanent deformation is induced in the balls and inner/outer races of bearings. The magnitude of this deformation increases with increase in load. Permissible magnitude of permanent deformation controls the allowable static load magnitude. Experience shows that total permanent deformation of 0.0001 × d (where d is the ball or roller diameter) at most heavily stressed balls and race can be tolerated.

For calculation of static load bearing capacity, Indian Standard I.S. 3823 is referred. These formulae are not required during bearing selection process. However manufacturer's catalogue gives static load carrying capacities of bearings based on the design, material and manufacturing by manufacturer. **Static load capacity is the maximum static radial load on the bearing that can be withstood by it without exceeding permanent deformation of 0.0001 × d on ball and race at its most heavily stressed contact.** The Stribeck's equation gives the static load carrying capacity of the bearing. This equation is discussed in later section.

3.3.2 Dynamic Load Carrying Capacity [C]

When the ball or roller bearing is under consideration, the contact between the balls (or rollers) and the inner and outer races (or ring) generate Hertz's contact stresses between them. For a properly lubricated, clean and sealed bearing, metal fatigue is the only criterion of failure. Metal fatigue involves millions of stress alternations successfully endured. Common life measures are; number of revolutions of the inner ring until the first sign or evidence of fatigue crack and number of hours of use at a certain standard angular speed until the first sign or evidence of fatigue. Dynamic load carrying capacity of the bearing is based on the fatigue life of the bearing. Life of a single bearing is difficult to predict. For life measurement of bearing, statistical average for a group of bearings is prominent in practice. The rating life of a group of approximately identical bearings is defined as the number of revolutions that 90% of the bearings will complete or exceed before the evidence of first fatigue crack. Rating life is also known as minimum life, catalogue life, L_{10} life or B_{10} life. Life of individual ball bearing may or may not be different than rating life. It is proved that life which 50% of a group of bearings will exceed or complete, is five times the rating or L_{10}.

The dynamic load carrying capacity of bearing is defined as radial load in radial bearings or thrust load in thrust bearings that can be carried for a life of one million revolutions by 90% of the bearings from a group of identical bearings. This dynamic load carrying capacity is dependent on the assumption that inner race is rotating and the outer race is stationery. Most of the manufacturer's catalogue provide ready to use information or values of dynamic load capacity.

3.4 STRIBECK'S EQUATION

This equation deals with the static load carrying capacity of the bearing. Following are the assumptions made in analysis of static load carrying capacity of the bearing.

- The inner and outer races of the bearings are rigid. This assumption is made as circular shape of the races may deviate from the fundamental circular profile.
- There is equal interspacing between the balls.
- Balls of a roller bearing in the upper half do not support any load magnitude.

The static load equation is derived based on Hertz equation for contact stresses which states that $\delta \propto (F)^{2/3}$ where F is the radial load and δ is the deflection of the ball.

Fig. 3.8 below, shows the inner race of a roller bearing and forces acting on it. These forces are acting through the rolling elements or balls, which support the static load C_0. For the analysis of static load on bearing single row of balls on races is considered. Referring the figure, the equation for equilibrium of forces in vertical direction is deduced as

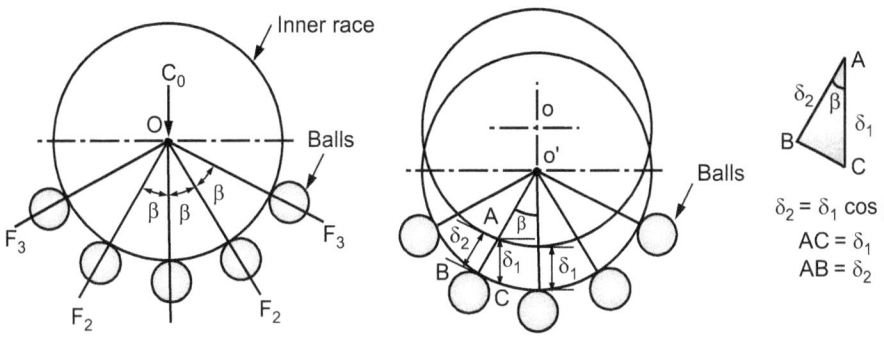

(a) Static Load on Inner Race   **(b) Deflected Inner Race**

Fig. 3.8

If C_0 is the total static load acting, central ball will take maximum load (= F_1) and subsequent balls will share F_2, F_3 ......

The vertical equilibrium of forces gives

$$C_0 = F_1 + 2F_2 \cos \beta + 2F_3 \cos(2\beta) + \ldots \qquad \ldots (3.1)$$

According to first assumption made in the analysis, only the balls take deformation and there is no deformation in the inner and outer races.

Let δ_1 be the deflection that occurs in the most heavily stressed ball which lies on the axis through which C_0 is acting. It is because of this deflection, the inner race gets deflected with respect to outer race through the same amount δ_1. Due to this the centre of inner ring moves from O to O', without deformation in the fundamental circular profile of inner ring.

Now let δ_1, δ_2 and δ_3 be the radial deformations occurring in respective balls.

As shown in Fig. 3.8 (b), $\delta_2 = \delta_1 \cos \beta$. The assembly is of bearing is subjected to contact stresses. As per Hertz's theory of contact stresses $\delta \propto (F)^{2/3}$. $\delta = B(F)^{2/3}$, B = Constant of proportionality.

Hence $\delta_1 = B(F_1)^{2/3}$ and $\delta_2 = B(F_2)^{2/3}$.

Thus,
$$\frac{\delta_2}{\delta_1} = \left(\frac{F_2}{F_1}\right)^{2/3}; \Rightarrow F_2 = F_1 (\cos \beta)^{3/2} \qquad \ldots (3.2)$$

Similarly it can be proved that $F_3 = F_1 (\cos 2\beta)^{3/2}$ and so on...

Using these values in (3.1), we get

$$C_0 = F_1 + 2 F_1 (\cos \beta)^{3/2} \cos \beta + 2 F_1 (\cos 2\beta)^{3/2} \cos(2\beta) + \ldots$$

$$C_0 = F_1 [1 + 2 (\cos \beta)^{5/2} + 2 (\cos 2\beta)^{5/2} + 2 \cos (3\beta)^{5/2} + \ldots]$$

This can be written as $C_0 = F_1 M;$ ... (3.3)

where, $M = [1 + 2 (\cos \beta)^{5/2} + 2 (\cos 2\beta)^{5/2} + 2 \cos (3\beta)^{5/2} + \ldots]$

If Z is the number of balls, the angular relation between the ball angle and the number of balls is given as $\beta = \dfrac{360}{Z}$. ... (3.4)

Thus, β dpends on Z. The number of balls in a standard bearing generally is 8, 10, and 12, 15 or higher. So evaluating the β values for various values of Z, M can be calculated. It is observed that, the ratio (Z/M), is almost constant. Stribeck suggested a constant value of 5 for the ratio (Z/M).

Hence; $$M = \frac{1}{5}Z \qquad \ldots (3.5)$$

Using equation (3.5) in (3.3), we get

$$C_0 = \frac{1}{5} Z F_1 \qquad \ldots (3.6)$$

Experimental evaluation shows that the force F_1 needed to produce a given permanent deformation in the balls is given as

$$F_1 = kd^2 \qquad \ldots (3.7)$$

Where k is a factor depending upon radii of curvature and material properties including modulii of elasticity of material; d is the ball diameter. From equations (3.6) and (3.7); we get

$$C_0 = kd^2 Z/5 \qquad \ldots \text{Stribeck's equation.}$$

3.5 EQUIVALENT BEARING LOAD (F_e)

In most of the practical situations, the force acting on the bearing possesses two components as radial and thrust. These two loads may be present in any proportions and therefore it is necessary to convert these two components into single equivalent which can be compared with the dynamic load carrying capacity. The expression for the equivalent dynamic load is given as

$$F_e = X V F_r + Y F_a$$

where,
- F_e = Equivalent dynamic load in N
- F_r = Radial load component in N
- F_a = Thrust or axial load component in N
- V = Race rotation factor

X and Y are the radial and thrust load factors. Their values are directly given or selected from manufacturer's catalogue. The values depend upon the geometry of bearings, number of balls, ball diameter and the relative values of F_a, F_r and C_0.

Value of race rotation factor V depends upon whether inner or outer race rotates.

V = 1; when inner race rotates and outer race is stationery.

V = 1.2; when outer race rotates and inner race is stationery.

The value of V = 1.2 is actually an acknowledgement that fatigue life is reduced for these operations. In most of the applications the inner race rotates and the outer race is stationary. (For example: ceiling fan, wherein the outer race is fixed in housing and the inner race rotates with fan spindle). However the value of V is unity for self aligning bearings whether inner or outer race rotates.

For the case when the bearing is subjected to pure radial and axial loads, the value of equivalent load becomes $F_e = F_r$ and $F_e = F_a$.

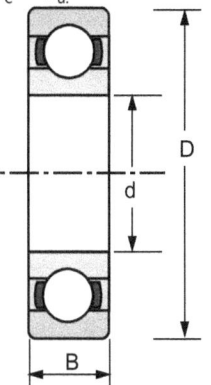

Fig. 3.9: Single Row Deep Groove Ball Bearing: Details

Table 3.2: Details of Single Row Deep Groove Ball Bearing

d mm	D mm	B mm	C N	C_0 N	Designation
10	26	8	4620	1960	6000
	30	9	5070	2240	6200
	35	11	8060	3750	6300
12	28	8	5070	2240	6001
	32	10	6890	3100	6201
	37	12	9750	4650	6301
15	32	9	5590	2500	6002
	35	11	7800	3550	6202
	42	13	11400	5400	6302
17	35	10	6050	2800	6003
	40	12	9560	4500	6203
	47	14	13500	6550	6303
	62	17	22900	11800	6403
20	42	12	9360	400	6004
	47	14	12700	6200	6204
	52	15	15900	7800	6304
	72	19	30700	16600	6404

contd. ...

d mm	D mm	B mm	C N	C₀ N	Designation
25	47	12	11200	5600	6005
	52	15	14000	6950	6205
	62	17	22500	11400	6305
	50	21	35800	19600	6405
30	55	13	13300	6950	6006
	62	16	19500	10000	6206
	72	19	28100	14600	6306
	90	23	4360	24000	6406
35	62	14	15900	8500	6007
	72	17	25500	13700	6207
	80	21	33200	18000	6307
	100	25	55300	31000	6407
40	68	15	16800	9300	6008
	80	18	30700	16600	6208
	90	23	41000	22400	6308
	110	27	63700	36500	6408
45	75	16	21200	12200	6009
	85	19	33200	18600	6209
	100	25	52700	30000	6309
	120	29	76100	45500	6409
50	82	16	21600	13200	6010
	90	20	35100	19600	6210
	110	27	61800	36000	6310
	130	31	87100	52000	6410
55	90	18	28100	17000	6011
	100	21	43600	25000	6211
	120	29	71500	41500	6311
	10	33	99500	63000	6411
60	95	18	29600	18300	6012
	120	22	47500	28000	6212
	130	31	81900	48000	6312
	150	35	108000	69500	6412
65	100	18	30700	19600	6013
	120	23	55900	34000	6213
	140	33	92300	56000	6313
	150	37	119000	78000	6413

3.5.1 Load-Life Relationship

The inter-relationship between the dynamic load carrying capacity, equivalent dynamic load and the bearing life is given by

$$L_{10} = (C/F_e)^a$$

L_{10} = Rated bearing life measured in million revolutions

C = Dynamic load carrying capacity in N

a = 3 for ball bearings

a = 10/3 for cylindrical and tapered roller bearings

Rearranging the above equation for rated life as;

$$C = F_e (L_{10})^{1/a}$$

For ball bearings $C = F_e (L_{10})^{1/3}$ and for cylindrical and tapered roller bearings $C = F_e (L_{10})^{0.3}$.

3.6 SELECTION OF BEARING LIFE

The desired bearing life is required to be specified for the purpose of deciding the size of the bearing. Life expectancy of bearing for a given application is expressed from past experience. For vehicles and many other applications, rotational speed is not constant but varies as per load conditions and functional requirements. Hence the bearing life is expressed in million revolutions. Based on past experiences, the desired bearing life for wheeled applications are mentioned in table 3.3 below.

Table 3.3: Values of Life in Million revolutions for general applications

Sr. No	Life in million revolutions	Applications
1.	50	Road vehicles - Medium category
2.	100	Road vehicles - Heavy vehicles, trucks
3.	500	Off road vehicles - Trolley cars, tractors

For applicactions in which the speed of rotation is constant, the expected life is measured in terms of hours of service. The recommended bearing life for such applications is given in table 3.3 below.

Table 3.4: Guidelines for bearing life in hours for common applications

Sr. No	Expected service in hours	Applications
1.	4000-8000	Intermittent machine applications: as lifting tackles, hand tools, drills, mixer - grinders, household appliances etc.
2.	12,000-20,000	Electric motors, gear drives and applications in which machines are used for stipulated hours of service as 8, 10 or 12.
3.	40,000-60,000	Pumps, compressors, and similar applications where machines are used for 24 hours of service per day and continuous operations.

These above mentioned values provide only a general guidance. However for some specific application the designer must account for past experiences, time and cost involved in replacement, repair of bearings and sometimes even breakdown costs.

3.7 LOAD FACTOR IN ROLLING CONTACT BEARINGS

The force analysis of bearing is done by taking into consideration the forces acting in vertical and horizontal planes. However the equations derived do not account for the dynamic loads and the other operational variations. To account for these and such other related factors, the elementary load values are multiplied by load application factors depending on the equipment. Guidelines for selection of load factors are given in table 3.5 below.

Table 3.5: Load Application factor values for gear, belt and chain drives

Sr. No	Load Application Factor	Drives	
1.		**Belt Drives**	
	2	i.	V- Belts
	3	ii.	Single Ply leather belt
	3.5	iii.	Double Ply Belt
	1.5	Chain drives	
2.		**Gear Drives**	
	1.2 to 1.4	Electric motors, turbo-compressors	
	1.4 to 1.7	I.C. Engines and Compressors	
	2.5 to 3.5	Hammer mills	

3.8 DESIGN FOR CYCLIC LOADS AND SPEEDS

For certain applications, bearings are subjected to cyclic loads and speeds. Considering a simplified approach we may consider that, a ball bearing having dynamic load capacity = C, operates under the following conditions:

(i) Radial load of F_1 (N) having life = L_1 (at F_1), completes n_1 rotations
(ii) Radial load of F_2 (N) having life = L_2 (at F_2), completes n_2 rotations
(iii) Radial load of F_3 (N) having life = L_3 (at F_3), completes n_3 rotations
(Where n_1, n_2, n_3 may be available as a % of total revolutions also).

Let L be the life in million revolutions under above conditions for this bearing.

Since, $L_1 = (C/F_1)^3$; $\quad \dfrac{1}{L_1} = \dfrac{F_1^3}{C^3}$

For one revolution, $1/L_1$ life is consumed
Therefore,

Fraction of life completed by F_1 is $\dfrac{n_1}{L_1}$ and will be $\dfrac{n_1}{L_1} = n_1\left(\dfrac{F_1^3}{C^3}\right)$

Fraction of life completed by F_2 is $\dfrac{n_2}{L_2}$ and will be $\dfrac{n_2}{L_2} = n_2\left(\dfrac{F_2^3}{C^3}\right)$

If the equivalent load = F_{eq} and total cycles covered are = $n = n_1 + n_2 + n_3$

Cumulative fraction of life completed = $\dfrac{n}{L} = n\left(\dfrac{F_{eq}^3}{C^3}\right)$

Equating effect of F_1, F_2, F_3 .... with F_{eq}

$$n_1 F_1^3/C^3 + n_2 F_2^3/C^3 + ...+ = n \cdot F_{eq}^3/C^3 \qquad \ldots (3.8)$$

Therefore,

$$F_{eq} = \sqrt[3]{\dfrac{n_1 \cdot F_1^3 + n_2 \cdot F_2^3 + n_3 F_3^3}{n_1 + n_2 + n_3}}$$

Once equivalent load value is known, we can find corresponding life 'n'.
When the load varies continuously with time, the above equation is rewritten as

$$F_e = \sqrt[3]{\left\{\left[\int_0^N F^3\, dN\right] \bigg/ \left[\int_0^N dN\right]\right\}}$$

$$F_e = \sqrt[3]{\left\{\left[\dfrac{1}{N}\int_0^N F^3\, dN\right]\right\}} \qquad \ldots (3.9)$$

For applications in which the bearings are subjected to combined axial and radial loads, these loads must be first converted into equivalent loads for the above calculations.

3.9 BEARING WITH A PROBABILITY OF SURVIVAL OTHER THAN 90%

For applications involving risk to human life, or where number of such bearings are used in a given system, it becomes mandatory to select a bearing that possesses reliability of more than 90% (R_{90} = 0.9). The relationship between bearing life and reliability is given by a stastical curve known as Wiebull distribution.

For Wiebull distribution,

$$R = e^{-\left(\frac{L}{a}\right)^b}$$

In the above equation R is the reliability, L is life and a and b are constants. Rearranging the above equation we get;

$$\text{Log}_e(1/R) = (L/a)^b \qquad \ldots (3.10)$$

When we consider 90% reliability of the bearing i.e. R_{90}, corresponding life is L_{10}, then the above equation is rewritten as

$$\text{Log}_e(1/R_{90}) = (L_{10}/a)^b \qquad \ldots (3.11)$$

Dividing equation (3.10) by (3.11), we get

$$(L/L_{10}) = \{[\log_e(1/R)]/[\log_e(1/R_{90})]\}^{1/b} \qquad \ldots (3.12)$$

Values of constants a and b are obtained by imposing the condition $L_{50} = 5L_{10}$

The values are a = 6.839, b = 1.169.

3.10 LUBRICATION AND MOUNTING OF BEARINGS

3.10.1 Lubrication of Rolling Contact Bearings

Rolling motion between the balls and races generates friction and heat. Lubrication is essential in antifriction bearings in order to reduce the friction between balls and races, including the other objectives as heat dissipiation (generated due to friction), avoid corrosion and protection of bearing from other particles. Oil and grease are two major types of lubricants used for lubrication.

Advantages of Oil over Grease as Lubricant are:
- Oil, being less viscous than grease carries frictional heat more easily and effectively than grease.
- Being in liquid state, oil feeds more contact areas under bearing load.
- It flushes dirt, corrosion and foreign particles from the bearing.

However, effective oil sealing arrangement has to be provided.

Grease lubricated bearings require less maintenance cost, are not subjected to leakage and rust. Also these bearings need simple housings.

Guidelines for Selecting Lubricant are:
- Temperature at the bearings is an important criteria. For applications involving temperature less than 100°C, grease provides excellent sealing action and lubrication, whereas oils have to be used in applications involving temperature more than 100°C.
- Greases are not preferred at high linear speeds. Where the product of bore (dimensions in mm) and speed (in rpm) is less than 200,000 grease is preferred and for higher values of product, lubricating oils are recommended.
- Grease is suitable for low operational speeds and moderate load magnitudes, whereas lubricating oils are preferred for heavy-duty applications.
- For applications like gear boxes where central lubricating system is employed lubricating oil is used.

3.10.2 Mounting of Rolling Contact Bearings

Bearing mouting is a complicated process involving a wide range of considerations ranging from manufactrinng to assembley considerations. Considerable expertise is required to select optimum mountings. Bearings provide housing for shafts. Usually bearings are mounted over shafts with tighter interference fit whereas bearings are usually fitted in the housing with a push fit. Bearing catalogues recommend suitable fits for the type of application.

Mounting of Bearings Over Shaft:

(a) Cold Mounting:

Bearings up to a 100 mm outside diameter can be cold mounted using a sleeve and a hammer or a press.

(b) Temperature Mounting:

Temperature mounting is the method of obtaining an interference fit by first introducing a temperature differential between the parts to be fitted. The required temperature differential can be obtained by heating one part and/or cooling the other part.

(c) Hydraulic Mounting:

Used for cold mounting a tapered bore bearing. It is based on forcing oil between the interfering surfaces, thereby greatly reducing the required axial force.

Radial Location:

Inner race of the bearing is fitted on shaft by means of interference fit. Similarly outer race is also fitted with interference fit. This intereference fit is responsible for prevention of wear and relative motion between inner race and the shaft. The degree of tightness of interference selected for outer race is less as compared with inner one. If the degree of tightness is insufficient than required, then the bearing is subjected to creep. For bearing creep refers to the small relative motion of the outer race relative to seat.

The bearings therefore are required to be located axially such that neither the shaft nor the bearings can move axially. Care has to be taken at the same time to ensure that there is provision for expansion of the shaft and there by provision for one of the bearings to move axially. Thus, in case a pair of bearing is mounted on same shaft, the outer race of one of the bearings is permitted for axial shift in order to withstand axial deflection due to thrust load or temperature variation.

Methods for Axial Location for the Bearing:

There are various methods employed to locate bearings axially. (Ref. Fig. 3.10). These can be:

(1) A step on the shaft or in the housing.
(2) Use of circlip on the shaft.
(3) Use of locking plate on the shaft.
(4) Having threads on the shaft and use of locking nut.
(5) Use of end cap in the housing, thus locating outer race and many more.

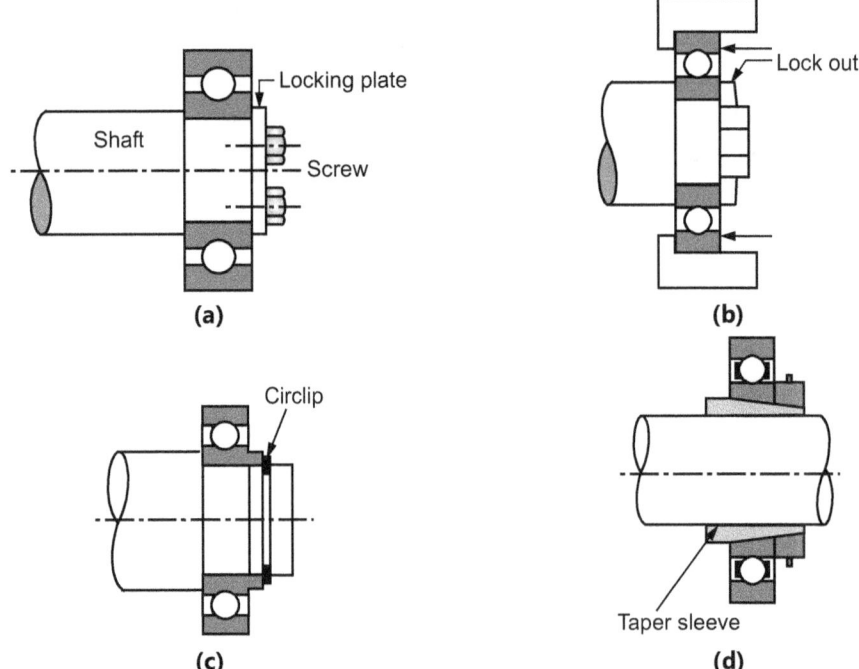

Fig. 3.10: Bearing-Axial Location Methods

Preloading of Bearings:

A bearing is fitted on a shaft and located inside a housing and has some clearance between different parts of the ball bearing. This clearance results into noise and vibrations during running. The preloading is a process wherein a thrust load is applied to remove axial or radial clearance within the bearing parts. This also helps in controlling rotational accuracy.

Optimum preload is essential. Excessive preload results in generation of excessive heat and also reduces fatigue life. Insufficient preload causes fretting corrosion. Values of optimum preload are estimated based on contact stresses at ellipse area between ball and race.

All applicatons do not require preloading since a positive clearance is desirable. However for applications such as machine tool spindle bearings, pinion bearings in automobils, a negative clearance is essential to increase running accuracy.

Advantages of Preloading:
- Eliminates radial and axial play.
- Eliminate unnecessary clearances, which induce rigidity to the bearings.
- By reducing the clearances, controls the rotational accuracy of the bearing.

Methods of Preloading:
1. Bearings with a tapered bore are suitable for radial preloading since, by driving the bearing up on to its tapered seat reduces radial clearances and achieves preloading.

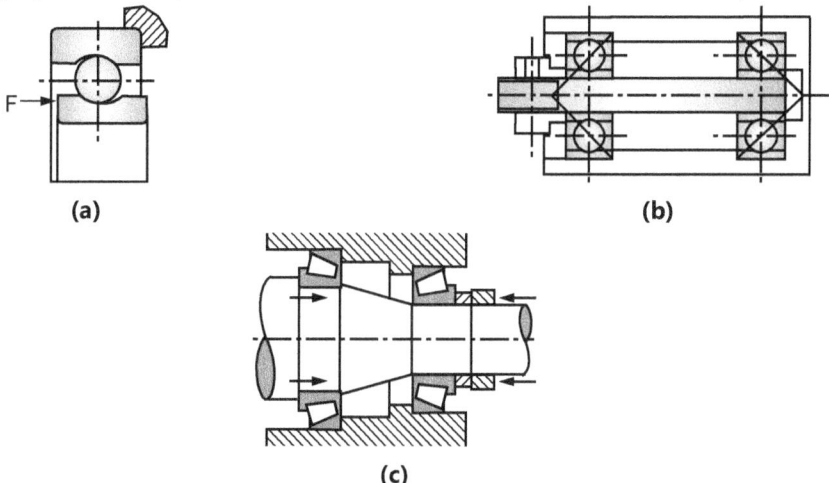

Fig. 3.11: Bearing - Preloading Methods

2. Figs. 3.11 (a) and 3.11 (b) shows a methodology wherein axial thrust is given on inner race while holding the outer race against a rigid surface. Reduces axial clearance and provides preloading.

   Fig. 3.9 (c) shows a typical taper roller beaing mounting whereby tightening the lock nut radial clearances will be reduced. Preloading values have to be accurately determined beforehand.

Types of Failures in Rolling Contact Beaings:

Theoretically, point or line contact occurs in a bearing which results into large values of contact stresses. Pitting and wear failures are therefore unavoidable over a period of time.

Therefore even when they are used under ideal conditions, bearings do fail by deterioration of material due to rolling fatigue. Pitting occurs due to excessive contact stresses and are basically designed to avoid this. Increasing surface hardness can extend the life.

Scoring is another fundamental problem which can occur with lubrication failure. Excessive heat is generated resulting in stick slip phenomenon. A bearing is said to have failed with the occurance of the first failure in the inner ring, outer ring or rolling element due to repeated stresses. However in order to get a satisfactory rated life from a bearing following modes of failures and their causes should be understood.

Main causes of bearing failures are:
- Wrong bearing selection (Check the type of bearing as well as its size).
- Faulty installation. (Too close or loose fittings, excessive misalignment - can lead to creep failure).
- Lubrication provided being inadequate. (lubrication method, type of lubricant, presence of corrosive additives, sealing provision – can lead to rust, corrosion wear or seizure).
- Foreign material contamination (during installation or working leading to abrasive wear).
- Extreme working conditions (speed and temperature – can lead to dry running).
- Abnormal shock loads (ball distortion – can lead to noisy operation).

To understand bearing failure causes, experience with bearings, its lubrication and understanding of the characteristics of the equipment are required.

Bearing Selection from the Catalogue:

Bearing selection process gets divided in two steps:

1. **Selection of the type of bearing based on design requirement:**

   This depends on
   (a) Absolute as well as relative magnitudes of radial and axial loads on the bearing.
   (b) Provision required to take misalignment based on likely assembly and installation environment.
   (c) Lubrication provision that can be made and ease of accesibilty.
   (d) Speeds, working temperature and expected life.

   Bearing manufacturer's catalogue gives selection guideline. For example, a single row deep groove (SRDG) ball bearing can withstand radial as well as axial load and can also take misalignment. Whereas, if the radial loads are heavy, cylindrical roller bearings could be the choice. Taper roller bearings can take radial as well as axial loads.

   Type of bearing is selected by considering above requirements.

2. Selection of the size of bearing:

Static and dynamic load carrying capablilities are published in the catalogue for every size of bearing. Required life of the bearing at specified reliability is decided by the application. The size of bearing is decided by iterative process to get optimum design. The selection process discussed here is mainly for the SRDG bearings which can be extended to cylindrical and spherical roller bearings by using prescribed tables from manufacturer's catalogue.

Seletion steps are described below:

(1) The shaft diameter is already calculated based on Bending Moment and torque. Bearing bore diameter is thus finalized.

(2) Find axial (F_a) and radial (F_r) load values for the bearing.

(3) Decide the type of bearing to be used as discussed earlier.

(4) Bearings are available in different series (light, medium, heavy). Select a light series of bearing from the catalogue to start with for the given bore size and find static load capacity '$Co_{cat.}$' And Dynamic load capacity 'C_{cat} from catalogue for the selected bearing.

(5) Referring to the table from manufacturer, find values of radial load factor (X) and axial load factor (Y). For the values of (F_a/C_o) for the selected bearing, find 'e'. Compare (F_a/F_r) value with 'e' and accordingly find X and Y using the table

Table 3.6: Single Row Deep Groove Ball Bearing

F_a/C_o	(F_a/F_r) < e		(F_a/F_r) > e		e
	X	Y	X	Y	
0.025				2.00	0.22
0.056				1.71	0.26
0.084				1.55	0.28
0.13	1.0	0.0	0.56	1.4	0.31
0.28				1.15	0.38
0.50				1.0	0.44

(6) Find equivalent load $F_{eq} = V \cdot X \cdot F_r + Y \cdot F_a$

Here V is the rotation factor =1 when inner race is rotating and = 1.2 when outer race is rotating.

(7) Knowing F_{eq} and desired bearing life at 90% reliability, find required value of 'C' (C_{reqd}) using the relation. $C = F_{eq} \cdot L^a$

(8) If $C_{cat} > C_{reqd}$, selection is suitable to get desired life.

(9) If $C_{cat} < C_{reqd}$, try next higher series for the same diameter and repeat steps from step 4, till we reach step 8. The next higher series bearing has same bore but larger outer diameter and ball size. Thus, it has also larger dynamic load capacity but it is costlier.

Iterative procedure is essential to arrive at optimum results.

Mounting of Taper Roller Bearing:

As already seen, in case of taper roller bearings, the load carrying member i.e. the taper roller has its axis at an angle w.r.t. shaft axis. Thus, even when the load is purely radial, it has components in axial direction and thus a thrust load. Moreover the construction of a taper roller bearing is such that the cone is a separable element and therefore the axial load must be carried by bearing at the other end. Thus, these bearings are used in pair. Two mounting methods are common. (Refer Fig. 3.12).

(A) Face to Face and

(B) Back to Back.

Thus, as the name suggests either the front sides (face) of the two bearings will be facing each other or the backs will be facing each other. Back to back arrangement is preferred when distance between two bearings is short and moment loads are applied. Face to face is popular because mounting is easier when interference is essential for inner ring.

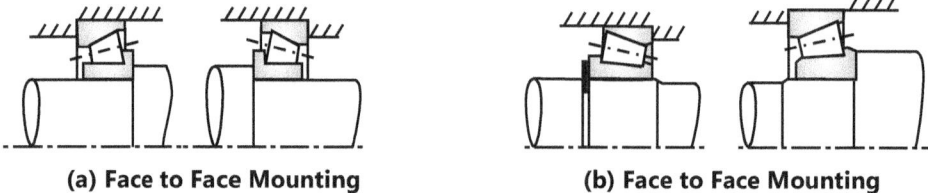

(a) Face to Face Mounting (b) Face to Face Mounting

Fig. 3.12

Table 3.7: Data on Taper Roller Bearing

d mm	D mm	B mm	C N	C_0 N	Designation	e	Y
20	42	15	22900	28700	32004X	0.37	1.6
	47	14	26000	30500	30204	0.35	1.7
	52	15	31900	36800	30304	0.3	2.0
	52	21	41300	31500	32304	0.3	2.0

contd. ...

d mm	D mm	B mm	C N	C₀ N	Designation	e	Y
25	47	15	25500	33700	32005 X	0.43	1.4
	52	15	29200	35500	30205	0.37	1.6
	62	17	41800	48800	30305	0.30	2.0
	62	17	35800	42700	31305	0.83	0.72
	62	24	56100	71800	32305	0.30	2.0
30	55	17	33600	41500	32006 X	0.43	1.4
	62	16	38000	46900	30206	0.37	1.6
	62	20	47300	61600	32206	0.37	1.6
	72	19	52800	63500	30306	0.31	1.9
	72	19	44600	53400	31306	0.83	0.72
	72	27	72100	95700	32304	0.31	1.9
35	62	18	40200	56100	32007 X	0.46	1.3
	72	17	48400	59800	30207	0.37	1.6
	72	23	61600	82800	32207	0.37	1.6
	80	21	68200	82100	30307	0.31	1.9
	80	21	57200	71800	31307	0.83	0.72
	80	31	89700	123000	32307	0.31	1.9
40	68	19	49500	73600	32908 X	0.37	1.6
	80	18	58300	71600	32208	0.37	1.6
	80	23	70400	92000	32208	0.37	1.6
	90	23	80900	103000	30308	0.35	1.7
	90	23	69300	85600	31307	0.83	0.72
	90	33	110000	153000	32307	0.35	1.7
45	75	20	55000	81000	32808 X	0.40	1.5
	85	19	62700	81000	30209	0.40	1.5
	85	23	74800	103000	32209	0.40	1.5
	100	25	101000	132000	30309	0.35	1.7
	100	25	85800	110000	31309	0.83	0.72
	100	36	132000	188000	32309	0.35	1.7
50	80	20	57200	83300	32018 X	0.43	1.4
	90	20	70400	95700	30218	0.43	1.4
	90	23	76500	105000	32210	0.43	1.4
	110	27	117000	153000	30310	0.35	1.7
	110	27	99000	128000	31310	0.83	0.72
	110	40	161000	234600	32310	0.35	7.7

For a given taper roller bearing (Table 3.7)

For $\dfrac{F_a}{F_r} > e \rightarrow$ X = 0.4 and Y = from table

$\dfrac{F_a}{F_r} < e \rightarrow$ X = 1.0 and Y = 0

Equivalent Load and Selection of Taper Roller Bearing:

Consider a back to back arrangement shown below with radial loads F_{1r}, F_{2r} on two bearings and external thrust load T.

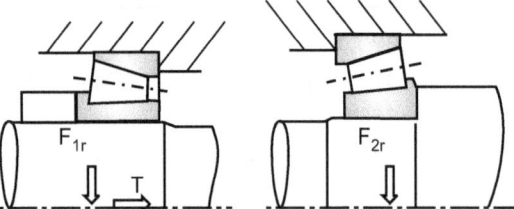

Fig. 3.13: Back to Back Mounting (Radial and Axial Load)

Radial load on bearing 1 = F_{1r}

Total axial load on bearing 1 = F_{1a}

F_{1a} = Thrust on bearing 1 due to radial load on bearing 2 + External thrust

$$F_{1a} = \dfrac{0.5 \times F_{2r}}{Y_2} + T$$

Similarly,

Radial load on bearing 2 = F_{2r}

Total axial load on bearing 2 =

F_{2a} = Thrust on bearing 2 due to radial load on bearing 1 − External thrust

$$F_{2a} = \dfrac{0.5 \times F_{1r}}{Y_1} - T$$

Having found radial loads on bearings 1 and 2, equivalent loads can be determined.

Equivalent load on bearing 1:

$$F_{eq1} = \left[X_1 \cdot F_{1r} + Y_1 \left(\dfrac{0.5 \times F_{2r}}{Y_2} \right) + T \right] K_1 \quad \text{or} \quad F_{1r} \times K_1$$

Whichever is larger.

Similarly,

Equivalent load on bearing 2:

$$F_{eq2} = \left[X_2 \cdot F_{2r} + Y_2 \left(\dfrac{0.5 \times F_{1r}}{Y_1} \right) + T \right] K_1 \quad \text{or} \quad F_{2r} \times K_1$$

Whichever is larger.

Having found equivalent loads the life of the bearing can be found as in case of SRDG bearings using the relation $L_{10} = (C/F_{eq})^3$. The method is typical and can be used for face to face arrangement by taking into consideration axial thrust directions.

Example: For an automobile application with shaft diameter of 35 mm and back to back taper roller bearing arrangement, the radial load on the LH side bearing is 2000 N and on the RH side bearing it is 1600 N. The external thrust is 1200 N towards RH side. Taper roller bearing 30207 is selected and the expected life is 800 million revolutions minimum. Comment on the suitability of the bearings. Take load application factor as 1.4.

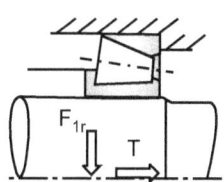
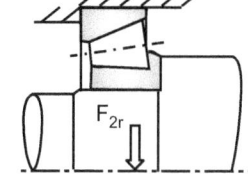

Fig. 3.14

F_{1r} = 2000 N, F_{2r} = 1600 N, T = 1200 N

Referring to the table 3.7 for selected bearing, 30207

C_0 = 59800 N; C = 48400 N

From the table, X = 0.4, Y = 1.6, e = 0.37

Consider bearing No. 1 on LH side

Radial load on LH side bearing 1 = F_{1r} = 2000 N

Total axial load on bearing 1 =

F_{1a} = Thrust on bearing 1 due to radial load in bearing 2 + External thrust

$$F_{1a} = \frac{0.5 \times F_{2r}}{Y_2} + T = \frac{0.5 \times 1600}{1.6} + 1200 = 1700 \text{ N}$$

Since $\dfrac{F_{1a}}{F_{1r}} = \dfrac{1700}{2000} > e$

∴ X_1 = 0.4 and Y_1 = 1.6

$$F_{eq1} = \left[X_1 \cdot F_{1r} + Y_1 \left(\frac{0.5 * F_{2r}}{Y_2} + T \right) \right] K_1 \quad \text{or} \quad = F_{r1} \times K_1$$

F_{eq1} = [0.4 × 2000 + 1.6 (1700)] 1.4 = 4928 N

or F_{eq1} = 2000 × 1.4 = 2800 N

Thus, F_{eq1} = 4928 N

Consider bearing No. 2 on RH side.

Radial load on RH side bearing 2 = F_{2r} = 1600 N

Total axial load on bearing 2 =

F_{1a} = Thrust on bearing 1 due to radial load on bearing 2 + External thrust

$$F_{2a} = \frac{0.5 \times F_{1r}}{Y_2} - T = \frac{0.5 \times 2000}{1.6} - 1200 = -575 \text{ N}$$

$$F_{eq2} = \left[X_1 \cdot F_{2r} + Y_1 \left(\frac{0.5 \times F_{1r}}{Y_1} + T \right) \right] K_1 \quad \text{or} \quad = F_{r2} \times K_1$$

F_{eq1} = [0.4 × 1600 + 1.6 (−575)] 1.4 = −392

or $\qquad$ = 1600 × 1.4 = 2240 N

Thus, $\qquad F_{eq2}$ = 2240 N

Taking maximum equivalent load as 4928 N

$$L = \left(\frac{C}{P}\right)^3 = \left(\frac{59800}{4928}\right)^3 = 1786.86 \text{ million revolutions.}$$

Minimum requirement is 800 million revolutions.

Hence, the bearing is adequate.

Selection of the proper type and size of bearing is the key to successful operation of machinaries.

SOLVED EXAMPLES

Example 3.1: A cylindrical roller bearing is subjected to a radial load of 5000 N. The desired life of the bearing with 90% reliability is 15,000 hours. The load application factor is 1.5. If the shaft rotates at 1440 rpm, calculate the required basic dynamic load rating of the bearing.

Solution: Given data: Type of bearing: Cylindrical roller

F_r = Radial load = 5000 N;

F_a = 0 N (Axial load)

L_{10h} = 15000 hours

K_a = 1.5 (Load application factor)

n = 1440 rpm

Radial load factor, X = 1 $\qquad$ ... (1)

(Since the bearing is subjected to pure radial load).

Axial load factor, Y = 0

(Since bearing is not subjected to any axial load).

Equivalent dynamic load (F_e),

Since the shaft (inner race) rotates V = 1.0

F_e = (XVF$_r$ + YF$_a$) K$_a$

$\qquad$ = (1 × 1 × 5000 + 0 × 0) 1.5

$\qquad$ = 7500 N

Rating life of bearing,
$$L_{10} = \frac{L_{10h} \times 60 \times n}{10^6} = \frac{15000 \times 60 \times 1440}{10^6} = 1296 \text{ million revolutions}$$

Required basic dynamic load capacity, (C) is given by
$$L_{10} = \left(\frac{C}{F_e}\right)^a$$

$$1296 = \left(\frac{C}{7500}\right)^{\frac{10}{3}}$$

$$C = 64393.61 \text{ N}$$
$$C = 64.393 \text{ kN}$$

Example 3.2: A 22 kW, 1440 rpm electric motor is directly coupled to a shaft of 25 mm diameter, which is supported by two cylindrical roller bearings. The shaft transmits power to another line shaft through the flat pulley of 300 mm diameter, which is placed mid-way between the two bearings. The coefficient of friction between the belt and pulley is 0.3, while the angle of lap is 180°. The belt is horizontal. The load factor is 1.5. If the expected life is 50,000 hours, select the bearings from manufacturer's catalogue.

Bearing No.	NU2205	NU2305
Basic dynamic capacity 'C' kN	15.99	31.39

Solution: Given data:

Type of bearing = Cylindrical roller bearing
kW = Power transmitted by electric motor = 22×10^3 W
n = Speed of shaft = 1440 rpm
d = Diameter of shaft = 25 mm
D = Diameter of pulley = 300 mm
μ = Coefficient of friction = 0.3
θ = Angle of lap = 180° = π radians
K_a = Load application factor = 1.5.
L_{10h} = Rating life of bearing = 50000 hours

(i) Select suitable bearing for ends of shaft

Radial load and axial load (F_a)

$$\frac{P_1}{P_2} = e^{\mu\theta} = e^{0.3\pi} = 2.566$$

∴ $P_1 = 2.566 \, P_2$

(ii) Belt speed V_B:

$$V_B = \frac{\pi D n}{60 \times 1000} = \frac{\pi \times 300 \times 1440}{60 \times 1000} = 22.62 \text{ m/sec}$$

(iii) Power transmitted by belt drive

$$\text{Power} = (P_1 - P_2) V_B$$
$$22 \times 10^3 = (2.566 P_2 - P_2) \times 22.62$$
$$P_2 = 621.07 \text{ N}$$
$$P_1 = 2.566 P_2 = 1593.7 \text{ N}$$

(iv) Total horizontal force, (F) on pulley:

$$F = P_1 + P_2$$
$$= 1593.7 + 621.07$$
$$= 2214.8 \text{ N}$$

(v) Radial load on each bearing (F_r):

$$F_r = \frac{F}{2} = \frac{2214.8}{2} = 1107.4 \text{ N}$$

(vi) Axial load on each bearing $F_a = 0$:

$$K_a = 1.5$$
$$F_{eq} = (XVF_r + YF_a) K_a = (1 \times 1 \times 1107.4 + 0) \times 1.5$$
$$= 1661.11 \text{ N}$$
$$L_{10} = \frac{L_{10h} \times 60 \times N}{10^6} = \frac{50000 \times 60 \times 1440}{10^6} = 4320 \text{ million revolutions}$$
$$L_{10} = \left(\frac{C}{F_e}\right)^a ; \quad 4320 = \left(\frac{C}{1661.1}\right)^{10/3}$$
$$\therefore \quad C = 20466 \text{ N}$$

Hence, we select bearing NU2305 having dynamic load capacity, C = 31.39 kN.

Example 3.3: The radial load carried on ball bearing is 2500 N for the first five revolutions and reduces to 1500 N for the next ten revolutions. The load variation then repeats itself. The expected life of the bearing is 25 million revolutions. Determine dynamic load carrying capacity of the bearings:

Solution:

Type of bearing : Single row deep groove ball bearing

F_1 = Radial load acting during first element = 2500 N

F_2 = Radial load acting during second element = 1500 N

N_1 = Number of revolution in first element = 5

N_2 = Number of revolution in second elemnt = 10

L_{10} = Rating life of bearing = 25 million revolution

DESIGN OF MACHINE ELEMENTS - II   ROLLING CONTACT BEARINGS

To find 'C':

Equivalent dynamic load for entire work cycle (F_e)

$$F_e = \left(\frac{N_1 (F_1)^3 + N_2(F_2)^3}{N_1 + N_2}\right)^{1/3}$$

$$= \left[\frac{5 \times (2500)^3 + 10 (1500)^3}{5 + 10}\right]^{1/3} = 1953.80 \text{ N}$$

Basic dynamic load capacity of bearing (C)

$$L_{10} = \left(\frac{C}{F_e}\right)^3$$

$$25 = \left(\frac{C}{1953.80}\right)^3$$

$$C = 5712.95 \text{ N}$$

Example 3.4: A single row deep groove ball bearing is subjected to the following work cycle. Reliability is 90%, consider 4 bearings and calculate reliability of system.

Fraction of cycle	Radial load F_r kN	Thrust load F_a kN	Radial factor 'X'	Thrust factor 'Y'	Race rotating	Service factor	Speed rpm
1/10	1.5	0.25	1.0	0	Inner	1.2	400
1/4	1.0	0.75	0.56	2.0	Outer	1.8	500
1/2	5.0	1.1	0.56	2.0	Inner	1.5	600
Remaining	1.0	–	1.0	0	Outer	2.0	800

Desired life of bearing: 15000 hours.
Select bearing from the following data. Find n_{avg}.

Number	6011	6211	6311	6411
Dynamic capacity	28.1 kN	43.6 kN	71.5 kN	99.5 kN

Given Data:

Type of bearing = Single row deep groove ball bearing
Desired life of bearing = 15000 hours.

For 1st cycle: $F_1 = (X_1 V_1 F_{r1} + Y_1 F_{a1}) \cdot K_{a1}$

$$= (1 \times 1 \times 1500 + 0 \times 250) \times 1.2$$

$$F_1 = 1800 \text{ N}$$

Revolutions $N_1 = \dfrac{1}{10} \times \left(\dfrac{L_{10h} \times 60}{10^6}\right) n_1 = \dfrac{1}{10}\left(\dfrac{15000 \times 60}{10^6}\right) \times 400$

$= \dfrac{1}{10} \times (0.9) \times 400$

$N_1 = 36$ million revolutions

For 2nd cycle:
$F_2 = (X_2 V_2 F_{r2} + Y_2 F_{a2}) K_{a2}$
$= (0.56 \times 1.2 \times 1000 + 2 \times 750) \times 1.8$
$= 3909.6$ N

$N_2 = \dfrac{1}{4}\dfrac{L_{10h} \times 60 \times n_2}{10^6} = \dfrac{1}{4} \times \dfrac{15000 \times 60 \times 500}{10^6} = \dfrac{1}{4}(0.9) \times 500$

$N_2 = 112.5$ million revolutions

For 3rd cycle:
$F_3 = (X_3 V_3 F_{r3} + Y_3 F_{a3}) K_{a3}$
$= (0.56 \times 1 \times 5000 + 2 \times 1100) \times 1.5 = 7500$ N

$N_3 = \dfrac{1}{2} \times \dfrac{L_{10h} \times 60 \times n_3}{10^6} = \dfrac{1}{2} \times \left(\dfrac{15000 \times 60}{10^6}\right) \times 600 = \dfrac{1}{2} \times 0.9 \times 600$

$N_3 = 270$ million revolutions

For 4th cycle:
$F_4 = (X_4 V_4 F_{r4} + Y_4 + F_{a4}) K_{a4} = (1 \times 1.2 \times 1000 + 0) \times 2$
$F_4 = 2400$ N

$N_4 = 0.15 \times \dfrac{L_{10h} \times 60 \times n_4}{10^6} = 0.15 \times \left(\dfrac{15000 \times 60}{10^6}\right) \times 800$

$= 0.15 (0.9)(800)$

$N_4 = 108$ million revolutions

Equivalent dynamic load for entire working cycle,

$$F_e = \left[\dfrac{N_1(F_1)^a + N_2(F_2)^a + N_3(F_3)^a + N_4(F_4)^a}{N_1 + N_2 + N_3 + N_4}\right]^{1/a}$$

$$= \left[\dfrac{36 \times (1800)^3 + 112.5(3909.6)^3 + 270 \times (7500)^3 + 108 \times (2400)^3}{526.5}\right]^{1/3}$$

$F_e = 6147.74$ N

Rating life of bearing, (L_{10})

$L_{10} = N = N_1 + N_2 + N_3 + N_4$

$= 36 + 112.5 + 270 + 108 = 526.5$ million revolutions

$L_{10} = \left(\dfrac{C}{F_e}\right)^3$

$526.5 = \left(\dfrac{C}{6147.74}\right)^3$

$C = 49641.56$ N

∴ 6311 bearing number with dynamic capacity 71.5 kN selected for given work cycle application.

Average speed of bearing, (n_{avg})

$$n_{avg} = \frac{\text{Total life of bearing in revolution}}{\text{Total life of bearing in minutes}}$$

$$= \frac{526.5 \times 10^6}{15000 \times 60}$$

$$n_{avg} = 585 \text{ rpm}$$

Reliability of total system,

$$R_s = (R)^{N_s} = (0.9)^4 = 0.6561$$

$$R_s = 65.61\%$$

Example 3.5: A single row deep groove ball bearing operates with the following work cycle.

Element time %	Radial load (F_r) kN	Thrust Load (F_a) kN	Radial Factor X	Thrust Factor Y	Race Rotating	Service Factor	Speed r.p.m.
40	4.0	1.0	0.56	1.4	Inner	1.8	720
20	2.5	1.0	0.56	1.6	Outer	2.0	1440
40	No load	No load	–	–	Outer	–	720

If the expected life of the bearing is 15000 hours with a reliability of 95%. Calculate the basic dynamic load rating of the bearing so that it can be selected from the manufacturer's catalogue based on 90% reliability.

If there are 6 such bearings in a system, what is the probability that all bearings will survive for 15000 hours.

Solution: Typ of bearing – Single row deep groove ball bearing.

L_{05h} = Rating life of bearing at 95% reliability = 15000 hours

N_s = Number of bearings = 6

$P_1 = (X_1 V_1 F_{r1} + Y_1 F_{a1}) \cdot K_{a1} = (0.56 \times 1 \times 4000 + 1.4 \times 1000) \times 1.8$

$P_1 = 6552 \text{ N}$

$N_1 = 0.4 \times \left(\frac{L_{10h} \times 60}{10^6}\right) \times n_1 = 0.4 \times \left(\frac{L_{10h} \times 60}{10^6}\right) \times 720$

$N_1 = 0.01728 \, L_{10h}$ million revolutions

$P_2 = (X_2 V_2 F_{r2} + Y_2 F_{a2}) \cdot K_{a2} = (0.56 \times 1.2 \times 2500 + 1.6 \times 1000) \times 2$

$P_2 = 6560 \text{ N}$

$N_2 = 0.2 \times \frac{L_{10h} \times 60 \times n_2}{10^6} = 0.2 \times \frac{L_{10h} \times 60 \times 1440}{10^6}$

DESIGN OF MACHINE ELEMENTS - II   ROLLING CONTACT BEARINGS

$$N_2 = 0.01728\, L_{10h} \text{ million revolutions}$$

$$P_3 = (X_3 V_3 F_{r3} + Y_3 F_{a3}) \cdot K_{a3} = 0 \text{ N}$$

$$N_3 = 0.4 \times \frac{L_{10h} \times 60 \times n_3}{10^6} = 0.4 \times \frac{L_{10h} \times 60 \times 720}{10^6}$$

$$N_3 = 0.01728\, L_{10h} \text{ million revolutions}$$

$$F_e = \sqrt[3]{\frac{N_1 P_1^3 + N_2 P_2^3 + N_3 P_3^3}{N_1 + N_2 + N_3}}$$

$$= \sqrt[3]{\frac{[0.01728 \times (6552)^3 + 0.01728\, (6.560)^3 + 0.0178\, (0)^3]\, L_{10h}}{3 \times (0.01728)\, L_{10h}}}$$

$$F_e = 5.7272 \text{ kN} = 5727.2 \text{ N}$$

(i) Rating life of the bearing for 90% reliability (L_{10h}):

$$\frac{L_{5h}}{L_{10h}} = \left[\frac{\log_e (1/R_{95})}{\log_e (1/R_{90})}\right]^{\frac{1}{1.7}}$$

$$\frac{15000}{L_{10h}} = \left[\frac{\log_e (1/0.95)}{\log_e (1/0.90)}\right]^{1/1.17}$$

$$L_{10h} = 27751.44 \text{ hours}$$

(ii) Rating life of bearing for 90% reliability, (L_{10})

$$L_{10} = N = N_1 + N_2 + N_3$$

$$= 0.01728 \times L_{10h} + 0.01728 \times L_{10h} + 0.01728\, L_{10h}$$

$$= 0.05184 \times L_{10h}$$

$$= 0.05184 \times 27751.44$$

$$\mathbf{L_{10} = 1438.63 \text{ million revolutions}}$$

Basic dynamic load capacity, (C)

$$L_{10} = \left(\frac{C}{F_e}\right)^a$$

$$1438.63 = \left(\frac{C}{5727.2}\right)^3$$

$$\mathbf{C = 64653.5 \text{ N} = 64.65 \text{ kN}}$$

Reliability of the system (R_s)

$$R_s = (R)^{N_s} = (0.95)^6$$

$$R_s = 0.7351$$

$$\mathbf{R_s = 73.51\%}$$

DESIGN OF MACHINE ELEMENTS - II — ROLLING CONTACT BEARINGS

Example 3.6: A single row deep groove ball bearing is used to support the lay shaft of a four speed automobile gearbox. It is subjected to the following loads in respective speed ratios.

Gear	Axial Load (N)	Radial Load (N)	% Time Engaged
1st gear	3400	4500	2%
2nd gear	800	3400	5%
3rd gear	100	2800	23%
4th gear	Nil	Nil	70%

The lay shaft is fixed to the engine shaft and rotates at 1600 rpm. The static and dynamic load carrying capacities of the bearing are 11800 N and 17300 N respectively. The bearing is expected to be in use for 4500 hours of operation. Find out the reliability with which life could be expected.

Refer the following data.

X and Y factors for single row, deep groove ball bearings

F_a/C_o	$(F_a/F_r) \le e$		$(F_a/F_e) > e$		e
	X	Y	X	Y	
0.025	1	0	0.56	2.0	0.22
0.040	1	0	0.56	1.8	0.242
0.070	1	0	0.56	1.6	0.27
0.130	1	0	0.56	1.4	0.31
0.250	1	0	0.56	1.2	0.37
0.500	1	0	0.56	1.0	0.44

Solution: Type of bearing: Single row deep groove

n = Speed of shaft rotation = 1600 rpm
C_o = Basic static load capacity = 11800 N
C = Basic dynamic load capacity = 17300 N
L_h = Life of bearing = 4500 hours

For 1st gear: $\dfrac{F_a}{C_o} = \dfrac{3400}{11800} = 0.288 \rightarrow e = 0.37 + \dfrac{(0.07) \times (0.038)}{0.25}$

$e = 0.3806$ (By interpolation)

$\dfrac{F_a}{F_r} = \dfrac{3400}{4500} = 0.755$ which is $> e$

∴ From above chart, X = 0.56 and Y is obtained by interpolation.

$$Y = 1.2 - \frac{(0.288 - 0.25) \times (1.2 - 1.0)}{(0.5 - 0.25)} = 1.1697 \approx 1.17$$

For remaining cases interpolation is not required since (F_a/F_r) < e. Hence, X and Y values are read from chart. Below shown table finds X and Y for all the cases.

Radial Load (F_r)N	Axial Load (F_a)N	F_a/F_r	F_a/C_o	e	X	Y	Gear
4500	3400	0.755	0.2669	0.3747	0.56	1.17	1st gear
3400	800	0.1769	0.0487	0.2487	1	0	2nd gear
2800	100	0.0231	6.36×10^{-3}	< 0.22	1	0	3rd gear
Nil	Nil	0	0		1	0	4th gear

Equivalent dynamic (Radial) load during 1st gear (F_1)

$$F_1 = (X_1 \cdot V_1 \cdot F_{r1}) + Y_1 \cdot F_{a1}) \cdot K_a$$
$$= 0.56 \times 4500 + 1.17 \times 3400) \times 1$$
$$F_1 = 6498.0 \text{ N}$$

Revolutions of bearing during 1st gear

$$N_1 = 0.02 \times \frac{L_{10h} \times 60 \times n_1}{10^6} = 0.02 \times \frac{L_{10h} \times 60 \times 1600}{10^6}$$

$$N_1 = 1.92 \times 10^{-3} L_{10h} \text{ million revolutions}$$

$$F_2 = (X_2 \cdot V_2 \cdot F_{r2} + Y_2 \cdot F_{a2}) \cdot K_{a2}$$
$$= (1 \times 1 \times 3400 + 0) \times 1$$

Parallely

$$F_2 = 3400.0 \text{ N}$$

$$N_2 = 0.05 \times \frac{L_{10h} \times 60 \times n_2}{10^6} = 0.05 \times \frac{L_{10h} \times 60 \times 1600}{10^6}$$

$$N_2 = 4.8 \times 10^{-3} L_{10h} \text{ million revolutions}$$

$$F_3 = (X_3 \cdot V_3 \cdot F_{r3} + Y_3 \cdot F_{a3}) \cdot K_a$$
$$= (1 \times 1 \times 2800 + 0) \times 1$$
$$F_3 = 2800 \text{ N}$$

$$N_3 = 0.23 \times \frac{L_{10h} \times 60 \times n_3}{10^6} = 0.28 \times \frac{L_{10h} \times 60 \times 1600}{10^6}$$

$$N_3 = 0.0221 L_{10h} \text{ million revolutions}$$

$$F_4 = (X_4 \cdot V_4 \cdot F_{r4} + Y_4 \cdot F_{a4}) \cdot K_a$$
$$F_4 = 0$$

$$N_4 = 0.7 \times \frac{L_{10h} \times 60 \times n_4}{10^6} = 0.7 \times \frac{L_{10h} \times 60 \times 1600}{10^6}$$

$$N_4 = 0.0672 L_{10h} \text{ million revolutions}$$

Equivalent dynamic (radial) load during entire work cycle (F_e).

$$F_e = \sqrt[3]{\frac{N_1 F_1^3 + N_2 F_2^3 + N_3 F_3^3 + N_4 F_4^3}{N_1 + N_2 + N_3 + N_4}}$$

$$F_e = \sqrt[3]{\frac{1.92 \times 10^{-3} \times L_{10h} \times 6498.5^3 + 4.8 \times 10^{-3} L_{10h} \times 3400^3 + 0.0221 \, L_{10h} \times 2800^3 + 0.0672 \times L_{10h} \times 0^3}{1.92 \times 10^{-3} L_{10h} + 4.8 \times 10^{-3} L_{10h} + 0.022 \, L_{10h} + 0.0672 \, L_{10h}}}$$

$$F_{eq} = \sqrt[3]{12.51} = 2.32 \text{ kN} = 2322 \text{ N}$$

(i) Rating life of bearing (L_{10}):

$$L_{10} = \left(\frac{C}{F_e}\right)^P = \left(\frac{17300}{2322}\right)^3 = 413.6 \text{ million revolutions}$$

L_{10} = 413.6 million revolutions

Actual revolutions completed by bearing during entire work cycle (L).

$$L = \frac{4500 \times 60 \times 1600}{10^6} \qquad \ldots \left(\frac{L_h \times 60 \times n}{10^6} = L\right)$$

L = 432 million revolutions

Reliability of bearing (R)

$$\frac{L}{L_{10}} = \left[\frac{\log_e (1/R)}{\log_e (1/R_{90})}\right]^{1/1.17}$$

$$\frac{432}{413.6} = \left[\frac{\log_e (1/R)}{\log_e (1/0.90)}\right]^{1/1.17} \Rightarrow R = 0.895$$

R = 89.5%

Example 3.7: The following data is given for a belt drive.

Diameter of pulley = 250 mm
Shaft diameter = 20 mm
Power transmitted = 5 kW
Speed = 720 rpm
Ratio of belt tensions = 3 : 1
Load factor = 3

Assume the pulley to be placed centrally with the belt tension acting vertically downwards. The required reliability of the bearing is 95% with life of 10,000 hours. Find the dynamic capacity of the bearing, when the bearings are selected from the manufacturer's catalogue, which lists dynamic load carrying capacity at 90% reliability.

Solution: Type of bearing – Single row deep groove

$$D = 250 \text{ mm}$$
$$d = 20 \text{ mm}$$
$$\text{Power} = 5 \text{ kW}$$
$$n = 720 \text{ rpm}$$
$$\frac{P_1}{P_2} = 3$$
$$K_a = 3$$
$$L_h = 10{,}000 \text{ hours}$$

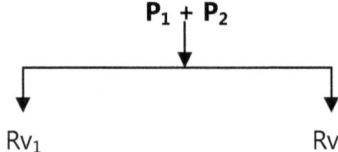

Belt tension
$$\frac{P_1}{P_2} = 3, \quad P = 3P_2$$

Belt speed (v)
$$v = \frac{\pi \cdot D \cdot n}{60000}$$
$$v = \frac{\pi \times 250 \times 720}{60000}$$
$$v = 9.4248 \text{ m/s}$$

Power transmitted by belt
$$kW = (P_1 - P_2) \cdot v$$
$$5 \times 10^3 = (3P_2 - P_2) \cdot 9.4248$$
$$P_2 = 265.26 \text{ N}$$
$$P_1 = 3P_2 = 795.77 \text{ N}$$

Radial load at each bearing
$$Rv_1 = Rv_2 = \frac{P_1 + P_2}{2} = \frac{795.77 + 265.26}{2} = 530.52 \text{ N} = F_r$$

Axial load = 0 N (= F_a)
$$K_a = 3$$
$$F_e = (X \cdot V \cdot F_r + Y \cdot F_a) \cdot K_a \quad \ldots \text{(Equivalent dynamic radial load)}$$
$$= (1 \times 1 \times 530.52 + 0) \times 3$$
F_e = 1591.56 N

Rating life of bearing (L_{10})

$$L = \frac{L_h \times 60 \times n}{10^6} = \frac{10000 \times 60 \times 720}{10^6}$$

L = 432 million revolutions

Now,
$$\frac{L}{L_{10}} = \left[\frac{\log_e (1/R)}{\log_e (1/R_{90})}\right]^{1/1.17}$$

$$\frac{432}{L_{10}} = \left[\frac{\log_e (1/0.95)}{\log_e (1/0.90)}\right]^{1/1.17}$$

L_{10} = 799.24 million revolutions

Basic dynamic load capacity (C),

$$L_{10} = \left(\frac{C}{F_e}\right)^P$$

$$799.24 = \left(\frac{C}{1591.56}\right)^3$$

C = 14770.06 N = 14.8 kN

Thus, bearing with basic dynamic load capacity greater than 14.8 kN should be selected for this application.

Example 3.8: A transmission shaft is supported by two deep groove ball bearings at two ends. The C.D. between the bearings is 160 mm. A load of 300 N acts vertically downwards at 60 mm distance from the left hand bearing whereas a load of 550 N acts horizontally at 50 mm distance from right hand bearing. Shaft speed is 3000 rpm and expected life of the bearings is 7000 hours with a reliability of 95%. It is intended to use same bearing at both ends of the shaft. Calculate dynamic load rating of the bearing so that it can be selected from manufacturer's catalogue. Load application factor is 1.5.

Solution: Type of bearing – Single row deep groove

$$n = 3000 \text{ rpm}$$
$$L_h = 7000 \text{ hours}$$

Considering vertical plane

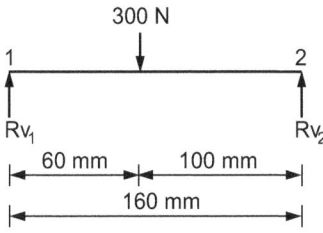

Fig. 3.15

Taking moment at point 1, i.e. $\Sigma M_1 = 0$

$$-300 \times 60 + Rv_2 \times 160 = 0$$
$$Rv_2 = 112.5 \text{ N}$$
$$\Sigma F_y = 0$$
$$\therefore \quad Rv_1 + Rv_2 - 300 = 0$$
$$Rv_1 = 300 - 112.5$$
$$\mathbf{Rv_1 = 187.5 \text{ N}}$$

Consider horizontal plane

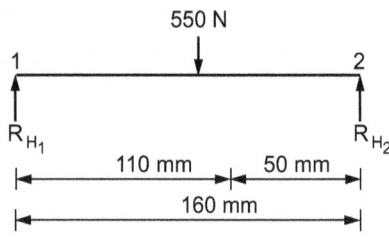

Fig. 3.16

Taking moment at point 1

i.e.
$$\Sigma M_1 = 0$$
$$-550 \times 110 + R_{H2} \times 160 = 0$$
$$\mathbf{R_{H2} = 378.13 \text{ N}}$$
$$\Sigma F_x = 0$$
$$R_{H1} + R_{H2} - 550 = 0$$
$$R_{H1} = 550 - 378.13$$
$$\mathbf{R_{H1} = 171.88 \text{ N}}$$

Resultant radial load at bearing 1
$$F_{r1} = \sqrt{Rv_1^2 + R_{H1}^2} = \sqrt{187.5^2 + 171.88^2}$$
$$\mathbf{F_{r1} = 254.36 \text{ N}}$$

Resultant radial load at bearing 2.
$$F_{r2} = \sqrt{Rv_2^2 + R_{H2}^2} = \sqrt{112.5^2 + 378.13^2}$$
$$\mathbf{F_{r2} = 394.51 \text{ N}}$$

Axial load on bearings 1 and 2 is zero.
$$K_a = 1.5$$

Equivalent dynamic load (P_e)

At bearing 1
$$F_{e1} = (XVF_{r1} + Y \cdot F_{a1}) \cdot K_a = (1 \times 1 \times 254.36 + 0) \times 1.5$$
$$\mathbf{F_{e1} = 381.54 \text{ N}}$$

At bearing 2

$$F_{e2} = (X \cdot V \cdot F_{r2} + Y \cdot F_{a2}) \cdot K_a = (1 \times 1 \times 394.51 + 0) \times 1.5$$

$$F_{e2} = 591.77 \text{ N}$$

Rating life of bearing, (L_{10})

$$L = \frac{L_h \times 60 \times n}{10^6} = \frac{7000 \times 60 \times 3000}{10^6}$$

$$L = 1260 \text{ million revolutions}$$

$$\frac{L}{L_{10}} = \left[\frac{\log_e (1/R)}{\log_e (1/R_{90})}\right]^{1/1.17}$$

$$\frac{1260}{L_{10}} = \left[\frac{\log_e (1/0.95)}{\log_e (1/0.90)}\right]^{1/1.17}$$

$$L_{10} = 2331.12 \text{ million revolutions}$$

Basic dynamic load capacity (C)

$$L_{10} = \left(\frac{C}{F_e}\right)^p$$

$$2331.12 = \left(\frac{C}{591.77}\right)^3$$

$$C = 7846.47 \text{ N}$$

Example 3.9: A shaft is supported on two bearings A and B which are 250 mm apart. A gear is attached at a distance of 100 mm on the right from left hand side bearing A. Weight of pulley is 100 N which is attached at an overhang of 150 mm on the right of the right hand side bearing B. Horizontal belt tensions are 498 N and 166 N respectively. Horizontal tangential force component for the gear is 497 N which is directed same as belt tensions. Vertically downwards radial force component for the gear is 181 N. The load factor for application is 2.5 and expected life of bearing is 8000 hours. If the shaft speed is 720 rpm. Find dynamic load capacity for bearings A and B so that they can be selected from manufacturer's catalogue.

Solution: Type of bearing – Single row deep groove

P_1 = 498 N
P_2 = 166 N
F_t = Tangential force on gear = 497 N
F_r = Radial force on gear = 181 N
K_a = 2.5
L_{10h} = 8000 hours
n = 720 rpm
W = 100 N = Weight of pulley

Considering vertical plane

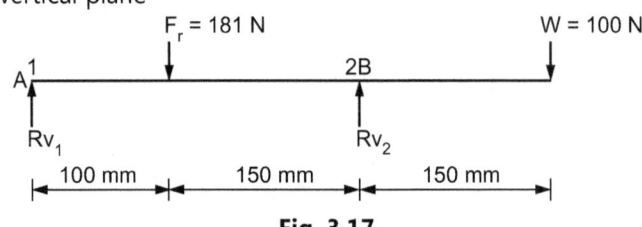

Fig. 3.17

Taking moment at point 1,
$$\Sigma M_1 = 0$$
$$-181 \times 100 + R_{v_2} \times 250 - 100 \times 400 = 0$$
$$\mathbf{R_{v_2} = 232.4 \ N}$$
$$\Sigma F_y = 0$$
$$R_{v_1} - 181 + 232.4 - 100 = 0$$
$$\mathbf{R_{v_1} = 48.6 \ N}$$

Considering horizontal plane

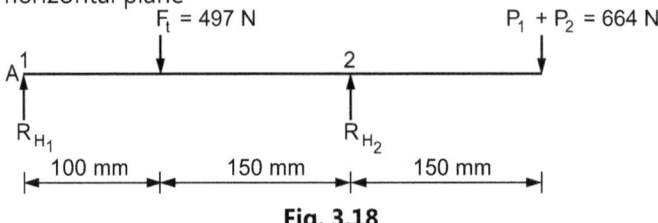

Fig. 3.18

Taking moment at point 1,
$$\Sigma M_1 = 0$$
$$R_{H2} \times 250 - 497 \times 100 - 664 \times 400 = 0$$
$$\mathbf{R_{H2} = 1261.2 \ N}$$
$$\Sigma F_x = 0$$
$$R_{H1} + R_{H2} - 497 - 664 = 0$$
$$\mathbf{R_{H1} = -100.2 \ N}$$
$$F_{r1} = \sqrt{(R_{v_1})^2 + (R_{H1})^2} = 111.36 \ N$$
$$F_{r2} = \sqrt{(R_{v_2})^2 + (R_{H2})^2} = 1282.43 \ N$$
$$K_a = 2.5$$
$$F_{e1} = (X \cdot V \cdot F_{r1} + Y \cdot F_{a1}) \cdot K_a$$
$$= (1 \times 1 \times 111.36 + 0) \times 2.5$$
$$\mathbf{P_{e1} = 278.4 \ N}$$
$$F_{e2} = (X \cdot V \cdot F_{r2} + Y \cdot F_{a2}) \cdot K_a$$
$$= (1 \times 1 \times 1282.43 + 0) \times 2.5$$
$$\mathbf{P_{e2} = 3206.08 \ N}$$

Rating life of bearing (L_{10})

$$L_{10} = \frac{L_{10h} \times 60 \times n}{10^6} = \frac{8000 \times 60 \times 720}{10^6}$$

L_{10} = 345.6 million revolutions

For bearing 1

$$L_{10} = \left(\frac{C_1}{F_{e1}}\right)^P \Rightarrow 345.6 = \left(\frac{C_1}{278.4}\right)^3 \Rightarrow \mathbf{C_1 = 1953.71\ N}$$

For bearing 2

$$L_{10} = \left(\frac{C_2}{F_{e2}}\right)^P = \left(\frac{C_2}{3206.08}\right)^3$$

$$L_{10} = 345.6$$

C_2 = 22499.12 N

Example 3.10: Using a constant $k = 60.8 \times 10^6$ N/mm² in the Stribeck's equation, compute the static capacity of a single row deep groove ball bearing series 208 with 9 balls having diameter of 12 mm.

Solution: As per Stribeck's equation of static capacity for ball bearing,

$$C_o = \frac{Kd^2Z}{5}$$

$$C_o = \frac{60.8 \times 10^6 \times 12^2 \times 9}{5}$$

$C_o = 1.5759 \times 10^{10}$ N

Example 3.11: An equivalent radial load on a bearing varies continuously from 0 to 20 kN in a sinusoidal manner. Determine the dynamic load rating at 90% reliability, if the bearing is to have a life of 20 million revolutions at a reliability of 99%. Assume shaft speed as 1000 rpm.

Use life reliability relationship as

$$\frac{L}{L_{10}} = \left[9.491 \log_e\left(\frac{1}{R}\right)\right]^{1/1.17}$$

Solution: Type of bearing – Single row deep groove ball bearing

$$P_{max} = 20 \times 10^3$$
$$L_{o1} = \text{Rating life of bearing} = 20 \text{ million revolutions}$$
$$n = 1000 \text{ rpm}$$

Equation for variable load is given by,

$$P = P_{max} \cdot \sin^2(\theta/2)$$
$$= P_{max} \cdot \left(\frac{1 - \cos\theta}{2}\right)$$

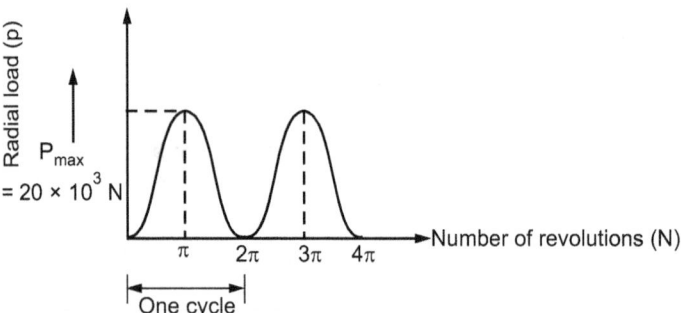

Fig. 3.19

Considering the work cycle for $\theta = 0$ to $\theta = 2\pi$

We have,

$$P_e = \left[\frac{1}{N}\int P^p \cdot dN\right]^{1/P}$$

$$P_e = \left[\frac{1}{N}\int P^3 \, dN\right]^{1/3}$$

$$= \left[\frac{1}{2\pi}\int_0^{2\pi} (P_{max})^3 \times \frac{(1-\cos\theta)^3}{8} \, d\theta\right]^{1/3}$$

$$= \frac{P_{max}}{2}\left[\frac{1}{2\pi}\int_0^{2\pi} (1-\cos\theta)^3 \cdot d\theta\right]^{1/3}$$

$$= \frac{P_{max}}{2}\left[\frac{1}{2\pi}\int_0^{2\pi} (1 - 3\cos\theta + 3\cos^2\theta - \cos^3\theta) \cdot d\theta\right]^{1/3}$$

$$= \frac{P_{max}}{2}\left[\frac{1}{2\pi}\int_0^{2\pi} \left\{1 - 3\cos\theta + 3\left[\frac{1+\cos 2\theta}{2}\right] - \cos\theta(1-\sin^2\theta)\right\} \cdot d\theta\right]^{1/3}$$

$$= \frac{P_{max}}{2}\left[\frac{1}{2\pi}\int_0^{2\pi} \left(\frac{5}{2} - 4\cos\theta + \frac{3}{2}\cos\theta + \sin^2\theta \cdot \cos\theta\right) d\theta\right]^{1/3}$$

$$= \frac{P_{max}}{2}\left[\frac{1}{2\pi}\left[\frac{5}{2}\theta - 4\sin\theta + \frac{3}{2}\cdot\frac{\sin^2\theta}{2} + \frac{\sin^3\theta}{3}\right]_0^{2\pi}\right]^{1/3}$$

Unit 3 | 3.42

$$= \frac{P_{max}}{2}\left[\frac{1}{2\pi}\left(\frac{5}{2}\times 2\pi - 0 + 0 + 0\right)\right]^{1/3} = \frac{P_{max}}{2}\left[\frac{5}{2}\right]^{1/3}$$

$$= \frac{20\times 10^3}{2}\left[\frac{5}{2}\right]^{1/3} \Rightarrow P_e = 13572.09 \text{ N}$$

$$\frac{L}{L_{10}} = \left[9.491 \log_e\left(\frac{1}{R}\right)\right]^{1/1.17}$$

$$\frac{20}{L_{10}} = \left[9.491 \log_e\left(\frac{1}{0.99}\right)\right]^{1/1.17}$$

L_{10} = 149.02 million revolutions

Basic dynamic load capacity, (C)

$$L_{10} = \left(\frac{C}{P_e}\right)^P$$

$$149.02 = \left(\frac{C}{13572.09}\right)^3$$

C = 71955.1 N

Example 3.12: A deep groove ball bearing operating under a constant load rotates at 700 rpm for 50% of cycle time, 1000 rpm for 30% of cycle time and 1500 rpm for rest of the cycle. The outer race of the bearing rotates. Considering load factor as 1.3 and radial and axial loads to be 3.0 kN and 1.5 kN, determine expected life bearings with 95% reliability, if the dynamic load capacity of the bearings is 45 kN. Consider radial load factor X = 0.56 and axial load factor, Y = 1.71.

Solution:

Rotation factor, V = 1.2 (since outer race is rotatory)
Load factor i.e. service factor = 1.3
Equivalent load

$$F_{eq} = 1.3\ (X\ V\ F_r + Y\cdot F_a)$$
$$= 1.3\ (0.56 \times 3.0 \times 1.2 + 1.71 \times 1.5)$$
$$= 5.955 \text{ kN}$$

(This load is constant)
Average shaft speed

$$= \frac{700 \times 0.5t + 1000 \times 0.30t + 1500 \times 0.2t}{(0.5t + 0.3t + 0.2t)}$$

N_{av} = 950 rpm

Rated life is given by

$$C = F_e L^{1/3}$$

∴ $$L = \left(\frac{C}{F_e}\right)^3 = \left(\frac{45}{5.955}\right)^3 = 431.51 \text{ million revolutions}$$

This is L_{10} life i.e. at 90% reliability.

Life at 95% reliability will be given by

$$\frac{L}{L_{10}} = \left[\frac{\log_e\left(\frac{1}{R_{95}}\right)}{\log_e\left(\frac{1}{R_{90}}\right)}\right]^{\frac{1}{1.17}}$$

$$= \left[\frac{\log_e\left(\frac{1}{0.95}\right)}{\log_e\left(\frac{1}{0.9}\right)}\right]^{\frac{1}{1.17}}$$

$$= [0.4868]^{1/1.17}$$

$$\frac{L}{L_{10}} = 0.540$$

∴ $L = 0.540 \times L_{10} = 0.54 \times 431.51$

$= 233$ million revolutions

∴ Life in hours $= \dfrac{233 \times 10^6}{950 \times 60} = 4087.7$ hours

Example 3.13: A shaft rotating at 1000 rpm is supported in bearings at its ends. Left side bearing has a radial load of 2500 N and axial load of 1200 N. Right side bearing has a radial load of 3000 N and axial load is zero. For commonisation it is proposed to use single row deep groove ball bearing 6307 with static load capacity as 18000 N and dynamic load capacity of 33200 N. What is expected trouble free life in hours.

Use following table for radial and thrust factors.

$\left(\dfrac{F_a}{C_o}\right)$	$\left(\dfrac{F_o}{F_r}\right) \leq e$		$\left(\dfrac{F_a}{F_r}\right) > e$		e
	X	Y	X	Y	
0.04	1	0	0.56	1.8	0.24
0.07	1	0	0.56	1.6	0.27
0.130	1	0	0.56	1.4	0.31

Considering L.H. bearing

$F_a = 1200$, $F_r = 2500$, $\dfrac{F_a}{F_r} = 0.48$, $F_a = 1200$, $C_o = 18000$, $\dfrac{F_a}{C_o} = 0.066$

'e' for $\dfrac{F_a}{C_o} = 0.066$ is between 0.24 to 0.27

∴ $\dfrac{F_a}{F_r} > e$

∴ $X = 0.56$

Value of Y is found by interpolation for $\dfrac{F_a}{C_o} = 0.066$

$$Y = 1.8 - \dfrac{(1.8 - 1.6) \times (0.066 - 0.04)}{(0.07 - 0.04)}$$

$$= 1.627$$

Radial load factor, $X = 0.56$

Axial load factor, $Y = 1.627$

∴ $(F_{eq})_{LH} = V \cdot X \cdot F_r + Y \cdot F_a$ (With V = 1 for inner race rotating)

$(F_{eq})_{LH} = 1 \times 0.56 \times 2500 + 1.627 \times 1200$

$= 1400 + 1952.4$

$= 3352.4$ N

Considering RH bearings:

$(F_{eq})_{RH} = 3000$ N (Since there is no axial load, X = 1)

∴ Load on LH bearing is critical

$F_{eq} = 3352.4$ N

Bearing life which can be expected is given by

$$C = F_e L^{1/3}$$

∴ $$L = \left(\dfrac{C}{F_e}\right)^3$$

$$= \left(\dfrac{33200}{3352.4}\right)^3$$

$= 971.285$ million revolutions

Life in hours at 1000 rpm will be

$$= \dfrac{971.285 \times 10^6}{60 \times 1000}$$

$= 16188$ hours

EXERCISE

1. What is preloading of bearing? How it is achieved. **(May 2013)**
2. What is the objective of preloading? Explain mounting and preloading of a taper roller bearing with appropriate sketch. **(October 2012)**
3. Discuss equivalent dynamic load and load life relationship for rolling contact bearing. **(October 2012)**
4. What is the objective of bearing preloading?

5. Explain the mounting and preloading of a taper roller bearing with appropriate sketch. **(April 2009, 2012; October 2011)**
6. Derive Stribeck's equation for static capacity of a rolling contact bearing. **(April 2009, 2012; October 2011)**
7. Discuss "Load-Life" relationship for rolling contact bearings. **(April 2010)**
8. Discuss preloading of rolling contact bearingas. **(April 2010)**
9. Compare ball bearing with roller bearing. **(April 2012, October 2011)**
10. Derive the expression for the equivalent load for the rolling contact bearing operating under cyclic loads in usual notation.
11. What are the basic principles to be followed in bearing mounting. **(October 2011)**
12. What do you understand by rating and median life of the bearing.
13. Write short note on lubrication of bearing. **(October 2011)**

✸✸✸

Unit IV
WORM GEARS

4.1 WORM/ WORM GEARS

Simplest way to obtain large speed reduction with high torque in a compact space is with worm gear drives.

A worm drive is a cylindrical worm with a shallow spiral thread that engages with the worm gear in a non-intersecting perpendicular axes configuration. Worm and gear have same hand of helix. Worm is like a screw and can have single or multiple starts. Meshing action is combined rolling and sliding.

 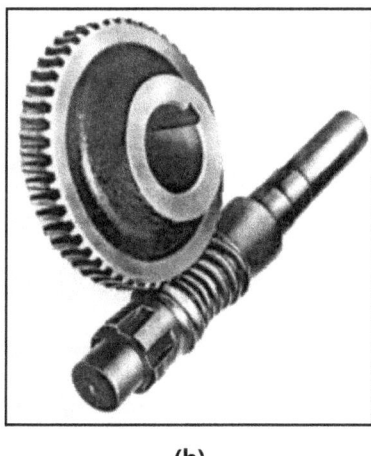

(a) (b)

Fig. 4.1: Typical Worm and Worm Wheel Set in Mesh

Advantages of worm/Worm Gear Pair:
- Worm gear drives are used for higher speed ratios ranging from 10 : 1 to 100 : 1.
- Attains high reduction ratio in single pair. This gives a compact arrangement. For this reason worm gear drives are very common in industrial applications where compactness is important.
- It can be designed for irreversibility. This makes it specially important for applications where irreversibility is a critical requirement.
- Operation is smooth and silent.

Limitations:
- The efficiency of worm – worm gear is however low and therefore they are not usually used for transmitting very large powers. (usually < 75 kW).

- Low efficiency results into more heat generation. The temperature rise of the lubricant limits the power transmission capacity of the gear pair.
- Gear is usually made of Phosphor Bronze which is a costly material.

Worm-Worm Gear Materials:

Since sliding is predominant in case of worm gear drive, different materials are used for worm and worm wheel. Worm material is hardened and made of better grade material. Worm wheel teeth are difficult to manufacture and therefore are made of soft material.

Worm undergoes more number of contact stress cycles than the worm gear and therefore a stronger material is usually selected for worm.

Materials for Worm:

Carbon Steel: They are inexpensive and strong but susceptible to corrosion.

Alloy Steel: They have superior strength, durability and corrosion resistance. They can also be hardened.

Worm Gear Materials:

Cast iron: It provides durability and ease of manufacture.

Brass: This material is inexpensive, easy to mold and corrosion resistant.

Bronze: This is an alloy consisting primarily of copper and other metals. The addition of other metals (usually tin), produces an alloy much harder than plain copper.

Phosphor bronze is an alloy of copper with 3.5 to 10% of tin and up to 1% phosphorus. Phosphor bronze has high toughness, strength, low coefficient of friction, and fine grain. The phosphorus also improves the fluidity of the molten metal and thereby improves the castability.

Aluminium bronze: 5 to 11% aluminium is added to copper as the main alloying element. The alloy has excellent wear resistance and industrial applications.

Selection of material will depend on the application details. Following guideline can be used.

(a) **Light duty:** For lighter loads and low speed application, worm is made of steel and worm.

(b) **Medium duty:** For such an application, worm is made of case hardened steel and wheel of phosphor bronze.

(c) **Heavy duty:** For heavy duty application, worm is made of alloy steel and wheel of phosphor bronze chilled to increase hardness.

4.2 WORM/WORM GEARS – DIMENSIONS AND PROPORTIONS

Worm:

Axial Pitch (p_x): It is the distance from any point on one thread to the corresponding point on the adjacent thread, measured parallel to the worm axis.

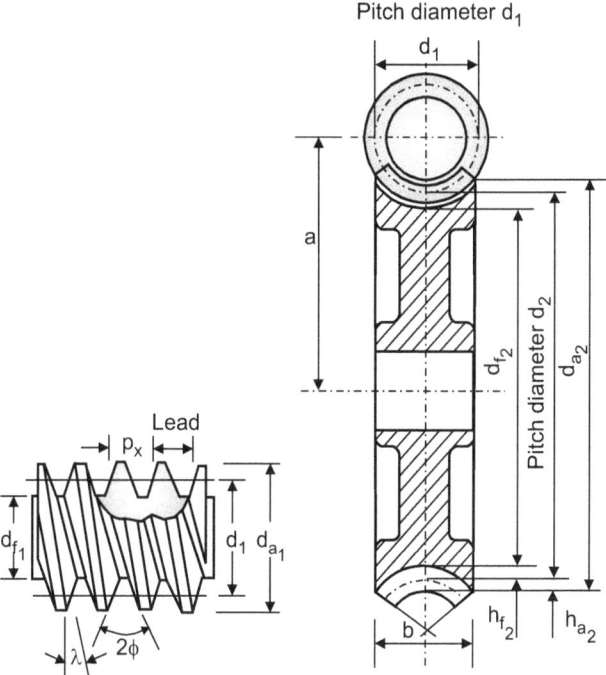

Fig. 4.2: Worm and Worm Wheel - Major Dimensions

Lead (L): It is the linear distance travelled by a thread when one complete revolution is given to the worm.

Then lead, $\qquad L = Z_1 \times p_x \qquad$ ... (4.1)

where Z_1 is the number of starts on the worm.

For a single start worm, lead is equal to the axial pitch and for double start worm thread, lead is twice the axial pitch and so on. Axial pitch of the worm is equal to the circular pitch of the worm gear.

Lead Angle λ:

It is the angle between the tangent to the thread helix on the pitch cylinder and the plane normal to the axis of the worm.

Lead angles (λ) are usually selected in the range 9° to 45°, since angles smaller than 9° result in rapid wear of worm tooth and very low efficiency.

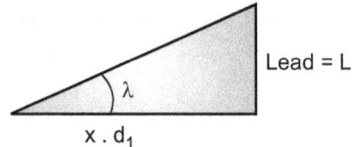

Fig. 4.3: Thread Helix on Worm

Helix angle of worm (ψ_w): It is the angle between the tangent to the thread helix on the pitch cylinder and the axis of the worm. Thus,

Helix angle, $\psi = 90 - \lambda$

Velocity Ratio:

Let,

$$N_1 = \text{Worm speed (rpm)}$$
$$N_2 = \text{Worm gear speed (rpm)}$$
$$D = \text{Pitch circle diameter of worm gear}$$

Linear Velocity of the Worm:

$$V_1 = \frac{L \times N_1}{60}$$

Linear Velocity of the Worm Gear:

$$V_2 = \frac{\pi \times d_2 \times N_2}{60}$$

Since $V_1 = V_2$ $L \times N_1 = \pi \times d_2 \times N_2$

Therefore, Velocity Ratio:

$$V_R = \frac{N_1}{N_2} = \frac{\pi \times d_2}{L}$$

Since, $\pi \times d_2 = Z_2 \times p_c$ and $L = Z_1 \times p_x$

$$V_R = \frac{Z_2 \times p_c}{Z_1 \times p_x} = \frac{Z_2}{Z_1} \text{ (Since } p_c = p_x\text{)} \qquad \ldots (4.2)$$

$$V_R = \frac{\text{Number of teeth in gear}}{\text{Number of starts on worm}}$$

Other Relations:

Axial pitch, $p_x = \pi \times m = \dfrac{\text{Lead}}{Z_1}$ where, m is the module in mm.

With multi start threads, the velocity ratio reduces but the efficiency increases. For velocity ratios above 30, usually single start worm will be preferred.

Table 4.1: Selection of Velocity ratio Vs No of starts on worm

Number of starts on Worm (Z_1)	1	3	4
Velocity Ratio (i)	12-36	8-12	6-10

Diametral Quotient (q): It is defined as the ratio of pitch circle diameter of worm to its module.

$$q = \frac{d_1}{m} \qquad \ldots (4.3)$$

where, d_1 = Pitch circle diameter of the worm

As can be seen, for a given value of module, the worm diameter 'd_1' increases as 'q' increases. Worm diameter serves as a shaft diameter to carry bending moment as well as torque. A larger 'q' will therefore result in a stronger worm but at the same time size as well as the cost goes up.

Values of standard module are: 1, 1.25, 1.5, 2, 2.5, 3, 4, 5, 6, 8, 10, 12, 16, 20 mm.

Values of q range from 8 to 18. Higher values used usually for low modules.

Standard values are 8, 10, 12.5, 16, 20, 25.

Transverse Pressure Angle (ϕ_t): It is the pressure angle measured in plane of rotation (transverse plane) of gear.

Normal Pressure Angle (ϕ_n): It is the pressure angle measured in the plane perpendicular to the teeth (normal plane) of gear.

$\tan \phi_t = (\tan \phi_n / \cos \lambda)$ OR $\tan \phi_t = (\tan \phi_n / \cos \phi_g)$

ϕ_n value is standard value selected from: 14.5°, 20°, 25°, 30°

Efficiency of worm/worm gear drive depends on values of coefficient of friction (μ), lead angle (λ) and pressure angle (ϕ_n). Greater normal pressure angles are selected for larger lead angles.

Normally selected values are:

Lead angle (λ)	4-15°	15-30°
Pressure angle (ϕ_n)	14.5°	20°

Face Width of Gear Tooth (b):

Referring to the Fig. 4.4, showing worm/worm gear pair, tangent to the pitch circle of the worm intersects its addendum circle at B and B_1. BB_1 is the minimum width that should be provided on the worm gear.

Let
b = Width of the gear tooth (mm)
d_{a1} = Addendum circle diameter of the worm
d_1 = Pitch Circle Diameter of the worm
h_{a1} = Addendum of the worm

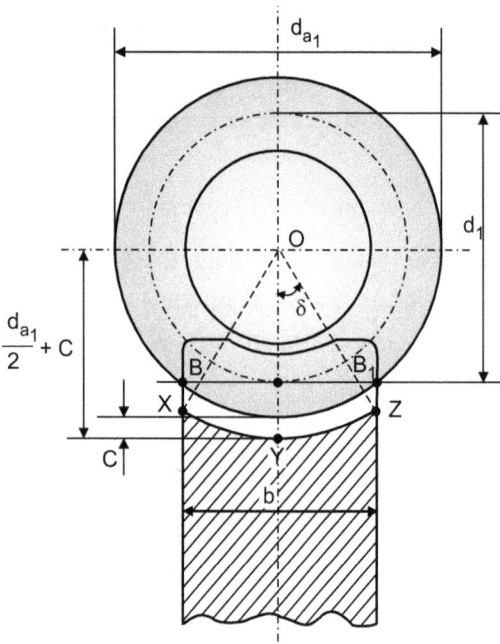

Fig. 4.4: Gear Width

Width 'b' should be $\geq BB_1$

$$BB_1 = 2 \cdot BC = 2 \cdot \sqrt{OB^2 - OC^2} = 2 \cdot \sqrt{\left(\frac{d_{a1}}{2}\right)^2 - \left(\frac{d_1}{2}\right)^2} = \sqrt{d_{a1}^2 - d_1^2}$$

Since $d_{a1} = d_1 + 2h_{a1}$

$$b \geq \sqrt{4 \cdot d_1 \cdot h_{a1} + 4 \cdot h_{a1}^2}$$

$$b \geq 2\sqrt{q \cdot m \,(m) + m^2} \geq 2 \cdot m \sqrt{q + 1}$$

Thus $b \geq 2 \cdot m \sqrt{q + 1}$ ... (4.4)

A minimum width of $0.73 \times d_1$ is recommended for the worm gear.

Thus, $b \geq 2 \cdot m\sqrt{q + 1}$ OR $0.73 \times d_1$

whichever is larger.

Table 4.2 shows proportions and major dimensions for a worm and worm wheel.

Table 4.2: Standard Proportions of Worm and Worm Wheel

Worm		
Addendum of Worm	h_{a1}	$= m$
Dedenum of Worm	h_{f1}	$= (2.2 \cos \lambda - 1) \cdot mm$
Outer Diameter	d_{a1}	$= d_1 + 2 \cdot h_{a1}$
Root Diameter	d_{f1}	$= d_1 - 2 \cdot h_{f1}$
Length of Worm	L_w	$= \pi \cdot m \cdot (4.5 + Z_g/50)$
Worm Wheel		
Addendum of Wheel	h_{a2}	$= 2(\cos \lambda - 1) \cdot m$
Dedenum of Worm	h_{f2}	$= (1 + 0.2 \cos \lambda) \cdot m$
Outer Diameter	d_{a2}	$= d_2 + 2 \cdot h_{a2}$
Root Diameter	d_{f2}	$= d_2 - 2 \cdot h_{f2}$
Clearance	C	$= 0.2 \cos \lambda$
Face Width	b	$=$

4.3 GEAR ENVELOPING AND RIM CONSTRUCTIONS

Single Enveloping:

In a single enveloping worm set width of the worm gear is cut into concave surface. This partially encloses the worm. As can be seen from the Fig. 4.5 (a), only the middle thread on the worm will have full engagement and the side threads have partial engagement. This is used in high speed and low load condition.

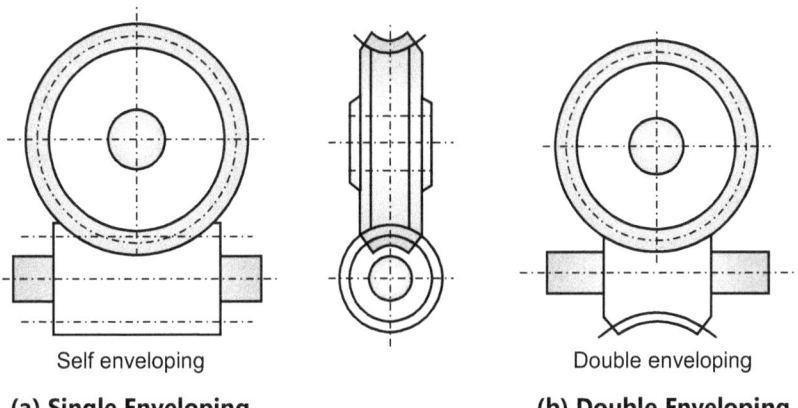

Self enveloping   Double enveloping

(a) Single Enveloping   **(b) Double Enveloping**

Fig. 4.5: Worm Gears

Double Enveloping:

In this case both, the width of the gear and the worm along its length, are cut with a concave shape to get better engagement as shown in Fig. 4.5 (b). With this both the worm and worm gear partially enclose each other. There are more teeth in contact and there is area contact rather than line contact. This permits higher load transmission.

Double enveloping gears are difficult to manufacture and mount compared with the single enveloping gears because of critical alignment requirements. They are used for higher load transmissions.

Worm wheel rim construction:

The following Fig. 4.6 shows different rim constructions for a worm wheel.

First arrangement shows straight teeth cut on a rim with a form cutter. This along with a straight worm will give no enveloping condition. This will give low efficiency and is used for very light service involving low load and intermittent service.

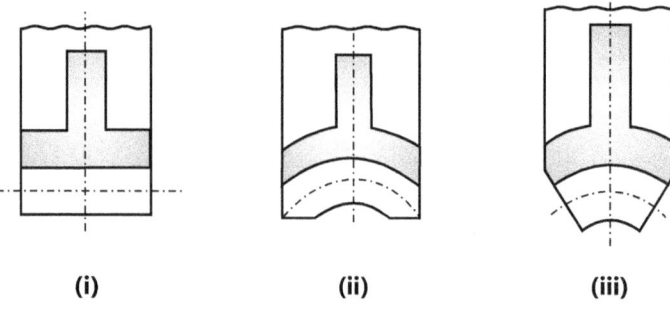

(i)   (ii)   (iii)

Fig. 4.6: Wheel Rims

In second arrangement, teeth are cut with a hob and ends of the gear teeth are cut parallel to the gear axis. This arrangement along with a straight worm will give single enveloping arrangement.

The third arrangement, in which worm gear teeth are cut radially towards the worm axis, characterises worm envelopment. This arrangement is used for heavy services.

First arrangement is easiest to manufacture but will give least efficiency on the other hand third arrangement is most difficult will give maximum efficiency. Alignment during mounting is also requires closer tolerances and hence is costly.

4.4 STRENGTH OF WORM AND WORM GEAR

Lewis Equation for Strength of Gear tooth (Beam Strength), S_b:

The approach used to find beam strength is similar to that of spur gears.

Since the material of the worm possesses higher mechanical properties than those of the worm wheel, the calculations are done to determine the strength of the worm wheel teeth only. The maximum load (S_b), which a worm wheel tooth can transmit, considering the tooth as a cantilever beam, is given as

$$S_b = \sigma_b \cdot b \cdot Y \cdot m_n = \sigma_b \cdot b \cdot Y \cdot m \cdot \cos\lambda \qquad \ldots (4.5)$$

where σ_b is the strength of the gear tooth material (N/mm^2) which is its maximum permissible bending stress. This could be taken as $= \frac{1}{3} \cdot S_{ult}$

b: Width of the gear wheel (mm) : Minimum of $b = 0.73 \times d_1$ or $b = 2m\sqrt{q+1}$

Y: Lewis form factor = 0.314 for 14.5° pressure angle

= 0.393 for 20° pressure angle

Buckingham's Wear Load Capacity of Gear tooth (Wear Strength) S_w:

Wear load capacity is calculated for worm and worm wheel pair as such and not for individual worm or worm wheel. Buckingham suggested following equation to find wear load rating in a worm gearing.

$$S_w = d_g \cdot b \cdot K_w \qquad \ldots (4.6)$$

where, K_W (N/mm^2) is the worm gear load stress factor (or wear constant). The factor depends on combination of material pair for worm and pressure/ lead angle.

Table 4.3: Typical Values of K_w can be taken as below

Worm	Worm Gear	K_w (N/mm^2)
Steel	Phosphor Bronze	0.51
Hardened Steel	Cast Iron	0.42
Hardened Steel	Phosphor Bronze	0.68
Hardened Steel	Chilled Phosphor Bronze	1.0

4.5 FORCE ANALYSIS OF WORM GEAR DRIVE

Consider a worm – worm wheel drive shown in Fig. 4.7 with worm rotating in anticlockwise direction. The worm shown has right hand threads and the worm is considered driver, as this will be the normal case.

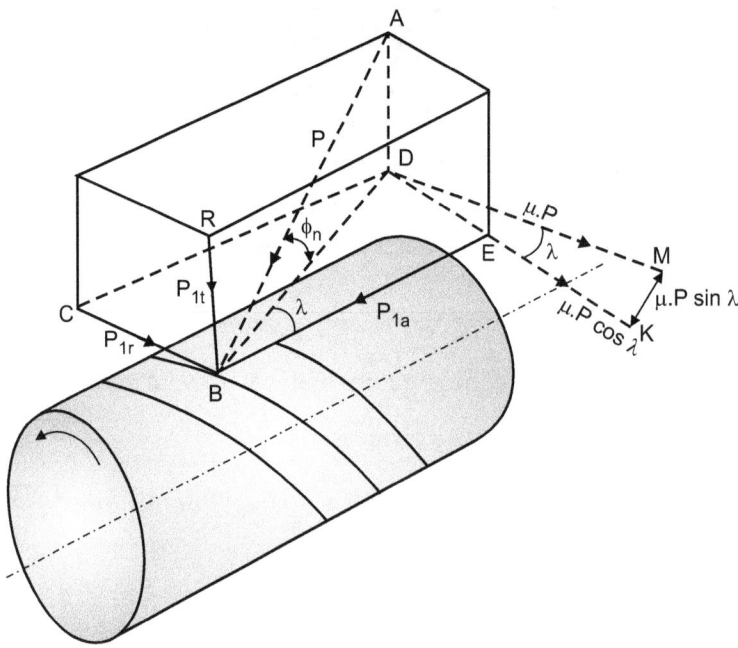

Fig. 4.7: Force Analysis : Forces on Worm

Let

P: be the normal resultant force acting between worm and worm wheel teeth

ϕ_n: Normal pressure angle

λ: Lead angle on worm (Helix angle on the worm gear)

P acts along AB which is perpendicular to BC and acts at an angle ϕ_n.

Components of P acting on the worm are as shown in the Fig. 4.7. Resolving P in the plane ABD.

Radial force P_{1r} = RB = AD = $P \cdot \sin \phi_n$ ... (4.7)

Normal force, BD = AB $\cos \phi_n$ = $P \cdot \cos \phi_n$ ... (4.8)

Normal force can be further resolved into

P_{1t} = CB = DE = BD $\cdot \sin \lambda$ = $P \cdot \cos \phi_n \cdot \sin \lambda$ ... (4.9)

P_{1a} = BE = BD $\cdot \cos \lambda$ = $P \cdot \cos \phi_n \cdot \cos \lambda$ ... (4.10)

Friction cannot be neglected between worm and worm wheel since there is sliding plus rolling action. Considering friction between and worm wheel, frictional force (μ.P) acts perpendicular to P and is considered to be acting in the plane of sliding. Frictional force (μ.P) as shown in Fig. 4.7 acts along DM which is perpendicular to BD. The direction of μ.P is such that it is opposing anticlockwise motion of worm at point B. Thus direction will be form D to M.

Friction force DM is further resolved as below.
Along, DK = $\mu \cdot P \cdot \cos \lambda$ (in the same direction as tangential force P_{1t}) and
Along, KM = $\mu \cdot P \cdot \sin \lambda$ (in the direction opposite to axial force P_{1a})
Superimposing frictional component on P_{1t} and P_{1a},
Total forces will be,

$$P_{1a} = P \cdot \cos \phi_n \cdot \cos \lambda - \mu \cdot P \cdot \sin \lambda = P(\cos \phi_n \cdot \cos \lambda - \mu \cdot \sin \lambda) \quad \ldots (4.11)$$
$$P_{1t} = P \cdot \cos \phi_n \cdot \sin \lambda + \mu \cdot P \cdot \cos \lambda = P(\cos \phi \sin \lambda + \mu \cdot \cos \lambda) \quad \ldots (4.12)$$
$$P_{1r} = P \cdot \sin \phi = P_{2r} \quad \ldots (4.13)$$

Prom this, P_{1a} and P_{1r} can be expressed in terms oP P_{1t} as

$$P_{1a} = P_{1t} \frac{(\cos \phi_n \cdot \cos \lambda - \mu \cdot \sin \lambda)}{(\cos \phi_n \cdot \sin \lambda + \mu \cdot \cos \lambda)} \quad \ldots (4.14)$$

$$P_{1r} = P_{1t} \frac{\sin \phi_n}{(\cos \phi_n \cdot \sin \lambda + \mu \cdot \cos \lambda)} \quad \ldots (4.15)$$

In practice knowing power transmission from the worm, values of P_{1t} will be known. $P_{1t} = \left(\dfrac{M_{1t}}{\dfrac{d_1}{2}}\right)$. Once value of P_{1t} is known, values of P_{1a} and P_{1r} can be found out using above relationships.

Fig. 4.8 shows the forces P_{1r}, P_{1t}, P_{1a} which are the radial, tangential and axial forces on the worm.

Equal and opposite forces will be acting on the worm wheel

$$\begin{aligned} P_{2t} &= P_{1a} \\ P_{2a} &= P_{1t} \\ P_{2r} &= P_{1r} \end{aligned} \quad \ldots (4.16)$$

and these are shown in the Fig. 4.8.

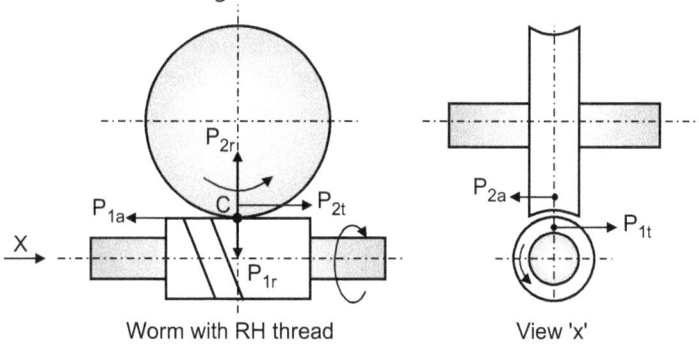

(a) **Worm with RH Threads** (b) **View - X**

Fig. 4.8: Forces on Worm Gear

Thus, the tangential, radial and axial components of forces on worm and worm wheel can be found out.

In practice designer will be required to establish the force and directions without going into force analysis every time. Before deciding the direction of forces of the worm and the worm wheel, it is necessary to first establish the direction of rotations of wheel.

Direction of Rotation for Worm and Gear:

In Fig. 4.9, consider worm to be rotating in anticlockwise direction as seen from left side and let the worm be having LH threads. Worm is considered similar to a thread and the worm wheel as a nut. Applying LH thumb rule, with fingers curling in the direction of rotation, worm will tend to move to right. The worm is not allowed to move axially and therefore will push the gear towards left side and thus the wheel will rotate clockwise. These directions of movements can be imagined about the contact point 'C' in Fig. 4.9.

If the hand of helix on worm was RH instead of LH, then we apply RH thumb rule and the directions of P_{2t} and P_{1a} would have been exactly opposite.

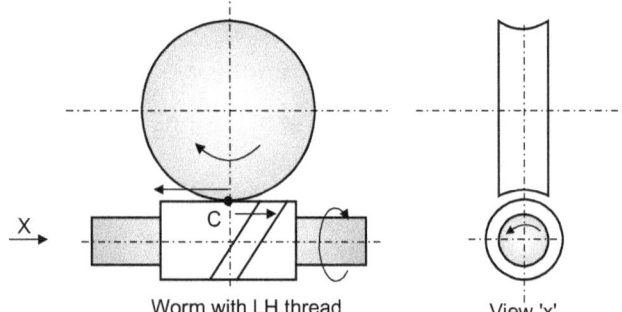

Worm with LH thread   View 'x'

Fig. 4.9: Worm and Gear Rotation Directions

Direction of Forces for Worm and Gear:

Once the directions of rotation are established, force directions can now be decided.

Force on the driver member is opposite to direction of motion.

Force on the driven member is in the direction of motion. The direction of motion is to be determined at the contact point 'C' shown in the Fig. 4.10.

Fig. 4.10 shows the worm gear pair with its direction of rotation as obtained in Fig. 4.9. The worm gear linear direction of motion is toward left as seen at point 'C'. Hence tangential force P_{2t} is also towards left. The axial force P_{1a} is in opposite to P_{2t} (to the right.).

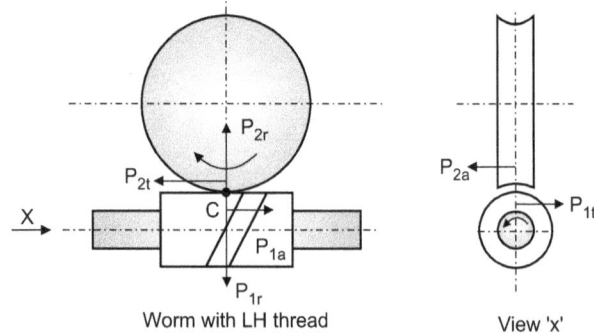

Worm with LH thread   View 'x'

Fig. 4.10: Worm and Worm Gear Force Directions

As seen from view X, worm (driving) is rotating in anticlockwise direction. Hence at the contact point, linear direction of motion of the worm is to the left. Hence tangential force P_{1t} is towards right. Axial force P_{2a} will be towards left.

Radial forces P_{1r} and P_{2r} are separating forces. Hence their directions will be from the contact point towards respective centers.

It can be seen that only P_{1t} and P_{2t} are useful components as they transmit torque. The radial and axial components are present and have to be sustained by the shaft and the bearings. These are considered during design of shaft and bearings.

4.6 COEFFICIENT OF FRICTION AND SLIDING VELOCITY

Thus to find the force components, it is necessary to know the coefficient of friction between the worm and worm wheel. The coefficient of friction depends on gear pair materials, lubricant used, accuracy of mounting and the sliding velocity (rubbing velocity) between the two.

Typical values of coefficient of friction for well lubricated gears are indicated below.

Table 4.4

Rubbing Velocity m/sec	1	2	3	4	5	6
Coefficient of friction	0.06	0.05	0.04	0.038	0.032	0.03

Sliding velocity is the relative velocity between worm and worm wheel. Consider top view of a worm with its axis A-A and the gear with axis B-B and that the position of worm is above the gear (Fig. 4.11). The direction of rotations of the worm and the gear are as marked in the figure. Velocities of worm (V_1) and gear (V_2) will then be as shown and sliding velocity will be

$$V_s = V_1 - V_2 \qquad \ldots (4.17)$$

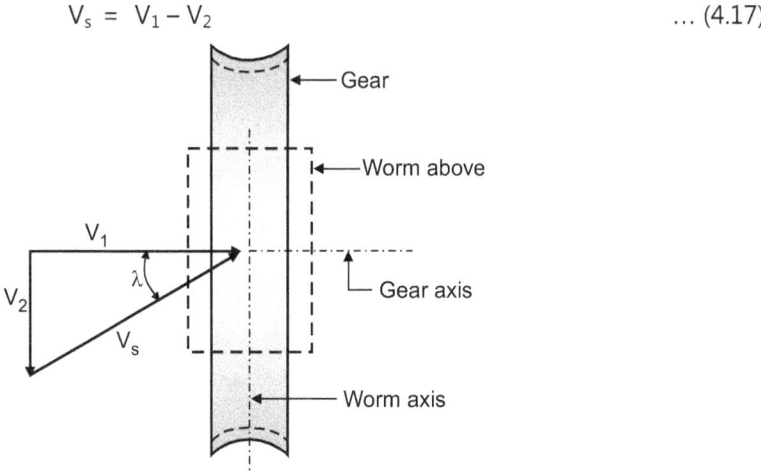

Fig. 4.11: Worm-Gear Sliding Velocity

Pitch line velocity of the worm is given by $V_1 = \dfrac{\pi \cdot d_1 \cdot n_1}{60 \times 1000}$

As seen from the Fig. 4.11, $V_s = V_1/\cos \lambda$

Rubbing velocity is obtained as a function of worm velocity and the lead angle.

4.7 EFFICIENCY OF WORM/WORM GEAR PAIR

Efficiency of a worm gear can be considered as ratio of output power to input power. (refer Fig. 4.8).

$$\eta = \frac{\text{Output power}}{\text{Input power}} = \frac{(P_2t)\left(\dfrac{d_2}{2}\right) \cdot N_2}{(P_{1t})\left(\dfrac{d_1}{2}\right) N_1} \qquad \ldots (4.18)$$

Now, Speed ratio $\dfrac{N_1}{N_2} = i$

and
$$\frac{d_2}{d_1} = \frac{Z_2}{q} = \frac{\left(\dfrac{Z_2}{Z_1}\right)}{\left(\dfrac{q}{Z_1}\right)} = \frac{i}{\dfrac{1}{\tan \lambda}} = i \cdot \tan \lambda \qquad \ldots (4.19)$$

Substituting values from equation (4.19) into (4.18).

$$\eta = \frac{P_2 t}{P_1 t} \cdot \tan \lambda = \frac{P_{1a}}{P_{1t}} \cdot \tan \lambda \qquad \ldots (4.20)$$

Substituting values from equations (4.14) efficiency is given by

$$\eta = \frac{P_{1a}}{P_{1t}} \cdot \tan \lambda = \frac{(\cos \phi_n \cos \lambda - \mu \cdot \sin \lambda)}{(\cos \phi_n \cdot \sin \lambda + \mu \cdot \cos \lambda)} \cdot \tan \lambda$$

This can be written as

$$\eta = \frac{\cos \phi_n - \mu \cdot \tan \lambda}{\cos \phi_n + \mu \cot \lambda} \qquad \ldots (4.21)$$

Alternately ϕ_v, is defined as the Virtual friction angle, such that

$$\phi_v = \tan^{-1} [\mu/\cos \phi_n] \qquad \ldots (4.22)$$

On substituting in the above equation equation, η can be reduced to form

$$\eta = \frac{\tan \lambda}{\tan (\phi_v + \lambda)} \qquad \ldots (4.23)$$

For initial estimation, efficiency of a worm gear pair can taken as

Table 4.5: Worm Gear Efficiency versus Worm starts

70 to 75%	For (Z_1 = 1): Single start
75 to 85%	For (Z_1 = 2): Double start
80 to 85%	For (Z_1 = 3): Tripple start
85 to 95%	For (Z_1 = 4): Quadruple start

Efficiency of Worm/Worm gear drive (η):

Overall efficiency of the drive will be total effect of gearing efficiency, together with losses in bearings and losses due to churning of the oil. Thus gear drive efficiency will be

$$\eta = \eta_g \cdot \eta_b \cdot \eta_c$$

$$\eta \approx 0.95 \times \eta_g$$

Considering other two losses as 5%

where, η_g = Efficiency of the gear pair considering gearing losses.

η_b = Efficiency considering bearing losses.

η_c = Efficiency considering churning losses.

Combined efficiency at bearings and that due to churning is however quite large (≈ 0.95) compared to gear pair efficiency.

Self Locking Drive:

Usually for a worm gear drive, worm is the driving member and gear is the driven member. As in case of screw mechanism, self locking will be achieved if the coefficient of friction is greater than tangent of the lead angle. (Friction angle is more than the lead angle). Thus if $\mu > \tan \lambda$, self locking is achieved. This property is important and is used with advantage in many material handling equipments where self locking can prevent accidental rotations of the worm wheel.

Effective Load on Worm Gear Tooth:

Theoretical tangential force acting on the gear, depends on the rated power to be transmitted and the efficiency of worm-gear pair. The dynamic load acting on the gear due to inaccuracies in teeth cutting and tooth deflection is accounted for by the velocity factor. Velocity factor for worm-wheel is usually taken as:

$$C_v = \frac{6}{6 + V_g}$$

The load value has to be further modified by a load factor (application factor) C_s, depending on nature of load and uncertainty in load. Considering these factors, the tangential load P_t gets modified to effective load which is obtained as

$$P_{eff} = \frac{C_s \cdot P_{2t}}{C_v}$$

Taking into consideration the factor of safety (FS), the gear strength in bending (S_b) as well as wear strength (S_w) should both be either greater than or equal to (FS × P_{eff}).

Thus

$$S_b, S_w \geq (FS) \cdot P_{eff}$$

If the power transmitted is known, tangential tooth load on the worm wheel can be obtained from

$$P_{2t} = \frac{Power}{V_2}$$

4.8 THERMAL CONSIDERATION IN WORM GEAR DRIVE

The efficiencies of the worm- worm gear pair can be considerably smaller depending on the geometry and higher friction. Thus there is considerable loss of power and this energy gets converted to heat at the contact area between worm and worm gear. For example, if the efficiency is 70% then 30% of input power is converted into heat. With this the temperature at the contact point can increase. Lubrication in worm – worm gear pair therefore has to perform important task of carrying away the heat while reducing the friction. The increasing temperature limits the maximum power that can be transmitted by the pair. Thus heat generated must be equated to heat dissipated while limiting the temperature rise within acceptable limit. Depending on the lubricant selected, usually lubricants will work satisfactorily up to temperatures of 90°C. Considering ambient temperature of 40 to 45°C, temperature rise may be limited to about 45°C.

Heat Generated, $H_g = (1 - \eta) \cdot P_i$

Heat Dissipated $H_d = C.A.(\Delta T)$

where

C = Overall heat transfer coefficient of Gear Box casing walls W/ m² °C.

= 12 to 18 W/ m² °C for natural circulation of air.

20 to 30 W/m² °C for forced circulation of air with fins.

A = External surface area of the housing (m²).

ΔT = Permissible temperature rise of oil.

The heat dissipation capacity can be increased by
1. Providing fins on the outer surface of the housing so as to increase surface area.
2. Forced circulation by providing a fan on worm shaft.
3. Providing cooling system for lubricating oil.

4.9 WORM DRIVE - TYPE OF FAILURES

As in case of spur and helical gears, worm gears are also subjected to damage mainly on two accounts.

(a) Lack of proper lubrication and
(b) Surface pitting due to long operations at high loads.

Additionally, sliding cannot be totally avoided in a worm drive. The worm wheel usually suffers more damage than the worm. Principal modes of gearing failures are:

- Surface damage caused by initial pitting.
- Tooth wear.
- Seizing due to heavy loads and lack of lubrication.
- Fatigue pitting due to high loads exceeding endurance strength of the material.
- Tooth breakage after severe wear caused by weakening of the section of the gear tooth.

Remedies:
- Adequate wear strength to avoid fatigue pitting. Load should be lesser than the endurance limit for the material.
- Adequate beam strength for gear material.
- Material hardness can be increased so that endurance limit of the material can increase thus avoiding pitting.
- Ensure sufficient and appropriate lubrication to prevent corrosive fatigue, abrasive pitting.

Table 4.6: Recommended values of $Z_1/Z_2/q/m$ for worm gearing

Centre dis-tance (mm)	Transmission Ratio							
	10	15	20	25	30	40	50	60
80	–	2/30/10/4	2/42/(11)/3	–	1/30/10/4	1/42/(11)/3	–	1/62/(18)/2
100	4/40/10/4	2/30/10/5	2/40/10/4	2/54/(11)/3	1/30/10/5	1/40/10/4	1/55/(11)/3	1/64/16/2.5
125	4/40/10/5	2/31/10/6	2/40/10/5	2/52/10/4	1/31/10/6	1/40/10/5	1/52/10/4	–
160	4/43/10/6	2/30/10/8	–	2/54/10/5	1/30/10/8	–	1/54/10/5	1/62/(18)/4
200	4/40/10/8	2/30/10/10	2/40/10/8	–	1/30/10/10	1/40/10/8	–	–
250	4/40/10/10	–	2/40/10/10	2/52/10/8	–	1/40/10/10	1/52/10/8	–
315	4/43/(9)/12	2/30/(9)/16	–	2/53/10/10	1/30/(9)/16	–	1/53/10/10	1/60/(18)/8

SOLVED EXAMPLES

Example 4.1: A worn gear box with an effective surface area of 1.5 m² is operating in still air with a heat transfer coefficient of 15 W/m²°C. The temperature rise of lubricant is limited to 60°C. The worm gears are designated as 1/30/10/8. The worm shaft is rotating at 1440 rpm and the normal pressure angle is 20°. Calculate the power rating based on thermal consideration for the drive. Take coefficient of friction as 0.03.

Given data:
Area = A = 1.5 m², C = 15 W/m²°C, ΔT = 60°C, μ = 0.03
Gear pair: $Z_1 / Z_2 / q' / m$ 1 / 30 / 10 / 8   Speed = 1440 rpm ϕ_n = 20°

Solution: Lead angle of worm: $\tan \lambda = \dfrac{\lambda_1}{q} = \dfrac{1}{10} = 0.1$

Lead angle, λ = 5.71° and ϕ_n = 20°

Gear pair efficiency

$$\eta = \dfrac{\cos \phi_n - \mu \tan \lambda}{\cos \phi_n + \mu \cot \lambda}$$

$$= \dfrac{\cos 20.0° - 0.03 \tan 5.71}{\cos 20°.0 + 0.03 \cot 5.71}$$

$$= \dfrac{0.9396 - 0.03 \times 0.09998}{0.9396 + 0.03 \times 10} = 0.755$$

Equating heat balance

Heat generated = Heat dissipated

$(1 - \eta) (kW)_{i/p} = C \cdot A \cdot \Delta T$

$(1 - 0.755) (kW)_{i/p} = 15 \times 1.5 \times 60$

$(kW)_{i/p}$ = 5510 W

Power rating = 5.51 kW

Based on thermal consideration alone.

Example 4.2: A worm gear pair 2/40/10/4 is having phosphor bronze gear with ultimate tensile strength 300 MPa. The worm is made of steel with ultimate strength 740 MPa. The coefficient of friction between the worm and the worm gear is 0.03 and normal pressure angle 20°. The worm gear wear factor is 0.9 N/mm². The overall heat transfer coefficient for the gear box is 18 W/m²°C. The permissible temperature rise for lubricating oil is 50°C. The worm rotates as 720 rpm and service factor is 1.5.

Determine the input power rating based on beam strength, wear strength and thermal consideration.

Assume effective surface area of the gear box as 0.8 m² and factor of safety as 1.5.

Given data: $z_1/z_2/q/m \to 2/40/10/4$, $\quad i = \dfrac{z_2}{z_1} = 20$

$(S_{ult})_g = 300 \text{ N/mm}^2 \quad (S_{ult})_w = 740 \text{ N/mm}^2 \quad\quad \mu = 0.03$

$N_2 = \dfrac{720}{20} = 36 \text{ rpm}$

$\phi_n = 20° \quad\quad\quad K_w = 0.9 \text{ N/mm}^2 \quad\quad C = 18 \text{ W/m}^2°\text{C}$
$\Delta T = 50°\text{C} \quad\quad\quad N_1 = 720 \text{ rpm} \quad\quad\quad\quad C_s = 1.5$
$FS = 1.5 \quad\quad \text{Surface area, } A = 0.8 \text{ m}^2$

$\tan \lambda = \dfrac{z_1}{q} = \dfrac{2}{10} = 0.2; \lambda = 11.3°$

Solution:

(a) Beam strength, by Lewis equation is given by (to be applied to worm gear)

$$S_b = \sigma_b \cdot b \cdot Y \cdot M_n$$

where, σ_b = Permissible bending stress for gear material

$$\sigma_b = \dfrac{1}{3} \times 300 = 100 \text{ N/mm}^2$$

b = Gear width [larger of]

∴ $b = 0.73 \, d_1 = 0.73 \, (q \times m) = 0.73 \, (10 \times 4) = 29.2 \text{ mm}$

OR

$b = 2m\sqrt{q+1} = 2 \times 4\sqrt{10+1} = 26.5 \text{ mm}$

Hence we select $b = 29.2 \text{ mm}$

$Y = 0.484 - \dfrac{2.87}{z_g} = 0.484 - \dfrac{2.87}{40} = 0.4122$

$m_n = m \cos \lambda$

where, $\tan \lambda = \dfrac{z_1}{q} = \dfrac{2}{10}$

∴ $\lambda = 11.31°$

$m_n = 4 \times 0.98 = 3.922 \text{ mm}$

∴ Beam strength, $S_b = 100 \times 29.2 \times 0.4122 \times 3.922$

$$S_b = 4720 \text{ N}$$

Wear strength:

$S_w = d_g \cdot b \cdot K_w = (m \cdot Z_g) \cdot b \cdot K_w$
$\quad = 4 \times 40 \times 29.2 \times 0.9$

$$S_w = 4204.8 \text{ N}$$

Effective load:

$P_{eff} = P_2 t \times \dfrac{C_s}{C_v}$

$C_s = 1.5, \quad d_1 = q \times m = 40, \quad n_1 = 720$

Velocity factor, $C_v = \dfrac{6}{6+V_2} = \dfrac{6}{6+\left(\dfrac{\pi \cdot d_2 n_2}{60 \times 1000}\right)} = \dfrac{6}{6+\left(\dfrac{\pi \times 160 \times 36}{60 \times 1000}\right)}$

$= \dfrac{6}{6+0.30} = 0.952$

$P_{eff} = P_2 t \times \dfrac{1.5}{0.952} = \mathbf{1.576\ P_2 t}$

Equating beam strength with effective load considering FS = 1.5.

$S_b = (FS) \cdot P_{eff} = (1.5)\ 1.576 \cdot P_2 t$

$4720 = 1.5 \times 1.576 \times P_{2t}$

$\therefore \quad P_2 t = 1997\ N$ (in bending)

Equating wear strength with effective load considering FS

$S_w = (FS)\ P_{eff}$

$4204.8 = 1.5 \times 1.576 \times P_{2t}$

$P_2 t = 1779\ N$ (in wear)

Output power rating based on beam strength

$= (P_2 t) \times V_2 = \dfrac{1997 \times 0.30}{1000} = 0.599\ kW$

Output power rating based on wear strength

$= (P_2 t)_{wear} \times V_2 = \dfrac{1779 \times 0.3}{1000} = 0.534\ kW$

Worm/Gear pair efficiency:

$\eta = \dfrac{\cos \phi_n - \mu \tan \lambda}{\cos \phi_n + \mu \cot \lambda} = \dfrac{\cos 20° - 0.03 \tan 11.3°}{\cos 20° + 0.03 \cot 11.3°} = \dfrac{0.9336}{1.09}$

$= 0.856$

Input power rating based on beam strength $= \dfrac{0.599}{0.856} = \mathbf{0.7\ kW}$

Input power rating based on wear strength $= \dfrac{0.534}{0.856} = \mathbf{0.63\ kW}$

Input power rating based on heat dissipation:

Equating heat generated = Heat dissipated

$(1 - \eta)\ (Power)_{i/p} = C \cdot A \cdot \Delta T = 18 \times 0.8 \times 50$

$(Power)_{i/p} = \dfrac{18 \times 0.8 \times 50}{(1 - 0.856)} = 5000\ W = \mathbf{5.0\ kW}$

Example 4.3: A pair of worm and worm gear is designated as 1/30/10/10. The input speed of worm is 1200 rpm. The worm wheel is centrifugally cast and made from phospher bronze having ultimate strength 240 N/mm². Coefficient of friction between worm and worm teeth is 0.04. Application factor and factor of safety are 1.25 and 1.5 respectively. The tooth system is 20° full involute. Calculate power transmitting capacity based on beam strength.

Given data: Worm/worm gear → 1/30/10/10 → $z_1/z_2/q/m$, $i = \dfrac{z_2}{z_1} = 30$

Worm: $N_1 = 1200$ rpm, $d_1 = q \times m = 100$, $\tan \lambda = \dfrac{z_1}{q} = \dfrac{1}{10}$, $\lambda = 5.71°$.

Worm wheel: $S_{ult} = 240$ N/mm², $d_2 = m \times z_2 = 300$ mm, $N_2 = \dfrac{1200}{i} = 40$

$\mu = 0.04$, $C_s = 1.25$, $FS = 1.5$, $\phi_n = 20°$.

Solution: Beam strength: S_b

$$S_b = \sigma_b \cdot b \cdot Y \cdot m_n = \sigma_b \cdot b \cdot Y \cdot m \cdot \cos \lambda$$

where,
$$\sigma_b = \frac{1}{3} \times S_{ult} = 80 \text{ N/mm}^2$$

$$b = 0.73\, d_1 = 73 \text{ mm}$$

OR

$$b = 2m\sqrt{q+1} = 2 \times 10 \sqrt{(10+1)} = 66.3 \text{ mm}$$

Hence we select $b = 73$ mm (larger of the two)

$$Y = 0.484 - \frac{2.87}{z_2} = 0.484 - \frac{2.87}{30} = 0.388$$

$$m_n = m \cdot \cos \lambda = 10 \times 0.995 = 9.95 \text{ mm}$$

∴ $S_b = 80 \times 73 \times 0.388 \times 9.95 = 22546$ N

Effective load: P_{eff}

$$P_{eff} = \left[\frac{C_s}{C_v}\right] \cdot P_{2t}$$

$$C_v = \frac{6}{6 + V_g} = \frac{6}{6 + \left(\dfrac{\pi\, d_2 \cdot n_2}{60 \times 1000}\right)} = \frac{6}{6 + \left(\dfrac{\pi \times 300 \times 40}{60 \times 1000}\right)}$$

$$= \frac{6}{6 + 0.6283} = 0.905$$

$$P_{eff} = \left[\frac{1.25}{0.905}\right] P_{2t} = 1.381\, P_{2t}$$

Equating beam strength with effective load, considering FS,

$S_b = (P_{eff}) \cdot FS$
$S_b = (1.381)\, P_{2t}\, (1.5)$
$S_b = 2.07\, P_{2t}$

∴ $22546 = 2.07\, P_{2t}$

∴ $P_{2t} = 10892$ N

DESIGN OF MACHINE ELEMENTS - II — WORM GEARS

∴ Output power rating based on beam strength

$$= (P_{2t})_{bending} \times V_2$$
$$= \frac{10892 \times 0.6283}{1000} = 6.843 \text{ kW}$$

Worm/worm-gear pair efficiency:

$$\eta = \frac{\cos \phi_n - \mu \cdot \tan \lambda}{\cos \phi_n + \mu \cot \lambda} = \frac{\cos 20° - 0.04 \times \tan 5.71}{\cos 20° + 0.04 \cot 5.71}$$

$$= \frac{0.9396 - 0.04 \times 0.0999}{0.9396 + 0.04 \times 10} = 0.6984$$

Input power rating based on beam strength

$$= \frac{\text{Output power}}{\text{Efficiency}} = \frac{6.843}{0.6984} = 9.8 \text{ kW}$$

Example 4.4: A double start worm made of alloy steel is to mesh with worm gear to be made of phosphor bronze (σ_{ut} = 270 N/mm²). The gear pair is required to transmit 7 kW power from an electric motor running at 1500 rpm to a machine running at 60 rpm. The service factor is 1.25, while the factor of safety required is 1.5. The face width of the worm gear is 0.73 times the pitch circle diameter of worm. The worm gear wear factor is 0.7 N/mm², while the diametrical quotient is 10. The normal pressure angle is 14.5°. If the coefficient of friction between worm and worm gear teeth is 0.03, design the gear and find the power lost. Would you recommend a fan for the gear box? Assume the permissible temperature rise is 50°C.

Use following data:

- Lewis form factor: $Y = 0.39 - \dfrac{2.15}{Z_g}$
- Velocity factor: $C_v = \dfrac{6}{6 + V_g}$
- Area of housing: $A = 1.14 \times 10^{-4} \times (a)^{1.7}$ m²

where, a = Centre distance in mm

Given data: 7 kW at worm, $i = 25$, $\phi_n = 14\frac{1°}{2}$

Worm: $Z_1 = 2$, $N_1 = 1500$ rpm, $q = 10$, $\tan \lambda = \dfrac{Z_1}{q} = 0.2$.

Gear: $S_{ult} = 270$ N/mm², $N_2 = 60$ rpm, $b = 0.73\, d_1$
$K_w = 0.7$ N/mm², $Z_g = i \times Z_1 = 50$, $d_2 = 50 \cdot m$
$C_s = 1.25$, FS = 1.5, $\mu = 0.03$, $\Delta T = 50°C$

Solution:

Beam strength S_b: (For the gear tooth)

$$S_b = \sigma_b \cdot b \cdot Y \cdot m_n$$

$$\sigma_b = \frac{1}{3} \times 270 = 90 \text{ N/mm}^2$$

$$b = 0.73 \, d_1 = 0.73 \, q \cdot m = 7.3 \, m$$

$$Y = 0.39 - \frac{2.15}{Z_g} = 0.39 - \frac{2.15}{50} = 0.347$$

$$m_n = m \cdot \cos \lambda = m \, (0.98)$$

$$S_b = 90 \times 7.3 \, m \times 0.347 \times 0.98 \, m = 223.4 \, m^2$$

Wear Strength S_w:

$$S_w = d_g \cdot b \cdot K_w = 50 \cdot m \times 7.3 \, m \times 0.7 = 255.5 \, m^2$$

Since, $S_b < S_w$, gear is weaker in bending and therefore will be designed against bending failure.

Load on the gear tooth:

Efficiency of gear pair ($\phi_n = 14.5°$, $\mu = 0.03$, $\tan \lambda = 0.2$)

$$\eta = \frac{\cos \phi_n - \mu \tan \lambda}{\cos \phi_n + \mu \cdot \cot \lambda} = \frac{0.968 - 0.006}{0.968 + 0.15} = \frac{0.962}{1.118}$$

$$= 0.8605$$

Output power is,

$$= \text{Input power} \times \eta = 7 \times 0.8605 = 6.02 \text{ kW}$$

Tangential gear tooth load P_t

$$P_t = \frac{\text{Output power}}{V_g} = \frac{6.02 \times 10^3}{\left(\frac{\pi \times d_2 \times n_2}{60 \times 1000}\right)} = \frac{6.02 \times 10^3}{\left(\frac{\pi \times 50 \cdot m \times 60}{60 \times 1000}\right)}$$

$$= \frac{6.02 \times 10^3}{0.157 \, m}$$

$$= \frac{38344}{m} \text{ Newton}$$

Effective gear tooth load

$$P_{eff} = \left(\frac{C_s}{C_v}\right) P_t$$

where,
$$C_v = \frac{6}{6 + V_g} = \left(\frac{6}{6 + 0.157\, m}\right)$$

$$= \left[1.25 \times \frac{(6 + 0.157\, m)}{6}\right] \cdot P_t$$

$$= 0.208\,(6 + 0.157\, m) \cdot P_t$$

This should be equated to beam strength considering factor of safety.

$$S_b = (P_{eff})\, FS$$

$$223.4\, m^2 = 0.208\,(6 + 0.157\, m) \cdot P_t \times 1.5 = 0.3125\,(6 + 0.157\, m)\, P_t$$

∴ $$223.4\, m^2 = 0.3125\,(6 + 0.157\, m) \times \frac{38344}{m}$$

Simplifying,

$$223.4\, m^3 - 1882\, m - 71895 = 0$$

$$m^3 - 8.43\, m - 321.8 = 0$$

By trial and error, m = 7.3 mm ≅ 8.0 mm

Therefore, the gear pair can be designed as,

$$Z_1/Z_2/q/m \to 2/50/10/8$$

(b) Power lost

Input power $(1 - \eta) = 7 \times (1 - 0.8605)$

$$= 0.98\, kW$$

(c) Provision of forced circulation (Fan)

Gear box area = $A = 1.14 \times 10^{-4} \times a^{1.7}\, m^2$

Here, $$a = \frac{d_1 + d_2}{2} = \frac{q \cdot m + m \cdot Z_2}{2} = \frac{80 + 400}{2}$$

$$= 240\, mm$$

∴ $A = 1.27\, m^2$

Equating heat balance to find required value of overall heat transfer coefficient

Input power $(1 - \eta) = C_3 \cdot A \cdot \Delta T$

$$7 \times (1 - 0.8605) \times 10^3 = C \times 1.27 \times 50$$

∴ $C_{required} = 15.4\, W/m^{2\,\circ}C$

Since this is < 18 W/m²°C.

Natural circulation will be sufficient.

Example 4.5: A worm 'up' type 2/40/10/5 worm gear pair transmit 5 kW power from worm shaft rotating at 1440 rpm to worm gear shaft. The worm is left hand and rotates in anticlockwise direction, when viewed from right side. Coefficient of friction between worm and worm gear teeth is 0.05. Normal pressure angle is 20°. Determine.
(i) Components of forces acting on worm and worm gear and show their directions.
(ii) Efficiency of worm gear pair.
(iii) Power lost in friction.

Given data: $Z_1/Z_2/q/m \rightarrow 2/40/10/5$
Worm; 5 kW, 1440 rpm
$\mu = 0.05$, $\phi_n = 20°$, $d_1 = q \times m = 50$ mm

$$\tan \lambda = \frac{Z_1}{q} = \frac{2}{10}, \quad \lambda = 11.3°$$

Solution:

(i) Tangential force on the worm

$$P_{1t} = \frac{\text{Power}}{V_1} = \frac{5000}{(\pi \times 50 \times 1440/60 \times 1000)} = 1326.4 \text{ N} = P_{2a}$$

$$P_{1a} = \frac{\cos \phi_n \cos \lambda - \mu \sin \lambda}{\cos \phi_n \sin \lambda + \mu \cos \lambda} \cdot (P_{1t})$$

$$= \frac{\cos 20° \cos 11.3° - 0.05 \sin 11.3°}{\cos 20° \sin 11.3° + 0.05 \cos 11.3°} (P_{1t})$$

$$= \frac{0.921 - 0.00979}{0.184 + 0.049} (1326.4) = 5188 \text{ N} = P_{2t}$$

$$P_{1r} = \frac{\sin \phi_n}{\cos \phi_n \sin \lambda + \mu \cos \lambda} (P_{1t}) = \frac{0.342}{0.233} (P_{1t})$$

$$= \frac{0.342}{0.233} (1326.4) = 1947 \text{ N} = P_{2r}$$

Since worm is above the worm gear.

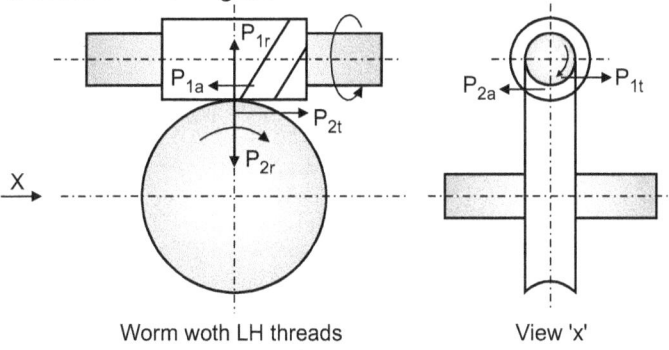

Worm woth LH threads   View 'x'
Fig. 4.12

For LH worm and given direction of rotation for worm, worm gear will rotate clockwise. Other forces and their directions will be as shown.

(ii) Efficiency of worm-worm gear pair:

$$\eta = \frac{\cos\phi_n - \mu \cdot \tan\lambda}{\cos\phi_n + \mu \cdot \cot\lambda}$$

$$= \frac{\cos 20° - 0.05 \times 0.2}{\cos 20° + 0.05 \times 5}$$

$$= \frac{0.8397}{1.1896}$$

$$\eta = 0.706$$

(iii) Power lost in friction:

$$= (1 - \eta) \text{ Power input}$$
$$= (1 - 0.706)\, 5 \text{ kW}$$
$$= \mathbf{1.47 \text{ kW}}$$

Example 4.6: A worm gear pair 2/52/10/4 transmits 10 kW power from an electric motor rotating at 720 rpm to a machine. The worm is right hand and rotates in clockwise direction when viewed from right side. Sketch the arrangement and show the components of tooth forces. The coefficient of friction between worm and worm wheel is 0.04, while the normal pressure angle is 20°. The overall heat transfer coefficient is 20 W/m²°C. The temperature rise of lubricating oil above the atmospheric temperature is 50°C. Determine:

(i) Components of tooth forces acting

(ii) Efficiency of worm gear pair

(iii) Minimum surface area of gear box

Is the drive self-locking? Comment. Assume worm is below the worm gear.

Given data:

Gear pair: 2/52/10/4 → $z_1/z_2/q/m$, $i = \dfrac{Z_2}{Z_1} = 26$

Worm: $N_1 = 720$ rpm, $d_1 = q \times m = 40$ mm, $\tan\lambda = \dfrac{Z_1}{q} = 0.2$, $\lambda = 11.31°$

Wheel: 10 kW, $\mu = 0.04$, $\phi_n = 20°$, $C = 20$ W/m²°C, $\Delta T = 50°C$

Solution:

P_{1t}: Tangential force on the worm

$$P_{1t} = \frac{\text{Input power}}{V_1} = \frac{10 \times 10^3}{\left(\dfrac{\pi d_1 N_1}{60 \times 1000}\right)} = \frac{10 \times 10^3}{\left(\dfrac{\pi \times 40 \times 720}{60 \times 1000}\right)}$$

$$P_{1t} = \frac{10 \times 10^3}{1.507} = 6632 \text{ N} = P_{2a}$$

$$P_{1a} = \frac{\cos \phi_n \cos \lambda - \mu \sin \lambda}{\cos \phi_n \sin \lambda + \mu \cos \lambda} \times (P_{1t})$$

$$= \frac{\cos 20° \cdot \cos 11.31° - 0.04 \sin 11.31°}{\cos 20° \sin 11.31° + 0.04 \cos 11.31°} \times (P_{1t})$$

$$= \frac{0.921 - 0.00784}{0.184 + 0.0392} (P_{1t})$$

$$P_{1a} = \frac{0.913}{0.2232} \times 6632 = 27128 \text{ N} = P_{2t}$$

$$P_{1r} = \frac{\sin \phi_n}{\cos \phi_n \sin \lambda + \mu \cos \lambda} (P_{1t}) = \frac{0.342}{0.2232} \times 6632$$

$$P_{1r} = 10162 \text{ N} = P_{2r}$$

$$\eta = \frac{\cos \phi_n - \mu \cdot \tan \lambda}{\cos \phi_n + \mu \cdot \cot \lambda}$$

$$= \frac{\cos 20° - 0.04 \tan \lambda}{\cos 20° + 0.04 \cot \lambda}$$

$$= \frac{0.9397 - 0.008}{0.9397 + 0.2}$$

$$= 0.817$$

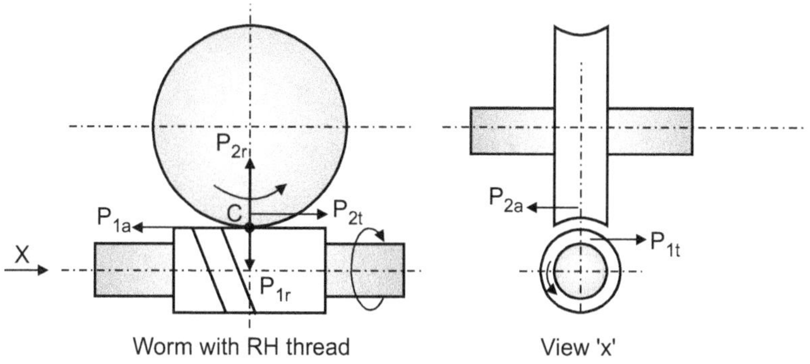

Worm with RH thread
(i)   (ii)   View 'x'   (iii)

Fig. 4.13

For RH worm and given direction of rotation for worm, worm gear would rotate clockwise.

Other forces and their directions, will be as shown.

Example 4.7: A worm/worm-gear pair is used to transmit from worm 5 kW power at 1500 rpm. Worm is two start having 60 teeth gear. The axial module is 6 mm and pressure angle is 14.5°. The diametral factor is 10. Worm gear material has ultimate tensile strength of 300 N/mm². Find the factor of safety in bending, wear and heat dissipation. Based on heat dissipation criteria the power transmission capacity is given by,

$$\text{Input kW} = \frac{a^{1.7}}{34.5\,(i+5)}$$

Take Lewis form factor: $Y = 0.39 - \dfrac{2.15}{Z_g}$

Assume: $K_w = 0.85$ N/mm², $\mu = 0.05$

Given data: 5 kW, Worm $N_1 = 1500$ rpm, $Z_2 = 60$, $Z_1 = 2$

$m = 6$ mm, $\phi_n = 14\tfrac{1}{2}°$, $q = 10$

Worm gear: $S_{ult} = 300$ N/mm², $\mu = 0.05$, $K_w = 0.85$

$\tan \lambda = \dfrac{Z_1}{q} = 0.2$, $d_2 = m \cdot Z_2 = 360$ mm, $N_2 = 50$

Solution: Beam strength: S_b

$$S_b = \sigma_b \cdot b \cdot Y \cdot m_n$$

$$\sigma_b = \frac{300}{3} = 100 \text{ N/mm}^2$$

$$b = 0.73\, d_1 = 0.73\,(q \times m) = 43.8 \text{ mm}$$

OR

$$b = 2m\sqrt{q+1} = 2 \times 6\sqrt{11} = 39.8 \text{ mm} \simeq 40 \text{ mm}$$

Hence we select $b = 43.8$ mm (Larger of the two)

$$Y = 0.39 - \frac{2.15}{60} = 0.354$$

$m_n = m \cos \lambda = 5.88$ mm

$S_b = 100 \times 43.8 \times 0.354 \times 5.88 = 9117$ N (in bending)

Wear strength: $S_w = d_2 \cdot b \cdot K_w$

$= (6 \times 60)\,(43.8)\,(0.85) = 13403$ N (in wear)

Effective load

$$P_{eff} = \left(\frac{C_s}{C_v}\right) P_{2t}$$

Velocity factor, $C_v = \dfrac{6}{6 + V_g}$

$$C_v = \dfrac{6}{\left(6 + \dfrac{\pi d_2 n_2}{60 \times 1000}\right)} = \dfrac{6}{\left(6 + \dfrac{\pi \times 360 \times 50}{60 \times 1000}\right)} = \dfrac{6}{6 + 0.942}$$

$$C_v = 0.864$$

Assuming service factor $C_s = 1$

$$P_{eff} = \left(\dfrac{1}{0.864}\right) P_{2t} = 1.158\, P_{2t}$$

Based on beam strength

$$P_{eff} = 1.158 \times 9117 = 10557 \text{ N (in bending)}$$

Based on wear strength

$$P_{eff} = 1.158 \times 13403 = 15521 \text{ N (in wear)}$$

Output power rating based on beam strength

$$= P_{eff} \times V_2 = \dfrac{10557 \times 0.942}{1000} = 9.94 \text{ kW}$$

Output power rating based on wear strength

$$= P_{eff} \times V_2 = \dfrac{15521 \times 0.942}{1000} = 14.62 \text{ kW}$$

Gear drive efficiency: η ($\phi_n = 14.5°$, $\mu = 0.05$, $\tan \lambda = 0.2$)

$$\eta = \dfrac{\cos \phi_n - \mu \tan \lambda}{\cos \phi_n + \mu \cot \lambda} = \dfrac{0.968 - 0.01}{0.968 + 0.25} = \dfrac{0.958}{1.218}$$

$$= 0.786$$

Input power based on beam strength

$$= \dfrac{9.94}{0.786} = 12.64 \text{ kW}$$

$$FS = \dfrac{12.64}{5} = \mathbf{2.528}$$

Input power based on wear strength

$$= \dfrac{14.62}{0.786} = 18.6 \text{ kW}$$

$$FS = \dfrac{18.6}{5} = \mathbf{3.72}$$

For heat dissipation

$$(kW) = \frac{a^{1.7}}{34.5(i+5)} \qquad \text{where, } a = \frac{d_1 + d_2}{2} = \frac{60 + 360}{2}$$

$$= \frac{210^{1.7}}{34.5(35)} = 7.35 \text{ kW} \qquad = 210 \text{ mm}$$

∴ FS based on heat dissipation

$$= \frac{7.35}{5} = 1.47$$

Example 4.8: A worm/worm-gear pair is designated as 1/30/10/10. The worm is rotating at 1000 rpm.

Find:

(a) Worm and worm gear dimensions.

(b) Centre distance between the worm and the gear.

(c) Estimate the value of coefficient of friction for the pair.

Use following relation.

Sliding velocity m/sec.	1	2	3	4	5	6
Coefficient of friction μ	0.042	0.032	0.029	0.027	0.025	0.023

Given data: $Z_1/Z_2/q/m \rightarrow 1/30/10/10$

$$\tan \lambda = \frac{Z_1}{q} = \frac{1}{10} = 0.1, \quad \lambda = 5.71°$$

$$d_1 = q \times m = 10 \times 10 = 100 \text{ mm}$$

$$d_2 = Z_2 \times m = 30 \times 10 = 300 \text{ mm}$$

Solution:

(a) **Worm:**

Addendum = h_{a1} = m = 10 mm

Dedendum = h_{f1} = (2.2 cos λ − 1) m = 11.89 mm

Outer diameter = d_{a1} = d_1 + 2h_{a1} = 120 mm

Root diameter = d_{f1} = d_1 − 2h_{f1} = 76.22 mm

Clearance = 0.2 m cos λ = 1.99 mm

Length of worm = $m\pi \left[4.5 + \frac{Z_2}{50} \right]$ = 160.22 mm

Worm wheel:

Addendum of wheel = $ha_2 = (2\cos\lambda - 1)m = 9.9$ mm

Dedendum of wheel = $h_{f2} = (1 + 0.2\cos\lambda)m = 11.99$ mm

Addendum diameter = $da_2 = d_2 + 2ha_2 = 319.8$ mm

Dedendum diameter = $df_2 = d_2 - 2hf_2 = 276.02$ mm

Face width, $b = 0.73 \quad d_1 = 73$ mm

(b) Centre distance between worm and gear

$$a = \frac{d_1 + d_2}{2} = \frac{100 + 300}{2}$$

$$= 200 \text{ mm}$$

(c) Sliding velocity

$$v_s = \frac{v_1}{\cos\lambda} = \frac{\frac{\pi d_1 N_1}{60 \times 1000}}{\cos 5.71°} = \frac{5.236}{0.995}$$

$v_s = 5.262$ m/sec.

From chart by interpolation coefficient of friction corresponding to sliding velocity of 5.262 m/sec.

$$\mu = 0.0245$$

Example 4.9: The worm of a worm/worm gear pair is required to transmit 6 kW power at 1500 rpm with a speed reduction of 30.

(a) Select a suitable pair based on heat capacity and

(b) Find the factor of safety for the worm gear based on beam strength.

Assume: Coefficient of friction = 0.04.

Pennissible bending stress for gear material = 80 N/mm².

Gear system is 20° full depth involute. Consider service factor as 1.0.

Use following data: Velocity factor $C_v = \dfrac{\sigma}{\sigma + v}$

Relationship for heat capacity based on centre distance between worm and gear.

$$(P_{input}) = \frac{a^{1.7}}{34.5\,(i + 5)}$$ where, a is centre distance in mm.

Centre distance a (mm)	Transmission Ratio (i)		
	20	30	40
100	2/40/10/4	1/30/10/5	1/40/10/4
125	2/40/10/5	1/31/10/6	1/40/10/5
160	–	1/30/10/8	–
200	2/40/10/8	1/30/10/10	1/40/10/8

Given data: Power: 6 kW, $N_1 = 1500$ rpm, $i = 30$, $\mu = 0.04$

Solution:

(a) Desired centre distance for 6 kW input power based on heat capacity.

$$P_{input} = \frac{a^{1.7}}{34.5\,(i+5)}$$

$$6 = \frac{a^{1.7}}{34.5\,(35)}$$

∴ $\quad a = 186.5$ mm

∴ We select $a = 200$ mm

∴ Selected gear pair from the table is

$$1/30/10/10 \rightarrow Z_1/Z_2/q/m$$

(b) $d_1 = q \times m = 100$ mm $\tan \lambda = \dfrac{Z_1}{q} = 0.1$

$d_2 = m \times Z_2 = 300$ mm

Beam strength: S_b

$S_b = \sigma_b \cdot b \cdot Y \cdot m_n$

σ_b = Allowable bending stress = 80 N/mm²

$b = 0.73 \times d_1 = 73$ mm

OR

$2m\sqrt{q+1} = 66.3$ mm

Hence we select $b = 73$ mm [Larger of the two]

Using standard relationship for Lewis form factor,

$$Y = 0.484 - \frac{2.87}{Z_g} = 0.484 - \frac{2.87}{30} = 0.388$$

$m_n = m \cos \lambda = 10 \cos 5.71° = 9.95$ mm

$S_b = 80 \times 73 \times 0.388 \times 9.95$

$\quad = 22546$ N

Gear pair efficiency ($\phi_n = 20°$, $\mu = 0.04$, $\tan \lambda = 0.1$)

$$\eta = \frac{\cos \phi_n - \mu \tan \lambda}{\cos \phi_n + \mu \cot \lambda} = \frac{0.9396 - 0.004}{0.9396 + 0.4} = 0.698$$

Output power = Input power $\times \eta = 6 \times 0.698$
= 4.2 kW

Gear tangential force ($d_2 = 300$ mm, $N_2 = 1500/30 = 50$ rpm)

$$P_t = \frac{\text{Output power}}{V_g} = \frac{4.2 \times 10^3}{\left(\frac{\pi d_2 N_2}{60 \times 1000}\right)} = \frac{4.2 \times 10^3}{\left(\frac{\pi \times 300 \times 50}{60 \times 1000}\right)} = \frac{4.2 \times 10^3}{0.785}$$

$P_t = 5348$ N

Effective force

$$P_{eff} = \left[\frac{C_s}{C_v}\right] P_t$$

With $C_s = 1$ and $C_v = \dfrac{6}{6 + V_g} = \dfrac{6}{6 + 0.785} = 0.884$

$$= \left[\frac{1}{0.884}\right] 5348 = 6050 \text{ N}$$

Equating beam strength with effective load considering factor of safety.

$S_b = (P_{eff})$ FS
22546 = 6060 × FS
FS = 3.72

Example 4.10: Design a worm/worm-gear pair based on wear strength and suggest minimum surface area to be provided for the gear box if it has to work with natural circulation. Single start worm is connected to 3.0 kW electric motor rotating at 1500 rpm. Required speed reduction is 30 between the worm and worm wheel. Wear stress factor for the gear material is 0.6 N/mm². Gear tooth system is 20° full depth involute and worm diametral quotient is 10. Consider service factor as 1.2 and required factor of safety is 1.4.

Permissible temperature rise for lubricant is 50°C. Use following data. Take coefficient of friction as 0.03.

Given data: $\mu = 0.03$, $\Delta T = 50°c$
Power: 8kW, $i = 30$, $\phi_n = 20°$, $C_s = 1.2$, FS = 1.4.
Worm: $Z_1 = 1$, $N_1 = 1500$, $q = 10$, $d_1 = q \cdot m = 10 \cdot m$.
Gear: $K_w = 0.6$, $N_2 = 50$, $Z_2 = \dfrac{1500}{50} = 30$, $d_2 = 30 \cdot m$

Solution: Wear strengths S_w:

$$S_w = d_2 \cdot b \cdot K_w$$
$$Z_2 = i \cdot Z_1 = 30 \times 1 = 30$$
$$d_2 = m \cdot Z_2 = 30 \cdot m$$
$$b = 0.73 \, d_1 = 7.3 \, m$$

OR

$$= 2m\sqrt{q+1} = 2m\sqrt{11} = 6.63 \, m$$

Hence we select $\quad b = 7.3 \, m$ (larger of the two)

$$S_w = 30 \cdot m \times 7.3 \times m \times 0.6$$
$$S_w = 131.4 \, m^2$$

Gear pair efficiency: ($\phi_n = 20°$, $\mu = 0.03$, $\tan \lambda = \dfrac{Z_1}{q} = 0.1$)

$$\eta = \frac{\cos \phi_n - \mu \tan \lambda}{\cos \phi_n + \mu \cot \lambda} = \frac{0.9396 - 0.003}{0.9396 + 0.3} = 0.755$$

∴ Output power is,

$$= \text{Input power} \times \eta = 8 \times 0.755$$
$$= 6.04 \, kW$$

Tangential gear tooth load P_t

$$P_t = \frac{\text{Output power}}{V_g} = \frac{6.04 \times 10^3}{\left(\dfrac{\pi d_2 N_2}{60 \times 1000}\right)} = \frac{6.04 \times 10^3}{\left(\dfrac{\pi \times 30 \cdot m \times 50}{60 \times 1000}\right)}$$

$$= \frac{6.04 \times 1000}{0.07854 \cdot m} = \frac{76904}{m} \, \text{Newton}$$

Effective gear tooth load, P_{eff}:

$$P_{eff} = \left(\frac{C_s}{C_v}\right) \cdot P_t$$

where, $\quad C_s = 1.2$

$$C_v = \frac{6}{6 + V_g} = \left(\frac{6}{6 + 0.0785 \, m}\right)$$

$$P_{eff} = \frac{1.2}{1} \times \frac{(6 + 0.0785 \, m)}{6} \cdot P_t$$

Equating P_{eff} with P_w = considering factor of safety

$$S_w = (P_{eff}) \cdot FS$$

$$131.4\, m^2 = \left[\frac{1.2}{1} \times \frac{(6 + 0.0785\, m)}{6} \times \frac{76904}{m}\right] 1.4$$

$$131.4\, m^3 = 1690\, m + 129199$$

$$m^3 - 12.85\, m - 983 = 0$$

Solving by trial and error we get m = 10.4 mm

We select next higher standard value as m = 12 mm

Heat dissipation:

$$\text{Heat generated} = P_{I/P}(1 - \eta)$$

$$= 8(1 - 0.755) = 1.96\, kW$$

$$\text{Heat generated} = C \cdot A \cdot \Delta T$$

where,

$$C = 18\, W/m^2{}°C \text{ (Assumed for natural circulation)}$$

$$= (18 \times A \times 50)\, W$$

Equating Heat generated = Heat dissipated

$$1.96 \times 10^3 = 18 \times A \times 50$$

$$A = 2.18\, m^2$$

EXERCISE

1. What are the types of failures in worm gearing and what remedies you propose to avoid such failures? **(May 2011)**

2. Why two dissimilar materials are used for worm and worm wheel. **(May 2011)**

3. Derive an expression for efficiency of worm gear pair.
   (November 2011, April 2009, October 2011, May 2012)

4. Explain following terms for worm and worm wheels. (a) Diameter quotient, (b) Self locking worm, (c) Rubbing velocity. **(May 2013)**

5. Why the soft material like Phosphor Bronze is chosen for worm gear and alloy steel for worm. **(May 2013)**

6. Derive an expression for effective face width of the worm wheel and length of the root of the worm wheel teeth. **(April 2009)**

7. Explain force analysis for a worm gear drive. **(April 2010)**

8. Discuss the thermal considerations in worm gear drive.
(April 2010, April 2012)

9. Derive equation for efficiency of worm gear in terms of lead angle and virtual friction angle. **(April 2012)**

10. Explain with neat sketch the difference between single Enveloping and double – Enveloping worm gear pair. **(October 2011)**

11. With neat sketches explain any two types of construction of worm gear.
(October 2011)

✱✱✱

Unit V

BELTS, ROPE AND CHAIN DRIVES

BELTS

5.1 INTRODUCTION

Belt, rope and chain drives are commonly known as *flexible machine elements or flexible drives*. Gear drives have many advantages. However when power is to be transmitted between two shafts at a considerable distance apart, the usage of gear drive results into incompatible solution in terms of space and manufacturing cost. For power transmission over a longer distance, flexible element drives prove to be advantageous.

Friction between the belt and pulley is responsible for power transmission. However in practical situations, some magnitude of slip is always present between belt and pulley. It is due to this reason that belt drive is not positive drive and hence it is not used in applications that require a constant velocity ratio. To certain extent flexible machine elements can be used as substitutes for gear and other rigid power transmission elements. More or less, these elements possess sufficient amount of elasticity, that helps in absorption/damping of shocks and vibrations. These elements can also tolerate a few degree of misalignment between driving and driven elements. Their applications include but are not limited to lathe machines, mopeds, positive displacement pumps, compressors, radiator cooling fans and many more. Few of the common types in use are flat, round, V and timing or toothed belt cross-sections.

Table 5.1: Details of typical fundamental belt types

Sr. No	Belt Cross-Section	Belt Type	Centre Distance	Remarks
1.	Flat		No Upper limit	Thickness up to 5 mm, joints are present.
2.	Round		No Upper limit	Diameter up to 20 mm. joints are present.
3.	V		Limited	Manufactured as endless. Width = 5 to 20 mm
4.	Timing/Toothed		Limited	Pitch: minimum 2 mm, manufactured as endless

5.2 MATERIALS AND CONSTRUCTION OF FLAT AND V-BELTS

Flat belts were traditionally made of leather or fabric and presently they are mostly made of rubber wherein they are fabric or cotton duck impregnated with rubber. Leather belts are made of excellent quality leather obtained by oak and mineral or chrome tanning process. Leather belts offer moderate and sometimes high coefficient of friction that result into enhanced power transmitting capacity. The number of layers present in a belt are called as plies. These belts are specified according to number of *plies* or *layers*, e.g. single-ply, double-ply, triple-ply and four-ply belts. A typical triple-ply belt is shown in Fig. 5.1 below.

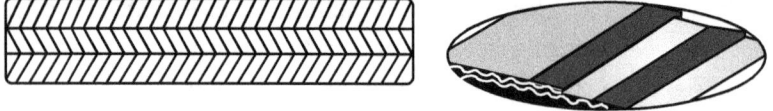

Fig. 5.1: A typical Triple-Ply Leather Belt

Fabric rubber belts are prepared by using a number of layers of canvas. Fabric functions as load transmission element, while the rubber acts as shield against damage and boosts coefficient of friction. Presence of rubber in the belt composition makes the different plies of fabric to act together as one belt. With advantages as high load carrying capacity, long service span and capacity to operate at speeds up to 250 m/sec, the fabric rubber belts are widely used in engineering applications. Different layers are built together by various methods.

Fig. 5.2: Fabric Rubber Belt

Ends of flat belts are joined using different processes as cementing, lacing and joining with metal fasteners. Flat belts are marketed in the form of coils and ends can be joined together to make them endless for a specific application as per required length. However care has to be taken to use proper joining method (as per manufacturer's recommendation), otherwise the belts will be weak at the joints and may not give rated capacity. The power rating of flat belts is specified as power transferred per ply of belt.

V-Belts: V belts may be completely rubber or polymer throughout the cross-section or there can be fibres of textile materials such as nylon or polyester or even steel embedded inside for achieving better strength. These type of belts mainly consist of three sections as

1. The load carrying layers of polyester/steel, located centrally near C.G of belt cross-section.
2. Layer of rubber that transfers load/force to cords from side walls.
3. Outer cover made of polychloroprene soaked with plastic.

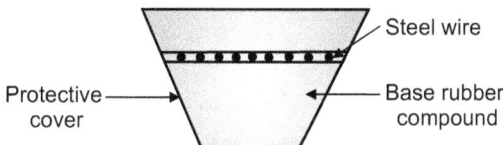

Fig. 5.3: Construction of V-Belt

Analysis of V-belt cross-section shows that the cords which are centrally located acts as load/force transfer members from driving to driven pulleys, thus resulting in power transmission. Furthermore as these steel wires or cords are located near the neutral axis, these are subjected to negligible amount bending stresses. Layers of rubber above the cords are subjected to tension and the layers below cords are subjected to compression and are known as tension and compression layers respectively. Usually, these belts are used as endless with factory manufactured belts to specific lengths. Multiple V belts are used for a specific power transmission when one belt is not adequate to transmit desired power. V belts are manufactured to various standards. Trapezoidal section sizes and manufacturer's guidelines need to be followed for their selection. These are very popular for industrial applications.

5.3 GEOMETRIC RELATIONSHIP FOR LENGTH OF BELT

Before proceeding for geometrical relation analysis of belt length, it is necessary to understand the open and crossed belt configurations.

Table 5.2

Sr. No	Open Belt Drive	Crossed Belt Drive
1.	The belt proceeds from driving to driven pulley without crossing.	The belt proceeds from top of driving to bottom of driven pulley and crosses over itself.
2.	*(diagram showing open belt drive with Pitch line, Belt thickness (t), Angle of contact, Effective surface, Pulley diameter (D), Driven pulley, Driving pulley, Shaft spacing (C))*	*(diagram showing crossed belt drive with Slack side, Driver pulley, Driven pulley, Tight side)*
3.	Driving and Driven pulleys rotate in same direction.	Driving and Driven pulleys rotate in opposite direction.

contd. ...

4.	Power transmission capacity is less as compared with the crossed belt drives.	Power transmission capacity is more as compared with the open belt drives.
5.	Magnitude of angle of wrap is less.	Magnitude of angle of wrap is more.
6.	Life of belt is more as compared with crossed belt drives.	Life of belt is less due to bending of belt in two different planes.
7.	Subjected to vibration and slip.	Free from vibration and slip.
8.	More popular than crossed belt drives	Less popular.

5.3.1 Derivation of Equation of Belt Length

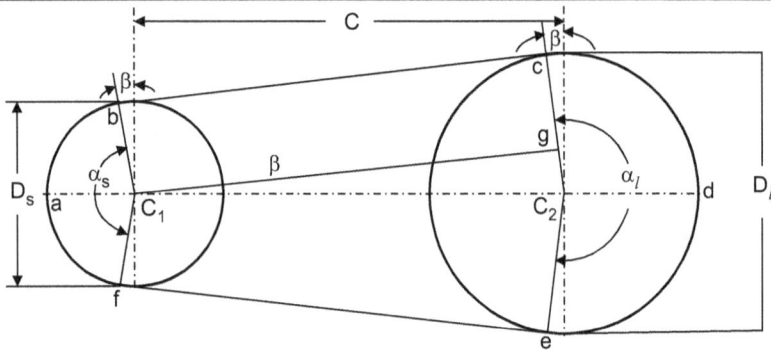

Fig. 5.4: Dimensional Details of Open Belt Drive

Referring the Fig. 5.4 of open belt drive, the belt dimensions are designated as under;

D_s = Diameter of small pulley (mm)

D_l = Diameter of large or big pulley (mm)

α_s = Angle of wrap for small pulley (degrees)

α_l = Angle of wrap for large or big pulley (degrees)

C = Centre distance (mm)

For open belting;

$$\sin \beta = \frac{D_l - D_s}{2C} \qquad \ldots (5.1)$$

$$\alpha_s = (180 - 2\beta) \Rightarrow \alpha_s = 180 - 2 \sin^{-1}\left(\frac{D_l - D_s}{2C}\right) \qquad \ldots (5.2)$$

$$\alpha_l = (180 + 2\beta) \Rightarrow \alpha_l = 180 + 2 \sin^{-1}\left(\frac{D_l - D_s}{2C}\right) \qquad \ldots (5.3)$$

Length of belt (L) for open belt drive is given as:

$$L = \text{arc (fab)} + l\text{(bc)} + \text{arc (cde)} + l\text{(ef)}$$

$$L = \frac{D_s}{2}(\alpha_s) + l(C_1 g) + \frac{D_l}{2}(\alpha_l) + l(C_1 g)$$

$$L = \frac{D_s}{2}(\pi - 2\beta) + C\cos\beta + \frac{D_l}{2}(\pi + 2\beta) + C\cos\beta$$

Rearranging the above equation

$$L = \frac{\pi(D_l + D_s)}{2} + \beta(D_l - D_s) + 2C\cos\beta \qquad \ldots (5.4)$$

For small values of β; $\beta = \sin\beta = \left(\frac{D_l - D_s}{2C}\right)$

$$\cos\beta = 1 - 2\sin^2\frac{\beta}{2} = 1 - (\beta^2/2) = (D_l - D_s)^2/8C^2$$

Using the above values in equation (5.4) and rearranging, we get

$$L = \frac{\pi(D_l + D_s)}{2} + \{(D_l - D_s)^2/2C\} + 2C - \{(D_l - D_s)^2/4C\}$$

$$L = 2C + \frac{\pi(D_l + D_s)}{2} + \{(D_l - D_s)^2/4C\} \qquad \ldots (5.5)$$

Equation (5.5) is the required expression for length of open belt drive.

Equation of Length for Crossed Belts:

Consider the crossed belt configuration. As can be seen from the figure, angle of lap on both pulleys is $\alpha_s = \alpha_l = 180 + 2\beta$.

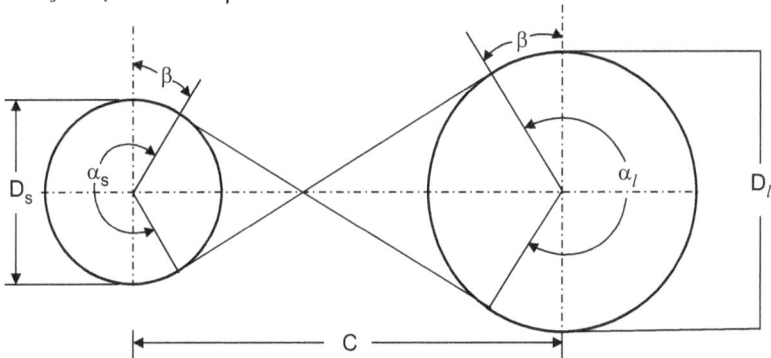

Fig. 5.5: Dimensional Details of Crossed Belt Drive

For evaluation of length of crossed belt drive,

$$\alpha_s = \alpha_l = (180 + 2\beta) \Rightarrow = 180 + 2\sin^{-1}\left(\frac{D_l - D_s}{2C}\right) \qquad \ldots (5.6)$$

Repeating the procedure followed for evaluation of length of open belt, we get length of crossed belt as

$$L = 2C + \frac{\pi(D_l + D_s)}{2}\{(D_l + D_s)^2/4C\} \qquad \ldots (5.7)$$

5.4 POWER RATING AND CONCEPT OF SLIP AND CREEP IN BELTS

5.4.1 Power Rating

Power rating (kW rating) for a flat belt is defined as the power transmission capacity of the belt per mm width per ply at 180° arc of contact. Consider e.g., the power rating (kW rating) of a flat belt is 0.015 kW, this means that a single ply of 1 mm width will transmit 0.015 kW power for 180° arc of contact with the pulley.

5.4.2 Concept of Slip and Creep in Belts

Creep is a typical phenomenon in belt drives. It is defined as a trivial relative motion of the belt as it passes over the pulley. As the belt moves from tight side to loose side over the pulley, it gets transferred from a zone of higher tension to lower one. It is due to this reduction of tension, belt is shortened and creeps over the surface of the pulley. This results into relative motion between belt and surface of pulley. Due to slight relative motion, the angular velocity of the driven pulley, evaluated from ratio of pulley diameters, is reduced. Creep phenomenon reduces the efficiency of the belt drive by 1% to 2%.

Slip phenomenon occurs due to overloads. During slipping action, the belt slides over entire arc of contact on the pulley. Slip phenomenon takes place when the difference in tensions of belt is less than force of frictional resistance on the rim of driven pulley, similarly reverse also holds true. If the force which belts deliver, exceeds the sum of limit of friction force between belt and pulley, slip will occur.

5.5 ANALYSIS OF BELT FORCES AND BELT TENSIONS

5.5.1 Belt Tension Analysis for Flat Belt

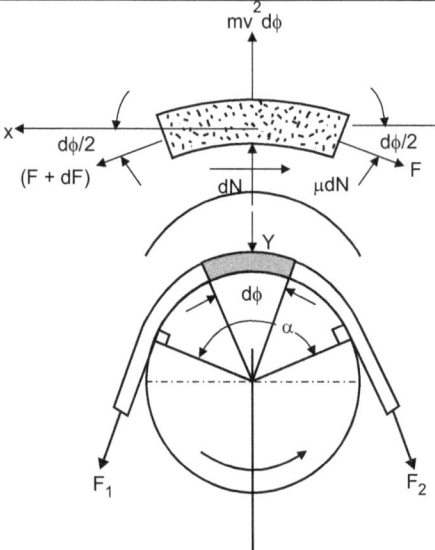

Fig. 5.6: Forces Acting on an Element of a Flat Belt

The forces acting on an element of a flat belt are shown in Fig. 5.6 above. Following notations are used in the analysis of belt tensions;

F_1 = Belt tension in the tight side (N)
F_2 = Belt tension in the loose side (N)
m = Mass of the one meter length of belt (kg/m)
v = Belt velocity (m/s)
f, μ = Coefficient of friction
α = Angle of wrap (radians)

Fig. 5.6 shows an element of belt subtending an angle dφ. This element is in equilibrium under the action of the following forces;

1. Tensions F and (F + dF) on loose and tight sides respectively.
2. The normal reaction dN between the surface of belt and pulley.
3. Frictional force f · dN (or μ · dN) at the belt pulley interface and
4. The centrifugal force ($mv^2 d\phi$) in radial outward direction

The centrifugal force acting on any element is given as

$$\text{Centrifugal force} = \text{Mass} \times \text{Acceleration} \qquad \ldots (5.8)$$

$$\text{Mass of the element is} = mr\, d\phi \qquad \ldots (5.9)$$

Also we know from fundamentals of kinematics of machines, that acceleration is given as

$$\text{Acceleration} = v^2/r \qquad \ldots (5.10)$$

From equations (5.8), (5.9) (5.10), the magnitude of centrifugal force is given as

$$\text{Centrifugal force} = mr\, d\phi * v^2 / r$$
$$= mv^2 d\phi$$

Writing the equilibrium by considering the forces in horizontal (X) and vertical (Y) directions; we get

$$(F + dF)\cos\left(\frac{d\phi}{2}\right) - F\cos\left(\frac{d\phi}{2}\right) - \mu dN = 0; \text{ Horizontal direction equilibrium}$$

$$(F + dF)\sin\left(\frac{d\phi}{2}\right) + F\sin\left(\frac{d\phi}{2}\right) - mv^2 d\phi - dN = 0; \text{ Vertical direction equilibrium}$$

For small values of $\left(\frac{d\phi}{2}\right)$, $\cos\left(\frac{d\phi}{2}\right)$ is nearly = 1 and $\sin\left(\frac{d\phi}{2}\right)$ is nearly = $\left(\frac{d\phi}{2}\right)$

Using these relations in horizontal and vertical equilibrium equations; we get
For horizontal equilibrium;

$$(F + dF) - F - \mu dN = 0$$

$$dF - \mu dN = 0 \Rightarrow dN = \frac{dF}{\mu} \qquad \ldots (5.11)$$

For vertical equilibrium;

$$(F + dF)\left(\frac{d\phi}{2}\right) + F\left(\frac{d\phi}{2}\right) - mv^2 d\phi - dN = 0$$

Neglecting second order differentials, i.e. $dF \times d\phi = 0$; we get

$$F\, d\phi - mv^2 d\phi - dN = 0 \qquad \ldots (5.12)$$

Using the value of dN from equation (5.11) in equation (5.12), and rearranging we get;

$$(F - mv^2)\, d\phi - \frac{dF}{\mu} = 0$$

$$\frac{dF}{F - mv^2} = \mu \cdot d\phi \qquad \ldots (5.13)$$

Equation 5.13 is called variable separable form; integrating the RHS and LHS and setting the limits as

$$\int_{F_2}^{F_1} \frac{dF}{F - mv^2} = \mu \int_0^{\alpha} d\phi$$

Integrating and using the upper and lower limits in the above equation, we get;

$$\frac{(F_1 - mv^2)}{(F_2 - mv^2)} = e^{\mu\alpha} \qquad \ldots (5.14)$$

The above equation is valid for high speed velocity belts. In case if the inertial force is negligible as compared to belt tensions equation (5.14).

$$\frac{F_1}{F_2} = e^{\mu\alpha} \qquad \ldots (5.15)$$

Further the power transmitted is given as

$$kW = \frac{(F_1 - F_2)\, v}{1000}$$

5.5.2 Belt Tension Analysis for V-belt

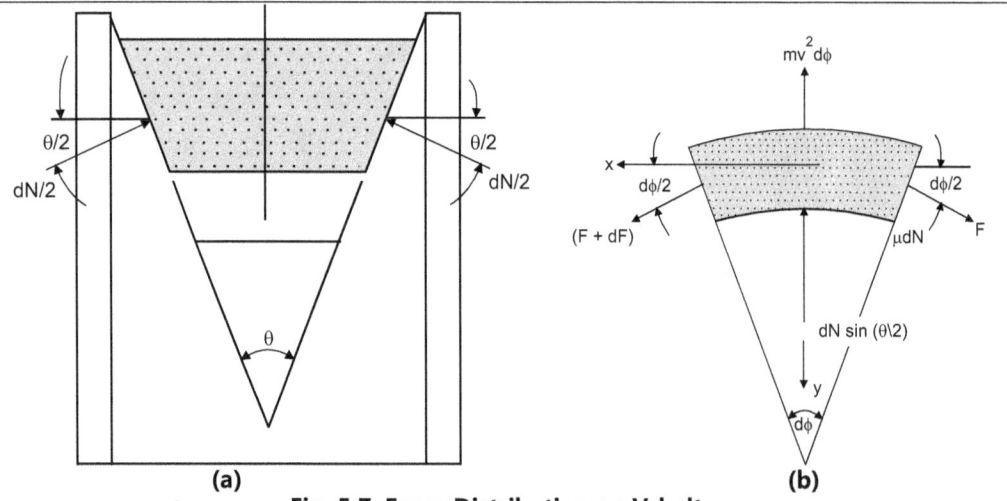

Fig. 5.7: Force Distribution on V-belt

In order to evaluate the magnitudes of belt tensions in terms of forces acting on the belt, the forces considered are shown in Fig. 5.7 above. Fig. 5.7 represents equilibrium condition of forces acting on v belt. Forces considered in flat belt analysis F, (F + dF) and $mv^2 d\phi$ remain same here also for the analysis of V belts. The sole difference is the magnitude of normal reaction dN, as it acts on both sides of v belt, its magnitude is assumed as (dN/2) on each side. Also the result reaction in X-Y plane is $dN \sin\left(\dfrac{\theta}{2}\right)$; where θ is called belt angle. As the magnitude of normal reaction is (dN/2); the total frictional force remains unchanged.

Writing the equilibrium by considering the forces in horizontal (X) and vertical (Y) directions; we get

$$(F + dF)\cos\left(\dfrac{d\phi}{2}\right) - F\cos\left(\dfrac{d\phi}{2}\right) - \mu dN = 0; \text{ Horizontal direction equilibrium}$$

$$(F + dF)\sin\left(\dfrac{d\phi}{2}\right) + F\sin\left(\dfrac{d\phi}{2}\right) - mv^2 d\phi - dN\sin\left(\dfrac{\theta}{2}\right) = 0; \text{ Vertical direction equilibrium}$$

For small values of $\left(\dfrac{d\phi}{2}\right)$, $\cos\left(\dfrac{d\phi}{2}\right)$ is nearly = 1 and $\sin\left(\dfrac{d\phi}{2}\right)$ is nearly = $\left(\dfrac{d\phi}{2}\right)$

Using these relations in horizontal and vertical equilibrium equations; we get

For horizontal equilibrium;

$$(F + dF) - F - \mu dN = 0$$

$$dF - \mu dN = 0 \Rightarrow dN = \dfrac{dF}{\mu} \qquad \ldots (5.16)$$

For vertical equilibrium;

$$(F + dF)\left(\dfrac{d\phi}{2}\right) + F\left(\dfrac{d\phi}{2}\right) - mv^2 d\phi - dN\sin\left(\dfrac{\theta}{2}\right) = 0$$

Neglecting second order differentials, i.e. $dF \times d\phi = 0$; we get

$$F\, d\phi - mv^2 d\phi - dN\sin\left(\dfrac{\theta}{2}\right) = 0$$

$$F\, d\phi - mv^2 d\phi - \dfrac{dF}{\mu}\sin\left(\dfrac{\theta}{2}\right) = 0 \qquad \ldots (5.17)$$

Using the value of dN from equation (5.16) in equation (5.17), and rearranging we get;

$$(F - mv^2)\, d\phi - \dfrac{dF}{\mu}\sin\left(\dfrac{\theta}{2}\right) = 0$$

$$\dfrac{dF}{F - mv^2} = \mu\, d\phi / \sin\left(\dfrac{\theta}{2}\right) \qquad \ldots (5.18)$$

Equation 5.19 is called variable separable form; integrating the RHS and LHS and setting the limits as

$$\int_{F_2}^{F_1} \dfrac{dF}{F - mv^2} = \left\{\mu / \sin\left(\dfrac{\theta}{2}\right)\right\} \int_{0}^{\alpha} d\phi$$

Integrating and using the upper and lower limits in the above equation, we get;

$$(F_1 - mv^2)/(F_2 - mv^2) = e^{\left(\frac{\mu\alpha}{\sin\frac{\theta}{2}}\right)} \qquad \ldots (5.19)$$

The above equation is valid for high speed velocity belts. In case if the inertial force is negligible as compared to belt tensions equation (5.19).

$$\frac{F_1}{F_2} = e^{\left(\frac{\mu\alpha}{\sin\frac{\theta}{2}}\right)} \qquad \ldots (5.20)$$

Furthermore the power transmitted is given as

$$kW = \frac{(F_1 - F_2)\,v}{1000}$$

A relative comparison between flat and V belts is given below.

Table 5.3: Comparison of flat and v belts

Sr. No.	Flat Belt	V Belt
1.	Simple and Inexpensive.	Costlier and periodic maintenance is needed.
2.	Low Power transmission capacity.	It can transmit more power than flat belts.
3.	Low velocity ratio (4 : 1).	High velocity ratio than flat belts (7 : 1)
4.	Operation is noisy.	Operation is smooth and noiseless.
5.	It can be used in open environment.	Used in closed environment where inclusion of dirt, dust is not expected.
6.	It can be used for long centre distances up-to 15 m, hence result into robust construction.	V belts are suitable shorter center distance and hence result in compact construction.
7.	Flat belt drives are horizontal.	It can be horizontal and vertical.
8.	Used in belt conveyors, baking machinery, stone crushers, brick manufacturing machinery, textiles, line shafts, flour mills, saw mills etc.	Used to drive compressors from electric motors, pumps, fans, blowers radiators, lathe machinery, mopeds etc.

5.6 MAXIMUM POWER CONDITION

The sole objective of belt drives, whether flat or V belt is to transmit power. Many factors are responsible for power losses in belt drives that include belt creep, friction between particles of belt, aerodynamic resistance for pulley motions, bearing friction, variation in belt material properties etc. For any type of belt to transmit maximum power (accounting the above mentioned factors) the initial tension in the belt and the belt velocity are the factors that can be varied to establish maximum power condition.

For the purpose of power transmission, an initial tension or pretension is provided to the belt. Let this initial tension be denoted by F_i. The magnitude of this pretension depends upon the characteristics of belt such as length of belt, belt material elasticity, centre distance and geometry of belt pulleys. For establishment of relation between the tensions on tight and slack sides and initial tension, it must be assumed that there is no variation in belt length before and after the application of initial tension and elasticity of the belt material is linear.

As the driving pulley starts rotating, the elongation on the tight side is in proportion with $(F_1 - F_i)$, further on loose side it is $(F_i - F_2)$. With reference to the assumption that the length of the belt is constant, we have;

$$(F_1 - F_i) = (F_i - F_2)$$

$$F_i = \frac{1}{2}(F_1 + F_2) \qquad \ldots (5.21)$$

We know that for a flat belt drive

$$\frac{(F_1 - mv^2)}{(F_2 - mv^2)} = e^{\mu\alpha}$$

Rearranging the above equation as; $\dfrac{(F_2 - mv^2)}{(F_1 - mv^2)} = e^{-\mu\alpha}$

Simplifying further

$$\frac{[(F_1 + F_2) - 2mv^2]}{(F_2 - F_1)} = \frac{(e^{-\mu\alpha} + 1)}{(e^{-\mu\alpha} - 1)} \qquad \ldots (5.22)$$

But $(F_1 + F_2) = 2F_i$

From equation (5.21); using in equation (5.22), we get

$$\frac{[2F_i - 2mv^2]}{-(F_1 - F_2)} = \frac{(e^{-\mu\alpha} + 1)}{(e^{-\mu\alpha} - 1)}$$

$$(F_1 - F_2) = [2F_i - 2mv^2] \times \frac{(1 - e^{-\mu\alpha})}{(1 + e^{-\mu\alpha})}$$

$$\text{Power} = v(F_1 - F_2) = [2F_i v - 2mv^3] \times \frac{(1 - e^{-\mu\alpha})}{(1 + e^{-\mu\alpha})} \qquad \ldots (5.23)$$

To obtain the maximum power condition, we differentiate the power with respect to belt velocity v, and equate it to zero. $\frac{d}{dv}(\text{Power}) = 0, \frac{d}{dv}(F_i v - mv^3) = 0$

$$\Rightarrow (F_i - 3mv^2) = 0 \text{ and}$$

Hence, the optimum velocity of the belt at which the maximum power is transmitted is given as $v = \sqrt{\frac{F_i}{3m}}$ required expression.

Alternatively maximum power can also be obtained in terms of tight side tension F_1:

We know that for a flat belt drive

$$\frac{F_1}{F_2} = e^{\mu\alpha} \quad \ldots (5.24)$$

If F_{max} is the maximum tension to which belt can be subjected

$$F_1 = F_{max} - F_c \quad \ldots (5.25)$$

where F_c is the centrifugal tension in belt $= m.v^2$

Power that can be transmitted by the belt

$$\text{Power} = (F_1 - F_2) \times v$$

$$= \left(F_1 - \frac{F_1}{e^{\mu\alpha}}\right) \cdot v = F_1\left(1 - \frac{1}{e^{\mu\alpha}}\right) \times v$$

$$= F_1 \cdot v \cdot C$$

where $C = \left(1 - \frac{1}{e^{\mu\alpha}}\right)$

Thus, $\quad \text{Power} = F_1 \cdot v \cdot C \quad \ldots (5.26)$

Substituting values of F_1 from (5.25)

$$\text{Power} = (F_{max} - F_c) \cdot v \cdot C = (F_{max} - m.v^2) \cdot v \cdot C = (F_{max} \cdot v - m \cdot v^3) \cdot C$$

For maximum power, $\frac{dp}{dv} = 0$

Hence, $(F_{max} - 3mv^2) = 0 \quad \ldots (5.27)$

Hence $(F_{max} - 3 \cdot F_c) = 0$ OR $F_{max} = 3 \cdot F_c \quad \ldots$ (a)

From equation 5.27, $\quad v = \sqrt{\frac{F_{max}}{3 \cdot m}} \quad \ldots$ (b)

From equation (5.25)

$$F_1 = F_{max} - F_c$$

$\therefore \quad F_1 = 3F_c - F_c = 2F_c \quad \ldots$ (c)

Equations (a), (b) and (c) in various forms express the conditions for maximum power transmission by a belt.

Initial tension in the belt: $F_i = \dfrac{F_1 + F_2}{2}$ ... (Neglecting centrifugal tension)

$$F_i = \dfrac{F_1 + F_2 + 2 \cdot F_c}{2}$$ ... (Considering centrifugal tension)

5.7 SELECTION OF FLAT AND V BELTS FROM MANUFACTURER'S CATALOGUE

5.7.1 Selection of Flat Belts

Proper belt selection for a given application needs information on (kW) power to be transmitted, input speed, speed ratio, nature and type of load, and the centre distance. The fundamental steps in flat belt selection are given below;

1. For optimum performance belt manufacturers recommend belt speed in the range of 18 to 22 m/s, consider e.g., 20 m/s and calculate the diameter of smaller pulley using the following relation

   $d = \dfrac{60{,}000 \times v}{\pi n}$; n is the speed (rpm) of smaller pulley or input speed

   Further evaluate the diameter of bigger pulley as

   $$D = d \times \dfrac{\text{Speed of input pulley}}{\text{Speed of output pulley}}$$

   After the values of smaller and larger diameters of pulleys are evaluated from the above equations; round-off the diameter values to nearest standard/preferred diameters. The standard diameters for the pulley are found by preferred series R20 and are rounded off. Hence, the preferred diameters are 100, 112, 125, 140, 160, 180, 200, 224, 250, 280, 315, 355, 400, 450, 500,.... These values are available in the manufacturer's catalogue. Having selected the pulley diameters, once again calculate the actual belt velocity. This velocity must be in the prescribed range (18 to 22 m/sec).

2. Different types of loads act on the belt. In order to account for the nature of load for the application under consideration, a modifying factor known as load correction factor is used. It is denoted by F_a. Using this factor the maximum power is evaluated. The values of load correction factor for different types of load are given in table 5.4 below

Table 5.4: Typical values of load correction factor

Sr. No.	Nature of Load	Value (F_a)
1.	Normal Load	1.00
2.	Intermittent Load	1.30
3.	Steady Load	1.20
4.	Impact or Shock load	1.50

The maximum power for the design purpose by considering the given application or load factor is calculated as:

$$\text{Design Power; (kW)}_{max} = F_a \text{ (kW)}$$

3. Determine the angle of wrap for smaller pulley using the relationship as

$$\alpha_s = (180 - 2\beta) \Rightarrow = 180 - 2\sin^{-1}\left(\frac{D-d}{2C}\right)$$

4. Belt manufacturers consider a value of 180° of arc of contact in developing the power transmitting capacities of the belt. However, the actual arc of contact will vary depending on the arrangement. The result of this is variation in tension in the belt (given by equation 5.15). To account for this, arc of contact factor F_d is considered for evaluating the power. The values for different wrap angles are given in table 5.5 below

Table 5.5: Values of contact arc factor

α_s (Degrees)	F_d	α_s (Degrees)	F_d	α_s (Degrees)	F_d
90	1.679	160	1.08	210	0.91
120	1.329	170	1.04	220	0.88
130	1.258	180	1.00	230	0.86
140	1.190	190	0.97	240	0.84
150	1.128	200	0.94	250	0.82

Calculate the corrected power by using

$$\text{(kW)}_{corrected} = \text{(kW)}_{max} \times F_d$$

5. Find the power rating from the catalogue for the belt type selected. Belt manufacturer indicates in the catalogue values of belt rating such as 0.023 kW per unit width of belt per ply at some standard velocity (say 10 m/sec).

6. The velocity for the application is determined in step 1 above, which could be different from the standard velocity. To account for this determine the corrected kW rating for the flat belt as

$$\text{Corrected kW belt Rating} = \frac{\text{Power rating per ply} \times \text{Correct belt velocity (v)} \frac{m}{s}}{10}$$

7. For the given number of plies in belt, further evaluate the belt width using the relation as

$$\text{(Belt width} \times \text{Number of plies)} = \frac{\text{kW corrected power}}{\text{Corrected kW belt rating}}$$

8. Standard belt widths are indicated by the manufacturer in the catalogue in the format such as:

| 3 ply | 25 mm | 40 mm | 50 mm | 63 mm |
| 4 ply | 40 mm | 44 mm | 50 mm | 63 mm |

9. The designer can conduct trials with 2/3/4 plies and find required widths. These widths can be compared with standard widths available and proper belt can be selected whose required width matches with standard width available.
10. Calculate the length of belt using the formula for length depending upon open or crossed belt drive.

5.7.2 Selection of V belts From Manufacturer's Catalogue

V-belts are prominently used in agitators, hammer mills, crusher, compressor fans, radiator fans and other similar applications. While selecting V belt from manufacturer's catalogue, prior information such as kW power to be transmitted (P), machine to be driven, operating hours per day, input rpm, speed ratio, desired center distance is needed. The steps in selection of V-belt are

1. Depending upon the details, such as type of driving unit, driven machine and operating hours per day, the **correction factor F_a** according to service is selected from the Table 5.6.

Table 5.6: Values of load correction factor for V-belt

Required Type of Service	Normal Magnitude of Torque for A.C. Motor			High Magnitude of Torque for A.C. Motor		
	Number of Operating shifts			Number of Operating shifts		
	1	2	3	1	2	3
Light duty	1.0 to 1.2			1.1 to 1.3		
Medium duty	1.1 to .3			1.2 to 1.4		
Heavy duty	1.2 to 1.4			1.4 to 1.6		

2. **Evaluate the design power** by using relationship as under;
Design Power = $F_a \times P$ (where, P = Power to be transmitted)
3. **V belt cross section** sizes such as A, B, C, D,........ are standardized by manufacturer to take different tensions at various speeds. A selection graph with design power as abscissa

and smaller pulley rpm speed as ordinate is published in the catalogue, to select the proper cross-section of the belt. Using this plot (Fig. 5.8) select the belt cross section (B, C, D etc.).

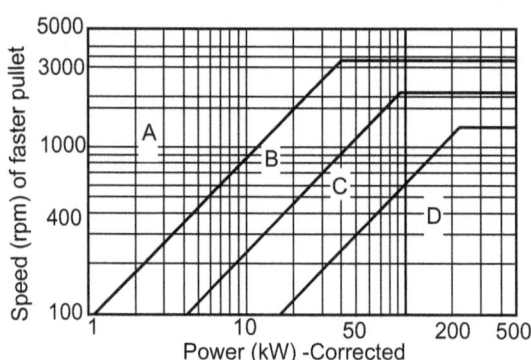

Fig. 5.8: Belt Cross Section Selection

4. **Select the recommended minimum pitch diameter of smaller pulley** for the belt type From the preferred pulley pitch diameters as below.

   B: 125, 132, 140, 150, 160, 170, 180, 200, 224, 250 ... (Recommended Minimum: 200)

   C: 200, 212, 224, 236, 250, 265, 280, 300, 315, 355... (Recommended Minimum: 315)

   D: 355, 375, 400, 425, 450, 475, 500, 530, 560, 600... (Recommended Minimum: 500)

   Knowing the speed ratio determine the pitch diameter of larger pulley. Select the closest standard pulley diameter from the above referred table. Find he velocity ratio obtained.

5. Knowing final pulley diameters, find **the length of belt** by using the relation

$$L = 2C + \frac{\pi(D+d)}{2} + \frac{(D-d)\times(D-d)}{4C}$$

   Preferred pitch lengths of belts are published in the manufacturer's catalogue such as

   B: 930, 1000, 1100, 1210, 1370, 1560, 1690...

   C: 1560, 1760, 1950, 2190, 2420, 2720...

   D: 2740, 3130, 3330, 3730, 4080, 4620...

   Select the length of the belt from preferred lengths that is closest to calculated length.

6. Using the value of standard length obtained from step 5, **find the correct centre distance** C, using relation $L = 2C + \frac{\pi(D+d)}{2} + \frac{(D-d)\times(D-d)}{4C}$ which becomes quadratic equation in terms of C.

7. Depending upon the type of cross-section and pitch length of the belt **select the correction factor (F_c)** for the pitch length obtained as under (Manufacturer's catalogue provides this information):
Lengths of belts with Correction factors
B: 930 (0.81), 1000 (0.83), 1100 (0.85), 1210 (0.87), 1370 (0.9), 1560 (0.92)…
C: 1560 (0.82), 1760 (0.84), 1950 (0.87), 2190 (0.9), 2420 (0.92), 2720 (0.94)…
D: 2740 (0.82), 3130 (0.86), 3330 (0.87), 3730 (0.9), 4080 (0.92), 4620 (0.94)…

8. Further **evaluate the arc of contact** for input pulley using the relation

$$\alpha_s = 180 - 2\sin^{-1}\left(\frac{D-d}{2C}\right)$$

Find correction factor F_d for arc of contact as under

α_s	130	142	160	171	180
F_d	0.86	0.89	0.95	0.98	1

9. Find power rating (P_r) from the table in the catalogue for the selected belt depending on the belt cross-section selected. Only typical values corresponding to standard motor speeds are indicated below.

Table 5.7: kW rating (P_r) for V-belt sections (B, C, D) at standard motor speeds and pulley diameters (sample cases)

Smaller pulley Speed	B Pulley diameter		C Pulley diameter		D Pulley diameter	
	125	160	200	250	355	400
720	1.61	2.48	4.65	6.81	16.26	19.9
960	2.02	3.13	5.76	8.46	19.26	23.45
1440	2.72	4.26	7.49	10.95	21.22	--
2880	3.96	6.11	--	--	--	--

10. Determine number of belts by using the relation

$$\text{Number of belts} = \frac{P \times F_a}{P_r \times F_c \times F_d}$$

F_a = Correction factor for industrial service
P_r = Rating power of single V belt
F_c = Belt length correction factor
F_d = Arc of contact correction factor

5.8 BELT TENSIONING METHODS

Whenever, a belt is mounted on pulleys it does not transmit any power on its own. This is due to absence of sufficient amount of friction. Hence, the belts are always provided with initial tension which increases the coefficient of friction and further results into power transmission. In course of service, the initial tension gets lost gradually due to many factors and hence there should be a provision to adjust the belt tensions as and when required. Hence, belt tensioning methods are needed. Various methods of belt tensioning are into existence as;

1. Cutting a short length of belt by the amount of slack, in case when the belt is laced. However, this method is not applicable to endless belts and is not convenient for regular tensioning. Usually, this method will be employed only when belt tensioning arrangement has reached its limits.
2. Using the adjusting screw (Usually on the driver pulley) the center distance between the pulleys is slightly increased. Typically an electric motor with its pulley may be mounted such that the motor position could be shifted using adjusting screw so as to periodically adjust the tension.
3. Usage of idler pulley mechanism is also into practice. In this, the idler pulley is located next to the input pulley and is held against the belt by its own and additional weight. Its position can be adjusted to provide a longer belt path as and when belt has slackened.
4. Referring the Fig. 5.9; another popular method known as Rockwood Belt drive is shown. From the figure it is observed that the adjustment in belt tension is done by variation in the eccentricity Z. Relationship between the tensions on tight and slack sides of the Rockwood belt drive is given as

$$Z = \frac{(T_t) \times y - (T_s) \times x}{W}$$

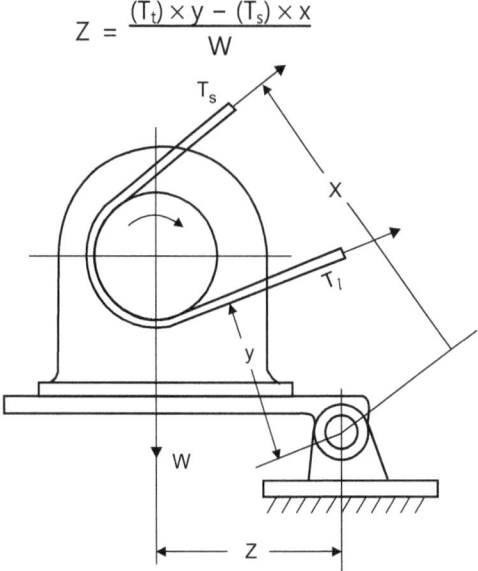

Fig. 5.9: Rockwood Belt Drive

5.9 CONSTRUCTION AND APPLICATIONS OF TIMING BELTS

These are actually flat belts with a series of evenly spaced circumferential teeth on the inner surface. These teeth consecutively mesh with the teeth on the pulley or sprocket as shown in Fig. 5.10 below. It is also known as synchronous belt, ribbed V-belt or toothed belt.

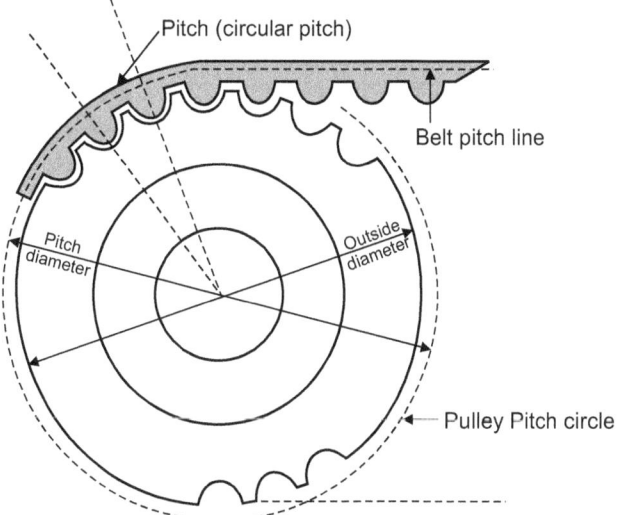

Fig. 5.10: Construction of Timing Belt

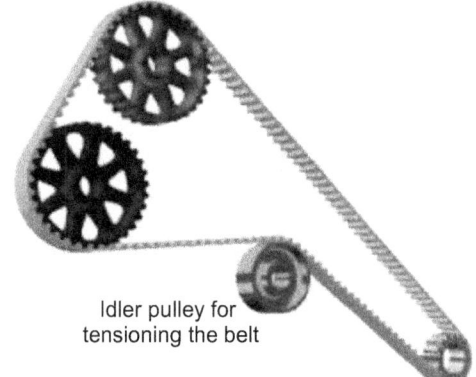

Fig. 5.11: Timing Belt Tensioning Arrangement

The timing belts are positive drives and combine high velocity characteristics of the belt drive with power transmission. The constituents of the timing belts include fibre (steel) cords to transmit load, protecting backing to steel wires especially made of rubber, teeth for engagement with the pulley or sprocket and cover to avoid wear of belts. Advantages of these drives include no slipping due to presence of teeth and high coefficient of friction. Such drives are used in applications that have high pitch line velocities up-to 80 m/s, do not require any arrangement for lubrication, no initial tension is needed, however these are costly as compared with the other belt drives and are sensitive to misalignment.

Timing belts are used in automobiles to drive camshaft from crankshaft. Sewing machines also employ V-belts, machine shop, wood working machines and other power transmission devices.

WIRE ROPES

5.10 CONSTRUCTION OF WIRE ROPES

Wire ropes are prominently used in material handling applications, wire rope hoists, winches and other similar applications where the component or the final product is to be carried or transferred from one place to other. Wire ropes also include stationary applications as bridge supports, and stays. Wire ropes offer high reliability, noiseless operation even at considerable velocities.

Wire rope Construction: Construction of wire ropes includes terms as wire, strands, core and rope. These are shown in Fig. 5.12.

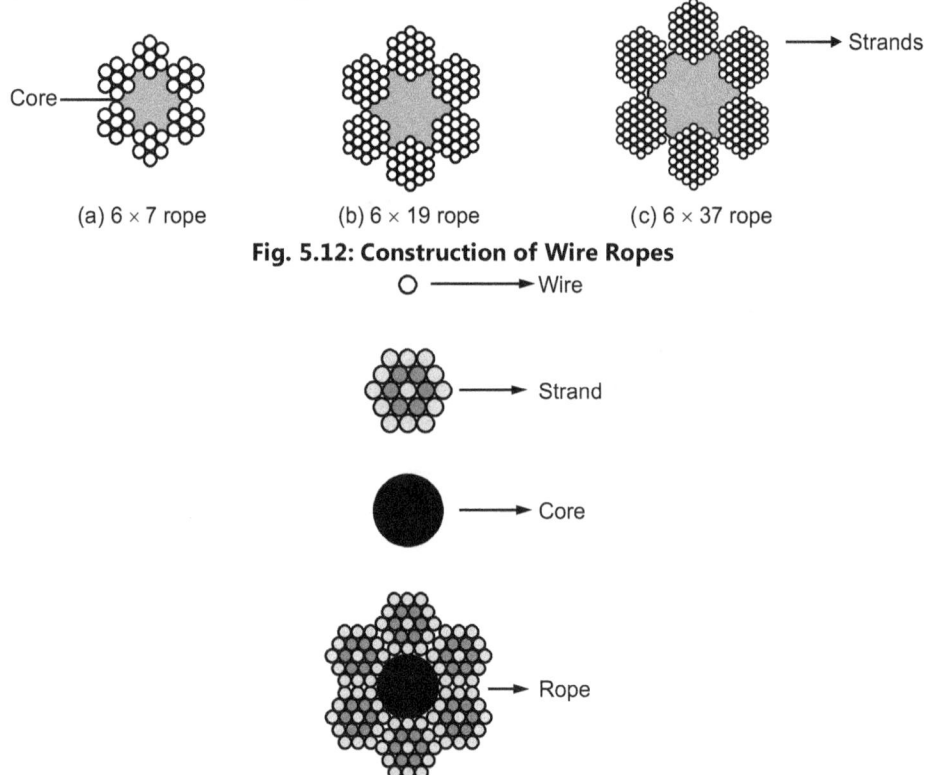

(a) 6 × 7 rope   (b) 6 × 19 rope   (c) 6 × 37 rope

Fig. 5.12: Construction of Wire Ropes

Fig. 5.13: Details of Wire Rope Construction

Fig. 5.13 above represents the exploded view of wire rope details. Numbers of wires are twisted into a strand, and further these strands are twisted around a core. Core is the central member or portion of the wire rope. Core material is usually fibre, wire and synthetic material. Fibre core includes natural fibers like sisal, hemp, jute or cotton. The fibre core is suitable for normal working conditions. The wire core is used in applications that include severe load and high temperature applications. The numbers of wires combined in each strand can be 7, 19 or 37 as mentioned in various standards for wire ropes; however numbers of strands are limited or restricted to six. Wire ropes are specified as 6X7 or 6X19 and 6X 37. In this specification, the first number shows number of strands while the second number designates number of wires in each strand. Also designated as 6/1, or 12/6/1 and 18/12/16/1.

5.11 LAY OF WIRE ROPES

The term "lay" refers to the style or mode in which the wires are helically laid into strands and strands into the rope. When the wires in the strand are twisted into the same direction as the strands then the rope is termed as 'Lang's Lay Rope' and when the wires are twisted into opposite direction to that of strands then the rope is termed as "regular or ordinary lay". Regular and Lang's lay are represented in Fig. 3.14 below.

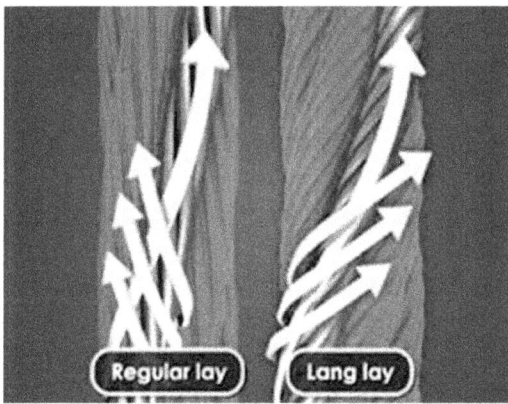

Fig. 5.14: Regular and Lang Lay Ropes

The regular as well as Lang's lay are again classified into right and left hand lays. These are represented in Fig. 5.15 below.

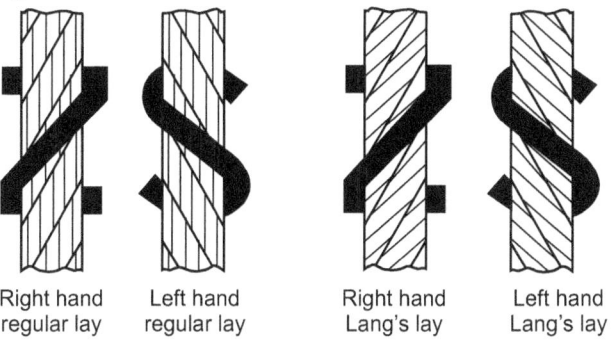

Fig. 5.15: Classifications of Lays

As compared with Lang's lay, the regular lay is more popular. They have the following advantages over Lang's Lay:
- More structural stability.
- More resistance to crushing and distortion.
- Less tendency to rotate under load.
- Less possibility of kinking.
- Easy handling during installation.

5.12 STRESSES IN WIRE ROPES

Rope appears to be a simple part but its stress analysis is complex as it needs considerations to various factors. There are mainly three types of stresses which need to be considered.

(a) Direct Tensile Stress:

The primary function of a wire rope is to raise or pull a load. During this pulling or raising operation, the individual wires in the rope are subjected to tensile stresses. In applications such as motorized hoist there are also jerk (shock) loads in addition to the rated load P_t.

The rated load P_t induces a direct tensile stress $\sigma_t = P_t/A$

Where A is the area of the steel wires within the rope cross section.

(a) Stress due to Bending:

During the load raising operation, the rope passes over the sheave or drum. The outer portion of rope which is passing over the drum is subjected to additional tensile stresses due to its bending over the curvature portion. The bending stresses in the individual wire is given as

$$\sigma_b = \frac{M_b \times Y}{I} \quad \ldots (5.28)$$

Here,

$$Y = \frac{d_w}{2}$$

Where, d_w is the wire diameter (mm)

The bending theory equation for an elastic material is given as $\frac{M_b}{I} = \frac{E}{r}$; where r is the radius of curvature.

Applying this to the rope and rope drum assembly, $\frac{M_b}{EI} = \frac{1}{R}$;

The radius R is the radius of sheave in this equation. Replacing R by D/2, we get

$$\frac{M_b}{EI} = \frac{2}{D} \quad \ldots (5.29)$$

From equations (5.28) and (5.29)

$$\sigma_b = \frac{E \times d_w}{D} \quad \ldots (5.30)$$

In the equation 5.30, E is the Modulus of elasticity for wire material. However, as already seen the construction of the wire rope is complex with wires strands going on a helical path and passing over a curvature on the sheave or drum. This is accounted by considering new modulus of elasticity as E_r, i.e. modulus of elasticity of rope. Hence, equation (5.30) becomes,

$$\sigma_b = \frac{E_r \times dw}{D}$$

While designing the wire ropes it is convenient to solve problems using equivalent bending load. This load will be hypothetical (or equivalent) tensile load that will induce same tensile stress as the bending stress. Hence, the equivalent bending load denoted as P_b will be given as

$$P_b = \sigma_b \cdot A$$

Equating $\quad \sigma_b = \dfrac{P_b}{A} = \dfrac{E_r \times dw}{D}$

Thus, the equivalent tensile load $P_b = \dfrac{A \times E_r \times dw}{D}$ and a bending stress of $\sigma_b = \dfrac{P_b}{A}$.

where A is the area of metallic cross-section of the wire rope.

(b) Bearing Stress (pressure):

Wire rope failures occurs due the fatigue or wear. The process of fatigue or wear is observed at the interface of rope and sheave. This fatigue is due to rubbing of the wire rope over sheave. When the rope passes over the sheave it bends and gets straightened which results in fluctuating stresses leading to fatigue failure. Wearing phenomenon is directly proportional to the amount of pressure between the rope and the sheave. If a rope (d_r) is wound over a sheave of diameter D and each of these ends have a load = P, then the rope bearing area is $D \times d_r$.

Considering the equilibrium of forces in vertical direction we have $2P = p \cdot (D \times d_r)$.

Thus bearing pressure $p = 2P/D \times d_r$

It is experimentally observed that if the wire rope material has 'S_{ult}' as its ultimate tensile strength, a substantial life can be expected for stress levels leading to $(p/S_{ult}) < 0.015$. These values are only indicative since variables are too many.

In practical situations a factor of safety of 8 is recommended and wire ropes along with other load handling devices undergo periodic checks to prevent any signs of early failure go unnoticed. Wire ropes are extensively lubricated to reduce wear.

5.13 SELECTION OF WIRE ROPES

Guidelines for selection of wire ropes are given as below:
1. Depending upon the type of application and the consequence of failure, cores are selected. Usage or selection of steel core in place of fibre core will certainly increase the strength of wire rope to certain extent.
2. Rope flexibility is also a parameter under consideration where the diameter of sheave is small or wherever ropes make number of bends. Consider e.g., wire rope 6×7 which includes few wires of large size. Thus, 6×7 wire ropes are suitable especially for carrying, transportation and similar applications. The remaining two types 6×19 and 6×37 are especially used in hoist and other similar applications due to their higher flexibility.
3. It is observed that large diameter wires as compared with smaller ones provide excellent wear resistance. This is the reason why 6×7 wires are seen in applications where the scratch resistance is of concern.

The factor of safety for wire ropes as per applications are categorized as in Table 5.8.

Table 5.8: Wire rope Factor of Safety for various applications

Sr. No	Application	Factor of Safety Range
1.	Jib hoist, lifting beams, guy ropes etc.	3.5 to 4.5
2.	Mobile platform, hoisting systems etc.	4 to 6
3.	Cranes and Hoists.	6 to 8

5.14 ROPE DRUM CONSTRUCTION AND DESIGN

When the load is lifted to its topmost position, wire rope is wound over the drum. Thus to accommodate this wire rope, the length of the drum depends on the height of lift. Fundamental function of a rope drum is to provide a bearing and contact surface to the rope while it passes over during its operation. Accordingly design considerations for rope drum include appropriate sizing, free run on the axle as per application requirement, grooves with suitable dimensions etc.

Different types of rope drum constructions are available. Most commonly seen are two types.
    (a) Drums with helical grooves and
    (b) Plain cylindrical drums without grooves.

Preferably grooved drums are used as compared with plain ones for hoisting installations. Grooved drums increase the bearing surface and this further prevents friction between the adjacent rope turns; resulting in less wear and increasing rope life. Material used for drum construction can be grey cast iron (FG200) or steel.

A grooved drum is shown in Fig. 5.16. Drum is provided with helical grooves so that the rope winds up uniformly on the drum. Radius of the helical groove should be selected so as to prevent jamming of the rope. Drums designed for two fall system (with two ropes on the drum) are provided with two helical grooves R.H and L.H. so that the ropes simultaneously move outside or inside thus maintaining the center line.

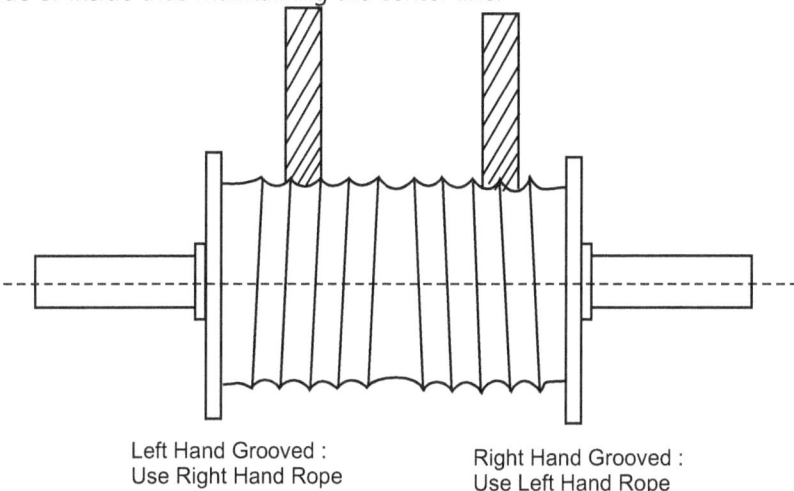

Left Hand Grooved : Use Right Hand Rope

Right Hand Grooved : Use Left Hand Rope

Fig. 5.16: Rope Drum and Wire

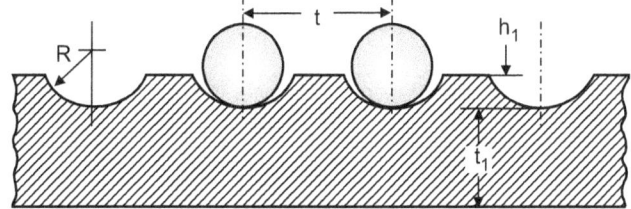

Fig. 5.17: Dimensional Details of Rope and Drum

Referring to Fig. 5.17 above the dimensional parameters of a rope drum and its assembly are given as under;

1. Pitch of the groove $t = d_r + $ (2 to 4 mm).
2. Thickness of shell of the cast iron drum is given by $t_1 = 0.02D + $ (5 to 10 mm).

   where d_r is nominal diameter of rope (mm) and D is drum diameter.

CHAIN DRIVES

5.15 INTRODUCTION

Chain drives are most reliable machine components that are widely used in industry. These drives are primarily used in power transmission and conveyance systems. Chain drive is a combination of chains, sprockets and a shaft mounting. Chain can be thought as a series of links to form loops; connected and fitted into one another. Basically, it consists of two sprockets or toothed wheels on which the loops of the chain fit and work as a drive for transmitting motion or power. Transmission chains have flexibility in one plane.

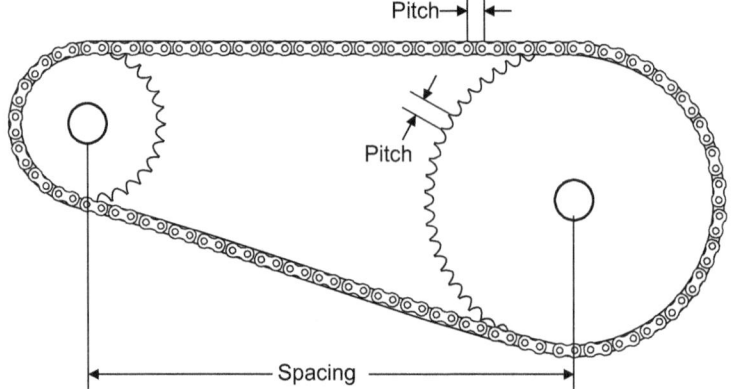

Fig. 5.18: Chain Drive

Chain drives offer the following advantages over belt drives:
- There is no slippage between chain and sprocket teeth.
- As the links are rigid bodies, there is negligible stretch in chain drives and hence chain drives can carry heavy loads.
- No or less sensitivity to external contaminants like dirt, dust, oil, grease etc.
- Can operate /work at elevated temperatures.
- Longer operating life as there is contact between hardened surfaces which are separated by oil film.
- Reliable drive and can take some amount of misalignment.

Some disadvantages of chain drive are:
- Wearing of links and sprocket teeth leads to elongation of chain.
- These drives need continual or frequent lubrication for certain applications.
- Replacement of sprockets is needed as and when worn out chains are replaced.
- These drives are limited to lower operating speeds than belt drives.

5.16 TYPES OF POWER TRANSMISSION CHAINS

Power transmission chains are applied in transmission of power from one shaft to another.

5.16.1 Roller Chains

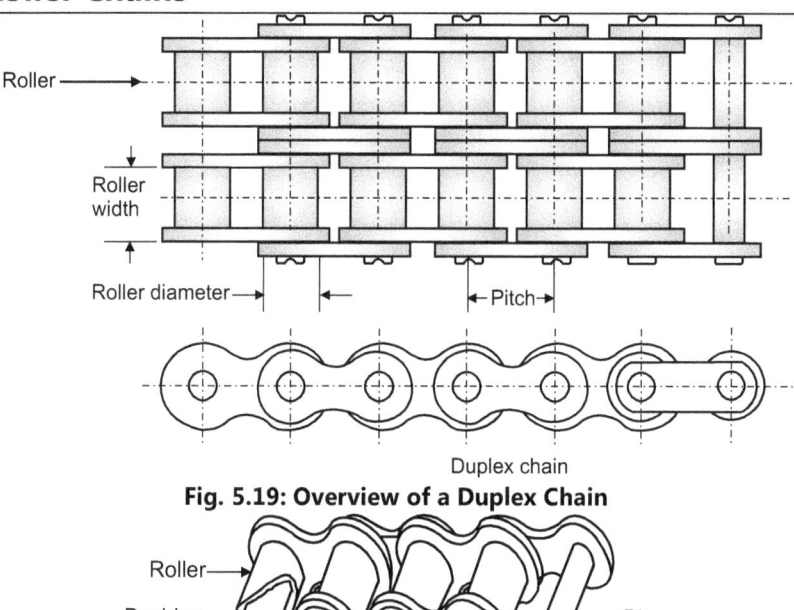

Fig. 5.19: Overview of a Duplex Chain

Fig. 5.20: Parts of a Simplex Roller Chain

The roller chain as shown in Figs 5.19 and 5.20 includes four fundamental parts.
1. Pin
2. Roller
3. Bush
4. Inner (bush) and outer (pin) link plates.

Roller chain drives work on rolling friction. The rolling friction is generated due to contact between the roller and the sprocket teeth. Pin is fitted to outer link plates and bush to inner link plates. Both these are fitted using pressing operation. Further, the rollers are fitted on the bushes, which turn freely during the engagement of teeth with the sprocket.

Materials:
1. Inner and outer link plates: Medium carbon steel.
2. Pin, bush and roller: Alloy steels.

Pitch of the chain is defined as the linear distance between the axes of adjacent rollers. These roller chains are available in single strand or multi strand constructions. (Duplex or triplex constructions)

5.17 CHAIN GEOMETRY

A chain engaged on sprocket wheel is shown in Fig. 5.21.

D: PCD of sprocket is defined as the diameter of an imaginary circle which passes through the centers of link pins as the chain is wrapped on the sprocket.

Pitch angle $\alpha = \dfrac{360}{z}$; where, z is the number of teeth on the sprocket.

From figure $\sin\left(\dfrac{\alpha}{2}\right) = \dfrac{p/2}{D/2}$ or $D = \dfrac{p}{\sin\dfrac{\alpha}{2}}$

Velocity ratio of the chain drive is given by $i = \dfrac{n_1}{n_2} = \dfrac{Z_2}{Z_1}$.

Where n_1, n_2 are rotational speeds of driving and driven shafts and corresponding Z_1 and Z_2 are the number of teeth on driving and driven sprockets. Velocity of the chain is one of the significant factor for chain life and operation in any application. The average velocity of the chain is $v = \dfrac{\pi D n}{60 \times 1000} = \dfrac{Z.p.n}{60 \times 1000}$.

Length of chain $L = L_n \times p$; L_n = Number of links in the chain.

If sometimes the chain length calculated results into odd number of links, an additional link known as offset link is attached. This additional link is generally weaker in terms of strength as compared with other links. Hence, preferably the chain length selected consists of even number of links. Chain tensioning provision is required for longer center distances between sprockets.

5.18 POLYGONAL EFFECT IN CHAINS

In any chain drive, the chain passes or rolls around the sprocket. The length of section of chain, that approaches sprocket, passes over sprocket, and leaves the sprocket, can be presumed as a chord of a circle. Engagement of sprocket and chain can be thought of as non-slipping belt that is wrapped around a rotating polygon. Fig. 5.21 shows this phenomenon with the aid of four teeth on sprocket. The same analysis will hold good for larger number of teeth as well. The link AB in the chain is assumed to be located at a distance of D/2 from sprocket centre and roller B has velocity at this point denoted by V_{max} and is given by

$$V_{max} = \dfrac{\pi D n}{60 \times 1000} \text{ m/s}$$

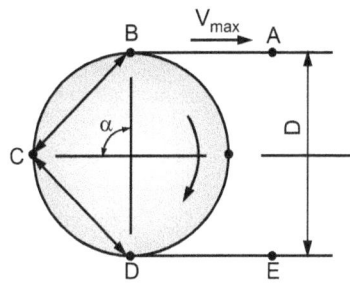
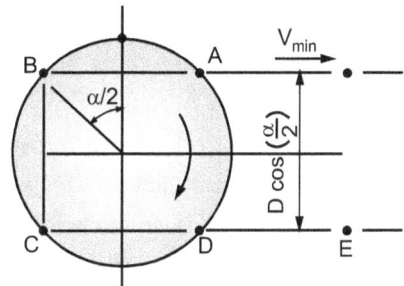

Fig. 5.21

Consider the link with advancement of angle α/2 as described in another figure. For this angular position the centroidal distance of the link AB is $\left(\dfrac{D}{2}\cos\dfrac{\alpha}{2}\right)$. The velocity of the link at this position is the minimum velocity V_{min}. The magnitude of this minimum velocity is given as

$$V_{min} = \dfrac{\pi D n \cos\dfrac{\alpha}{2}}{60 \times 1000}$$

It is thus obvious that velocity of the chain is not constant but varies between these two maximum and minimum limits of velocity. This is the reason for pulsating/fluctuating and jerking or momentary motions of chains. This is called polygonal effect.

The speed variation can be determined as the difference between the maximum and minimum velocities ($V_{max} - V_{min}$).

$$V_{max} - V_{min} = 1 - \cos\dfrac{\alpha}{2}; \text{ Here } \alpha = \dfrac{360}{z}$$

To reduce the speed variation it is clear from the above relation that number of teeth on the sprocket is to be increased. Guideline values for speed variation are given in table 5.9.

Table 5.9

Number of teeth	Speed Variation %
11	4
17	1.6
24	< 1

5.19 MODES OF FAILURE FOR CHAIN

There are various failure criterion for chain. These are described as;

1. **Excessive Tensile Load:** If the chain is subjected to excessive tensile load compared to its breaking load capacity, the chain can fail by breakage. The microscopic cracks in the link plate can develop further leading to its failure. Excessive load may be due to shock loads encountered, wrong chain selection, excessive misalignment in mountings etc.

2. **Excessive Chain Elongation**: Due to long running and normal wear and tear of the chain parts, the chain starts elongating. If chain extension becomes excessive, the chain starts riding over the sprocket and has a tendency to leave the sprocket. The chain length has to be corrected either through a chain tensioning arrangement or by removing an extra link.

3. **Wear:** The pin and bush are held together with the help of pin joint. This articulation is the prime reason for the wear of chain. Due to this wearing, the chain pitch is increased. This results in faulty engagement of teeth. As this wear increases beyond certain limit it becomes mandatory to replace the chain. This limit of elongation is fixed between 1.6 to 2.5%. Periodic lubrication with oil is important remedy for reducing wear as it creates a thin film of oil between the contacting surfaces.

4. **Fatigue:** During chain action, the chain passes through two sides i.e. tight side and loose side. At every turn on the sprockets, the chain is subjected to tensile force. This force is maximum on tight side and minimum on the slack side. Hence for one revolution of chain over the sprocket wheel, the chain is subjected to fluctuating stresses. This leads to fatigue failure of side link-plates. To avoid this type of failure, endurance limit of the link plates is kept more than the tensile stress for infinite life.

5. **Impact:** During power transmission, the rollers of the chain engage with the teeth. During engagement of rollers and teeth there is slight impact. Improper alignment at two sprockets can result into excessive loads. The magnitude of this impact when exceeds beyond limit, results in to failure of roller or bush. The magnitude of impact can be reduced either by reduction of tension on tight side or by increasing the number of teeth on the sprocket or proper alignment.

6. **Galling:** If the tension in the chain is high, microscopic welds are formed between the contacting surfaces/areas. These welds break as a result of relative motion between the contacting surfaces and leads to wear. This wear occurs even in the presence of lubricant. This results into stick-slip phenomenon between the pin and the bush.

5.20 LUBRICATION OF CHAINS

There are three fundamental methods of chain lubrication. These are designated as Type-A, Type-B and Type – C. The type relies on the power rating and velocity of the chain.

1. **Type-A Lubrication:** This is manual or drip lubrication method. In this, the lubricating oil is applied with the aid of brush or oil-can. Frequency of application of oil is so adjusted that the chain is not overheated as well as there is no discoloration. In the drip lubrication process; a pipe with small holes i.e. drip lubricator supplies the

oil. The oil emerges out in the form of drops and falls on the link plates. The distance for the travel of oil drop to chain is so adjusted that presence of wind does not affect the lubrication process. Presence of excessive wind may result is spreading of oil on the other surfaces. This method is suitable for low speed applications with velocity upto 2 m/sec.

2. **Type-B Lubrication:** This type of lubrication is called as disk or bath lubrication. In this method of lubrication, the lower side of the chain passes through a sump filled with oil upto the pitch line of the chain. In other method the whole chain is kept above the oil level in the sump and the oil is spilled or deposited on the chain with the help of disk which is attached to one of the shafts. This is known as disk lubrication. This method is suitable for medium speeds upto 5 m/sec.

3. **Type-C Lubrication:** In this method, a stream of lubricating oil is forced on the inside or slack side of the chain loop. A separate oil sump is provided to supply a continuous stream of oil. This method is also known as oil stream lubrication. Forced lubrication of this type is required for higher speeds and larger power transmission capabilities. Chain manufacturer's recommendations need to be followed.

SOLVED EXAMPLES

Example 5.1: A pulley of 1000 mm diameter is driven by an open type flat belt from 25 kW, 1440 rpm electric motor. The pulley on the motor shaft is 250 mm in diameter and the centre distance between the two shafts is 2.0 m. The allowable tensile stress for the belt material is 2 N/mm^2 and the coefficient of friction between the belt and pulley is 0.28.

The density of the belt material is 900 kg/m^3.

If the width of the belt is 125 mm, determine:
(i) The thickness of belt
(ii) The length of belt and
(iii) The initial tension required in the belt. **(May 2006, December 2008)**

Solution: Type of drive: Open type flat belt

D_l = Diameter of driven pulley = 1000 mm
Power = 25 kW
n = 1440 rpm
D_s = 250 mm
C = 2000 mm
σ_{tper} = Permissible tensile stress in belt = 2 N/mm^2
μ = 0.28
ρ = Density of belt material = 900 kg/m^3
b = Width of belt = 125 mm

To find:
(i) t, (ii) L, (iii) F_i

(i) Thickness of belt (t)

Velocity of belt (v)

$$v = \frac{\pi \times D_s \times n}{60 \times 1000} = \frac{\pi \times 250 \times 1440}{60 \times 1000}$$

$$v = 18.85 \text{ m/s}$$

Power to be transmitted by belt

$$\text{Power} = (F_1 - F_2) \cdot v$$

$$25 \times 10^3 = (F_1 - F_2) \times 18.85$$

$$F_1 - F_2 = 1326.26 \text{ N} \quad \ldots (1)$$

Angle of contact (α_s)

$$\beta = \sin^{-1}\left(\frac{D_l - D_s}{2C}\right)$$

$$= \sin^{-1}\left(\frac{1000 - 250}{2 \times 2000}\right)$$

$$\beta = 10.807° = 0.1886 \text{ rad}$$

$$\alpha_s = \pi - 2\beta = \pi - 2(0.1886)$$

$$\alpha_s = 2.7644 \text{ rad}$$

Limiting tension ratio

$$\frac{F_1}{F_2} = e^{\mu\alpha} = e^{0.28 \times 2.7644}$$

$$F_1 = 2.1685 \, F_2 \quad \ldots (2)$$

From equations (1) and (2),

$$2.1685 \, F_2 - F_2 = 1326.26$$

$$F_2 = 1135.04 \text{ N}$$

$$F_1 = 2461.33 \text{ N}$$

Centrifugal tension (F_c)

$$F_c = m \cdot v^2$$

$$= (\rho \times \text{Volume}) \cdot v^2$$

$$= \left(\rho \times \frac{b}{1000} \times \frac{t}{1000} \times 1\right) \times v^2$$

$$= \left(900 \times \frac{125}{1000} \times \frac{t}{1000} \times 1\right) \times (18.85)^2$$

$$F_c = 39.973 \, (t) \text{ N}$$

Total tension

$$F_t = F_1 + F_c$$

$$T_t = 2461.33 + 39.973 \, (t)$$

$$\sigma_{tper} = \frac{F_t}{b \cdot t}$$

$$2 = \frac{2461.33 + 39.973\,(t)}{125 \cdot t}$$

$$250\,t = 2461.33 + 39.973\,(t)$$

$$t = 11.72 \text{ mm}$$

$$t \cong 11.75 \text{ mm}$$

(ii) Length of belt (L):

$$L = 2C + \frac{\pi(D_l + D_s)}{2} + \frac{(D_l - D_s)^2}{4C}$$

$$= 2 \times 2000 + \frac{\pi(1000 + 250)}{2} + \frac{(1000 - 250)^2}{4 \times 2000}$$

$$L = 6033.807 \text{ mm}$$

$$L = 6034 \text{ mm}$$

(iii) Initial tension in belt (F_i):

$$F_c = 39.973 \times 11.75$$

$$\mathbf{F_c = 469.68 \text{ N}}$$

$$F_i = \frac{F_1 + F_2 + 2F_c}{2}$$

$$= \frac{2461.33 + 1135.04 + 2 \times 469.68}{2}$$

$$\mathbf{F_i = 2267.867 \text{ N}}$$

Example 5.2: Two parallel shafts are to be connected by an open flat belt. The diameter of pulleys are 400 mm and 800 mm and they are 1 m apart. The initial tension in belt when it is stationary is 2 kN. The mass of belt is 2 kg/m. The coefficient of friction between the belt and the pulley is 0.3. Calculate the power transmitted if smaller pulley rotates at 1000 rpm.

Also suggest the speed of the smaller pulley for maximum power transmission by the belt. Determine this maximum power. **(May 2010)**

Solution: Type of belt drive = Open type flat belt

$$D_s = 400 \text{ mm}$$
$$D_l = 800 \text{ mm}$$
$$C = 1000 \text{ mm}$$
$$F_i = 2000 \text{ N}$$
$$m = \text{Mass of belt} = 2 \text{ kg/m}$$
$$\mu = 0.3$$
$$n = 1000 \text{ rpm}$$

To find:
(i) kW, (ii) n for maximum power, (iii) kW_{max}

Power transmitted by belt:

Belt speed, $v = \dfrac{\pi \cdot D_s \cdot n}{60 \times 1000} = \dfrac{\pi \times 400 \times 1000}{60 \times 1000} = 20.94$ m/s

Centrifugal tension (F_c)
$$F_c = mv^2$$
$$= 2 \times 20.94^2$$
$$\mathbf{F_c = 877.298 \text{ N}}$$

Initial tension (F_i)
$$F_i = \dfrac{F_1 + F_2 + 2F_c}{2}$$
$$2000 = \dfrac{F_2 + F_1 + (2 \times 877.29)}{2}$$
$$F_1 + F_2 = 2245.4 \text{ N} \qquad \ldots (1)$$

Angle of contact (α_s)
$$\beta = \sin^{-1}\left(\dfrac{D_l - D_s}{2C}\right) = \sin^{-1}\left(\dfrac{800 - 400}{2 \times 1000}\right)$$
$$\beta = 11.53° \text{ or } 0.2013 \text{ rad}$$

For an open belt drive
$$\alpha_s = \pi - 2\beta = \pi - (2 \times 0.2013) = \mathbf{2.7388 \text{ rad}} = \alpha$$

Limiting tension ratio
$$\dfrac{F_1}{F_2} = e^{\mu\alpha}$$
$$\dfrac{F_1}{F_2} = e^{0.3 \times 2.7388}$$
$$F_1 = 2.2742 \, F_2 \qquad \ldots (2)$$

Tensions in belt due to friction (F_2) and (F_1) from equations (1) and (2)
$$2.2742 \, F_2 + F_2 = 2245.4$$
$$\mathbf{F_2 = 685.78 \text{ N}}$$
$$\mathbf{F_1 = 1559.601 \text{ N}}$$

(i) Power transmitted by the belt (kW)
$$\text{Power} = (F_1 - F_2) \cdot v$$
$$= (1559.601 - 685.78) \cdot 20.94$$
$$\text{Power} = 18297.82 \text{ W} = 18.297 \text{ kW}$$

(ii) Optimum speed of driving pulley

Maximum power transmission capacity of belt is obtained when
$$F_c = \dfrac{F_i}{3}$$

$$F_c = \frac{2000}{3} = 666.667 \text{ N}$$

$$F_c = m \cdot v^2 \quad \ldots V = \text{Optimum speed in m/s}$$

$$666.667 = 2(v)^2$$

$$v^2 = 333.33$$

$$\therefore v = \mathbf{18.26 \text{ m/s}}$$

$$v = \frac{\pi \cdot D_s \cdot \text{Optimum speed}}{60 \times 1000}$$

$$\therefore 18.26 = \frac{\pi \times 400 \times \text{Optimum speed}}{60000}$$

$$\therefore \text{Optimum speed} = 871.72 \text{ rpm}$$

Belt tensions due to belt friction (F_2) and (F_1)

Initial belt tension

$$F_i = \frac{F_2 + F_1 + 2F_c}{2}$$

$$2000 = \frac{F_2 + F_1 + (2 \times 666.667)}{2}$$

$$F_1 + F_2 = 2666.67 \text{ N} \quad \ldots (3)$$

From equations (2) and (3),

$$2.2742\, F_2 + F_2 = 2666.67$$

$$F_2 = 814.449 \text{ N}$$

$$F_1 = 1852.22 \text{ N}$$

(iii) Maximum power (kW_{max})

$$\text{Maximum power} = (F_1 - F_2) \cdot v$$

$$= (1852.22 - 814.449) \times 18.26$$

$$= 18949.71 \text{ W}$$

$$\text{Maximum power} = \mathbf{18.949 \text{ kW}}$$

Example 5.3: A horizontal flat belt is used to transmit 25 kW power from an electric motor running at 1440 rpm to a centrifugal water pump expected to run at 720 rpm. The required centre distance is 4.5 m. Select the flat belt for drive. Use the following data.

Recommended range of belt speed: 17.8 m/s to 22.9 m/s.

Standard pulley diameter: 90, 100, 112, 125, 140, 160, 180, 200, 224, 250, 280, 315, 355, 400, 450, 500, 560, 630, 710, 800 mm. Load correction factor: $F_a = 1.2$.

Arc of contact correction factor (F_d)

Arc of contact	120°	130°	140°	150°	160°	170°	180°
F_d	1.33	1.26	1.19	1.13	1.08	1.04	1.00

DESIGN OF MACHINE ELEMENTS - II BELTS, ROPE AND CHAIN DRIVES

Power rating per ply/mm width at 180° arc of contact and v = 10 m/s. For HI-SPEED BELT - 0.023 kW/ply/mm.

Number of plies and standard belt widths.

Number of ply	Standard belt widths 'b' mm
4	40, 44, 50, 63, 76, 90, 100, 125, 152
5	76, 100, 125, 152

(May 2006)

Solution: Type of drive = Open type flat belt drive

Power = 25×10^3 W

n = 1440 rpm

N = Speed of driven (big) pulley or pump = 720 rpm

C = Centre distance = 4500 mm

Assuming, v = 17.8 m/s

$$v = \frac{\pi \cdot D_s \cdot n}{60 \times 1000}$$

$$17.8 = \frac{\pi \times D_s \times 1440}{60000}$$

$$D_s = 236.08 \text{ mm}$$

Selecting nearest higher standard diameter

∴ $D_s = 250$ mm

Now, $\dfrac{N}{n} = \dfrac{D_s}{D_l}$

$$\frac{720}{1440} = \frac{250}{D_l}$$

∴ $D_l = 500$ mm

Actual belt speed

$$v = \frac{\pi \cdot D_s \cdot n}{60000}$$

$$v = \frac{\pi \cdot 250 \times 1440}{60000}$$

$$= 18.85 \text{ m/s}$$

Load correction factor (F_a) = 1.2

Design power = $F_a \times$ kW

= $1.2 \times 25 \times 10^3$

Design power = 30×10^3 W

Angle of contact (α_s):

$$\beta = \sin^{-1}\left(\frac{D_l - D_s}{2C}\right) = \sin^{-1}\left(\frac{500 - 250}{2 \times 4500}\right) = 1.5918°$$

$$\beta = 0.02778 \text{ rad}, \quad \alpha = 180° = 2 \times 1.5918 = 176.814$$

Arc of contact factor, $\quad F_d = 1.04 - \dfrac{(1.04 - 1.00)(170° - 176.8144°)}{(170° - 180°)}$

$$F_d = 1.0127$$

Power rating (kW rating)

$$\text{kW rating} = 0.023 \times 10^3 \text{ W/Ply/mm}$$

$$\text{Modified kW rating} = \frac{\text{kW rating}}{F_d} \times \frac{v}{10}$$

$$= \frac{0.023 \times 10^3}{1.0127} \times \frac{18.85}{10}$$

$$= 0.0428 \times 10^3 \text{ W/Ply/mm}$$

$$\text{Belt width} \times \text{Number of plies} = \frac{\text{Design power}}{\text{Modified kW rating}}$$

$$= \frac{30 \times 10^3}{0.0428 \times 10^3}$$

$$= 700.93 \text{ ply-mm}$$

For 4 plies, belt width $= \dfrac{700.93}{4} = 175.23$ mm

For 5 plies, belt width $= \dfrac{700.93}{5} = 140.187$ mm

Selecting number of plies $= 5$

Width of belt (b) $= 152$ mm

Length of belt (L)

$$L = 2C + \left(\frac{D_l + D_s}{2}\right) + \frac{(D_l - D_s)^2}{4C}$$

$$= 2 \times 4500 + \frac{\pi(500 + 250)}{2} + \frac{(500 - 250)^2}{4 \times 4500}$$

$$L = 10181.57 \text{ mm}$$

$$L = 10182 \text{ mm}$$

Example 5.4: A v-belt drive is used to transmit 38 kW power from a three phase induction motor to a centrifugal pump. Speed of the motor is 1440 rpm and the centrifugal pump is required to be operated at 360 rpm. For the motor pulley pitch diameter is 225 mm and the groove angle is 38°. Centre distance between the pulley is 1 m. Coefficient of friction for the belt pulley combination is 0.2 and the density of the belt material is 0.97 gm/cc. Allowable tension in the belt is 800 N.

Determine:
(i) Number of belts required.
(ii) Pitch length of the belt.
Assume C/S for the belt as shown in the Fig. 5.22.

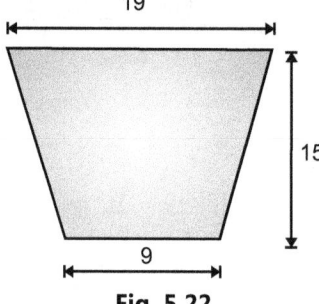

Fig. 5.22

Solution: Type of drive = Open type V-belt

Power = 38 kW

n = 1440 rpm

N = Speed of driven (big) pulley = 360 rpm

D_s = 225 mm

$\theta = 38°$ = Groove angle of pulley

C = 1000 mm

μ = Coefficient of friction = 0.2

ρ = 970 kg/m³

F_{max} = Maximum allowable tension = 800 N

To find:
(i) Number of belts required.
(ii) Pitch length of belt.

(i) Number of belts required:

Cross-sectional Area of V belt

$$A = \frac{1}{2} \times (9 + 19) \times 15$$

$$= 210 \text{ mm}^2$$

Velocity of belt (v)

$$v = \frac{\pi \cdot D_s \cdot n}{60 \times 1000} = \frac{\pi \times 225 \times 1440}{60000}$$

$$v = 16.96 \text{ m/s}$$

Centrifugal tension (F_c)

$$F_c = m \cdot v^2$$
$$= (\rho \cdot A) \cdot v^2$$
$$= (970 \times 10^{-6} \times 210) \times (16.96)^2$$
$$F_c = 58.62 \text{ N}$$

Speed ratio $\dfrac{N}{n} = \dfrac{D_s}{D_l}$

$$\dfrac{360}{1440} = \dfrac{225}{D_l}$$

$$\mathbf{D_l = 900 \text{ mm}}$$

Angle of contact (α_s)

$$\beta = \sin^{-1}\left(\dfrac{D_l - D_s}{2C}\right) = \sin^{-1}\left(\dfrac{900 - 225}{2 \times 1000}\right)$$

$$\beta = 19.7246° = 0.3442 \text{ rad}$$

$$\alpha_s = \pi - 2\beta = 2.453 \text{ rad}$$

Limiting tension ratio

$$\dfrac{F_1}{F_2} = e^{\left(\dfrac{\mu \cdot \alpha}{\sin \theta/2}\right)}$$

$$\dfrac{F_1}{F_2} = e^{\left(\dfrac{0.2 \times 2.453}{\sin 19}\right)}$$

$$F_1 = 4.5127\, F_2$$

$$F_{max} = F_1 + F_c$$

$$800 = F_1 = 58.62$$

$$\mathbf{F_1 = 741.4074 \text{ N}}$$

∴ $\quad\quad\quad\quad\mathbf{F_2 = 164.2935 \text{ N}}$

Power transmitted

$$\text{Power/belt} = (F_1 - F_2) \times v$$
$$= (741.4074 - 164.2935) \times 16.96$$
$$= 9787.85 \text{ W} = 9.787 \text{ kW}$$

$$\text{Number of belts required} = \dfrac{\text{kW}}{\text{kW/belt}}$$

$$= \dfrac{38}{9.787}$$

$$= 3.88$$

Number of belts required $\cong 4$

(ii) Pitch length of belt

$$L = 2C + \frac{\pi(D_l + D_s)}{2} + \frac{(D_l - D_s)^2}{4C}$$

$$= (2 \times 1000) + \frac{\pi(900 + 225)}{2} + \frac{(900 - 225)^2}{4 \times 1000}$$

$$L = 3881.052 \text{ mm}$$

L = 3882 mm

Example 5.5: A single v belt is used to transmit power from a grooved pulley of pitch diameter 200 mm running at 1500 rpm to a flat pulley of diameter 600 mm. The centre distance between the pulleys is 1000 mm. The mass of the belt is 0.3 kg per metre. The coefficient of friction between the belt and pulley is 0.25. The v-belt pulley groove angle is 38°. If the allowable tension in the belt is 800 N. Determine.
   (i) Power transmitting capacity of the belt, and
   (ii) Initial tension required in the belt.   **(December 2006)**

Solution: Type of drive = Open type V-belt
Number of belts = 1
D_s = 200 mm
D_l = 600 mm
n = 1500 rpm
C = 1000 mm
m = 0.3 kg/m
µ = 0.25
2θ = 38°
F_{max} = 800 N

To find: (i) kW, (ii) F_i
Angle of contact (α_s):

$$\beta = \sin^{-1}\left(\frac{D_l - D_s}{2C}\right) = \sin^{-1}\left(\frac{600 - 200}{2 \times 1000}\right)$$

$$\beta = 11.53° = 0.2014 \text{ rad}$$

$$\alpha_s = \pi - 2\beta = \pi - 2 \times 0.2014 = 2.7388 \text{ rad}$$

For driven flat belt

$$e^{\frac{\mu \cdot \alpha_s}{\sin \theta}} = e^{\frac{0.25 \times 2.7388}{\sin 19}} = 8.1915$$

$$\alpha_l = \pi + 2\beta = \pi + 2(0.2014) = 3.5444 \text{ rad}$$

$$e^{\mu \cdot \alpha_l} = e^{0.25 \times 3.5444} = 2.4256$$

Limiting tension ratio:

$$\frac{F_1}{F_2} = e^{0.25 \times 3.544} \quad \ldots (i)$$

$$F_1 = 2.4256 \, F_2$$

Velocity of belt

$$v = \frac{\pi \cdot D_s \cdot n}{60000} = \frac{\pi \times 200 \times 1500}{60000}$$

$$v = 15.71 \text{ m/s}$$

Centrifugal tension (F_c)

$$F_c = m \cdot v^2$$
$$= 0.3 \times (15.71)^2$$
$$\mathbf{F_c = 74.022 \text{ N}}$$
$$F_{max} = F_1 + F_c$$
$$800 = F_1 + 74.022$$
$$\mathbf{F_1 = 725.9588 \text{ N}}$$

From equation (1)

$$\mathbf{F_2 = 299.29 \text{ N}}$$

(i) Power transmitting capacity of belt (kW):

$$\text{Power} = (F_1 - F_2) \times v$$
$$= (725.9588 - 299.29) \times 15.71$$
$$\mathbf{Power = 6702.96 \text{ W}}$$
$$= 6.703 \text{ kW}$$

(ii) Initial tension (F_i):

$$F_i = \frac{F_1 + F_2 + 2F_c}{2}$$

$$= \frac{725.9588 + 299.29 + 2\,(74.022)}{2}$$

$$\mathbf{F_i = 586.6464 \text{ N}}$$

Example 5.6: A v belt drive is used to transmit 30 kW power from an electric motor running at 1440 rpm to a machine running at 480 rpm. The central distance between the shaft is 1 m. Groove angle for pulley is 38° and coefficient of friction between the belt and the pulley is 0.2. The density of the belt material is 1000 kg/m³ and allowable tensile stress for the belt is 1.53 N/mm². The c/s dimensions of the belt are as follows:

Width of the belt at the top: 37 mm.

Width of the belt at the bottom: 19 mm.

Depth of the belt: 25 mm.
Find: (i) Diameter of pulleys, (ii) Minimum number of belts required. Assume maximum power transmission capacity conditions for belts.

(December 2009)

Solution: Type of drive: Open type V-belt

$$\text{Total Power} = 30 \text{ kW}$$
$$n = 1440 \text{ rpm}$$
$$N = 480 \text{ rpm}$$
$$C = 1000 \text{ mm}$$
$$2\theta = 38°$$
$$\mu = 0.2$$
$$\rho = 1000 \text{ kg/m}^3$$
$$\sigma_t = 1.53 \text{ N/mm}^2$$
$$b_t = 37 \text{ mm (Width of belt at top)}$$
$$b_b = 19 \text{ mm (Width of belt at bottom)}$$
$$t = \text{Thickness of belt} = 25 \text{ mm}$$

To find: (i) D_l and D_s, (ii) Number of belts required.

$$A = \frac{1}{2} \times (37 + 19) \times 25$$

A = 700 mm²

Maximum permissible tension (F_{max})

$$F_{max} = \sigma_t \times A$$
$$= 1.53 \times 700$$

F_{max} = 1071 N

Centrifugal tension (F_c)

$$F_c = \frac{F_{max}}{3}$$
$$F_c = \frac{1071}{3} = 357 \text{ N}$$

Velocity of belt

$$F_c = m \cdot v^2$$
$$F_c = (\rho \cdot A) \cdot v^2$$
$$357 = \left(1000 \times \frac{700}{1000 \times 1000} \times 1\right) v^2$$

v = 22.58 m/s

$$v = \frac{\pi \cdot D_s \cdot n}{60000}$$

$$22.58 = \frac{\pi \times D_s \times 1440}{60000}$$

$$D_s = 299.518 \text{ mm}$$

$$\therefore \quad \mathbf{D_s = 300 \text{ mm}}$$

From speed ratio

$$\frac{N}{n} = \frac{D_s}{D_l}$$

$$D_l = \frac{1440 \times 300}{480}$$

$$\mathbf{D_l = 900 \text{ mm}}$$

Angle of contact (α_s)

$$\beta = \sin^{-1}\left(\frac{D_l - D_s}{2C}\right) = \sin^{-1}\left(\frac{900 - 300}{2 \times 1000}\right)$$

$$\beta = 17.45° \text{ or } 0.3046 \text{ rad}$$

$$\alpha_s = \pi - 2\beta = 2.5322 \text{ rad}$$

We know

$$\frac{F_1}{F_2} = e^{\frac{\mu \cdot \alpha_s}{\sin \theta}}$$

$$= e^{\frac{0.2 \times 2.5332}{\sin 19}}$$

$$F_1 = 4.7377 \, F_2 \qquad \ldots (1)$$

$$F_{max} = F_1 + F_c$$

$$F_1 = F_{max} - F_c$$

$$F_1 = 1071 - 357$$

$$\mathbf{F_1 = 714 \text{ N}}$$

$$\therefore \quad \mathbf{F_2 = 150.706 \text{ N}}$$

Power transmission capacity of each belt

$$\text{Power/belt} = (F_1 - F_2) \cdot v$$

$$= (714 - 150.706) \cdot 22.58$$

$$= \mathbf{12719.177 \text{ W} = 12.72 \text{ kW/belt}}$$

$$\text{Number of belts required} = \frac{\text{Total power to be transmitted (kW)}}{\text{Power transmission capacity of each belt (kW/belt)}}$$

$$\therefore \quad \text{Number of belts} = \frac{30}{12.72} = 2.35$$

$$\therefore \quad \mathbf{\text{Number of belts} = 3}$$

Example 5.7: The following data is given for an open type V-belt drive.
  Diameter of driving pulley = 120 mm
  Diameter of driven pulley = 240 mm
  Centre distance = 0.8 m
  Groove angle = 40°
  Mass of belt = 0.25 kg/m
  Maximum possible tension = 800 N
  Coefficient of friction = 0.18

Plot the graph of maximum tension and power transmitted against the belt velocity. Neglect power losses. **(December 2007)**

Solution: Type of drive = Open type V-belt drive
$$D_s = 120 \text{ mm}$$
$$D_l = 240 \text{ mm}$$
$$C = 800 \text{ mm}$$
$$2\theta = 40°$$
$$m = 0.25 \text{ kg/m}$$
$$F_{max} = 800 \text{ m}$$
$$\mu = 0.18$$

Angle of contact (α_s)
$$\beta = \sin^{-1}\left(\frac{D_l - D_s}{2C}\right) = \sin^{-1}\left(\frac{240 - 120}{2 \times 800}\right)$$
$$\beta = 4.3012° \text{ or } 0.07507$$
$$\alpha_s = \pi - 2\beta = 2.9914 \text{ rad}$$

Limiting tension ratio
$$\frac{F_1}{F_2} = e^{\frac{\mu \cdot \alpha_s}{\sin \theta}} = e^{\frac{0.18 \times 2.9914}{\sin 20}}$$
$$F_1 = 4.8274 \, F_2$$

Initial tension in belt (F_i).
Initial tension in the belt occurs at v = 0.
$$F_{max} = F_1 + F_c$$
$$800 = F_1 + mv^2$$
$$800 = F_1 + 0.25 \times (0)$$
$$F_1 = 800 \text{ N}$$
$$F_2 = 165.717 \text{ N}$$

Initial tension in belt,

$$F_i = \frac{F_1 + F_2 + 2F_c}{2}$$

$$= \frac{800 + 165.717}{2}$$

$F_i = 482.8585$ N

Belt tension on tight side

$$F_{max} = F_1 + F_c$$
$$F_1 = F_{max} - F_c$$
$$F_1 = F_{max} - mv^2$$
$$2F_1 = F_1 + F_2 = 2F_c$$
$$F_2 = 2(F_i - F_c) - F_1$$
$$= 2[F_i - m(v^2)] - F_1$$
$$F_2 = 2[482.8586 - mv^2] - [F_{max} - mv^2]$$
$$F_2 = 965.7172 - mv^2 - F_{max}$$
$$\frac{F_1}{F_2} = 4.8275$$

$$\frac{F_{max} - mv^2}{965.712 - mv^2 - F_{max}} = 4.8275$$

$$F_{max} - mv^2 = 4661.9998 - 3.8275 \times mv^2$$
$$F_{max} = 800 - 0.1642\,v^2$$

Belt tension on slack side

Tension on slack slide $= F_2 + F_c$

$$= 165.7172 - 0.0858\,v^2 + 0.25\,v^2$$
$$= 165.7172 + 0.1642\,v^2$$

$$\text{Power} = (F_1 - F_2) \times v$$
$$= \{[800 - 0.1642\,(v^2)] - [165.7172 + 0.1642\,v^2]\}\,v$$

$$\text{Power} = 634.2828\,v - 0.3284\,v^3$$

$$F_{max} = 800 - 0.1642\,(v)^2$$

At $v = 0$, $F_{max} = 800$ N

∴ The equation for power transmitted by belt is

$$\text{Power} = 634.2828\,(v) - 0.3284 \times v^3 \qquad \ldots \text{(a)}$$

At v = 0, kW = 0

$$v = \sqrt{\frac{F_i}{3m}}$$

For maximum power

$$v = \sqrt{\frac{482.8586}{3 \times 0.25}} = 25.3734 \text{ m/s}$$

Maximum power = $634.2828\, v - 0.3284\, v^2 = 15882.48$ W
Maximum power = 15.882 kW

Speed versus power chart is drawn below using equation (a).

Belt speed v (m/sec)	0	10	20	25.37	30	40	43.48
F_{max} (N)	800	783.6	734.6	694.3	652.2	537.3	482.4
kW	0	6.014	10.058	10.729	10.162	4.334	0

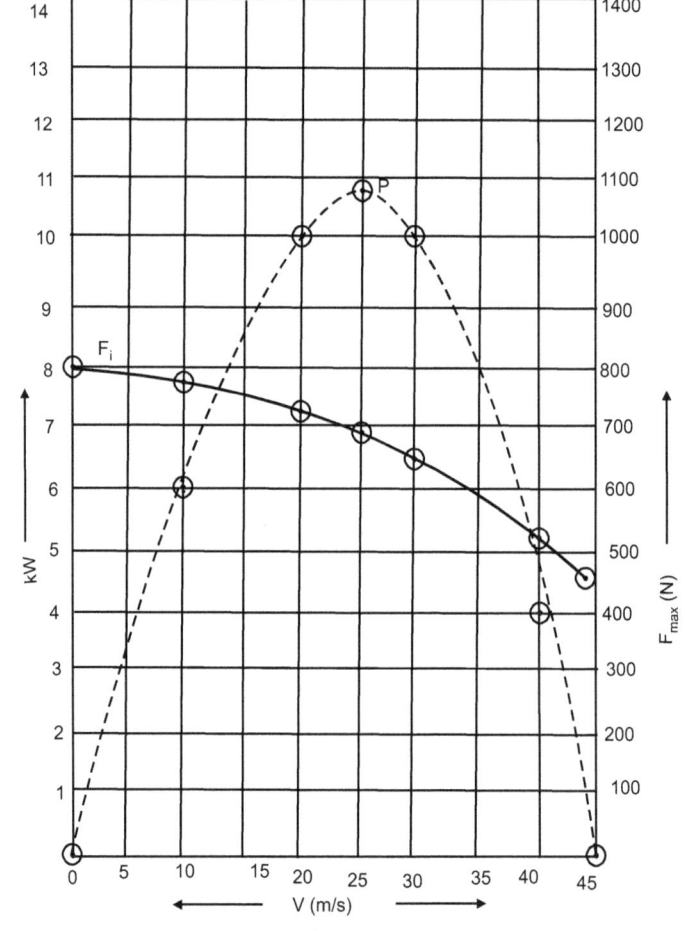

Fig. 5.23

EXERCISE

1. Explain the reasons for speed variations in chain drives. **(April 2009)**
2. Derive the condition for maximum power transmitting capacity of the belt. **(April 2009)**
3. Compare belt, chain and gear drives with respect to the power transmitting capacity, performance, losses and noise and areas of application. Give two applications of each drive. **(April 2009)**
4. Write a note on 'silent chains'. **(April 2009)**
5. Discuss different belt-tightening (tensioning) methods. **(April 2010)**
6. Derive a relation for optimum velocity of a belt for maximum power transmission capacity in terms of total tension in tight side of the belt and mass per unit length of the belt. **(April 2010)**
7. Discuss relative advantages and limitations of chain drives. **(April 2010. 2011)**
8. State and explain four basic-modes of failure in roller chain. **(April 2012)**
9. Explain stresses in wire rope with sketch. **(April 2012)**
10. Derive the condition for maximum power capacity of belt.
11. Explain polygonal effect in chain with sketch.
12. Draw neat sketch of rope drum construction and explain its design procedure. **(April 2012)**
13. Prove that, the maximum power transmitted by the belt at a given initial tension T_i.

    $$P(K_w) = \frac{(T_1 - T_2)}{1000}\sqrt{\frac{T_i}{3m}}$$

    where, T_1 and T_2 = Tension in tight and slack side (N), m - Mass per unit length of belt (kg/m). **(October 2011)**
14. What are inverted tooth chain? Sketch and explain their advantages over roller chains. **(October 2011)**

15. Write short note on construction and lay of wire ropes with sketch.

(October 2011)

16. Explain the procedure of selection of flat belt from manufacturer's catalogue.

(October 2011, 2012)

17. Discuss stresses developed in wire rope. **(October 2012)**

18. Explain any one belt tensioning method with suitable sketch.

(October 2012)

✸✸✸

Unit VI

SLIDING CONTACT BEARING

6.1 LUBRICATING OILS

All rotating and moving machinary parts consume energy that goes waste as frictional losses. Every attempt is therefore made by designers to reduce this friction.

Lubricants are widely used with the following purposes.

- Reduce frional losses and reduce wear at the point of contact.
- Dissipate heat generated due to friction.
- Reduce corrosion of parts.

Lubrcants are mainly of three types.

- Liquid lubricants – Lubricating oils.
- Semi solid Lubricants – Greases.
- Solid lubricants – For example, Graphite powder.

Solid lubricants are used for extreme temperature and load conditions. Semisolid lubricants are mainly used where frequent lubrication is not possible and not essential. Solid lubricants remain on the surface for a relatively longer period. Liquid lubricants are very widely used for wide range of applications. We will limit our discussion to liquid lubricants only in this chapter.

Liquid lubricant is any liquid that has reasonable viscosity. Vicosity should not be very high since it will limit its ability to flow and carry away the heat. Lubricants can be in solid, liquid or gaseous form. Liquid lubricants i.e. lubricating oils are most common in industrial applications.

6.2 PROPERTIES OF LUBRICATING OILS

As referred above, though main purpose of lubricating oil is to reduce friction and carryaway heat, simultaneously it must meet compatibility requirements with the environment in which it is working and also carry out secondary functions. Following are some of the most important properties of the lubricants.

Viscosity: This is the most important property of any lubricating oil. Viscosity is the resistance offered by a fluid to flow. Higher viscosity will introduce mobility problem for the lubricanting oil and low viscosity oils will not be able to retain the thin film on the part for a longer period. Desired viscosity for a given application will depend on speed of operation and the force between the contact parts. If a plate of area 'A' is moving with a velocity U on a film of lubricant of thickness 'h' and force F is required for this, as per Newon's viscosity law, shear stress in the fluid is proportional to the rate of change of U with respect to y. Thus,

$$\tau_x = \frac{F}{A} = \mu \frac{\partial u}{\partial y}$$

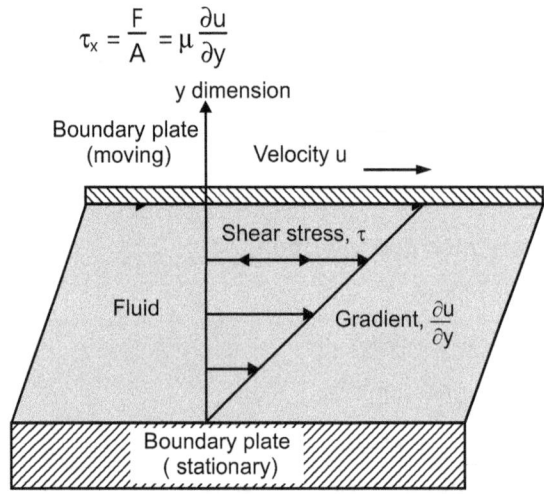

Fig. 6.1: Newton's Viscosity Law

The constant of proportionality µ (N-s/mm²) is called the absolute viscosity. A more convenient unit used is Poise giving absolute viscosity in dyne-s/cm². This also is a large unit and therefore popularly viscosity is stated in centi Poise (cP).

Thus,

$$\mu = \text{Absolute vicosity in N-s/mm}^2 \text{ or MPa-s}$$
$$Z = \text{Absolute viscosity in cP}$$

Converting $\quad \mu = z/10^9$

In laboratory, vicosity is measured in terms of time in seconds required for a given volume of oil to pass through a capillary tube of standard dimensions at a constant temperature. In USA, Saybolt Universal Viscometer is commonly used and time SUS (Saybolt Universal Seconds) is specified. Knowing this time t, in seconds, kinematic viscosity is obtained as

$$Z_k = \left(0.22 \times t - \frac{180}{t}\right)$$

From this absolute viscosity can be obtaind as $z = Z_k \cdot \rho$.

Viscosity is the resistance offered by the fluid to the relative motion of its particles. Absolute viscosity (µ) is the force and is measured in N-S/mm². With increase in temperature, the viscosity of oil decreases and the viscosity of the oil is determined by the operating temperature of the system. Ideally an oil should undergo minimum change in viscosity with temperature.

Viscosity Index: The viscosity of most oils change with temperature and this brings serious limitation on utility of a particular lubricant. Viscosity index is a measure of how much oil's viscosity changes with temperature. Oil with viscosity index as 100 undergoes minimum change in the viscosity with temperature. Whereas oil with viscosity Index as 0 undergoes maximum change in the viscosity .

The viscosity Index for a oil is measured as

$$V.I. = \frac{L - U}{L - H} \times 100$$

Where,

L = Viscosity of oil at 38°C whose viscosity index is to be determined

U = Viscosity of oil at 38°C whose viscosity index is zero

H = Viscosity of oil at 38°C whose viscosity index is 100

In simple terms higher the viscosity index, more stable is the viscosity. Where large temperature changes are expected, it will be essential to use oil with higher Viscosity Index.

Society of Automotive Engineers (SAE) has esablished a viscosity grading system for lubricating oils. Lubricating oils are designated with SAE grades or numbers that indicate their viscosity range. Winter grade oils suitable for low temperature applications are designated with suffix W (for example, SAE 20W. Their viscosities are measured at 0°F (−18°C). Higher SAE number indicates that oil is more viscous.

Typical values could be

SAE 40 – 80 SUS

SAE 90 – 100 SUS

Table 6.1: Typical oil viscosities in SUS

SAE Grade	Viscosity Range at 210°F (99°C) in SUS
Motor Oils	
SAE 20	45-58
SAE 30	58-70
SAE 40	70 85
SAE 50	85-110

contd. ...

Gear Oils	
SAE 90	75-120
SAE 140	120-200
SAE 250	200 and above

Thermal Conductivity: The lubricating oil should have high thermal conductivity so that it can efficiently carry away heat from the source to the surrounding.

Pour Point: This is the lowest temperature at which oil will flow. Lower the pour point, better it is. This will extend suitability of oil for low temperature applications.

Flash Point: This is the temperature at which oil will give out ignitable vapours. Obviously higher flash point is desirable.

Fire Point: This is the temperature at which oil can catch fire.

Oxidation Stability: Lubricating oils may react with Oxygen in air to produce oxides. Oxide products if insoluble remain in the system as particles and can create clogging, wearing out of different parts.

Foaming: Foaming is formation of gas bubbles on the surface of lubricating oil. It can lead to disturbances in regular supply of oil and can cause related problems.

Acidity and Alkalinity: Acidity within a lubricating oil is susceptible to rise in course of time due to combustion or oxidation. For some applications alkalinity is introduced in the lubricant for neutralising the acidity.

Oiliness: Oiliness is the property by virtue of which oil sticks with the contact surface. This helps to avoid metal to metal contact in case of boundary lubrication. Higher the oilinee, lower will be the coefficient of friction.

6.3 LUBRICATING OIL ADDITIVES

Additives are special compounds which are added to the lubricating oil for improving chemical and physical properties so as to improve the lubricant performance. Additives comprise upto 5 to 10% of the base oil by weight. Engine oils, gear box oils, hydraulic oils commonly use different additives for optimum performance.

The additives may be grouped under different actions they perform:

1. **Controlling chemical breakdown:** Such as antioxidants, detergent activities, corrosion inhibitor.
2. **Viscosity improvers:** Viscosity modifiers, anti-pour depressants.
3. **Lubricity modifiers:** Friction modifiers, extreme pressure additives, anti-wear additives.
4. **Contamination control:** Anti-foam agent.

Extreme pressure additives: In applications where the contact parts are under very high loads, there is a risk of breakdown of oil film. Compounds of sulphur, phosphorous and chlorine are added. They form a coating on the surface of the part that redues the shear resistance. This also reduces wear and scoring, thus improving the performance of the system.

Rust and corrosion inhibitors: These additives form a protective barrier on the part surface. They protect the part from Oxygen, water and reduce corrosion rate.

Viscosity Index Improvers: Viscosity of lubricating oil reduces at higher temperatures. With this, adequate lubricant does not stay on the part. These additives help the lubricating oil to maintain a acceptable level of viscosity even at higher temperatures. A stable oil film improves lubrication performance.

Anti Wear Additives: These compounds form a protective layer on the surface of the product and reduce the wear of the parts.

Friction Modifiers: These additives form a layer on the part surface that has crystal structure consisting of molecular layers. These layers reduce the coefficient of friction resulting in improvinng efficiency and controlling temperature rise.

Anti-oxidants: Oxidation causes oxide products to get in circulation alongwith lubricating oil causing clogging. Anti-oxidants inhibit oxidation process of oils.

Detergents: Strong acids present in the lubricant are neutralised by detergents.

Dispersants: These additives keep the foreign particles in the lubricant in the dispersed form in the oil.

6.4 SELECTION OF LUBRICATING OILS

Lubricating oils can be catagorised into natural oils, mineral oils and synthetic oils.

(A) Natural Oils: These can be:

1. Vegetable oils – Castor oil, Rapeseed oil etc.
2. Animal oils – Animal fats, Whale oil etc.

These are environmentally favourable lubricants and have excellent lubrication performance and are used since ancient times. Their use in industrial applications as lubricants is however limited due to low oxidation and thermal stabilty, poor performance at low temperatures and narrow range of available viscosities. Suitable anti-oxidants can be used as additives to improve their performance. These are suitable for maximum temperatures upto 120°C.

(B) Mineral Oils:

Obtained by refining of petroleum products. Mineral oils are made up of mainly hydro carbon type compounds. They can be used upto a temperature of 200°C. They exhibit good performance and are available in large quantity. These are the most commonly used oils as lubricants in industrial applications.

Synthetic Oils: Requirements of lubricants for extreme applications involving high temperature, pressures and humidity has resulted in development of synthetic oils. These can be of many types including synthetic hydrocarbons, fatty acid esters, silicone, chloroflurocarbon and many more. They can be used upto temperature of 400°C. Their use in industrial applications is limited due to higher costs. However for extreme applications they remain the only choice.

Applications:

Motor oil: This is a lubricant used in I.C. enegines of various vehicles, generators etc. They contain oil with special additives such as extreme pressure additives to reduce friction and wear and tear of moving parts. These are mainly mineral oils with suitable additives. They have however low fire resistance and poor bio-degradability.

Various mechanisms in a I.C. Engine which are covered by motor oils are crank shaft in engine bearings, camshaft in camshaft bearing, piston – cylinder engagement, piston pin in small end of connecting rod etc.

Typical recommended oil is:

SAE 40 – For medium and heavy motor oil.

Gear Oil: These lubricants are used in gear box. Main function is to reduce friction, wear and provide corrosion protection. They are mainly mineral based. Extreme pressure (EP) additives, oxidation inhibitors, anti-foaming agents could be added as additives depending on the application. Synthetic oils are also used for extreme working conditions.

Typical recommended oils are:

SAE 20 – Oil for light transmission gears.

SAE 40 – Oil for medium transmission gears.

Hydraulic Oil:

Hydraulic pumps, cylinders, tanks and related subsystems use hydraulic oils which works both as a medium as well as lubricant.

Important properties required from the oil are thermal and chemical stability, good lubrication, low flash point, low foaming etc.

Mineral based oils are most commonly used along with suitable additives in the form of detergents, anti-foaming, anti-corrosion property enhancers.

Turbine Oil:

Neopentyl polyol esters, (type of Synthetic lubricant) are used as gas turbine engine lubricant. They have superior thermal and oxidation stability.

Chain Lubricants:

The lubricant used for chain lubrication should not be thick as it will not penetrate inaccessible locations and thin lubricants don't last long. Many times a special lubricant which is a mix of thick lubricant with a volatile solvent is used to overcome this problem. This mix is easy to apply and would also enter intricate locations.

Wire Rope Lubricants:

Wire rope lubricants have two main functions:

1. Reduce the friction between individual wires which have relative motion when it bends and provide corrosion protection and lubrication on exterior surfaces as well as in the core.
2. Wire rope lubricants can be petroleum based or vegetable oil based.

6.5 PROPERTIES AND SELECTION OF BEARING MATERIALS

Bearing Material Properties: When a bearing is working as a full fledged hydrodynamic bearing there is no metal to metal contact, however there is pressure due to oil film. In addition, during the start, there is partial metal to metal contact under load and bearing will be operating under thin film lubrication where metal to metal contact may be present. Bearing material is required to demostrate the following properties besides availabilty and low cost.

- **High compressive strength:** The bearing material should withstand high pressures without undergoing any change in shape i.e. distortion.
- **Low coefficient of friction:** The bearing material in combination with journal material should exhibit low value of coeffieient of friction. This will reduce energy losses in friction and would limit temperature rise for the system.
- **Fatigue Strength:** The bearing material should have good fatigue strength to resist external shock and varying loads.
- **Conformabilty:** The bearing material should have ability to yield and adopt its shape to that of the journal and thus increase the bearing pressure area. Material should have therefore good conformability. It helps to accommodate misalignment. Relatively softer materials are better in this regard.
- **High Corrosion Resistance:** The oxide products of many lubricating oils corrode bearing materials. The bearing material should have high corrosion resistance. Otherwise during idle period and in case of failure of lubrication, bearing may experience excessive corrosion.

- **Compatibility:** A good combination of shaft and bearing material is necessary since in running condition they should not produce localised welds leading to either scoring or seizure.
- **High embeddability:** Bearing material should be soft to allow foreign material to get embeded in the lining. Thus high embeddability is desired. Materials with high hardness will have low embeddability.
- **High thermal conductivity:** This would ensure efficient heat transfer away from the bearings to the surrounding. This will further ensure that lubricant temperature will not exceed its allowable value. Lubrication performance will be enhanced with this.
- **Lower Relative Hardness:** Compared to the shaft material the bearing material should usually be softer. However at the same time it should be hard enough to resist abrasive wear of its own surface. This is because bearings are easier and economical to replace compared to the shaft.
- **Availability:** Ready material availabity is always an important criteria in engineering to ensure productcion continuity and even for replacement requirement.
- **Cost:** Cost of a material i.e. econmic consideration is the ultimate deciding factor in any engineering application.

Bearing Materials:

Bearing materials have conflicting requirements as seen above. Materials needs to be having satisfactory compressive strength and fatigue strength to withstand external loads. Simultaneously it should be soft to exhibit good embeddability and conformability.

Bearing Construction:

Bearings in industrial applications would vary in their construction from a very simple arrangement to a very complex system involving detail design aspects.

- A hole made in a cast iron part can work as a bearing supporting a pin or a shaft.
- More common method adopted is a press fitted bush inside a solid part. The bush may be a single piece or made in two halves.

Figs 6.2 (a) and (b) shows constructions of a simple sleeve bush in two different ways. Constructions show a solid bush which could be either press fitted or screwed in a solid housing.

Bush in Fig. 6.2 (a) could be made-up of a bearing material such as cast iron, phosphor Bronze or a sintered metal.

Bush in Fig. 6.2 (b) is made-up of two different materials. The thicker material shown is a supporting material. In a typical application this material could be suitable quality steel or cast iron.

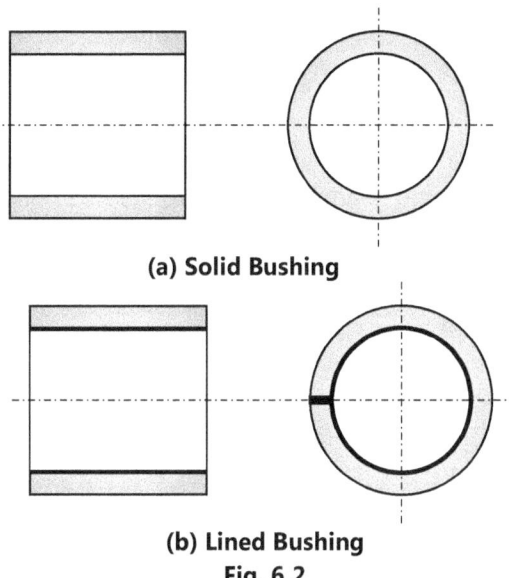

(a) Solid Bushing

(b) Lined Bushing

Fig. 6.2

The material shown in dark is the bearing material. This could be a lining material such as Babbit that is deposited over the supporting material. This gives a combination of strong support material with a soft Babbit which can demonstrate embeddability and conformability. This aspect should be clear while selecting bearing material.

Bushed Journal Bearing: In some of the applications designer may select to use a special housing (a) A single piece base (Fig. 6.3) with bush press fitted or b) A split type plummer block also called as a pedestal where bush is also split and assembled in the housing.

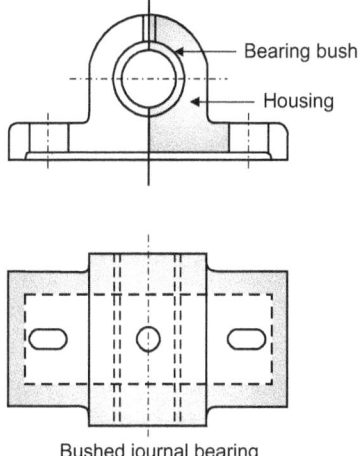

Bushed journal bearing

Fig. 6.3: Bushed Journal Bearing

The selection depends on severity of application, ease of mounting, lubrication method and frequency.

Bearing Materials:

Various bearing materials are available. The selection of appropriate bearing material will depend on various factors such as load, speed, shaft material, lubrication requirement and provision.

Some of the commonly used bearing materials for hydrodynamic bearings are:

- **Cast Iron:** Cast iron bearings can be used with hardened steel shaft. This results in low coefficient of friction and less wear. This provides a low cost solution.

- **Bronze:** These are copper alloys. These can be copper – tin, copper–lead, leaded bronze alloys. Compared to babbits, copper alloys bearing materials show superior load capacity, better wear resistance and high temperature performance. However, scoring resistance of babbits is superior. The bearings are required to be replaced when they wear out considerably.

  Copper lead alloys are used for heavy load applications such as diesel engines in trucks and off road vehicles. Leaded bronze is preferred for intermediate loads and speed applications such as machine tools, home appliances, farm machinery etc.

  Tin bronzes have high hardness requiring reliable lubrication. These are used in high load, low speed applications such as rolling mill bearings, gear bushings for off road vehicles.

- **Babbit:** One of the most popular bearing materials is babbit or white metal. Babbit material is deposited over the support material with thickness ranging from 0.025 to 2.5 mm. Babbits exhibit high embeddability, good conformability, good corrosion resistance. Babbits may be lead based or tin based. Tin based babbits have higher corrosion resistance but are more costly. Both materials have less strength.

  Babbit bearings are used in many high speed rotating equipment such as compressors, turbines, gear drives working in environment where rolling contact bearings may have limitations.

  Typical application is such as in marine gear box. Connecting rod big end bearing of an I.C. Engine may have a shell lined with bronze with additional layer of Babbit.

- **Sintered metal:** In industrial applications very often there are situations where bush bearings have to work with thin boundary lubrication. Bearings may be located at dificult to access locations. Sintered metal bushes come very handy for such applications. Sintered metal bushes are factory manufactured with oil impregnation. These materials have porous structure and hence have the capacity to retain the lubricant oil within them. Sometimes such bushings also use oil soaked casings in which these bushes are held.

- **Plastic:** Palstics can operate under lubrication free behaviour. These are low weight, corrosion resistant and maintenance free. However these materials get heated when operated beyond their specified parameters. Common plastics are nylon, Polytetrafluroethylene (PTTE), Ultra high molecular weight polyethylene (UHMWPE).
- Plastic Bearings are used in machines similar to Xerox machines, farm equipment, medical equipments, food and packaging machines.

6.6 HYDRODYNAMIC LUBRICATION

Two surfaces having relative motion are separated by a thin film of lubrication thus providing liquid lubrication.

Liquid lubrication can be (a) Hydrodynamic type, (b) Hydrostatic type, (c) Squeeze film lubrication. Difference lies mainly in the manner in which the pressure between two surfaces is created. The pressure created helps journal to carry load but avoids metal to metal contact with the bearing.

Hydrostatic Lubrication: Here the pressure is generated externally by a pump. The flow of pressurised lubricant is capable of withstanding higher loads whether the shaft is rotating or not. The system is sophisticated, requires higher cost and needs maintenance.

Squeeze Film Lubrication: Two surfaces are seperated by a thin film of oil. The surfaces are in reciprocatory relative motion in a perpendicular direction. The pressure is built up due to inertia of the liquid film.

The lubrication is said to be **hydrodynamic** when the two surfaces separated by fluid film are set in relative motion, oil pressure gets developed which can sustain load without any metal to metal contact. In this chapter we will be restricting our discussion on hydrodynamic lubrication only.

6.7 THEORY OF HYDRODYNAMIC LUBRICATION

When a journal is rotating inside a bush bearing and no oil is supplied between the two, one would easily expect a higher coefficient of friction. Now if oil is supplied between the two surfaces, the friction coefficient should come down. 'Tower' was conducting experiments based on this to arrive at optimum design parameters. During experimentation, to his surprise, he observed a pressure built up within oil film between journal and bearing. He confirmed this by measurements. The reasons were not known that time. Reynolds was able to offer a mathematical solution to this phenomenon. Theory of **hydrodynamic lubrication** is based on differential equation derived by Reynolds. **Typical value of 'f' which can be expected is in the range of 0 – 0.003.**

Petroff's Hydrodynamic lubrication:

Petroff in 1883 published his work on hyrodynamic lubriation. He assumed that journal is concentric to the bearing and there is no side flow of lubricant. These assumptions are valid only if load is light, rotational speed is high and lubricant viscosity is high.

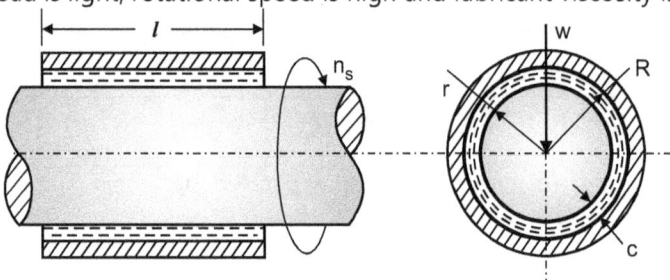

Fig. 6.4: Hydrodynamic Lubrication

Let

W = Radial load on the journal (N) n_s = Speed of the journal, rps
R = Radius of the bearing (mm)   r = Radius of journal (mm)
l = Bearing length, (mm)   c = Radial clearance = R − r
p = W/2·r·l Bearing pressure (N/mm^2)
U = 2·π·r·n_s Journal velocity (mm/sec)
A = 2·π·r·l Surface area of journal (mm^2)
f = Coefficient of friction

According to Newton's equation for viscous flow

$$F = \mu \cdot A \cdot \frac{dU}{dy} = \mu \cdot A \cdot \frac{U}{c}$$

Substituting
$$F = \mu \cdot (2 \cdot \pi r \cdot l) \frac{2 \cdot \pi \cdot r \cdot n_s}{c} \quad \ldots (6.1)$$

Frictional torque on the journal

$$T_f = F \cdot r = \frac{4 \cdot \pi^2 \cdot r^3 \cdot \mu \cdot l \cdot n_s}{c} \quad \ldots (6.2)$$

If 'f' is the friction coefficient, frictional torque is also given by

$$T_f = f \cdot W \cdot r = f \cdot (p \cdot 2r \cdot l) \cdot r = 2 \cdot f \cdot p \cdot l \cdot r^2 \quad \ldots (6.3)$$

Equating equations (6.2) and (6.3)

$$f = 2 \cdot \pi^2 \left(\frac{\mu \cdot n_s}{p}\right)\left(\frac{r}{c}\right) \quad \ldots \text{Petroff's equation} \ldots (6.4)$$

The equation has two important dimensionless variable: ($\mu \cdot n_s/p$) called as bearing modulus and clearance ratio, (r/c), in the range of 500 to 1000. Petroff's equation gives reasonable values of 'f' for light loads. With increase in load and decrease in speed, journal gets eccentric and results deviate.

Power lost in friction: $(kW)_f = (2 \cdot \pi \cdot n_s \cdot T_f / 10^6)$

6.8 MECHANISM OF PRESSURE DEVELOPMENT

To understand the mechanism of pressure build-up within a fluid flow, consider a **stationary surface and another parallel surface** moving with velocity 'U' separated by fluid film. The velocity of the fluid, having laminar flow, varies linearly (refer Newtons law of viscosity) from zero at stationary surface to U at the moving surface. The velocity distribution at both the inlet and outlet sections is identical and there is no pressure build-up within the fluid. Thus, the moving plate cannot support any load as the fluid has not built up any pressure.

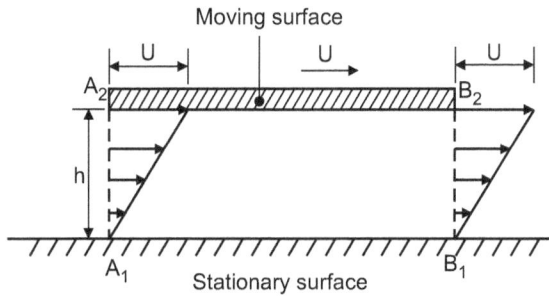

Fig. 6.5: Velocity Distribution – Parallel Surfaces

Now consider a stationary surface not parallel with top plate and the top plate moving at velocity U. As shown in Fig. 6.6, the velocity will be 'U at A_2 and B_2 and will be zero at A_1, B_1. If the velocity distribution along A_1A_2 and B_1B_2 is considered linear as in previous case, flow at outlet will be less than the flow at inlet (since $B_1B_2 < A_1A_2$). Thus, continuity condition will not be satisfied. Therefore, there will be a pressure built-up in the fluid film until flow continuity is maintained. The velocity distribution will be as shown to maintain flow continuity. The pressure induced flow opposes velocity induced flow at A_1A_2 and assists velocity induced flow at B_1B_2. Thus, due to pressure built-up two non parallel plates having relative movement and separated by a fluid film will be able to support a thrust load. Somewhere inbetween at section C_1C_2, velocity distribution will be linear and across this section there will be no pressure induced flow.

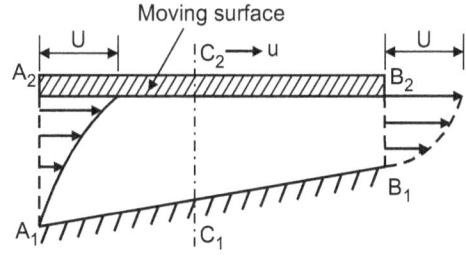

Velocity distribution - Non-parallel surface

Fig. 6.6: Velocity Distribution – Non-parallel Surfaces

Hydrodynamic Lubrication Between Journal and Bearing:

Cosider a journal initially static inside a bearing (Fig. 6.7). Load W is applied on the journal. The gap between journal and bearing is filled with enough oil. Because of the load, the journal will be touching the bearing surface as shown in Fig. 6.7 (a).

Now when the journal starts rotating in anticlockwise direction, initially when the speed is low, it tries to climb over the surface of bearing. The fluid starts flowing due to shaft rotation. There is also a pressure bult up due to **wedge** (similar to non-parallel plates referred above) and a small gap is created between the journal and bearing surface. Refer Fig. 6.7 (b).

Further when the speed increases, the pressure build-up throws the journal to the other side till a balance is obtained. The pressure buid-up in the oil film is shown in Fig. 6.7 (c). The values of pressure and its distribution are arrived at by applying Reynold's equation.

Thus in hydrodynamic lubrication, pressure is built-up by the wedge action when the journal rotates at high speeds. This pressure supports load 'W' and avoids metal to metal contact between the journal and bearing. Since there is no metal to metal contact, the coefficient of friction is the result of viscous resistance to flow of fluid. Thus coefficient of friction is very low. This is the principle of hydrodynamic lubrication.

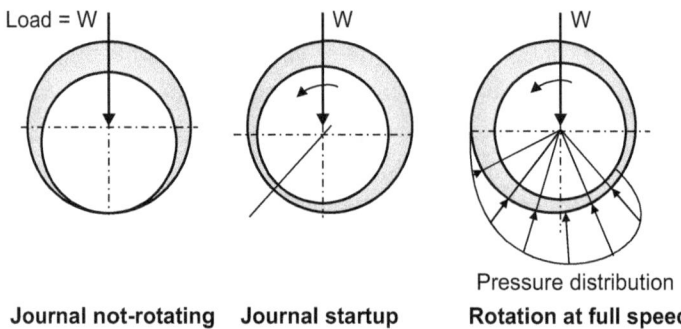

Journal not-rotating   Journal startup   Rotation at full speed

Fig. 6.7: Hydrodynamic Lubrication

6.9 REYNOLD'S EQUATION

Reynold's equation is based on the following assumptions:
- The fluid is Newtonian. Lubricant obeys Newton's law of viscosity.
- Fluid viscous forces are large compared to intertia forces.
- Lubricant is incompressible and has constant viscosity.

- Fluid body forces are negligible.
- Flow is laminar.
- Lubricant film is thin and pressure across the film is constant.
- Film thickness is very small compared to length and width and hence curvature effects are negligible.
- There is a constant supply of the lubricant.

Consider a fluid element of dimensions dx, dy, dz as shown in Fig. 6.8.

Fig. 6.8 (a) shows the fluid element between journal and bearing under consideration.

Fig. 6.8 (b) shows the same element shown oriented along X and Y axes. The boundaries of journal and bearing are now shown as two non-parallel surfaces. This simulates the wedge shape (between AA' and BB') created in Fig. 6.8 (a) by journal and bearing surfaces.

X is the axis in the direction of motion of the fluid element due to rotational velocity of the journal.

Y is the axis in the radial plane.

Z is the axis parallel to axis of the journal.

u, v, z are the velocities of the fluid element in X, Y, Z directions respectively.

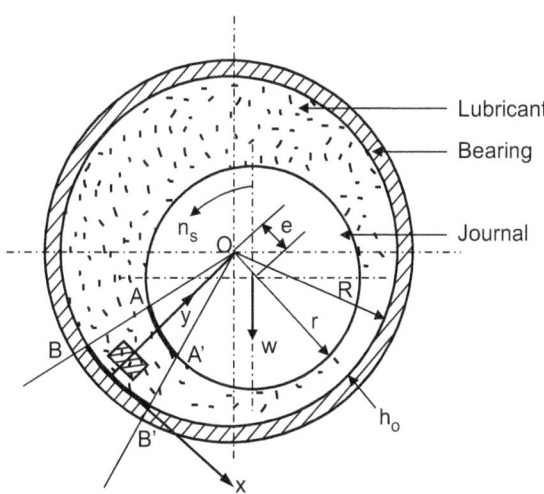

(a) Shaft Rotating in a Hydrodynamic Bearing

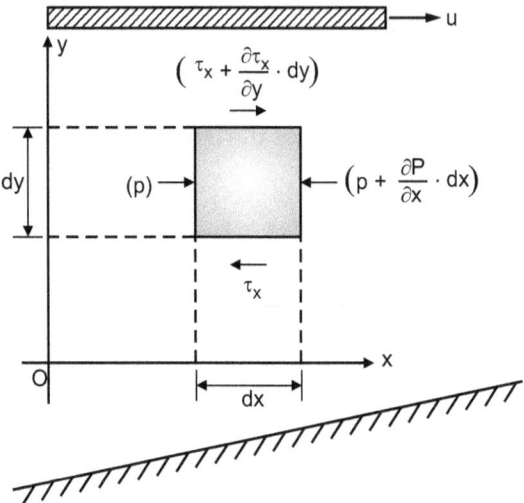

(b) Forces on Fluid Element

Fig. 6.8

Due to the pressure built-up by the flow through two non-parallel surfaces, the fluid element on its face parallel to Y axis is subjected to normal force due to pressure 'p' which undergoes a incremental rise on another face at distance dx.

The fluid element on its face parallel to X axis is subjected to shear force due to shear stress τ_x which undergoes a incremental rise on another face at distance dy for equilibrium.

The body forces, inertia forces are neglected.

Considering equilibrium of forces in X direction

$$p \cdot dy \cdot dz + \left(\tau_x + \frac{\partial \tau_x}{\partial y} \cdot dy\right) dx\, dz - \tau_x \cdot dx\, dz - \left(p + \frac{\partial p}{\partial x} \cdot dx\right) \cdot dy\, dz = 0 \quad \ldots (6.5)$$

$$\therefore \quad \frac{\partial p}{\partial x} = \frac{\partial \tau_x}{\partial y} \quad \ldots (6.6)$$

Applying Newton's law of viscosity

$$\tau_x = \mu \frac{\partial u}{\partial y} \quad \ldots (6.7)$$

Substituting equation (6.7) in equation (6.6), we obtain

$$\mu \frac{\partial^2 u}{\partial y^2} = \frac{\partial p}{\partial x} \quad \ldots (6.8)$$

Equation (6.8) gives fluid pressure variation in x direction

Integrating twice
$$u = \frac{1}{\mu} \cdot \frac{\partial p}{\partial x} \times \frac{y^2}{2} + C_1 \cdot y + C_2 \quad \ldots (6.9)$$

Using boundary conditions

u = 0 at y = 0 and u = U at y = h

We get,
$$u = \frac{U \cdot y}{h} + \frac{1}{2 \cdot \mu} \cdot \frac{\partial p}{\partial x}(y^2 - h \cdot y) \qquad \ldots (6.10)$$

Equation (6.10) gives velocity distribution of lubricant in the film in x direction as a function of y, h and pressure gradient $\frac{\partial p}{\partial x}$ at a point between y = 0 and y = h.

Similarly considering forces in the Z direction
$$w = \frac{1}{2 \cdot \mu} \cdot \frac{\partial p}{\partial z}(y^2 - h \cdot y) \qquad \ldots (6.11)$$

General continuity equation for incompressible flow gives,
$$\frac{\partial u}{\partial x} + \frac{\partial v}{\partial y} + \frac{\partial w}{\partial z} = 0$$

Since there is no flow in y direction, $\frac{\partial v}{\partial y} = 0$ and above equation reduces to
$$\frac{\partial u}{\partial x} + \frac{\partial w}{\partial z} = 0 \qquad \ldots (6.12)$$

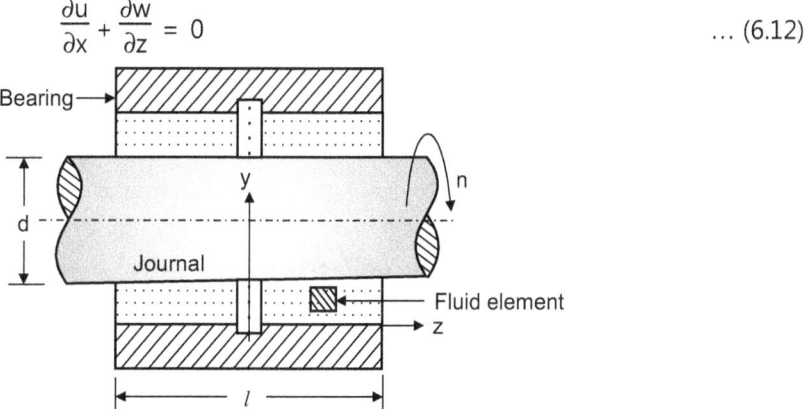

Fig. 6.9: Rotating Journal in Hydrodynamic Bearing

Integrating the equation w.r.t. y between 0 to h gives
$$\int_0^h \frac{\partial u}{\partial x} dy + \int_0^h \frac{\partial w}{\partial z} dy = 0 \qquad \ldots (6.13)$$

Since for definite integrals sign of differentiation and integration can be interchanged
$$\frac{\partial}{\partial x} \int_0^h u \, dy + \frac{\partial}{\partial z} \int_0^h w \, dy = 0 \qquad \ldots (6.14)$$

Where u and w are given by equations (6.10) and (6.11)

Substituting the values of u and v from above and integrating we get

$$\frac{\partial}{\partial x}\left[h^3 \frac{\partial p}{\partial x}\right] + \frac{\partial}{\partial z}\left[h^3 \frac{\partial p}{\partial z}\right] = 6\mu U \left(\frac{\partial h}{\partial x}\right) \qquad \ldots (6.15)$$

This is Reynolds equation for a two dimensional flow (in X and Z direction). The detailed steps in integration are avoided here and can be referred from a standrad text book on Tribology.

Reynolds Equation:
- Theoretically, exact solution can be obtained if bearing is assumed to be infinitely long or very short.
- There is no exact analytical solution to Reynolds equation for bearings with finite length.
- Approximate solutions using numerical methods are available for bearings with finite dimensions.

Bearing Parameter ($\mu \cdot N_s/P$):

The term ($\mu \cdot N_s/P$), a dimensionless group is of significant importance in the design of bearing. A given journal bearing assembly during its operation may undergo fluctuations in speed, load and system temperature. When the journal starts rotation from rest, there is metal to metal contact between the journal and the bearing and the coefficient of friction is large. As the speed slowly picks up the journal starts carrying oil along with it and slowly the pressure starts getting built up. The journal gets separated from the bearing surface by a thick layer of lubrication. This is called thick film lubrication and the coefficient of friction reduces. The effect of speed, load and temperature variation on coefficient of friction is best explained by a graph – (Fig. 6.10) showing variation in coefficient of friction on Y axis and a dimensionless parameter ($\mu \cdot N_s/P$) on X axis.

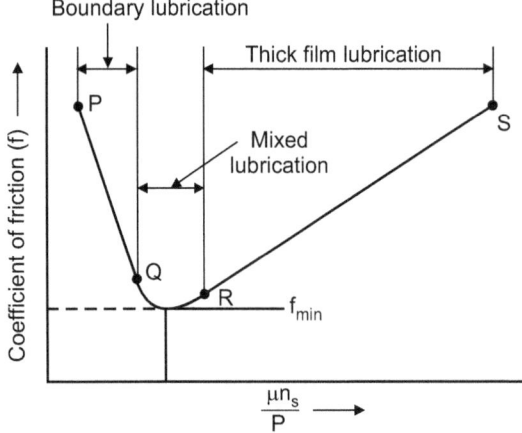

Fig. 6.10: Coefficient of Friction Versus $\left(\dfrac{\mu \cdot n_s}{p}\right)$

The graph is divided in three regions. Region I where for low values of ($\mu \cdot N_s/P$), coefficient of friction is large. This is boundary lubrication or thin film lubrication. The value of ($\mu \cdot N_s/P$) corresponding to lowest value of coefficient of friction is called **Bearing Modulus**. For higher values of ($\mu \cdot N_s/P$), the coefficient of friction increases and this is the thick film or hydrodynamic lubrication region. Inbetween region is called mixed lubrication. This is the unstable region. In this region, if load increases or speed decreases for any reason, ($\mu \cdot N_s/P$) decreases. This increases the coefficient of friction as seen for mixed region. With increase in coefficient of friction, there is increase in heat and the temperature increases. This reduces viscosity. With this ($\mu \cdot N_s/P$) decreases further and the cycle continues. Thus there is a cascading effect and the system can end up running with very high value of coefficient of friction. It is therefore recommended to avoid this region. Preferred value for operational value of ($\mu \cdot N_s/P$) is 3 to 4 times the value of Bearing Modulus. Still higher values can be taken if operating conditions are not steady.

Thick film lubrication is to be always preferred since:
1. There is no metal to metal contact thus leading to low coefficient of friction.
2. This is a stable region.
3. Coefficient of friction can be as low as 0.0012.

It may clearly be understood that the above discussion holds good only for a hydrodynamic bearing. Every application involving a bush bearing is not a case of hydrodynamic bearing. In fact many applications (where speeds may be low, loads may be high, lubricant supply can not be as requied) will be running in thin or boundary film lubrication since it may be more econmical to do so.

Design of Hydrodynamic Journal Bearing with Finite Dimensions

Design Variables: While designing a hydrodynamic bearing, based on machine operation and materials selected, designer has already arrived at certain values such as

- l: Length of the bearing
- n_s: Speed of the shaft in Revolutions/sec.
- p: Bearing pressure [= W/ ($l \times d$)]
- r: Radius of the shaft
- W: Load on the shaft
- β: Arc of bearing

Based on his experience and judgments he further selects values for

- C: Radial clearance between journal and bearing
- μ: Viscosity of oil

Performance Variables: Selection of above variables results into obtaining values of performance variables. For a hydrodynamic bearing these are:

- f: Coefficient of friction
- Q: Flow rate of oil (mm^3/sec.)
- ΔT: Temperature rise in lubricant
- h_0: Minimum oil film thickness

Each of the above variables will have a desired and acceptable range. If these requirements are met, design will be final. Otherwise designer needs to make suitable changes in design variables and recheck the output performance variables.

6.10 RAIMONDI AND BOYD METHOD

- There is no exact analytical solution to Reynolds equation for bearings with finite length. Exact solutions are available only for infinitely long or very short bearings.
- Approximate solutions using numerical methods are available for bearings with finite dimensions.
- Raimondi and Boyd obtained numerical solution of two dimensional Reynolds equation for a finite bearing.
- In this method performance of the bearing is expressed in terms of dimensionless parameters. Solution gives unique inter relationship between these groups.
- Results are available in the form of charts and tables.

Nomenclature of Hydrodynamic Bearing:

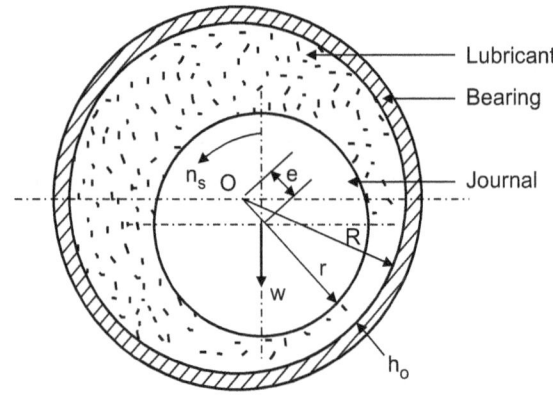

Fig. 6.11: Hydrodynamic journal bearing - Geometry

- e = Eccentricity between centers of bearing and journal.
- R = Radius of the bearing (mm), r = Radius of journal (mm)
- h_o = Minimum film thickness (mm) c = Radial clearance = $R - r$
- $R = e + r + h_o$
- $c = R - r = e + h_o = c \cdot \varepsilon + h_o$ $\varepsilon = 1 - (h_o/c)$

Dimensionless Parameters:

- Length to diameter ratio: l/d
- Minimum film thickness to clearance ratio: h_o/c
- Eccentricity ratio: $\varepsilon = e/c$

- Sommerfeld Number (OR Bearing characteristics number): S

$$S = \left(\frac{r}{c}\right)^2 \frac{\mu \cdot n_s}{p}$$

μ = Viscosity of the lubricant (N-s/mm²)
n_s = Journal speed (rev/s)
p = Unit bearing pressure (N/mm²)
r = Shaft radius in mm
c = Radial clearance in mm

- **Coefficient of Friction Variable:**

$$(CFV) = \left(\frac{r}{c}\right) \cdot f$$

where 'f' is the coefficient of friction.

- **Flow Variable:**

$$(FV) = \frac{Q}{r \cdot c \cdot n_s \cdot l}$$

Q = Flow of the lubricant mm³/sec.
l = Length of the bearing (mm)
n_s = Journal speed rev/sec.

- **Flow ratio:** Q_s/Q

Where Q_s is the side flow in the bearing and Q is the flow in circulation (mm³/sec.)

Values for parameters p/p_{max} and angle ϕ giving minimum film thickness plane orientation can also be obtained.

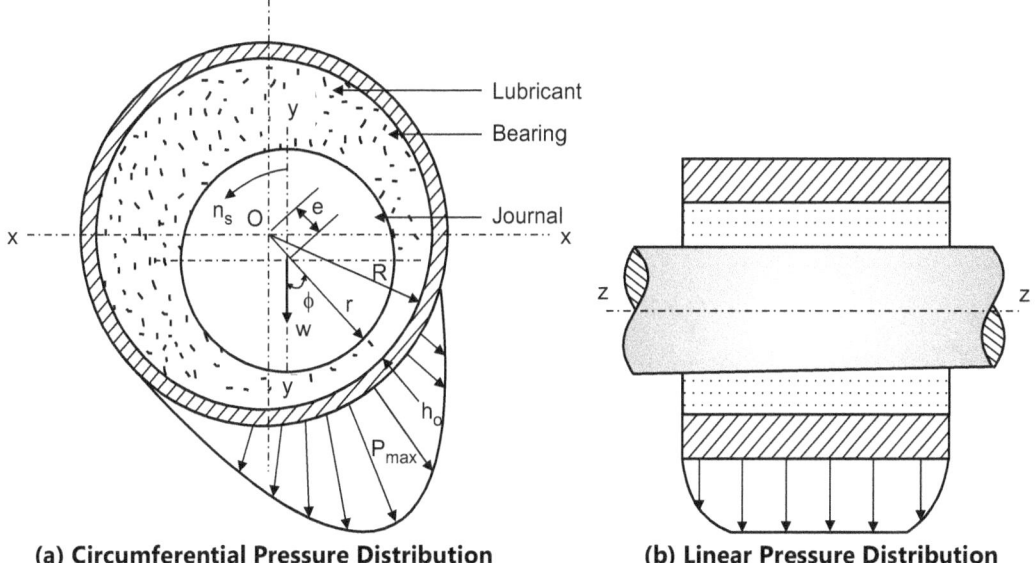

(a) Circumferential Pressure Distribution   (b) Linear Pressure Distribution

Fig. 6.12: Hydrodynamic Journal Bearing

DESIGN OF MACHINE ELEMENTS - II   SLIDING CONTACT BEARING

Design Approach:

1. For a selected $\left(\dfrac{L}{d}\right)$ ratio and bearing angle, table 6.2 gives unique relationship between dimensionless design parameters and preference variable if the bearing is to operate under hydrodynamic condition.

2. By referring to the table, knowing one of the dimensionless parameters, values of other perforamnce variables can be found out. Frictional losses and temeprature rise of lubricant can now be estimated.

Power Lost in Overcoming Friction:

Frictional Torque: The frictional torque required to be overcome will be equal to the frictional force ($= f \cdot W$) multiplied by journal radius.

$$\therefore \quad T_f = f \cdot W \cdot r \; (N.mm)$$

$$\textbf{Frictional Power} = (kW)_f = (2 \cdot \pi \cdot n_s \cdot T_f) \, 10^{-6}$$

$$= (2 \cdot \pi \cdot n_s \cdot f \cdot W \cdot r) \, 10^{-6} \; (kW)$$

This is the power required to overcome friction at bearing.

Since friction energy will get converted into heat, this is also the **Heat Generated = Hg**, (kJ/s).

Heat Dissipation: H_d

The hydrodynamic bearing assembly must dissipate the heat generated for reaching a stable equilibrium situation. Till that happens the temperature will keep increasing. If it is assumed that the total heat is carried away by the flow of lubrication

$$H_d = m \cdot C_p \cdot \Delta T$$

Where,

m = Mass flow rate of lubricating oil (kg/s) = $(\rho \cdot Q / 10^9)$

ρ = Mass density (kg/m³)

C_p = Specific heat of lubricating oil (kJ/kg°C)

ΔT = Temperature rise of lubricating oil

Q = Flow rate (mm³/sec.)

For heat balance at equilibrium

$$\text{Heat generated} = \text{Heat dissipated}$$

$$(2 \cdot \pi \cdot n_s \cdot f \cdot W \cdot r) \, 10^{-6} = \rho \cdot Q \cdot C_p \cdot \Delta T / 10^9$$

$$\Delta T = \left[\dfrac{2 \cdot \pi \cdot n_s \cdot f \cdot W \cdot r}{\rho \cdot Q \cdot C_p}\right] \times 10^3$$

This gives the temperature rise for the lubricant over the inlet temperature. This is an important parameter since most of the lubricants will not perform satisfactorily above temperatures of about 100°C. Assuming inlet temperature of 45°C, the rise in temperature may have to be restricted to about 55°C.

Temperature Rise in Terms of Dimensionless Parameters:

The same temperature rise calculated above can also be calculated using the dimensionless parameters which are obtained during the design of bearing using the charts.

As seen above, the temperature rise is given by

$$\Delta T = \left[\frac{2 \cdot \pi \cdot n_s \cdot f \cdot W \cdot r}{p \cdot Q \cdot C_p}\right] \times 10^3$$

The various dimensionless parameters are

$$(CFV) = \left(\frac{r}{c}\right) f$$

$$\therefore \quad f = CFV \left(\frac{c}{r}\right)$$

$$(FV) = \frac{Q}{r \cdot c \cdot n_s \cdot l}$$

$$\therefore \quad Q = FV \, (r \cdot c \cdot n_s \cdot l)$$

Substituting values of 'f' and Q from above in expression for ΔT.

with $p = N/mm^2$;

ρ = Specific gravity

C_p = kJ/kg°C

$$\Delta T = \frac{4 \cdot \pi \cdot r}{\rho \cdot C_p} * \frac{(CFV)}{(FV)}$$

Above temperature rise was obtained considering total heat is carried by the oil that is in circulation alone. Sometimes if the side flow is considerable, heat carried by the oil that is leaving the bearing can also be taken into consideration for estimating the oil temperatures.

Total Flow of Lubricating oil:

$$Q = Q_c + Q_s$$

Where,

Q_c = Circumferential flow due to relative motion

Q_s = Axial flow due to side leakage

Let T_1 be the inlet temperature of the lubricating oil
T_2 be the outlet temperature of the lubricating oil
Then, $\quad \Delta T = T_2 - T_1$

It is assumed that Q_s, axial flow due to side leakage, takes place at $T_{av} = \dfrac{(T_1 + T_2)}{2}$

Temperature rise of axial flow: $T_{av} - T_1 = \left[\dfrac{(T_1 + T_2)}{2}\right] - T_1 = \dfrac{\Delta T}{2}$

Taking into account the axial flow, the rate of heat dissipation and temperature rise can be modified.

Heat generated in this case is same as determined earlier.

$$\begin{aligned}\text{Heat dissipated} \quad H_d &= \dfrac{\rho \cdot Q_c \cdot C_p \cdot \Delta T}{10^9} + \dfrac{\rho \cdot Q_s \cdot C_p \cdot \Delta T/2}{10^9} \\ &= \dfrac{\rho \cdot (Q - Q_s) \cdot C_p \cdot \Delta T}{10^9} + \dfrac{\rho \cdot Q_s \cdot C_p + \Delta T/2}{10^9} \\ &= \dfrac{\rho \cdot C_p \cdot \Delta T}{10^9}\left[Q - Q_s + \left(\dfrac{Q_s}{2}\right)\right] \\ &= \dfrac{\rho \cdot C_p \cdot \Delta T}{10^9}\left[Q - \dfrac{Q_s}{2}\right]\end{aligned}$$

With this, the temperature rise for the lubricant can be found out.

Parameters of Bearing Design: Designer has to select various parameters in the process of designing a hydrodynamic bearing. The parameters and considerations in their selection are discussed below.

Minimum film thickness h_o:

Minimum permissible oil thickness, h_0, depends on surface finish, nature of load and viscosity. If surface finishes on the journal and shaft are rough, it would require larger value for h_0 to avoid metal to contact. This otherwise would run the bearing under thin film lubrication and reduce load carrying capacity. If a better surface finish is obtained, it increases load carrying capacity, however machining cost also increases. Designer has to strike a balance. Lower limit for h_0 is $(0.0002) \times r$ to $(0.0003) \times r$, where r is the radius of the shaft.

Bearing Pressure p:

The maximum acceptable bearing pressure depends mainly on the material used for the bearing. Nature of load, such as, whether it is fluctuating or steady, whether journal starts rotation on 'no' load or 'full' load also decides the permissible value. Depending on the nature of loading permissible range is 0.3 to 15 N/mm². Typical values for few common applications are as below.

- Automobile engine - main bearing: 0.8 to 2.0 N/mm².
- Automobile engine - crank pin bearing: 7.0 to 10.5 N/mm².
- Rotary Motors: Upto 1.5.
- Machine Tools: Upto 2.0.

Values of allowable bearing pressures for materials can be referred from related material standards or design data handbooks. Proper material selection depends on the application, bearing material compatibilty with shaft material and above all the economy.

Clearance 'c': Radial clearance, which is the difference in the radii of bearing and journal, should be small to provide required velocity gradient for the fluid which is nesessary to build sufficient pressure. However, smaller 'C' requires better finish on journal and bearing to avoid metal to metal contact between the two. Recommended values are

C = 0.001 (r) to 0.004 (r).

Length to Diameter Ratio l/d:

A higher l/d ratio for bearing means higher load capacity and stability, however flow rate Q decreases. This increases the temperature of the lubricant, thereby limiting load carrying capacity. A lower value for l/d means higher lubricant flow and lower temperature. However the pressure developed is not uniform along shaft length and drops considerably thereby reducing the load carrying capacity. Commonly used ratios are 1, 1/2. Charts for various design parameters are available for different values of l/d ratios.

Table 6.2: Dimensionless Parameters for Various $\left(\dfrac{l}{d}\right)$ Ratios

[l/d]	ε	$\dfrac{h_o}{c}$	$\dfrac{\mu \cdot n_s}{p}\left(\dfrac{r}{c}\right)^2$	$\left(\dfrac{r}{c}\right) \cdot f$	$\dfrac{Q}{r \cdot c \cdot n_s \cdot l}$	$\dfrac{Q_s}{Q}$
			S	CFV	FV	FR
∞	1	0	0	0	0	0
	0.97	0.03	---	---	---	0
	0.9	0.1	0.0115	0.756	0.411	0
	0.8	0.2	0.021	0.961	0.760	0
	0.6	0.4	0.0389	1.20	1.56	0
	0.4	0.6	0.0626	1.52	2.26	0
	0.2	0.8	0.123	2.57	2.83	0
	0.1	0.9	0.240	4.8	3.03	0
	0	1.0	∞	∞	3.147	0

contd. ...

l/d							
1	1.0	0	0	0	0		1.0
	0.97	0.03	0.00474	0.514	4.82		0.973
	0.9	0.1	0.0188	1.05	4.74		0.913
	0.8	0.2	0.0446	1.70	4.62		0.842
	0.6	0.4	0.121	3.22	4.33		0.680
	0.4	0.6	0.264	5.79	3.99		0.497
	0.2	0.8	0.631	12.8	3.59		0.280
	0.1	0.9	1.33	26.4	3.37		0.150
	0	1.0	∞	∞	3.142		0
(1/2)	1.0	0	0	0	---		1.0
	0.97	0.03	0.00609	0.610	5.88		0.980
	0.9	0.1	0.0313	1.60	5.69		0.939
	0.8	0.2	0.0923	3.26	5.41		0.874
	0.6	0.4	0.319	8.10	4.85		0.730
	0.4	0.6	0.779	17.0	4.29		0.552
	0.2	0.8	2.03	40.9	3.72		0.318
	0.1	0.9	4.31	85.6	3.43		0.173
	0	1.0	∞	∞	3.142		0

Design Procedure for Hydrodynamic Bearing:

The design will in general follow the following steps:

1. Load on the shaft, its speed and journal (shaft) diameter will be known once the shaft for a particular application with known loads is designed for a given application.
2. Length of the journal that will be supported in the bearing can be decided by selecting appropriate l/d ratio. Usual value will be in the range of 1 to 1.25. Depending on other design constraints, some other ratio may become essential.
3. Select bearing material depending on design application and find permissible pressure value for the material from design data book.
4. Knowing dimensions and load values, check the actual pressure value (= $W/l \times d$) to be less than permissible value. Make suitable changes if required.
5. Select appropriate lubricant based on its suitability for the application and acceptable viscosity. Find bearing modulus value ($\mu \cdot N_s/p$).

6. Once one of the dimensionless parameters is known, values of other dimensionless parameters can be obtained from the table. Various performance parameters can now be checked for their acceptable ranges. If the parameters do not fall in acceptable range, one of the design parameters need to be changed and iterative process has to be followed.

7. Check bearing parameers h_o and c for their acceptable values for the given conditions.

8. Determine coefficient of friction and check its acceptability.

9. Determine flow rate and temperatue rise for lubricant.

10. Find the power lost in friciton.

SOLVED EXAMPLES

Example 6.1: A shaft 80 mm in diameter rotates concentrically in a 100 mm long sleeve at 1000 rpm and supports a load of 5000 N. If the lubricant used has a viscosity of 30 cP and the radial clearance is 0.1 mm, find the coefficient of friction and the power loss. Assume Petroff's equation holds good for the given arrangement.

Solution:

Bearing pressure, $p = \dfrac{W}{l \times d} = \dfrac{5000}{100 \times 80} = 0.625 \text{ N/mm}^2$

Speed in revolutions per second, $n_s = \dfrac{\text{rpm}}{60} = \dfrac{1000}{60} = 16.67$

Coefficient of friction

$$f = 2\pi^2 \left(\dfrac{\mu \cdot n_s}{p}\right) \dfrac{r}{C}$$

$$= 2\pi^2 \left(\dfrac{30 \times 10^{-9} \times 16.67}{0.625}\right) \left(\dfrac{40}{0.1}\right)$$

$$f = 0.00632$$

Frictional torque

$$T_f = f \cdot W \cdot r = 0.00632 \times 5000 \times 40$$

$$= 1264 \text{ N·mm}$$

Power loss $(kW)_f = \dfrac{2\pi \cdot n_s \cdot T_f}{10^6}$

$$= \dfrac{2\pi \times 16.67 \times 1264}{10^6}$$

$$= 0.133 \text{ kW} = 133 \text{ W}$$

DESIGN OF MACHINE ELEMENTS - II   SLIDING CONTACT BEARING

Example 6.2: Find the maximum radial load that the journal can carry and can still operate at hydrodynamic condition for following data of a hydrodynamic bearing.

Journal diameter = length = 60 mm.

Radial clearance = 0.06 mm.

Minimum film thickness = 0.006 mm

Journal speed = 1440 rpm

The lubricant used has specific gravity of 0.9. Its specific heat is 1.75 kJ/kg°C and the viscosity is 20 cP.

For the above calculated load find the power lost in friction and the resultant temperature rise.

Given data: $l = d = 60$ mm

Radial clearance, $C = 0.06$ mm

$h_o = 0.006$ mm

Journal speed, $n_s = \dfrac{1440}{60} = 24$ rps

Viscosity, $\mu = 20$ cP $= 20 \times 10^{-9}$ N·sec/mm²

$C_p = 1.75$ kJ/kg°C

Specific gravity = 0.9

Solution:

(a) Dimensionless parameter $\left(\dfrac{h_o}{C}\right) = \dfrac{0.006}{0.06} = 0.1$

Corresponding to $\left(\dfrac{h_o}{C}\right) = 0.1$ values for other dimensionless parameters can be read from table.

Sommerfeld Number, $S = 0.0188$

Now, $S = 0.0188 = \dfrac{\mu \cdot n_s}{P}\left(\dfrac{r}{C}\right)^2 = \dfrac{20 \times 10^{-9} \times 24}{P}\left(\dfrac{30}{0.06}\right)^2$

Solving, $P = 6.38$ N/mm²

Bearing pressure, $P = \dfrac{W}{\text{Projected area}} = \dfrac{W}{60 \times 60} = 6.38$

Load, $W = 22968$ N

DESIGN OF MACHINE ELEMENTS - II

SLIDING CONTACT BEARING

(b) Friction Variable $\left(\dfrac{r}{C}\right)f = 1.05$

$$\therefore \quad f = \dfrac{1.05 \times 0.06}{30} = 0.0021$$

Power lost in friction:

$$(kW)_f = \dfrac{2\pi \cdot n_s \cdot f \cdot W \cdot r}{10^6} = \dfrac{2\pi \times 24 \times 0.0021 \times 22968 \times 30}{10^6}$$

$$= 0.218 \text{ kW}$$

(c) Assuming that total heat is carried away by the total amount of flow:

$$FV = \dfrac{Q}{r \cdot C \cdot n_s \cdot l} = 4.74$$

$\therefore \quad$ Flow rate, $Q = 4.74 \times 30 \times 0.06 \times 24 \times 60 = 12286 \text{ mm}^3/\text{sec}$

Heat dissipated $= m \cdot C_p \cdot \Delta T = (\rho \cdot Q) C_p \cdot \Delta T \times 10^{-9}$

$$= (900 \times 12286) \, 1.75 \times \Delta T \times 10^{-9}$$

Equating heat generated = Heat dissipated

$$= (900 \times 12286) \, 1.75 \times \Delta T \times 10^{-9}$$

$$\Delta T = 11.26°C$$

Example 6.3: A Babbit lined steel back bush bearing is used to support a shaft of diameter 50 mm. The radial load on the bearing is 2044 N. The oil filter restricts clearance at the bearing as 50 microns. The length of the bearing is 50 mm. Shaft rotates at 950 rpm. The oil used has a viscosity of 25 cP at operating temperature. Calculate,

(a) Coefficient of friction
(b) Minimum oil film thickness
(c) Requirement of oil flow
(d) Power lost in friction
(e) Temperature rise, assuming that heat generated is carried away by the total oil flow.

Assume specific gravity of oil as 0.86. Specific heat of oil is 1.85 kJ/kg°C.

Given data: $l = d = 50$ mm. Hence, $\left(\dfrac{l}{d}\right) = 1$, Load = 2044 N,

$$\mu = 25 \text{ cP} = 25 \times 10^{-9} \text{ N-s/mm}^2, \quad n_s = \dfrac{950}{60} = 15.83 \text{ rps}$$

Radial clearance, $C = 50$ microns $= 0.05$ mm

Solution:

Bearing pressure, $P = \dfrac{W}{l \times d} = \dfrac{2044}{50 \times 50} = 0.8176 \text{ N/mm}^2$

Sommerfeld Number, $S = \left(\dfrac{\mu \cdot n_s}{P}\right)\left(\dfrac{r}{C}\right)^2$

$= \left(\dfrac{25 \times 10^{-9} \times 15.83}{0.8176}\right)\left(\dfrac{25}{0.05}\right)^2 = 0.121$

Once one of the dimensionless parameters is known, values of other dimensionless parameters can be read from table for $\left(\dfrac{l}{d}\right) = 1$ and $S = 0.121$.

Thus,

(1) $\left(\dfrac{r}{C}\right) f = 3.22$. Substituting $\left(\dfrac{25}{0.05}\right) \times f = 3.22$

Coefficient of friction, $f = 0.00644$

(2) $\dfrac{h_o}{C} = 0.4$ with $C = 0.05$

Minimum film thickness, $h_o = 0.02$ mm

(3) $\dfrac{Q}{r \cdot C \cdot n_s \cdot l} = 4.33$

Gives $Q = 4.33 \times 25 \times 0.05 \times 15.83 \times 50$

$= 4284 \text{ mm}^3/\text{sec} = 4.284 \times 10^{-6} \text{ m}^3/\text{sec}$

$= 4284 \times 10^{-6}$ litre/sec

$= 4284 \times 60 \times 10^{-6} = 0.257$ l/min

(4) Power lost in friction: (Heat generated)

$(kW)_f = (2 \cdot \pi \cdot n_s \cdot f \cdot W \cdot r) \times 10^{-6}$

$= (2 \cdot \pi \cdot 15.83 \times 0.00644 \times 2044 \times 25) \times 10^{-6}$

$= 0.0327$ kW

(5) Neglecting effect due to side leakage (Heat carried by total oil flow in circulation)

Heat generated $= 0.0327$ kW $=$ Heat dissipated

Heat dissipated $= m \cdot C_p \cdot \Delta T = H_d$

where, $m = \rho \cdot Q = 860 \times 4284 \times 10^{-9} = 0.003684$ kg/sec.

$H_d = 0.003684 \times 1.75 \times \Delta T = 0.0327$

$\Delta T = 5.07°C$

DESIGN OF MACHINE ELEMENTS - II SLIDING CONTACT BEARING

Example 6.4: Following data is given for a full hydrodynamic bearing.

Journal diameter = 80 mm
Bearing length = 40 mm
Journal speed = 1500 rpm
Viscosity of the lubricant = 25 cP
Minimum film thickness = 15 microns
Specific gravity of lubricant = 0.86
Specific heat of lubricant = 2.09 kJ/kg°C

Considering the application, designer intends to provide $H_8 e_8$ fit between the journal and bearing. Use following tolerance values.

	Tolerance in mm	
Diameter 80 mm	H8	e8
	+ 0.046	− 0.060
	+ 0.000	− 0.106

Calculate:
(a) Load carrying capacity of the bearing.
(b) Side leakage.
(c) Temperature rise considering side leakage.

Given data: L = 40 mm, d = 80 mm, N = 1500, $n_s = \dfrac{1500}{60} = 25$ rps, $h_o = 0.015$ mm.

Solution: Average hole diameter: D_{av}

$$D_{av} = \frac{80.000 + 80.046}{2} = 80.023 \text{ mm}$$

Average shaft diameter: d_{av}

$$d_{av} = \frac{(80 - 0.06) + (80 - 0.106)}{2} = 79.917 \text{ mm}$$

∴ Diameter clearance = $2C = D_{av} - d_{av}$

$2C = 80.023 - 79.917$

$C = 0.053$ mm

Minimum film thickness h_o = 0.015 mm.

∴ Minimum film thickness variable $\left(\dfrac{h_o}{C}\right) = \dfrac{0.015}{0.053} = 0.283$

From table, values of other non-dimensional parameters are to be obtained by interpolation.

$\left(\dfrac{l}{d}\right)$	$\dfrac{h_o}{C}$	S	$\left(\dfrac{r}{C}\right)f$	$\dfrac{Q}{r \cdot C \cdot n_s \cdot l}$	$\dfrac{Q_s}{Q}$
$\left(\dfrac{1}{2}\right)$	0.4	0.319	8.10	4.85	0.730
	0.2	0.0923	3.26	5.41	0.874

$$\dfrac{h_o}{C} = 0.283$$

In this case values of other dimensionless parameters are to be obtained by interpolation.

Considering similar triangles ABC and ADE.

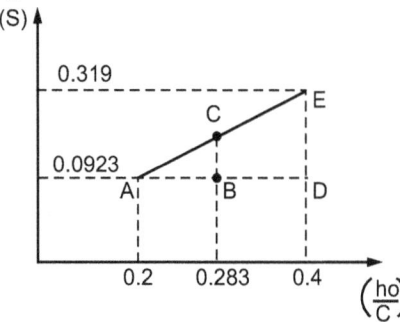

Fig. 6.13

Sommerfeld Number:

$$S = 0.0923 + \left[\dfrac{0.283 - 0.2}{0.4 - 0.2}\right](0.319 - 0.0923)$$

$$= 0.0923 + [0.415](0.2267)$$

$$S = 0.1863$$

Coefficient of friction variable $CFV = \left(\dfrac{r}{C}\right)f$

$$CFV = 3.26 + [0.415](8.10 - 3.26) = 5.269$$

Flow variable $FV = \dfrac{Q}{r \cdot C \cdot n_s \cdot l}$

$$FV = 5.41 - [0.415](5.41 - 4.85) = 5.178$$

Flow ratio, $FR = \dfrac{Q_s}{Q}$

$$FR = 0.874 - [0.415](0.874 - 0.730) = 0.814$$

(a) Load carrying capacity

$$S = \frac{\mu \cdot n_s}{P}\left(\frac{r}{C}\right)^2$$

$$0.1863 = \frac{25 \times 10^{-9} \times 25}{P}\left(\frac{40}{0.053}\right)^2$$

Bearing pressure $P = 1.91\ \text{N/mm}^2$

$$P = \frac{W}{l \times d} = \frac{W}{40 \times 80}$$

Load capacity, $W = 6112\ \text{N}$

(b)

$$FV = \frac{Q}{r \cdot C \cdot n_s \cdot l} = 5.178$$

$\therefore\quad Q = 5.178 \times 40 \times 0.053 \times 25 \times 40 = 10978\ \text{mm}^3/\text{sec}$

$$FR = \frac{Q_s}{Q} = 0.814$$

$Q_s = 0.814 \times 10978 = 8936\ \text{mm}^3/\text{sec}$

$\quad\ = 8936 \times 10^{-6} \times 60 = 0.536\ \text{litres/min.}$

(c) Heat generated:

$$CFV = \left(\frac{r}{C}\right)f = 5.269$$

Coefficient of friction $f = 5.269 \times \dfrac{0.053}{40} = 0.00698$

$(kW)_f$ = Heat generated

$$= \frac{2\pi \cdot n_s \cdot f \cdot W \cdot r}{10^6} = \frac{2\pi \times 25 \times 0.00698 \times 6112 \times 40}{10^6}$$

$$= 0.268\ \text{kW}$$

Heat dissipated $= \dfrac{\rho \cdot C_p \cdot \Delta T}{10^9}\left[Q - \dfrac{Q_s}{2}\right]$

$$= \frac{860 \times 2.09 \times \Delta T}{10^9}\left[10978 - \frac{8936}{2}\right] = 0.0117 \cdot \Delta T$$

Equating heat generated = Heat dissipated

$\quad 0.268 = 0.0117\ \Delta T$

$\quad \Delta T = 22.9°C$

Example 6.5: For al full hydrodynamic bearing following data applies:

Radial load = 5 kN
Journal diameter = 50 mm
Bearing length = 50 mm
Journal speed = 1440 rpm
Minimum oil film thickness = 0.01 mm

Bearing hole and shaft are machined with following tolerances.

Hole 50 $^{+0.025}_{+0.00}$ Shaft 50 $^{-0.075}_{-0.050}$

Suggest viscosity for the lubricant to be selected.

Given data: W = 5000 N, $l = d$ = 50 mm, N = 1500 rpm, h_o = 0.01 mm

Solution: Average hole diameter = 50.0125 mm

$$\text{Average shaft diameter} = \frac{49.925 + 49.95}{2} = 49.9375 \text{ mm}$$

Average diameter clearance = 2C = 50.0125 − 49.9375

2C = 0.075 mm

Radial clearance, C = 0.0375 mm

Minimum film thickness variable:

$$\left(\frac{h_o}{C}\right) = \frac{0.01}{0.0375} = 0.2667$$

Sommerfeld Number 'S' can be obtained by interpolation from table.

$$S = 0.0446 + \left[\frac{0.2667 - 0.2}{0.4 - 0.2}\right](0.121 - 0.0446)$$

$$= 0.0446 + [0.3335](0.0764)$$

$$S = 0.07$$

$$\text{Bearing pressure, } P = \frac{W}{l \times d} = \frac{5000}{50 \times 50} = 2 \text{ N/mm}^2$$

$$n_s = \frac{1440}{60} = 24 \text{ rps}$$

$$\therefore \quad S = 0.07 = \left(\frac{\mu \cdot n_s}{P}\right)\left(\frac{r}{C}\right)^2$$

$$0.07 = \frac{\mu \times 24}{2}\left(\frac{25}{0.0375}\right)^2$$

$$\mu = 13.1 \times 10^{-9} \text{ N·sec/mm}^2$$

Desired viscosity is 13.1 cP.

Example 6.6: A 100 mm diameter ground steel journal rotates at 1440 rpm in a bronze bushing 100 mm long. For the hydrodynamic lubrication, minimum oil thickness is to be maintained as five times the sum of the roughness of journal and bearing. Use following data for roughness values. Radial clearance between journal and bearing is 60 microns.

	Process	Roughness values
Shaft	Grinding	1.6 microns
Bearing	Boring	0.8 micron

Determine the maximum radial load the journal can carry to operate under hydrodynamic condition and the total amount of oil flow. Consider oil viscosity as 18 cP.

Given data: $d = l = 100$ mm, $N = 1440$ rpm, $C = 0.06$ mm, Viscosity = 18 cP, $h_o = 5 \times$ (Roughness on journal and bearing 0.

Solution: Minimum oil film thickness:

$$h_o = 5(1.6 + 0.8) = 12 \text{ microns} = 0.012 \text{ mm}$$

$$\frac{h_o}{C} = \frac{0.012}{0.06} = 0.2$$

Corresponding to this value of dimensionless parameter, referring to Table for $\frac{l}{d} = 1$.

(a) $S = 0.0446$, $FV = 4.62$

$$S = \frac{\mu \cdot n_s}{p} \left(\frac{r}{C}\right)^2$$

$$0.0446 = \frac{18 \times 10^{-9} \times 24}{p} \left(\frac{50}{0.06}\right)^2$$

$$p = 6.73 \text{ N/mm}^2$$

Bearing pressure, $p = \dfrac{W}{l \times d}$

$$6.73 = \frac{W}{100 \times 100}$$

Load which bearing can carry = 67300 N

(b) $FV = 4.62 = \dfrac{Q}{r \cdot C \cdot n_s \cdot l}$

$$Q = 4.62 \times 50 \times 0.06 \times 24 \times 100$$

$$= 33264 \text{ mm}^3/\text{sec.}$$

$$= 33264 \times 10^{-6} \times 60 = 1.995 \text{ litres/min}$$

Example 6.7: A hydrodynamic bearing has a diameter and length of 75 mm. The radial load on the bearing is 20 kN. The journal speed is 1500 rpm and the radial clearance is 60 microns. If the viscosity of the oil is 25 cP, determine.

(i) Minimum oil film thicikness

(ii) Probable coefficient of friction

(iii) Power lost in friction

(iv) Quantity of oil in circulation

(v) Side leakage

(vi) If the make up oil is supplied at 30°C, find the average oil temperature.

Assume specific gravity of oil as 0.86 and the specific heat as 2.09 kJ/kg°C.

Given data: $l = d = 75$ mm. Hence, $\left(\dfrac{l}{d}\right) = 1$, Load $= 20 \times 10^3$ N,

$$\mu = 25 \text{ cP} = 25 \times 10^{-9} \text{ N-s/mm}^2, \quad C = 60 \text{ microns} = 0.06 \text{ mm}$$

$$n_s = \dfrac{1500}{60} = 25 \text{ rps}$$

Solution: Bearing pressure, $P = \dfrac{W}{l \times d} = \dfrac{20000}{75 \times 75} = 3.555 \text{ N/mm}^2$

$$\text{Sommerfeld Number, } S = \left(\dfrac{\mu \cdot n_s}{P}\right)\left(\dfrac{r}{C}\right)^2$$

$$= \left(\dfrac{25 \times 10^{-9} \times 25}{3.555}\right)\left(\dfrac{37.5}{0.06}\right)^2 = 0.06867$$

Values of other dimensionless parameters can be obtained from table for $\left(\dfrac{l}{d}\right) = 1$ and $S = 0.06867$. In this case, values are to be obtained by interpolation considering linear variation.

(i)
$$\dfrac{h_o}{C} = 0.2 + \left[\dfrac{0.06867 - 0.0446}{0.121 - 0.0446}\right](0.4 - 0.2)$$

$$= 0.2 + [0.315](0.2)$$

$$= 0.2 + 0.063 = 0.263$$

∴ Minimum oil film thickness

$$h_o = 0.263 \times 0.06$$
$$h_o = 0.01578 \text{ mm}$$

(ii) **Probable coefficient of friction:**

$$\left(\frac{r}{C}\right)f = 1.70 + [0.315](3.22 - 1.70)$$
$$= 1.70 + 0.4788$$
$$\left(\frac{r}{C}\right)f = 2.18$$

Hence, $f = 2.18 \times \dfrac{0.06}{37.5} = 0.003488$

Flow variable $\dfrac{Q}{r \cdot C \cdot n_s \cdot l} = 4.62 - [0.315](4.62 - 4.33)$

$$= 4.529$$

$$FR = \frac{Q_s}{Q} = 0.842 - [0.315](0.842 - 0.680)$$
$$= 0.791$$

(iii) **Power lost in friction:** (Equal to heat generated H_g)

$(kW)_f = 2\pi \cdot n_s \cdot f \cdot W \cdot r = 2 \times \pi \times 25 \times 0.00348 \times 20 \times 10^3 \times 37.5 \times 10^{-6}$

$$= 0.41 \text{ kW}$$

(iv) **Quantity of oil in circulation:**

$$\frac{Q}{r \cdot C \cdot n_s \cdot l} = 4.529$$

∴ $Q = 4.529 \times 37.5 \times 0.06 \times 25 \times 75$
$$= 19107 \text{ mm}^3/\text{sec}$$
$$= 19107 \times 10^{-6} \times 60 \text{ mm}^3/\text{min}$$
$$= 1.146 \text{ litre/min}.$$

(v) **Side leakage:**

$$\frac{Q_s}{Q} = 0.791$$

∴ $Q_s = 0.791 \times 19107$
$$= 15114 \text{ mm}^3/\text{sec}$$

(vi) Average oil temperature:

Heat dissipated considering side leakage is given by,

$$H_d = \frac{\rho \cdot C_p \cdot \Delta T}{10^9}\left[Q - \frac{Q_s}{2}\right]$$

$$H_d = \frac{\rho \cdot C_p \cdot \Delta T}{10^9}\left[19107 - \frac{15114}{2}\right]$$

Equating heat generated = Heat dissipated

$$0.41 = \frac{860 \times 2.09}{10^9}\Delta T\,[19107 - 7557]$$

∴ Temperature rise $\Delta T = 19.74°C$

∴ Average oil temperature = Inlet oil temperature + $\frac{\Delta T}{2}$

$$= 30 + \frac{19.74}{2} = 39.9°C$$

Example 6.8: Following data is given for a 360° hydrodynamic bearing. Radial load is 20 kN and diameter of the journal is equal to the length of bearing which is 80 mm. The radial clearance between the journal and bearing is 0.08 mm. If the inlet temperature of the oil is 40°C, find the coefficient of friction and minimum film thickness. The shaft rotates at 1500 rpm. Assume specific gravity of oil as 0.86 and specific heat of the lubricant as 1.75 kJ/kg°C.

Temperature/viscosity relationship is given below.

Temperature (T°C)	38	40	42	43	44	45	46	47	48	49	50
Z (cP)	56	53.5	51	49.5	48	46.5	45.5	44.5	43.5	42	40.5

Assume all the heat is carried away by the total fluid flow.

Given data: W = 20000 N, $l = d = 80$ mm, C = 0.08 mm,

N = 1500 rpm, $n_s = \frac{1500}{60} = 25$ rps

Solution:

(1) Since total heat is to be considered as carried by total oil flow, it will be more convenient here to find temperature rise in terms of variables CFV and FV. The relation is given by,

$$\Delta T = \left(\frac{4\pi \cdot p}{\rho \cdot C_p}\right) \frac{CFV}{FV}$$

(2) Since viscosity is varying with temperature, we will take trial 1 assuming average temperature as 45°C.

Bearing pressure

$$p = \frac{W}{l \times d} = \frac{20000}{80 \times 80} = 3.125 \text{ N/mm}^2$$

$$S = \frac{\mu \cdot n_s}{P}\left(\frac{r}{C}\right)^2 = \frac{\mu \times 10^{-9} \times 25}{3.125}\left(\frac{40}{0.08}\right)^2 = 2 \times 10^6 \cdot \mu$$

Trial 1: Average temperature = 45° C

μ = Viscosity as per above table for 45°C is 46.5×10^{-9} N·sec/mm^2

∴ Sommerfeld number,

$$S = 2 \times 10^6 \times 46.5 \times 10^{-9} = 0.093$$

Referring to the table for $\frac{l}{d} = 1$ and S = 0.093, the values of dimensionless variables CFV and FV are to be obtained by interpolation.

∴

$$CFV: \left(\frac{r}{C}\right)f = 1.7 + \left[\frac{0.093 - 0.0446}{0.121 - 0.0446}\right](3.22 - 1.7)$$

$$= 1.7 + [0.633](1.52) = 2.663$$

$$FV: \frac{Q}{(r \cdot C \cdot n_s \cdot l)} = 4.62 - [0.633](4.62 - 4.33)$$

$$= 4.62 - [0.633](0.29) = 4.43$$

Now, temperature rise of the lubricant can be found as,

$$\Delta T = \left(\frac{4\pi \cdot p}{\rho \cdot C_p}\right) \frac{CFV}{FV}$$

$$= \left(\frac{4\pi \times 3.125}{0.86 \times 1.75}\right) \times \frac{2.663}{4.43} = (26.09)(0.601) = 15.69°C$$

∴ Actual T_{ow} = $40 + \frac{15.69}{2} = 47.84°C$

Since this is considerably higher than assumed temperature 45° C, we go for next trial.

Trial 2: Assume average temperature as 47°C

μ = Viscosity is 44.5×10^{-9} N·sec/mm²

∴ $\quad S = 2 \times 10^6 \times \mu = 2 \times 10^6 \times 44.5 \times 10^{-9} = 0.089$ Nsec/mm²

$$CFV: \left(\frac{r}{C}\right) f = 1.7 + \left[\frac{0.089 - 0.0446}{0.121 - 0.0446}\right](93.22 - 1.7)$$

$$= 1.7 + [0.581](1.52) = 2.58$$

$$FV: \frac{Q}{(r \cdot C \cdot n_s \cdot l)} = 4.62 - [0.581](0.29) = 4.45$$

Temperature rise of the lubricant

$$\Delta T = \left(\frac{4\pi \cdot p}{\rho \cdot C_p}\right)\left(\frac{CFV}{FV}\right) = (26.09)\left(\frac{2.58}{4.45}\right)$$

$$= 15.12$$

∴ $\quad$ Actual $T_{av} = 40 + \dfrac{15.12}{2} = 47.56$°C

This is close to assumed temperature of 47°C. Hence we accept results of trial 2. As found above

(A) Coefficient of friction: $\left(\dfrac{r}{C}\right) f = 2.58$

∴ $\quad f = 2.58 \times \dfrac{0.08}{40} = 0.00516$

(B) Minimum film thickness:

By interpolation $\quad \dfrac{h_o}{C} = 0.2 + [0.581](0.4 - 0.2) = 0.2 + 0.116 = 0.316$

∴ $\quad h_o = 0.316 \times 0.08 = 0.0253$ mm

Example 6.9: Following data is given for a 360° hydrodynamic bearing. Radial load = 20 kN. Bearing diameter = Length = 60 mm. Journal speed is 1500 rpm. Radial clearance between journal and bearing is 0.08 mm. Temperature/viscosity relationship as shown below.

Temperature	38	40	41	42	43	44	45	46	47	48	49	50	51	52
Viscosity	58.5	56	53.5	51	48.5	46	44	42	40	38	36	34	32	30

Assuming inlet oil temperature as 38°C, specific gravity of oil is 0.86 and specific temperature of the lubricant is 1.75 kJ/kg°C; find power lost in friction and oil flow required.

Given: W = 20000 N, $l = d$ = 60 mm, C = 0.08 mm, N = 1500 rpm,

$$p = \frac{W}{l \times d} = \frac{20000}{60 \times 60} = 5.55 \text{ N/mm}^2, \quad n_s = \frac{1500}{60} = 25.$$

$$S = \frac{\mu \cdot n_s}{P}\left(\frac{r}{C}\right)^2 = \frac{\mu \times 10^{-9} \times 25}{5.55}\left(\frac{30}{0.08}\right)^2 = (0.633 \times 10^6)\mu$$

Solution:

Trial 1: Assume $T_{av} = 45°C$, $\mu = 44 \times 10^{-9}$

$$S = (0.633 \times 10^6)(44 \times 10^{-9}) = \mathbf{0.02785}$$

$$\left(\frac{r}{C}\right)f = 1.05 + \left[\frac{0.02785 - 0.0188}{0.0446 - 0.0188}\right] \times (1.7 - 1.05)$$

$$\left(\frac{r}{C}\right)f = 1.05 + [0.35] \times (0.65) = 1.2775$$

$$f = 1.2775 \times \frac{0.08}{30}$$

$$= 0.0034$$

$$\frac{Q}{r \cdot C \cdot n_s \cdot l} = 4.74 - [0.35] \times (4.74 - 4.62) = 4.712$$

$$Q = 4.712\,(30 \times 0.08 \times 25 \times 60) = 16963 \text{ mm}^3/\text{sec}$$

$$\left(\frac{Q_s}{Q}\right) = 0.919 - [0.35] \times (0.919 - 0.842) = 0.892$$

$$Q_s = 0.892 \times 16963 = 15131 \text{ mm}^3/\text{sec}$$

Heat generated $= 2\pi \cdot n_s \cdot f \cdot W \cdot r \times 10^{-6}$ kW

Heat dissipated $= \dfrac{\rho \cdot C_p \cdot \Delta T}{10^9}\left[Q - \dfrac{Q_s}{2}\right]$

Equating the two values,

$$2\pi \times 25 \times 0.0034 \times 20000 \times 30 \times 10^{-6} = \frac{860 \times 1.75 \times \Delta T}{10^9}[16963 - 7565.5]$$

$$0.320 = 0.014\,\Delta T$$

$$\Delta T = 22.8°C$$

∴ Average temperature $= T_{inlet} + \dfrac{\Delta T}{2} = 38 + \dfrac{22.8}{2} = 49.4°C$

Since this is considerably higher than the assumed temperature of 45°C, we go for next trial.

Trial 2: Assume $T_{av} = 48°C$

For $T = 48°C$, viscosity is 38×10^{-9} N·sec/mm²

$$\therefore S = \left(\frac{\mu \cdot n_s}{P}\right)\left(\frac{r}{C}\right)^2 = (0.633 \times 10^6)\mu$$

$$= (0.633 \times 10^6)\, 38 \times 10^{-9} = 0.024$$

$$\left(\frac{r}{C}\right)f = 1.05 + \left[\frac{0.024 - 0.0188}{0.0446 - 0.0188}\right](1.7 - 1.05)$$

$$= 1.05 + [0.201](0.65) = 1.181$$

$$\therefore f = 1.181 \times \frac{0.08}{30} = 0.003148$$

$$\frac{Q}{r \cdot C \cdot n_s \cdot l} = 4.74 - [0.201](0.12) = 4.716$$

$$Q = 4.716 \times (30 \times (0.08)) \times 25 \times 60)$$

$$= 4.716 \times (3600) = 16978 \text{ mm}^3/\text{sec}.$$

$$\frac{Q_s}{Q} = 0.919 - [0.201] \times (0.077) = 0.903$$

$$Q_s = 0.903 \times 16978 = 15331 \text{ mm}^3/\text{sec}$$

Equating Heat generated = Heat dissipated

$$\frac{2\pi \cdot n_s \cdot f \cdot W \cdot r}{10^6} = \frac{\rho \cdot C_p \cdot \Delta T}{10^9}\left[Q - \frac{Q_s}{2}\right]$$

$$\frac{2\pi \times 25 \times 0.003148 \times 20000 \times 30}{10^6} = \frac{860 \times 1.75 \times \Delta T}{10^9}\left[16978 - \frac{15331}{2}\right]$$

$$0.2966 = 0.014\, \Delta T$$

$$\Delta T = 21.2°C$$

$\therefore$ Average temperature

$$= \text{Inlet temperature} + \frac{\Delta T}{2}$$

$$= 38 + \frac{21.2}{2} = 48.6°C$$

This is close to assumed average temperature of 48°C.

It will be safe to consider average temperature as 48.3°C.

(A) Power lost in friction:

$$(kW)_f = \frac{2\pi \cdot n_s \cdot f \cdot W \cdot r}{10^6}$$

$$= \frac{2\pi \times 25 \times 0.003148 \times 20000 \times 30}{10^6}$$

$$= 0.2966 \text{ kW}$$

(B) Required oil flow (As calculated above)

$$Q = 16978 \text{ mm}^3/\text{sec}$$

$$= \frac{16978 \times 60}{10^6}$$

$$= 1.018 \text{ litre/min.}$$

EXERCISE

1. Derive an expression determining the temperature increase in lubricant, when the side leakage is considered. **(May 2011)**

2. Explain the construction of hydrodynamic bearings and journals with the help of sketches. **(May 2011)**

3. Write a short note on selection of hydrodynamic bearing design variables. **(November 2011)**

4. Derive with usual notations $\varepsilon = 1 - h_o/c$. **(November 2011)**

5. Discuss in detail the lubrication regimes. **(November 2011)**

6. Write desirable properties of bearing material. **(May 2012)**

7. State assumptions made in Petroff's equation and derive it. **(May 2012)**

8. State assumptions made in deriving Reynold's equation. **(May 2012)**

9. Sketch pressure distribution in infinitely short hydrodynamic bearing. **(May 2012)**

10. What is infinitely long and short journal bearing? State conditions and Reynold's equation for long and short journal bearing. **(May 2013)**

11. Write notes on:
    (a) Additive for mineral oils
    (b) Properties of bearing materials. **(May 2013)**

12. (a) What is infinitely long and short journal bearing? State conditions and write Reynold's equation for long and short journal bearing.

    (b) Write notes on:

       (i) Additive for mineral oils

       (ii) Properties of bearing materials. **(October 2013)**

13. (a) Explain the mechanism of pressure development in oil film and draw radial and axial pressure distribution for hydrodynamic journal bearing. **(October 2012)**

14. (a) Derive from first principal Reynold's equation with usual notation.

$$\frac{\partial}{\partial x}\left(h^3 \frac{\partial p}{\partial x}\right) + \frac{\partial}{\partial y}\left(h^3 \frac{\partial p}{\partial y}\right) = 6\mu u \frac{\partial h}{\partial x}$$

(May 2013)

✶✶✶

www.ingramcontent.com/pod-product-compliance
Lightning Source LLC
Chambersburg PA
CBHW082036230426
43670CB00016B/2672